Safeguarding the Quality of Forensic Assessment in Sentencing

This edited collection provides an interdisciplinary and cross-national perspective on safeguarding the quality of forensic assessment in sentencing offenders.

Taking an in-depth look at seven different Western countries, each chapter provides an overview of the role of assessment in sentencing offenders, as well as a focus on formal ways in which the respective country's legal system and disciplinary associations safeguard the quality of forensic assessment. Each chapter explores how to assure better decision making in general and in individual cases based on assessments of psycholegal concepts such as mental disorder/insanity, criminal responsibility, and dangerousness.

Combining the perspectives of lawyers or legal scholars, and clinicians working in the field, this book is essential for those working in and with forensic assessment.

Michiel van der Wolf is a professor of Forensic Psychiatry at Leiden University and associate professor in Criminal Law at the University of Groningen, the Netherlands.

International Perspectives on Forensic Mental Health
A Routledge Book Series

Edited by Patricia Zapf
Palo Alto University

The goal of this series is to improve the quality of health care services in forensic and correctional settings by providing a forum for discussing issues and disseminating resources related to policy, administration, clinical practice, and research. The series addresses topics such as mental health law; the organisation and administration of forensic and/or correctional services for persons with mental disorders; the development, implementation, and evaluation of treatment programs and interventions for individuals in civil and criminal justice settings; the assessment and management of violence risk, including risk for sexual violence and family violence; and staff selection, training, and development in forensic and/or correctional systems. The book series will consider proposals for both monographs and edited works on these and related topics, with special consideration given to proposals that promote evidence-based best practices and that are relevant to international audiences. Workbooks and manuals targeted towards practitioners and reflecting evidence-based practice and intervention will also be considered.

Published Titles

Handbook of Violence Risk Assessment
Edited by Randy K. Otto & Kevin S. Douglas

Sexual Predators: Society, Risk and the Law
Robert A. Prentky, Howard E. Barbaree & Eric S. Janus

Learning Forensic Assessment, Second Edition
Edited by Rebecca Jackson and Ronald Roesch

Evaluating Juvenile Transfer and Disposition Law, Science, and Practice
Kirk Heilbrun, David DeMatteo, Christopher King, Sarah Filone

Handbook of Forensic Mental Health Services
Ronald Roesch, Alana N. Cook

A Treatment Manual for Justice Involved Persons with Mental Illness Changing Lives and Changing Outcomes
Robert D. Morgan, Daryl Kroner, Jeremy F. Mills

Safeguarding the Quality of Forensic Assessment in Sentencing. A Review Across Western Nations
Edited by Michiel van der Wolf

Forthcoming Titles

Minority Groups and Marginalization in Forensic Mental Health Care
Edited by Jack Tomlin and Birgit Vollm

Safeguarding the Quality of Forensic Assessment in Sentencing

A Review Across Western Nations

Edited by Michiel van der Wolf

NEW YORK AND LONDON

Cover image: Getty Images

First published 2022
by Routledge
605 Third Avenue, New York, NY 10158

and by Routledge
4 Park Square, Milton Park, Abingdon, Oxon, OX14 4RN

Routledge is an imprint of the Taylor & Francis Group, an informa business

© 2022 selection and editorial matter, Michiel van der Wolf; individual chapters, the contributors

The right of Michiel van der Wolf to be identified as the author of the editorial material, and of the authors for their individual chapters, has been asserted in accordance with sections 77 and 78 of the Copyright, Designs and Patents Act 1988.

"The Open Access version of this book, available at www.taylorfrancis.com, has been made available under a Creative Commons Attribution-Non Commercial-No Derivatives 4.0 license."

Trademark notice: Product or corporate names may be trademarks or registered trademarks, and are used only for identification and explanation without intent to infringe.

Library of Congress Cataloging-in-Publication Data
A catalog record for this title has been requested

ISBN: 978-1-138-57762-6 (hbk)
ISBN: 978-1-138-57764-0 (pbk)
ISBN: 978-1-351-26648-2 (ebk)

DOI: 10.4324/9781351266482

Typeset in Bembo
by MPS Limited, Dehradun

Contents

Acknowledgements   xi

1 Introduction   1
MICHIEL VAN DER WOLF

    1.1   Origin and core idea of the book 1
    1.2   Scope of the approach 2
    1.3   Explaining the outline 4
        1.3.1   Introduction of the legal system and the tradition of assessment 4
        1.3.2   Overview of the role of forensic assessment in sentencing offenders 4
        1.3.3   Safeguards for the quality of forensic assessment 4
        1.3.4   Safeguards 'against' the limited quality of forensic assessment 5
        1.3.5   Safeguarding the quality of decision making when confronted with disagreement between experts 5
        1.3.6   Critical reflections 5

**2 Contemplations and discussions on the quality of forensic assessment in
sentencing: Puzzling pieces for decision makers**   6
MICHIEL VAN DER WOLF & MICHIEL DE VRIES-ROBBÉ

    2.1   Introduction: 'state of the art' 6
    2.2   Background knowledge: context and quality of assessment 7
        2.2.1   The origins of forensic assessment in (criminal) law 7
        2.2.2   Types and measures of quality 8
        2.2.3   Legal context: additional biases 10
    2.3   The assessment of mental disorder 12
        2.3.1   Definition, diagnosis, and classification 12
        2.3.2   Validity, utility, and reliability 13
    2.4   The assessment of insanity/criminal responsibility 14
        2.4.1   Concept, criteria, and divisibility 14
        2.4.2   Utility and reliability 15
    2.5   The assessment of risk 17
        2.5.1   Purpose 17
        2.5.2   Risk of what type of behaviour is being assessed? 17
        2.5.3   Single versus team-based assessment 18

vi Contents

2.5.4   *Clinical versus structured risk assessment 18*
2.5.5   *Actuarial versus structured professional judgement 19*
2.5.6   *Static factors versus dynamic factors 20*
2.5.7   *Risk factors versus protective factors 21*
2.5.8   *The importance of context 21*
2.5.9   *Front-end and back-end assessments 22*
2.5.10   *Risk communication and scenarios 22*
2.5.11   *Change over time 23*
2.5.12   *Generalisability 24*
2.5.13   *Age 25*
2.5.14   *The certainty of uncertainty 25*
2.6   *In sum 26*

3 An English perspective   34

ADRIAN GROUNDS & NICOLA PADFIELD

3.1   *Introduction 34*
    3.1.1   *The legal system 34*
    3.1.2   *The related tradition of forensic assessment 35*
3.2   *Short overview of the role of assessment in sentencing offenders 37*
    3.2.1   *Sentences and execution 37*
    3.2.2   *Decisions within sentencing and execution 41*
    3.2.3   *Concepts to be assessed 42*
    3.2.4   *Forensic assessment and procedure 45*
3.3   *Safeguards for the quality of forensic assessment 46*
    3.3.1   *Requirements in law and policy 46*
    3.3.2   *Disciplinary and ethical requirements 49*
    3.3.3   *Requirements for the evaluator 50*
    3.3.4   *Enforcement of requirements 52*
3.4   *Safeguards 'against' the limited quality of forensic assessment 54*
    3.4.1   *Questioning the assessment by the defence 54*
    3.4.2   *Questioning the assessment by the court 55*
    3.4.3   *Other questioning of the assessment 55*
3.5   *Safeguarding the quality of decision making when confronted with disagreement between experts 56*
    3.5.1   *Dealing with disagreement 56*
    3.5.2   *Best practices 56*
3.6   *Critical reflections 57*

4 An American perspective   63

CHRISTOPHER KING, LAUREN GROVE, BROOKE STETTLER & SHARON KELLEY

4.1   *Introduction 63*
    4.1.1   *The legal system 63*
    4.1.2   *The related tradition of forensic assessment 66*
4.2   *Short overview of the role of assessment in sentencing offenders 67*
    4.2.1   *Sentences and execution 67*

4.2.2 Decisions within sentencing and execution 74
4.2.3 Concepts to be assessed 74
4.2.4 Forensic assessment and procedure 75
4.3 Safeguards for the quality of forensic assessment 77
4.3.1 Requirements in law and policy 77
4.3.2 Disciplinary and ethical requirements 77
4.3.3 Requirements for the evaluator 78
4.3.4 Enforcement of requirements 78
4.4 Safeguards 'against' the limited quality of forensic assessment 79
4.4.1 Questioning the assessment by the defense 79
4.4.2 Questioning the assessment by the court 81
4.4.3 Other questioning of the assessment 81
4.5 Safeguarding the quality of decision making when confronted with disagreement between experts 81
4.5.1 Dealing with disagreement 81
4.5.2 Best practices 85
4.6 Critical reflections 86

5 A Canadian perspective 98
MICHELLE S. LAWRENCE & DAVID W. MORGAN

5.1 Introduction 98
5.1.1 The legal system 98
5.1.2 The related tradition of forensic assessment 99
5.2 Short overview of the role of assessment in sentencing offenders 101
5.2.1 Sentences and execution 101
5.2.2 Decisions within sentencing and execution 103
5.2.3 Concepts to be assessed 106
5.2.4 Forensic assessment and procedure 110
5.3 Safeguards for the quality of forensic assessment 111
5.3.1 Requirements in law and policy 111
5.3.2 Disciplinary and ethical requirements 112
5.3.3 Requirements for the evaluator 112
5.3.4 Enforcement of requirements 112
5.4 Safeguards 'against' the limited quality of forensic assessment 113
5.4.1 Questioning the assessment by the defense 113
5.4.2 Questioning the assessment by the court 113
5.4.3 Other questioning of the assessment 114
5.5 Safeguarding the quality of decision-making when confronted with disagreement between experts 114
5.5.1 Dealing with disagreement 114
5.5.2 Best practices 115
5.6 Critical reflection 116

viii Contents

6 An Australian perspective 121

JAMIE WALVISCH & ANDREW CARROLL

6.1 *Introduction 121*
    6.1.1 *The legal system 121*
    6.1.2 *The tradition of forensic assessment 122*
6.2 *Overview of the role of assessment in sentencing offenders 123*
    6.2.1 *Sentences and execution 123*
    6.2.2 *Decisions within sentencing and execution 124*
    6.2.3 *Concepts to be assessed 128*
    6.2.4 *Forensic assessment and procedure 128*
6.3 *Safeguards for the quality of forensic assessment 129*
    6.3.1 *Requirements in law and policy 129*
    6.3.2 *Disciplinary and ethical requirements 133*
    6.3.3 *Requirements for the evaluator 134*
    6.3.4 *Enforcement of requirements 135*
6.4 *Safeguards 'against' the limited quality of forensic assessment 136*
    6.4.1 *Questioning the assessment by the defense 136*
    6.4.2 *Questioning the assessment by the court 136*
    6.4.3 *Other questioning of the assessment 137*
6.5 *Safeguarding the quality of decision-making when confronted with disagreement between experts 137*
    6.5.1 *Dealing with disagreement 137*
    6.5.2 *Best practices 138*
6.6 *Critical reflections 138*

7 A German perspective 146

JOHANNES KASPAR & SUSANNE STÜBNER

7.1 *Introduction 146*
    7.1.1 *The legal system 146*
    7.1.2 *The related tradition of forensic assessment 147*
7.2 *Short overview of the role of assessment in sentencing offenders 148*
    7.2.1 *Sentences and execution 148*
    7.2.2 *Decisions within sentencing and execution 150*
    7.2.3 *Concepts to be assessed 153*
    7.2.4 *Forensic assessment and procedure 157*
7.3 *Safeguards for the quality of forensic assessment 159*
    7.3.1 *Requirements in law and policy 159*
    7.3.2 *Disciplinary and ethical requirements 161*
    7.3.3 *Requirements for the evaluator 161*
    7.3.4 *Enforcement of requirements 163*
7.4 *Safeguards 'against' the limited quality of forensic assessment 163*
    7.4.1 *Questioning the assessment by the defense 163*
    7.4.2 *Questioning the assessment by the court 164*
    7.4.3 *Other questioning of the assessment 165*

Contents   ix

7.5 *Safeguarding the quality of decision-making when confronted with disagreement between experts 165*
    7.5.1 *Dealing with disagreement 165*
    7.5.2 *Best practices 165*
7.6 *Critical reflections 166*

8 A Swedish perspective   175

TOVA BENNET, MALIN HILDEBRAND KARLÉN & LENA WAHLBERG

8.1 *Introduction 175*
    8.1.1 *The legal system 175*
    8.1.2 *The related tradition of forensic psychiatric investigation 176*
8.2 *Short overview of forensic psychiatric investigations in sentencing offenders 178*
    8.2.1 *Sentences and execution 178*
    8.2.2 *Decisions within sentencing and execution 180*
    8.2.3 *Concepts to be assessed 180*
    8.2.4 *Forensic assessment and procedure 183*
8.3 *Safeguards for the quality of forensic psychiatric assessment 185*
    8.3.1 *Requirements in law and policy 185*
    8.3.2 *Disciplinary and ethical requirements 186*
    8.3.3 *Requirements for the evaluator 190*
    8.3.4 *Enforcement of requirements 191*
8.4 *Safeguards 'against' the limited quality of forensic assessment 191*
    8.4.1 *Questioning the assessment by the defense 191*
    8.4.2 *Questioning the assessment by the court 191*
    8.4.3 *Other questioning of the assessment 192*
8.5 *Safeguarding the quality of decision-making when confronted with disagreement between experts 193*
    8.5.1 *Dealing with disagreement 193*
    8.5.2 *Best practices 193*
8.6 *Critical reflections 193*
    8.6.1 *Current threats to the quality of the forensic assessment 193*
    8.6.2 *Concluding remarks 194*

9 A Dutch perspective   200

MICHIEL VAN DER WOLF, HJALMAR VAN MARLE & SABINE ROZA

9.1 *Introduction 200*
    9.1.1 *The legal system 200*
    9.1.2 *The related tradition of forensic assessment 201*
9.2 *Short overview of the role of assessment in sentencing offenders 203*
    9.2.1 *Sentences and execution 203*
    9.2.2 *Decisions within sentencing and execution 208*
    9.2.3 *Concepts to be assessed 211*
    9.2.4 *Forensic assessment and procedure 215*
9.3 *Safeguards for the quality of forensic assessment 216*
    9.3.1 *Requirements in law and policy 216*

x Contents

    9.3.2   *Disciplinary and ethical requirements 217*

    9.3.3   *Requirements for the evaluator 219*

    9.3.4   *Enforcement of requirements 219*

  9.4   *Safeguards 'against' the limited quality of forensic assessment 220*

    9.4.1   *Questioning the assessment by the defense 220*

    9.4.2   *Questioning the assessment by the court 221*

    9.4.3   *Other questioning of the assessment 222*

  9.5   *Safeguarding the quality of decision-making when confronted with disagreement between experts 222*

    9.5.1   *Dealing with disagreement 222*

    9.5.2   *Best practices 224*

  9.6   *Critical reflections 224*

10 Comparative analysis 230

MICHIEL VAN DER WOLF

  10.1   *Introduction 230*

    10.1.1   *The legal system 230*

    10.1.2   *The related tradition of forensic assessment 233*

  10.2   *Short overview of the role of assessment in sentencing offenders 235*

    10.2.1   *Sentences and execution 235*

    10.2.2   *Decisions within sentencing and execution 237*

    10.2.3   *Concepts to be assessed 237*

    10.2.4   *Forensic assessment and procedure 240*

  10.3   *Safeguards for the quality of forensic assessment 240*

    10.3.1   *Requirements in law and policy 240*

    10.3.2   *Disciplinary and ethical requirements 242*

    10.3.3   *Requirements for the evaluator 244*

    10.3.4   *Enforcement of requirements 245*

  10.4   *Safeguards 'against' the limited quality of forensic assessment 246*

    10.4.1   *Questioning the assessment by the defense 246*

    10.4.2   *Questioning the assessment by the court 248*

    10.4.3   *Other questioning of the assessment 250*

  10.5   *Safeguarding the quality of decision-making when confronted with disagreement between experts 250*

    10.5.1   *Dealing with disagreement 250*

    10.5.2   *Best practices 253*

  10.6   *Conclusions and critical reflections 254*

Contributors   258

Index   262

Acknowledgements

As the coming about of this edited volume became a much longer story than expected when the project was conceived, I have to acknowledge the many 'safeguards' that were in place for the eventual materialisation of the book.

First and foremost, I owe a lot of gratitude to the former series' editor Ron Roesch for welcoming and encouraging the project, as he – and the selected peer reviewers – were convinced of the value of the book as part of the International Perspectives on Forensic Mental Health book series. Not losing sight of this value was probably the strongest safeguard in seeing the project through. The current series' editor Patricia Zapf also has to be credited for playing an important part in the final stages of the process, especially in picking up the pace. As over the course of the project, I have been in touch with three consecutive editors from the publisher, my appreciation goes out to all of them for the pleasant cooperation.

Another important safeguard was the enthusiasm of the authors of the country chapters in this book. Especially my requirement that both the legal and behavioural scientific discipline would be represented in the author teams has led to inspiring collaborations, as expressed in their feedback. As the countries for this review were selected based on their investment in forensic mental health, shown also by their presence in international conferences on the subjects, it is no surprise that I met most of these authors that way. Working with these highly esteemed members of my network has been the most fulfilling element of this project, for which I owe them many thanks. Hopefully we can get together physically again in 2022 to present the book at these conferences, as we presented our preliminary results with a small selection of authors on the online conference of the International Association of Forensic Mental Health Services in 2021 already.

In addition, I am indebted to the Dutch Research Council (NWO), as my research time for this book was funded through a Veni-grant as part of its Talent Programme. This edited volume is part of a larger research project on how to deal with both the human rights boundaries of sentencing mentally disordered and/or dangerous offenders and the behavioural scientific limitations of forensic assessment. As the grant is intended to further the development of early career scholars, in facilitating exactly that – amongst other things a professorship in forensic psychiatry – already before finishing the project, at least part of the late arrival of the book is explained by pleasant circumstances.

This book has been published open access thanks to the financial support of the Open Access Book Funds of the NWO and the University of Groningen.

A salute to my colleagues in Groningen and Leiden, and my former colleagues in Rotterdam, for continued motivating collaborations.

And finally, in speaking of safeguards for quality of life, I have to end on the personal note of thanking my family for their uplifting presence and infinite support through ups and (lock)downs.

May 2022

Chapter 1

Introduction

Michiel van der Wolf

1.1 Origin and core idea of the book

At the heart of this book lie several consistent participatory observations made in criminal courts within the Netherlands. In our jurisdiction, the possibility exists for experienced legal experts – including academic legal scholars – to serve as deputy judges in a court consisting of three legally qualified judges. This is considered a win–win situation, as, on the one hand, the academic gets valuable insights in legal practice and will be able to add law in action to law in books in his teachings and research. On the other hand, the court is not only provided with an inexpensive increase of capacity, but also with the expert knowledge that scholars tend to have. As I have been fortunate in the past almost ten years to serve as a deputy judge for about a dozen days a year, I have been able to inform the court from within on legal aspects concerning forensic assessment of psycholegal concepts related to sentencing, my area of expertise. Otherwise, I also learned that the dialogue between the disciplines needs much more translating than I am able to do, or than is appropriate for me to do without reversing roles – I was originally trained as a forensic psychologist – within the context of an individual case.

The most important observation is probably the impact that the assessment of psycholegal concepts can have on the length and type – in other words, the severity – of the sanction and, as a consequence, the life of an individual. Especially, since in our jurisdiction (see Chapter 9) the concept of dangerousness is an important factor in sentencing that in some contexts does not require expert evidence from other disciplines, I am often struck by the ease with which judges assess dangerousness intuitively – and extend sentences accordingly – as if the vast body of knowledge from decades of risk assessment research is not of relevance, if only as a test for their intuition.

Then again, if there is a forensic assessment in place, I am similarly often struck by the ease with which the conclusions of the behavioural scientific evaluator are followed by the judges, as if that same vast body of knowledge has not shown the relativity of these conclusions. Moreover, this is particularly true for a conclusion of high risk, whereas a conclusion of low risk – for example, in a case of (conditional) release – is received with much more scrutiny, even though again that body of knowledge teaches us that the latter is a scientifically much more robust conclusion than the former (see Chapter 2). As this may be understandable from the perspective of the different societal consequences between false negative and false positive decisions in such a case, in my opinion these are missed opportunities to narrow the gap between normative and empirical reality, which will eventually strengthen the transparency and objectivity of legal decision making based on psycholegal concepts.

On this note, it is important to stress that in safeguarding the quality of the dialogue between the relevant disciplines, it takes two to tango. As thus far, the mentioned observations may be regarded as somewhat critical towards legal decision makers, it is only fair

DOI: 10.4324/9781351266482-1

to mention that, in large, they are dependent on the input of behavioural scientists testifying before the court. Therefore, it won't come as a surprise that some of my other consistent observations are on their behalf. First of all, especially since they are experts representing science, I am often struck by an omission to provide a proper scientific underpinning for their conclusions. Especially on the issue of validity or reliability, or the presentation of alternative conclusions, they often seem to favour a firm conclusion over transparency concerning the scientific state of the art. As this may in part be due to the wish to provide clear and simple grounds for the decision to be made, it is in contrast with the legal duty to inform the court about the state of the discipline. A contrasting opinion, which may act as a remedy in situations like these, is a rarity within our jurisdiction. But, in the few cases in which I was involved, where conflicting counter-expertise was provided, I was struck by the fact that the presentation of a similarly firm, but different, conclusion was mainly substantiated by discrediting the first opinion, instead of referring to the limitations of the discipline, which allows for alternative views.

Out of the sum of these observations, the following question is derived: how to safeguard both the use and quality of forensic assessment as well as the quality of the sentencing decisions based on such assessments? As these observations were made within the specific Dutch context, in which particularly the inquisitorial nature of procedures is of influence, I was wondering what might be learned from safeguards in other jurisdictions. Since forensic assessment in the context of sentencing makes up a large part of the dialogue between the disciplines and the quality of the dialogue is a shared responsibility, both disciplinary and legal safeguards need to be taken into account. Therefore, this book will take both an international and interdisciplinary approach.

1.2 Scope of the approach

The classic comparative nature of the book is visible in the chapter outline, with chapters from country representatives as the main body flanked by introductory chapters and a comparative analysis from the editor. In any comparative project, the choice of jurisdictions is most important for the comparison to be relevant. For the aim of this book, those jurisdictions are chosen that are known to invest in forensic mental health research and practice. An indicator for this premise is, for example, that these seven countries are generally the suppliers of the largest delegations to international conferences on forensic mental health. Equally important is that these jurisdictions represent both the common law tradition (England & Wales, United States, Canada, and Australia) and the civil law tradition (Germany, Sweden, and the Netherlands), so that both inter- and intra-tradition differences can be observed. Even though, as a consequence of these choices it has become a review of Western nations, the fact that the 'practical problem' at hand is how to make an optimal use of forensic assessment in decision making related to sentencing, which is universal and independent of the legal system, should render the described best practices also of use in jurisdictions from other parts of the world. The model of analysis can be described as the functional method of comparative legal research. It is a model that does not primarily focus on rules or legal systems, but solutions to practical problems – such as the one mentioned for this project – within legal practice. Of course, in explaining observed differences, the societal and legal traditions or systems and sentencing regulations may come into play and a more law-in-context method may be needed in addition (see Chapter 10).

Not withstanding the fact that the word 'safeguard' may have a somewhat legal ring to it, as mentioned also instruments and practices that exist within the behavioural scientific disciplines aimed at warranting quality are part of the comparison. To cover this scope, combinations of authors are assembled in which both legal and behavioural scientific expertise is represented. Equally important, in the author combinations per country, both scholarly and practical professional experience is represented, to insure both an informed insider and critical outsider perspective.

From a legal perspective, safeguards related to this topic are generally described from a human rights perspective, for example, related to legal frameworks for dangerous offenders.[1] Generally, the limited validity of assessment is mentioned as a theoretical or ethical problem, but not much attention is given to how the legal context permits this limited validity to be dealt with in the interdisciplinary dialogue in legal practice. For example, if an assessment meets the ethical and formal criteria, how can a defendant/offender challenge the substantive outcome of an assessment? As the option of a second or third opinion or counter-expertise depends on the procedural and financial possibilities at hand, it is highly jurisdiction-specific and also related to the major distinction between adversarial and inquisitorial justice systems.

From a behavioural sciences perspective, most literature focuses on the state of the art of assessment from a somewhat universal scientific and clinical perspective.[2] Not often is this related to how the specific legal concepts used in different jurisdictions shape the forensic assessment in different ways. Criteria of mental disorder, dangerousness, insanity/responsibility, treatability/need for treatment, and other requirements for sentencing dangerous offenders may differ immensely in relation to the (legal) context, not to mention the specifics of the procedure in which the assessment takes place. And as, for example, dominant legal and political theory may also shape the legal context, this may also influence the practice of forensic assessment apart from scientific and clinical insights. The state of the art of the science generally does not equal the state of the art of the practice. And when ethical and formal demands concerning the assessment from within the behavioural scientific disciplines are mentioned, they are usually not confronted with those in other jurisdictions, in which different behavioural scientific frames of reference may be dominant. The question remains how in different countries the demands of law, policy, disciplinary and ethical codes and practice shape the assessment in different ways and what safeguards are in place to ensure the (formal) quality of the (evaluators doing the) assessment? In conclusion, this book aims to be complementary to existing knowledge – as also presented earlier in this series – especially in combining information from multiple disciplines, information from academic literature, and experiences within (legal) practice and information from different jurisdictions.

Even though the book is also about international differences in definition of relevant concepts, some defining of the scope of the contents is necessary at forehand. Already the term 'sentencing' may evoke different connotations related to its breadth. In this project, a broad perspective on sentencing is taken, which includes decision making on the imposition of sentences, on issues during the execution of sentences, like transfer, leave, etcetera, and on (conditional) termination of sentences. As the first category is often called front-end, and the last category is called back-end, maybe we can designate the in-between category as mid-way sentencing decisions. It means that decisions may be made by different authorities, with possible consequences for the forensic assessment. Also, in relation to another distinction in sentencing law, that between youth sentences and adult sentences, the choice is made to include both.

Forensic assessment is then considered as all expertise – either written or oral – provided in establishing psycholegal factors relevant to sentencing. Of course, dangerousness or risk is almost relevant to all decisions in sentencing. And while in the country chapters all other relevant concepts will be calendared, it won't come as a surprise that the assessment of concepts such as mental disorder, need for treatment and criminal responsibility are among the mentioned concepts. As in common law jurisdictions, legal insanity is part of the trial of fact, separate from the sentencing trial; in continental European jurisdictions criminal responsibility is traditionally very much related to sentencing. Therefore, for the comparison, the concept will be mentioned in all chapters, unlike, for example, fitness-to-stand trial, which may be mentioned as a relevant psycholegal factor in forensic assessment in general (while not strongly related to sentencing), or if deemed relevant in describing what possibilities exist to deal with mentally disordered offenders. The addition of these concepts to the vastly empirically studied concept of risk means that establishing the substantive quality of these assessments is even more fuzzy (science) than the area of risk assessment, because the validity of these concepts is much more difficult to study (see chapter 2). And, what does or should that mean for the possibilities of challenging the decision?

1.3 Explaining the outline

As all the country chapters aim at presenting the legal and disciplinary safeguards for insuring quality of the forensic assessment and the decision based upon it from a national perspective, it presupposes that some universal remarks can be made about the quality of forensic assessment. Chapter 2 aims at providing decision makers within sentencing (including execution) an overview of the contemplations and discussions related to the quality of forensic assessment in general, and to several specific psycholegal factors such as mental disorder, criminal responsibility and risk, which would be good to take notice of in making a legal decision possibly based upon such assessment.

From Chapter 3 onwards, the contents of the book will follow a classical comparative outline, with all seven country chapters following a similar structure to aid the comparison. The themes mentioned later form the pillars of the framework, as visible in the contents page of the book.

1.3.1 Introduction of the legal system and the tradition of assessment

In the introductory paragraphs, some relevant characteristics of the legal system, which impact forensic assessment, are discussed, as well as the tradition of forensic assessment, which exists in the country at hand.

1.3.2 Overview of the role of forensic assessment in sentencing offenders

In these paragraphs, it is explained what type of sentences are in place for which forensic assessment is required or used, and how – in broad strokes – these sentences are carried out. It is also described what type of decisions are being made, including all front-end (imposition), mid-way (prolongation of the execution, etcetera), and back-end (termination) decisions, and by what type of bodies. Moreover, it is calendared what psycholegal factors are relevant criteria in these decisions, and how the division of competences is between the disciplines involved in establishing these concepts. Finally, it is discussed how the forensic assessment is embedded in (criminal) procedure and dealt with in practice.

1.3.3 Safeguards for the quality of forensic assessment

In the following paragraphs, the focus is on what legal or policy requirements are in place for (different types of) forensic assessment, as well as what ethical or disciplinary requirements exist regarding these evaluations. It is also covered what specific requirements should safeguard the quality of the evaluator him- or herself. In addition, the question is answered as to which instruments are in place to enforce any of the requirements mentioned earlier, for example, within the trial or through disciplinary law.

1.3.4 Safeguards 'against' the limited quality of forensic assessment

In these paragraphs, the focus shifts from safeguards for the quality of assessment to safeguards 'against' its limited quality. At first, it is explained what possibilities and requirements exist for contesting an assessment. As the possibilities for (financial) legal aid may influence these possibilities, they are blended into this discussion. Finally, it is researched whether, next to the parties involved in the trial/case, other parties may be able to play a relevant part in this context.

1.3.5 Safeguarding the quality of decision making when confronted with disagreement between experts

As forensic assessment is intended to improve the quality of the decision at hand, the question may rise how difference of opinion is, or may be dealt with, in practice by the decision-making body. Next to legal possibilities, possible best practices for optimal decision making are shared.

1.3.6 Critical reflections

To conclude the country chapters, the authors mention what critical reflections exist in (national) literature or what critical reflections they might have themselves, related to the topic at hand.

The strict framework is meant to safeguard the quality of the comparison, as it is presented in the analysis in Chapter 10. Another safeguard for the quality of the information presented is, of course, the quality of the authors, which may be assessed through the author information in the appended list of contributors. This quality was, to a large extent, the ground for providing the authors with enough freedom to also add to the structure (in the third layer of numbering, 1.1.1) or to the presentation of information, for example, if deemed relevant from the perspective of their jurisdiction or their own expertise. In a sense, the critical reflections were provided as a means of picking their brains, as well as a means of forecasting in what ways current discussions may shape the field in the future.

Notes

1 See for an example in this series: McSherry, 2013.
2 See for an example in this series: De Ruiter and Kaser-Boyd, 2015.

References

De Ruiter, C., and Kaser-Boyd, N. (2015). *Forensic Psychological Assessment in Practice: Case Studies (International Perspectives on Forensic Mental Health)*. New York: Routledge.

McSherry, B. (2013). *Managing Fear: The Law and Ethics of Preventive Detention and Risk Assessment (International Perspectives on Forensic Mental Health)*. New York: Routledge.

Chapter 2

Contemplations and discussions on the quality of forensic assessment in sentencing: Puzzling pieces for decision makers

Michiel van der Wolf and Michiel de Vries Robbé

2.1 Introduction: 'state of the art'

A book on safeguards for the quality of forensic assessment in sentencing may suggest that there is something like a state of the art, the use of which is to be safeguarded. The term *state of the art*, in its metaphorical sense, is used for a most recent technique, which is therefore considered the best. As mentioned in Chapter 1, forensic assessment in this book is seen as 'all expertise – either written or oral – provided in establishing psycholegal factors', which in the context of the topic of this book should be relevant to sentencing. In essence, forensic assessment is labour of a diagnostic nature. Diagnosis literally means to discern or to distinguish, and is of course mainly associated with medical conditions. Whilst even in the context of somatic medical science, many a discussion may exist on what the state of the art is in diagnosing a certain pathology,[1] forensic assessment adds at least two layers of complexity to the diagnostic process, represented already in the term 'psycho-legal'.

The first layer is the realm of psychodiagnostics, which covers the discernment of psychopathology – both at the level of functioning and classification – as well as personality traits. Psychiatry, more than any other medical discipline, is prone to philosophical debate. Using the word *discipline* already avoids the debate whether psychiatry is even a science, or may be more suited among the humanities, with all its epistemological consequences.[2] Indeed, psychiatry and clinical psychology do not predominantly study physiological matter, but mind. Already the suggestion that our thoughts, feelings, desires, personalities, and behaviours are manifestations of the brain, as their physiological substrate, would be taking sides in another of such debates. But even those taking a neurobiological view on the discipline won't find it hard to admit that causes of many psychopathologies remain obscure, as the brain is the most complex organ in the human body, and despite all advances of the neurosciences is still largely unknown territory. Without clarity regarding origin or causality, symptomology concerning the mind is based mainly on deviance in functioning, incorporating among other things the risk of societal and normative influences. The misuse of psychiatry in this respect has a history of its own, but is in Western literature especially referred to in relation to the second layer of added complexity: the legal context.[3]

This context confronts the behavioural sciences involved in forensic assessment with a number of challenges, such as differences in language and definition, both between the disciplines but also between jurisdictions. Other differences are for example related to competence concerning the decisions involved, societal and political interests, and stakes added to – and dominant over – the interests of the individual, etcetera. This legal context also provides temporal challenges, as for sentencing the law is generally more interested in the past and the future, than it is in the present.

DOI: 10.4324/9781351266482-2

Therefore, in discussing forensic assessment, the term state of the art does not (only) refer to a most recent technique, but should be interpreted more in a literal sense: the current state of knowledge within the psycholegal disciplines, including the discussions and debates on what its quality is. Quite often in advising legal decision makers, they are left in the dark about many of these discussions, for example, because the advisor in question has already taken a side in a certain debate, or because (sense of) clarity is chosen over transparency. As this chapter aims mainly at illuminating these underlying discussions, it does not aim at providing integral reviews of the literature of the psychometric qualities of certain instruments or methods used in forensic assessment for example, but it will provide the background for understanding such reviews, as there is much more to the quality of the assessment as a whole. In doing that, it hopes to provide decision makers with essential pieces of the puzzle they have to find the best solution for.

In this chapter, first of all, the necessary backdrop to all these discussions will be set through discussing the origins of forensic assessment, types, and measures of quality and possible biases that come with the legal context. Next, discussions on the most common psycholegal concepts relevant for the quality of forensic assessment in sentencing will be described respectively (in its various definitions): mental disorder, criminal responsibility, and dangerousness. As will be explained in the upcoming paragraph, most attention related to the quality of assessment will go out to the last concept.

2.2 Background knowledge: context and quality of assessment

2.2.1 The origins of forensic assessment in (criminal) law[4]

As in the country chapters, the historical traditions in forensic assessment are addressed per country, this paragraph only addresses their common origins. The western world is often said to have a Judeo-Christian tradition, and this is particularly true for its (criminal) laws. The triangle of interrelated concepts that is still to a large extent the 'raison d'être' for forensic assessment in sentencing – mental disorder, criminal responsibility, and dangerousness – is already recognisable in Hebrew law and in (Christian) Church laws, which were actually highly influenced by the morals, myths, and laws of ancient Greece and Rome.[5] On the relation between disorder and responsibility, the Babylonian Talmud (written around 500 AD) mentions:

> *Idiots, lunatics and children below a certain age ought not to be held criminally responsible because they could not distinguish good from evil, right from wrong and were thus blameless in the eyes of God and man.*[6]

As in Hebrew law – similarly in Roman law and many medieval, both the English and Germanic Western European legal traditions – criminal acts were dealt with in a civil law manner, kinsmen of the insane offender were held liable for compensating the victim and were also held responsible for preventing future harm by the offender.[7] It underlines the ancient roots of the presumption of dangerousness, based on the (combined) stigma of offender and mentally disordered. Therefore, from its origins onwards, this triangle has always added both retrospective – criminal responsibility – and prospective complexity – dangerousness – to forensic assessment.

From then on, both developments in (criminal) law and developments in psychodiagnostics – also originating from the ancient Greek ideas of Hippocrates and Galenus which were mainly biological[8] – have shaped forensic assessment, often hand in hand as the introduction explained that both disciplines are prone to societal and normative influences. For example, the influence of the Church made both area's inherently 'theocratic'. In Medieval times, criminal law became separated from civil law, at first because not all crimes could be compensated, and later shaped by Christian thought under the influence of concepts of sin, personal ethical blame, and guilt. In England, for example, certain crimes which were punishable – even by death – because they could not be wiped out by compensation, could at first not entirely be excused, but through Church influence later could, by absence of intention and voluntariness: 'not out of own free will'.[9] That same influence had another effect on legal insanity through turning herecy into an offence. Some mentally disordered offenders were given harsher punishment than ordinary offenders, but only because they were mistaken for persons possessed by demons, even by doctors.[10] It shows that psychodiagnostics had mostly turned into demonology in those late Middle Ages. The Dutch doctor Johannes Wier is known to be the first to separate the mentally ill from the 'possessed' in the sixteenth century, as a predecessor of French doctor Philippe Pinel who is said to have freed the mentally ill from criminal chains in the dungeons of Bicêtre in the late eighteenth century.[11] The latter event is often being referred to as the birth of forensic psychiatry.

The rise of facilities for psychiatric care went hand-in-hand with the specialisation of the medical discipline. The (lead) psychiatrists of those facilities would also start to be asked for advice by courts. This practice would increase as diagnostics became more refined, and many recognised disorders would no longer be apparent to laypersons, including legal practitioners. The advancements in, also criminological, science would in the meantime also influence criminal law theory, as biological, psychological, and social causes for crime other than rational choice were identified. A modern school no longer propagated proportionate retribution of guilt as grounds for punishment, but dangerousness based on these causes. Obviously, this led to much more demand for advice on these causes in an individual case. The classical criminal law theory, based on responsibility, had led to the origin of forensic assessment – also from the humanitarian point of view of insanity/diminished responsibility as an exclusion criterion for the death penalty.[12] The modern theory however led to its bloom in the beginning of the twentieth century, also because dangerousness became an important concept throughout sentencing.[13] As, especially, the development of the criminal justice system and the consequential tradition of forensic assessment based on these developments differ from this point in time per jurisdiction, more modern historical context will be sketched in the respective country chapters.

2.2.2 Types and measures of quality

The quality of forensic assessment is evidently multifaceted. In the outline of the country chapters in this book, a distinction is made between the quality of the expert and the quality of an individual evaluation. The quality of the justice system itself also determines in part the quality of the assessment, for example, whether there are well-defined psycholegal concepts in place as the outcome of assessments, or whether in criminal procedure requirements regarding assessment exist.[14] From the safeguards described in the following chapters, it can be inferred that quality of forensic assessment can be divided in three major facets or types: contextual quality, procedural quality, and substantive quality.

Under the heading of contextual quality, we refer to the extent to which legal and ethical requirements that are relevant within the jurisdiction have been met in the entire process of the evaluation: from the appointment to possibly testifying in court. These requirements concerning the context of forensic assessment are described in the country chapters, and the extent to which they are followed is amongst other factors dependent on the type of justice system (explained in more detail in Chapter 10). As in an adversarial system, truth – including conclusions related to psycholegal concepts – is being sought through conflicting opinions; a lot of scrutiny is being directed to the opposing expertise, also on its contextual quality. In an inquisitorial system, where the same outcomes of forensic assessment are often being sought through consensus of opinion, scrutinising the opinion by the court – which is primary in doing the questioning – is less common and the contextual quality is often taken for granted. That is why, for example, it could occur that an omission to inform the defendant about their right to inspection and correction of the report was quite prevalent.[15] In contrast, the requirement of impartiality, which is common in both systems, may be somewhat at odds with adversarialism, considering its proneness to additional biases, as elaborated on in paragraph 2.3.

Procedural quality refers mainly to the adherence to disciplinary standards concerning the entire process of the evaluation: from the collection of data, inferences made on the basis of these data, and reporting and testifying on the conclusions based on these inferences. These disciplinary standards also safeguard the common requirement that an expert remains within the boundaries of his/her expertise. The minimisation of biases and the use of state of the art methods and tools, accepted within the discipline, are generally among such standards. With regards to having the required expertise, an English study on evaluations in juvenile cases, showed a remarkably low percentage of evaluators trained in diagnosing juveniles.[16] When it comes to reporting, again in inquisitorial systems, researchers have mentioned a lack of scrutiny, related to the soundness of argumentation for example, as a Dutch study showed.[17]

Eventually, the substantive quality of the conclusions or outcome of the evaluation is of course key, as advising that a psycholegal criterion, necessary for a certain decision in sentencing, is met or not met impacts legal decision making enormously. Again, especially research from inquisitorial systems shows very high rates of adaptation of conclusions from forensic assessment by decision makers.[18] The substantive quality of forensic assessment is often expressed in similar terms as used for psychodiagnostic tools, such as tests for personality or intelligence, through the psychometric measures of validity and reliability.

Validity relates to the question whether a test actually measures what it claims to measure. Especially for the prospective activity of assessing risk, the assessment may be verified (and researched) by an actual outcome in the future (for example a re-offense). Therefore, the quality of risk assessment is generally expressed through the measure of *predictive* validity. For other concepts, such as mental disorder and especially the retrospective activity of assessing legal insanity/criminal responsibility, no such outcome measure exists. In order to research the validity of conclusions on these matters, one has to resort to proxy-measures (elaborated on in paragraph 3.2), or 'softer' forms of validity, like *construct* validity or *face* validity. Construct validity refers to how well the test relates to underlying theoretical concepts, which given the lack of consensus about underlying theories for many psycholegal concepts is mainly researched when there is a widely accepted theory, such as the RNR principles for the assessment of forensic treatment effectiveness.[19] Face validity refers to how well the test or process (at face value) seems to appear to measure what it claims to measure, for example in the public's eye. Face validity for example plays a role in the discussion about the dichotomous versus dimensional nature of the responsibility doctrine.

The reliability of a test is related to the consistency (of the result) of a measuring test, or in other words: the extent to which a measure or process yields the same results independent from variations in other variables.[20] For example, between different points in time by the same evaluator over repeated measurements (*test-retest* reliability), or between different evaluators using the same test for the same individual (*interrater* reliability). Especially the latter is used in research related to forensic assessment, as the level of agreement between experts may be related to (the legal concept of) arbitrariness in decision making. More broadly in forensic science, reliability has been distinguished from 'biasability', with the first concept referring to the consistency of expert performance based on relevant information without bias, and the latter referring to decision making that is affected by irrelevant contextual information (which will be elaborated on in the next paragraph). The overall variability is then a function of both reliability and biasability.[21]

Highly relevant for forensic assessment is the finding that the levels of reliability and validity impact each other, especially in individual case decision making. If for example the interrater reliability of a method of risk assessment is low, the predictive validity of a single evaluation is also likely to be impaired.[22] And vice versa, if a concept has a low validity, for example as it is not that clearly defined, it will result in a lower interrater reliability. This latter effect may explain findings on the level of agreement between experts in assessing legal insanity.[23] Both examples will be elaborated on in following paragraphs.

As, of course, it is most important to know how well a test performs in an actual situation of decision making in the 'field', the concepts of *field* validity and field reliability are used to distinguish them from their counterparts based on research in the 'lab'. Studies show that field validity and reliability of tests, or tools, used in forensic assessment tend to be lower than their lab-counterparts, due to methodological issues.[24] It is, therefore, relevant to inquire into the type of research when evaluators report on reliability rates for tools they have used. However, as for specific tools (especially for risk assessment) such rates are generally available, this is much less the case for the more idiographic processes used in forensic assessment, which are less easily, and thus less frequently, researched.[25] Inferences resulting in individualised diagnoses, levels of dangerousness based on an 'offense analysis', or (levels of) criminal responsibility are examples of such processes. Nevertheless, it should be possible for an evaluator to comment at least qualitatively on the reliability of these processes (also based on literature), as is often required for the contextual quality of the report or testimony, even though – again especially in inquisitorial systems – this is often omitted.[26]

'Forensic psychiatry and forensic psychology are referred to as "soft sciences" for which satisfying levels of reliability and validity of findings are suspect'.[27] Nevertheless: 'The judicial system finds psychiatry and psychology, despite their limitations, to be relevant and useful, even indispensable, in a variety of legal issues for which an individual's mental functioning is relevant'.[28] These two quotes – both from the same source, written by Felthous – summarise the scrutinised yet firm position of forensic assessment. They also explain why in (both regular and) forensic psychodiagnostic research often the term 'utility' or 'usefulness' is distinguished from, and preferred, over the term validity.[29]

2.2.3 Legal context: additional biases

In any process of decision making, biases can come into play. Legal decision making, especially within criminal justice, has itself a bad reputation in that respect.[30] And as drawing conclusions based on the collection of information in forensic assessment is a process comparable to decision making, it is no exception. Already within psychodiagnostics outside the legal context, biases, and cognitive distortions have been identified as either: stemming from the structure of the human mental apparatus, expectancy-based, and stemming from learning and experience, or stemming from situational and systemic factors that distort information processing and cause errors in decision making.[31] The legal context of forensic assessment adds 'situational and systemic factors' in a number of ways. Zapf and Dror, for example, mention case-specific factors, such as irrelevant case information, reference materials, and case evidence.[32] In a study into the beliefs about bias among evaluators, these authors (and colleagues) describe how most evaluators expressed concern over cognitive bias but held an incorrect view on how to mitigate bias (through 'mere willpower'). In addition, they found evidence for a 'bias blind spot', meaning that more evaluators acknowledge bias in their peers' judgments than in their own.[33]

Even though indeed factors influencing the evaluators themselves are many, it is fair to mention that also factors stemming from the defendant, or from the tools evaluators use, add to the variability of outcomes of forensic assessments. Factors stemming from the defendant, which either unconsciously or consciously lead to distorted information, include cognitive distortions, transference, social desirability, and relevant in the legal context simulation, aggravation, or malingering as the stakes can be high.[34] Tools, such as the *DSM* classification system or for structured risk assessment, have also been criticised as being biased, for example racially.[35]

Related to the evaluator, several relevant biases should be mentioned in this context, as mentioned stemming from our nature, nurture, or the context. Bias is already ingrained in human nature, as our cognitive system is such that it processes information in an efficient and effective way. However, the shortcut mechanisms used to do so result in vulnerability to bias and error. Stereotyping is such a mechanism, which in forensic assessment has been demonstrated, for example, for gender, leading to different conclusions for men and women on certain psycholegal factors, depending also on diagnosis.[36] Other well-known mechanisms are primacy – and recency bias – placing too much weight on the first or last information perceived, availability bias – overestimating the probability of an event when other instances of that event or occurrence are easily recalled – and confirmation bias – tunnelling to conclusions that are in accordance with what we believe. In systems with a one-phase trial in which trial and sentencing are combined, confirming the believe that someone is guilty, will impact the evaluation of a defendant who denies the charges.[37]

What we believe may also be the result of nurture, evoking motivational biases or pre-existing attitudes – for example, a firm stance in debates on sentencing related issues such as capital punishment or preventive detention.[38] A very important bias in this context, related to association or affiliation bias, is what is called adversarial allegiance. There is ample evidence that within adversarial justice systems, outcomes of forensic evaluations may be dependent on which party has retained them.[39] Other well-known errors in drawing inferences within forensic assessment include circular reasoning – for example, establishing the mental disorder based on the offense – and base rate expectations. They may be related to case specifics, such as experiences in the interaction with the defendant – like countertransference, or other forms of affective bias.[40] But they could also be due to the evaluator's more general (professional) experiences and knowledge, which may work against him or her if recent insights from literature correcting earlier findings are not processed, or 'rater drift' occurs – the unintentional redefining of criteria, like legal tests which are not consulted for every evaluation because the evaluator considers them internalised.[41]

Decision makers within sentencing have to be aware of the possible impact of bias – either or not due to the legal context – in forensic assessment, as they should also be aware of bias in their own decision making. If suspicious of bias in an evaluation, they could ask for strategies used to mitigate the impact of bias, which have been developed within (forensic) behavioural sciences. Of course, the testing of alternative (or opposite) hypotheses is a well-documented one and the use of more nomothetic scientific knowledge, for example, structured tools. Similarly, training (about bias) and peer review of evaluations will also mitigate susceptibility for bias.[42] But, even with all the de-biasing strategies in the book, error can never be ruled out completely. Not only through the possible unawareness of one's own biases, but also because the state of the art in assessing psycholegal concepts will continue to allow it.

2.3 The assessment of mental disorder

2.3.1 Definition, diagnosis, and classification

'Assessing' a mental disorder, in some definition or another, may be relevant in sentencing, either as a criterion for a certain sanction, disposition, or transfer – sometimes in combination with (a degree of) legal insanity or culpability or need for treatment – or as a factor in determining the height of a sentence. In the latter sense, the concept may be used in two opposite directions: as a mitigating factor related to the concept of culpability or an aggravating factor related to the concept of dangerousness. As, on a group level, there is no evidence that mental disorder is related to incompetence or dangerousness, these consequences within sentencing have often been exposed as stigmatising.[43] However, at the level of specific disorders or through an idiographic approach that relation may well be established in an individual case.[44] The subject of stigma resonates however in the vast body of literature that understands (or denies) mental disorder as being a social construct, stretching from the heydays of antipsychiatry onwards.[45] As not all discussions on the concept of mental disorder are relevant in the context of this book, we focus on a few which may be relevant for the quality of assessment in the forensic context.

Among those who do acknowledge mental disorder as a reality, many different concepts or definitions exist. Already psychology and psychiatry have different ways of looking at the concept, based on their differences in methodology, as more of a deviance from the 'normal' in the bell curve or as an illness in the dichotomy opposing healthy. Traditionally, this can also be explained through the existence of different schools of thought, which all had definitions of mental disorder in line with their theory on behaviour in general. For example, psychodynamic, phenomenological, behavioural, and neurobiological views have all impacted the development of forensic assessment, to a point that nowadays generally a more eclectic biopsychosocial model remains. The fact that there has always been so much discussion on the origins of mental disorder, is one of the underlying factors for the a-theoretical classification system, such as the *DSM*.[46] A possible reason why, especially in forensic assessment, the influences of traditional schools of thought have resonated longer than in general psychodiagnostics may be that, especially for explaining offending behaviour, a mere classification does not provide as much help as an underlying theory.[47]

Another underlying factor for classification of disorders, either or not in a system such as the *DSM*, is traditionally the need for common language. Dating back to the days of Kraepelin, this development based on agreement at the level of description has paved the way for more universal and more nomothetic research.[48] For obvious reasons, however, the endeavour of classification has been criticised as being reductionistic and empiristic,[49] as well as rendering the psychiatric nomenclature with an appearance of validity. Indeed, the boundaries between different 'labels' as well as with 'normality' may be described as 'fuzzy' – exposed for example by the term 'comorbidity' and classifications ending with 'Not otherwise specified' – and the endeavour of diagnosing mental disorder as an 'epistemological uncertainty'.[50] Consequentially, for both clinical and legal decision making, a much more elaborate and individualised description of someone's functioning is needed as diagnosis.

When a mental disorder is itself defined in law, it is generally in a broad sense, rendering it less important what the exact (*DSM-*)classification is. However, it very much depends on the definition and whether there are categories mentioned, or explanatory notes issued on the scope of the definition, whether a certain classification can fall under the criterion.[51] In general, when it is defined in law, it also becomes a legal concept, meaning that it is in the end up to the legal decision maker to establish the concept, often on the advice of a behavioural expert. Nevertheless, when the definition itself is completely in line with dominant psychiatric terminology, this distinction in competencies becomes more artificial or even problematic.[52] Therefore, in some jurisdictions, to underline this division in competence – and to be independent of the volatile trends in psychiatric lingo – the legal concepts are distinctively not defined in language used within the psychiatric discipline.

As studies into the psychometric quality of diagnoses are generally narrowed down to *(DSM)* categories or labels, and its accessory (semi)structured tools or interviews, the nuances mentioned above might deny the relevance of these findings for forensic assessment. However, not only is classification part of the state of the art of diagnosing psychopathology, it also predetermines the outcome of any following assessment based on the disorder. For example, jurisdiction-specific regulations may disallow certain diagnoses, like substance intoxication or antisocial personality disorder, as the basis for legal insanity. Moreover, also scientific evidence – like the relationship between psychopathy and risk – or practical experience – for example, that legal insanity is mostly based on psychotic disorders – can have such a presorting effect. Therefore, the consequences of misdiagnosis in forensic assessment may be considerable.[53]

2.3.2 Validity, utility, and reliability

As mentioned, in determining the validity of a psychopathological classification, by lack of a certain outcome measure or Delphi oracle, researchers have to resort to proxies. Even though the labels are a-theoretical sometimes such proxies, for example, for psychotic disorders, are biological markers, or the effects of an established (pharmaco)therapy. However, personality disorders, for example, do not have well-established biological markers and do not evidence predictable responses to treatment.[54] There is a vast body of literature on the validity of antisocial personality disorder, often critical because of the overlap with offending behaviour. In recent years, the validity of this classification has been researched as predictive validity for institutional misconduct, with quite opposite results.[55] Of course, validity rates differ per diagnostic categories, but as they are often based on different proxies it is hard to compare such results. When an overview of the clinical utility of the *DSM* classification system is given, the verdict is also based on the intended argument. When, for example, protection is intended against critics 'who use its weaknesses to argue for the complete abolition of psychiatric diagnosis', the clinical utility is portrayed as great.[56] When, for example, other, more modern dimensional methods of diagnostic classification are being propagated, the clinical utility is called overestimated.[57] Forensic utility, as mentioned, may depend somewhat on the type of justice system, the type of decision, and the type of follow-up question. No wonder the DSM has a disclaimer in place that a classification in itself should not have any legal consequences. In general, however, in relation to other psycholegal concepts, mental disorder is one for which legal decision makers tend to really rely on the competence of behavioural experts.

As explained earlier, the limited validity of a concept also impacts the reliability, and the other way around. And researching reliability of diagnostic (categories of) classification has its own methodological obstacles – for example, the unethicality to keep evaluating an individual in person so that audiovisual registration is used – which have been pointed at to explain disappointing initial results of the reliability of DSM-5 classifications.[58] Considering that the forensic context may impact the diagnostic process (see paragraph 2.3), research in that field is most relevant in this respect. In the adversarial realm, however, studies are generally affected by adversarial allegiance and measure 'biasability' rather than reliability.[59] There is one jurisdiction, however, as explained in the American chapter, which provides for a naturalistic study into the agreement between nonpartisan evaluators. Hawaiian regulations state that the court will appoint three evaluators to a felony case in which forensic mental health assessment is called for. A first-of-a-kind analysis of 240 of such cases on six diagnostic categories showed perfect agreement between the three evaluators in fewer than one of five cases. There was also a difference between the diagnostic categories, with agreement on psychotic disorders being about 72%, agreement on cognitive disorders being highest (90%), and on personality disorders lowest (62%). As next to cognitive disorders, psychotic disorders (72%), substance-related disorders (65%), and mood disorders (65%) are most likely to impact a decision on legal insanity,[60] while for competency also intellectual disorders (95%) are relevant,[61] the authors conclude that 'in terms of field reliability, this means that evaluators reach a consensus on the most pertinent diagnostic categories for pretrial evaluations in fewer than half of all pretrial cases. This low level of agreement is likely to have serious implications for the psycholegal opinions made by the evaluators, and, in turn, the ultimate judicial dispositions made by the court'.[62] In short, evaluators are more likely to disagree than agree on a defendant's total diagnostic picture in pretrial forensic mental health evaluations.

In inquisitorial justices systems, such a naturalistic design is even harder to be found, as it is customary for multiple evaluators to try and reach a consensus before reporting, while initial dissenting opinions are generally not reported. Field reliability has therefore never been researched. A recent vignette-study from the Netherlands in which three actual reports of typical cases, stripped to the level of symptomatology, were presented to 52 evaluators, showed also a very high level of agreement on a case of a schizophrenic suspect of manslaughter, and much lower levels of agreement on personality disorders in addition with paraphilia or substance abuse, respectively, in cases of a grooming sex-offence and a robbery.[63] These differences in diagnoses had quite an impact in the assessed level of criminal responsibility and the sanctioning advise.

2.4 The assessment of insanity/criminal responsibility

2.4.1 Concept, criteria, and divisibility[64]

In general, as a first step in assessing legal insanity or (diminished) criminal responsibility, some definition of mental disorder is required. So, while all the contemplations of paragraph 3 similarly apply, the next steps add even more complexity. The first additional step is that the mental disorder has had to be present during the time of the offense. Retrospective diagnostics are alien to the regular clinical context, and few tools exist to assist this activity of reconstructing the offender's state of mind during the offense, other than logical inferences, for example, about the chronicity of the disorder diagnosed in the present in combination with information about its onset before the committed act. A second additional step common in provisions of the responsibility doctrine is a specification of the (functional) capacities that the disorder should have impaired at the time of the offence in order to establish legal insanity, often called a 'test'. In provisions in Western nations, it is common to find – either or both – a test of cognition and volition or control. On the other hand, in a few jurisdictions, provisions exist that require a more general causal relationship between the offence and (the product of) the disorder – sometimes called the 'product test'. On the basis of obvious criticisms related to determinism and a demand for restoration, some jurisdictions limit the use of the doctrine, re-label it, or have abolished it altogether. Already in this book all these different models are represented, suggesting that much more so than the concept of mental disorder it is highly culture-specific.[65] It has been argued that the precariousness of the doctrine and its connection to central aspects of criminal law seem to justify that a national support base is needed.[66] As this suggests a highly normative activity, it is generally accepted that it falls under the competence of the legal decision maker.[67] In several jurisdictions, there are (contextual quality) requirements, which enforce the delineation of the epistemological activity of the evaluator from the normative activity of the legal decision maker, for example, that no advice is given on the ultimate issue.[68]

Apart from the contemplations mentioned earlier, there are more elements surrounding this doctrine that hinder any universal endeavor to grasp the concept empirically: especially its embedding within criminal procedure and (related) discussions on its divisibility. In adversarial jurisdictions, legal insanity is a defense discussed at the trial of fact. Understandably, because of its consequence, it is a dichotomous – all or none – concept. In most inquisitorial jurisdictions of the European continent, the concept is viewed as an excuse, related to the level of culpability and punishability of the offender in relation to the offence. In these jurisdictions, the concept is considered a gradual concept, which could lead to a degree of mitigation of punishment up until a prohibition of punishment in case of a total lack of criminal responsibility. This distinction between adversarial and inquisitorial justice is actually more nuanced, as in adversarial jurisdictions doctrines of diminished responsibility may exist to mitigate the sentence in case of murder,[69] while at the sentencing stage culpability, viewed as a more dimensional concept, may well be mitigated due to mental disorder.[70]

Even though it has been suggested that dichotomous concepts are 'peculiarly foreign' to psychiatry, it is understood that the dichotomy used for the insanity defense is also being preserved to avoid more influence of psychiatrists in legal decision making.[71] The gradual or dimensional approach to responsibility may indeed have more 'face validity', but automatically adopts problems in the reliability of assessment. Indeed, in the Netherlands, there is a lively discussion on how many gradations can scientifically be distinguished.[72]

2.4.2 Utility and reliability

Because of the aforementioned aspects, a universal body of evidence, as there is for risk assessment, will never exist for the assessment of criminal responsibility. Moreover, as no sensible proxy is available for measuring this concept described as 'a legal fiction of a medical fiction',[73] validation will always be impaired. In addition, both legal standards and the psychiatric state of the art are constantly developing. When the need for evidence-based insanity evaluations is described, intended are 'a standard procedural approach, accuracy of diagnosis, and quality monitoring'.[74] With regards to the standardised approach – as the latter two have been discussed – in some countries, tools are in place. For example, guidelines from the American Academy of Psychiatry and the Law (AAPL) in which next to procedures also some substantive guidance is offered, for example, on how to relevantly assess impaired volition.[75] Some psychometric tools exist, like the Rogers Criminal Responsibility Assessment Scale (R-CRAS) from the United States,[76] and the Rating Scale of Criminal Responsibility for mentally disordered offenders (RSCRs) from China.[77] And most recent in Brazil, the 'criminal responsibility scale' has been constructed.[78] Validation of the tool is then being achieved through comparing the outcome of the tool with an expert's opinion, or through construct validity based on major components of existing evaluations.[79] In that sense, the structured method can never be more valid than the expert's opinion, while the question remains how valid that is. Since it is in the end a legal decision, one way of testing the expert's opinion to an external outcome is through the agreement with the legal decision maker. Since in adversarial systems, there are generally multiple, often different, opinions expressed in one case, it is less feasible to research such agreement affected by adversarial allegiance. However, in the Hawaiian system of three court-appointed experts, judges followed the majority opinion among evaluators in 91% of cases.[80] While in inquisitorial systems, generally one opinion is given – in case of multiple evaluators, based on consensus – research shows a similarly high percentage of following the expert's opinion by the decision maker.[81] In other words, the utility or usefulness of the (impartial) expert's opinion for legal decision making appears to be great, even though there may be some concern about its reliability.

A structured approach is often mentioned as beneficial for the reliability of the assessment,[82] and in doing that enhance the validity of assessments in a single case. However, the mentioned tools are not used in most parts of the world, and not even consistently in the countries they were created for. Reliability rates for such tools are therefore not indicative for field reliability of actual evaluations. For that, similarly designed (or the same) studies as those discussed in paragraph 3.2 are most notable. In 165, again, Hawaiian cases, three evaluators reached unanimous agreement regarding legal sanity in only 55.1% of cases. Agreement was higher when they agreed about diagnosing a psychotic disorder, and lower when a defendant was under the influence of drugs or alcohol at the time of the offense. The authors conclude that 'reliability among practicing forensic evaluators addressing legal sanity may be poorer than the field has tended to assume. Although agreement appears more likely in some cases than others, the frequent disagreements suggest a need for improved training and practice'.[83] That last remark could be tested a year later, when the Hawaiian state adopted more stringent certification standards, of which a rigorous training was part. The overall field reliability increased by 17%.[84] A study from 2015 showed an overall agreement of 63%, labelled as 'fair' or 'moderate', which was however much less than the agreement for competency to stand trial in the same study. This was explained through the retrospective nature of insanity evaluations, which makes it more complex and inferential in comparison to competency assessment. The level of agreement was said to be comparable to complex decision making in (somatic) medicine. 'As task complexity increases, "individuals may use heuristic-based strategies, with associated increases in effort, confusion, error rate, and consequent reduction in performance"'.[85]

When more gradations of criminal responsibility are acknowledged, and there are more (three) potential outcomes, logically agreement would be lower. In a Polish study on field reliability, which is a possibility because in Poland courts may ask for more than one evaluation, however, 57% agreement was reached. When the court asked for a second report knowing the outcome of the first, the conclusion was different in 47% of the cases.[86] This result may suggest that courts are able to identify poor evaluations, or that something exists which may be called 'inquisitorial allegiance': handing the court another conclusion when it is unsatisfied with the first. In the mentioned Dutch vignette study, agreement on the graded concept of criminal responsibility was not really related to agreement on the consequential sanctioning advice. Agreement on this advice was highest in the case of the schizophrenic defendant, even though there was more disagreement on criminal responsibility, with about two out of three of the evaluators drawing the conclusion of non-responsibility and one out of three that of diminished responsibility. In the case of the sex offender and the case of the robber, about four out of five evaluators assessed the defendant to be diminished responsible, and one out of five opted for fully responsible, while there was much more disagreement on the sanctioning advice – ranging from no treatment (in prison) to a severe safety- and treatment-order.[87] Arguably, given the enormous consequences of the dichotomous insanity decision, the sanctioning advice in inquisitorial justice is a better comparison than the graded responsibility assessment, yielding more disappointing results.

2.5 The assessment of risk

2.5.1 Purpose

Risk assessment serves different goals. In a legal sense, it is used predominantly to assess dangerousness. Although, historically, risk assessment was used mainly to predict future re-offending, in recent years, the focus has shifted to the prevention of new offenses through tailored interventions and risk management.[88] Assessment is merely the collection of relevant information that provides insight in the dangerousness of the individual case. Structured assessment (in contrast to unstructured assessment; see paragraph 2.5.4) can be seen as the coat rack to gather and organise this information. Each bit of information is regarded as a piece of the individual's risk puzzle. The task of the assessor is to collect the relevant pieces of information and combine these into a meaningful conclusion regarding the individual's risk. The more reliable the information, the better the quality of the assessment. When relevant information is missing, this should be highlighted in order for decision makers to be able to interpret the findings accordingly and, where necessary, request for additional information.

Risk assessment is often informed by the Risk-Needs-Responsivity model.[89] This model states that (forensic) interventions should: (1) be intensified if risks are more present; (2) focus on those factors most relevant for the individual case – the criminogenic needs; and (3) be offered in a manner that matches the responsivity or learning style of the individual. The complementing theoretical Good Lives Model[90] of rehabilitation states that an individual should work towards positive personal goals. Comprehensive risk assessment for an individual aims to provide insight into each of these aspects in order to be able to draw final conclusions regarding the overall level of risk and inform risk management and intervention decisions. It should be noted that risk assessment is a complex and time-consuming task, which requires extensive training and forensic expertise. As the assessor aims to 'foresee' the future based on the collected information and attempts to formulate a best judgement regarding future behaviour of the assessed individual in the anticipated context, almost by definition risk assessment is an extremely difficult undertaking. In the following paragraphs, several specifically complicating issues are being discussed.

2.5.2 Risk of what type of behaviour is being assessed?

When carrying out or interpreting risk assessment, it should be carefully considered what type of risk is being assessed. Dangerousness regarding what type of undesirable behaviour? Often, the most serious types of offending come to mind when risk is being assessed, such as bodily harm or sexual abuse. However, other types of violence towards others, such as domestic abuse, stalking, fire setting, or verbal threats, are generally also included in the definition of violence risk assessment.[91] While risk assessment measures often differentiate between physical and sexual violence, there are in fact specific assessment measures for a wide range of undesirable behaviours, such as intimate partner violence, stalking, extremist violence, honour-based violence, and so on. Although violent in nature, self-harm and aggression against objects are generally not regarded as 'violence'. Other risk assessment measures consider dangerousness much more broadly and include all types of criminal offending in their definition (e.g. LS/CMI[92]).

Although measures that focus on specific types of violence generally show somewhat more accurate predictive validities,[93] there is no right or wrong in the scope of an assessment measure. However, for both the assessor who formulates conclusions regarding risk and the decision maker who incorporates the assessment results in his judgement regarding dangerousness, it is of vital importance to clearly define the type of risk that is being evaluated, as the results of an assessment may be altogether different if an alternative definition of risk is employed. In addition, recidivism base-rates vary greatly between different types of offending behaviour. For example, recidivism in sexual violence is relatively rare, compared to recidivism in general criminal behaviour. Knowledge of base-rates for specific offending behaviours in different populations would provide useful background information for decision makers. Surprisingly, this type of information in the form of a base-rate overview is often not easily available. A complicating factor in this regard is the fact that recidivism may go unnoticed and thus official recidivism rates only remain a proxy for actual new offenses that have been committed.

2.5.3 Single versus team-based assessment

As the assessment concerns the collection, weighing, and integrating of relevant information regarding the individual, a risk assessment is as good as the information that is being regarded. Therefore, it is important for the assessor to make use of different sources of information, such as the individual's criminal and psychiatric records, behaviour observations, collateral information from family or friends, and self-reported reflections from interviews with the individual. However, even when multiple sources of information are used and assessors are experienced, they remain susceptible to blind spots, tunnel vision, the (dis)likability of the assessed, dishonest testimonials, or one-sided observations. In order to avoid these, unwanted biases risk assessments are sometimes carried out by multiple people. These team-based assessments help to bring information to the table from different angles, consider this more objectively, and come to a consensus rating regarding the case. Moreover, these discussions often serve as a valuable starting point for risk-management and treatment. Although time consuming and expensive, risk assessment carried out by multiple assessors generally produces more valuable and objective results.[94]

2.5.4 Clinical versus structured risk assessment

In day-to-day life, people carry out personal risk assessment all day long as minimising risk biologically increases the likelihood of survival. Similarly, psychiatrists and psychologists carry out mini-assessments regarding an individual's risk many times a day based on their experience and expertise. These implicit evaluations of risk are considered clinical or unstructured assessment. Although individualised and useful to avoid harmful behaviour in daily interactions, research has shown that unstructured risk assessment has fairly poor predictive validity when it comes to estimating an individual's future violence risk, due to the aforementioned biases that may occur. In the past decades, the science of risk assessment has advanced into structured risk assessment, which provides the assessor with group-level evidence-based guidelines regarding the specific topics to include in an individual assessment and offers clear instructions on how these topics should be evaluated. Validated structured risk assessment instruments have proven to substantially increase the predictive validity of a risk assessment over unstructured clinical judgement.[95] Perhaps somewhat in between these two approaches lies the structured offense analysis, which follows clear guidelines on how to collect information regarding an individual's specific offense and the circumstances that preceded the offense. This offense analysis concerns a structured yet personalised approach.

2.5.5 Actuarial versus structured professional judgement

Structured guidelines for risk assessment exist in various forms. Roughly two main categories of tools can be divided: actuarial measures and those following a structured professional judgement (SPJ) approach. Both kinds of tools include a list of factors that have empirically been shown to be related to an increased likelihood of future offending. The difference between the two approaches concerns the way conclusions are drawn from these empirically based factors.

2.5.5.1 Actuarial approach

In the actuarial approach, the different factors assessed receive a numerical rating (e.g. VRAG[96]). At the end of the assessment, the scores for each factor are tallied-up to come to an overall score on the measure. In more advanced actuarial tools, total scores are then compared to those of reference groups, in order for the assessor to be able to conclude whether the individual falls into a predetermined category of individuals with an increased likelihood of harmful behaviour. This way of actuarially adding up scores and comparison to other similar cases has the advantage that it is straight forward and less susceptible to rater bias and insightful in terms of caseload prioritisation. However, mechanically adding up scores leaves less room for an individualised view, as each concept receives an equal weight in the overall total score. Moreover, comparing to reference groups is only really useful if the individual is sufficiently similar in characteristics to the other individuals in the reference group (e.g. in terms of offending behaviour, psychopathology, gender, age, cultural background, setting, and country), which requires extensive databases of individual ratings, that are often not available in such detail. When interpreting the results from actuarial tools, decision makers should carefully consider whether the reference group that is being applied is indeed sufficiently similar to the assessed individual to warrant this kind of comparison and thus the validity of conclusions drawn from the assessment.

A final concern with this approach is the relative insensitivity to the context for which an assessment is carried out (see paragraph 2.5.8). The latest generation of actuarial tools (e.g. the Static-99R[97] and Stable-2007[98]) offers a more individualised view as the factors assessed are in themselves well-developed mini-judgements regarding specific concepts. However, the reference group issue and context insensitivity remain. Some tools even go as far as to conclude that based on the actuarial rating an individual belongs to a specific subgroup that, based on previous research regarding the applied reference group, has a specific likelihood of reoffending within a specific timeframe (i.e. 30% of this subgroup recidivates with a sexual offense within two years after discharge). This type of conclusion is quite prone to incorrect interpretation by decision makers and should be used with great caution, or better yet be avoided, as it creates an unjustified sense of certainty of the likelihood of future harmful behaviour.

2.5.5.2 Structured professional judgement approach

To overcome the overreliance on evidence gathered from previous research regarding specific groups of individuals, which may not be directly transferable to other individuals, and in an attempt to facilitate more individualised risk assessment, a new method was found in which the approach of assessing structured evidence-based factors is combined with the professional expertise of the assessor: SPJ. Through interpreting, weighing, and integrating the findings in the structured assessment, the assessor evaluates the individual case and comes to a well-informed final risk judgement regarding the likelihood of re-offending.

There have been many SPJ tools developed for a wide range of different outcomes (e.g. HCR-20^{V3}[99] for violent recidivism, SARA[100] for intimate partner violence, and SAVRY[101] for juvenile offending). Each of these relies on the assumption that a well-trained mental health care professional has the ability to formulate final judgements regarding risk based on carefully evaluating the presence or absence of the factors assessed in the structured checklist. In addition, it is possible for the assessor to add case-specific factors that are not present in the general list of factors. The careful consideration of the meaning and impact of each factor for the specific individual allows for a highly individualised assessment regarding the likelihood of future offending. However, this too has its pitfalls. The possibility for a rater to interpret factors based on his own professional insight or experience brings room for bias in terms of possible overreliance on the presence of specific factors and risk of subjectivity (e.g. a well-behaved assessee is not necessarily low risk).

Given that also in validation studies regarding SPJ measures, the mechanical adding of scores generally predicts future recidivism quite well at group level,[102] the assessor is advised not to stray too far from the overall observed ratings on the factors when arriving at the final conclusion. In order to prevent the actual addition of scores, some tools have moved to descriptive ratings only (e.g. HCR-20^{V3}). Other tools have included the option to highlight critical factors that appear of particular importance to the individual (e.g. START[103] and SAPROF[104]). Regardless, if the assessor does come to a very different conclusion than would be expected from the overall ratings on the factors, it should be carefully explained why this 'clinical override' is justified. It may, for example, be the case that one specific risk factor severely impacts the chance of recidivism (e.g. specific delusions), or that specific protective factors strongly reduce the likelihood of offending (e.g. a physical handicap or support that is in place). The flexibility of the SPJ approach also allows for the evaluator to take into account the influence of context on risk, which is a vital consideration (see paragraph 2.5.8).

Despite the seeming advantages of the SPJ approach, conclusions draw from this approach are unfortunately also prone to incorrect interpretation by decision makers. Many SPJ tools conclude with a final risk judgement regarding future undesirable behaviour (e.g. violence) in terms of 'low-moderate-high'. However, this final conclusion summed up in one word often leaves decision makers puzzled (e.g. how should one interpret 'moderate' risk? See paragraph 2.5.10).

2.5.6 Static factors versus dynamic factors

Many risk assessment tools include static or historical factors. These factors describe the individual's past behaviour or experiences. They are important from a diagnostic viewpoint as figuring out the historical puzzle pieces offers insight into an individual's route to offending behaviour (i.e. risk formulation[105]) and vulnerabilities that should be taken into account in risk management. Historical factors also generally predict quite well, past behaviour provides a fairly good indicator for future behaviour. However, from a psycholegal context, the sole reliance on historical information provides a one-sided view that does not allow for change and offers little optimism for rehabilitation.

Luckily, people can and do change, also those severely impacted by past unfavourable experiences. Therefore, in order to be able to evaluate changes in attitudes and behaviour as well as in contextual factors (e.g. situational and social influences) over time, most risk assessment tools also included dynamic or changeable factors. These factors often provide a more up-to-date picture of the individuals functioning and risks. Dynamic factors can either consider current or recent functioning, or can concern expected functioning in the near future. Many risk assessment measures compose a combination of historical factors and dynamic factors, to allow for a well-rounded view of the individual that offers room for change over time. Combining the historical findings with dynamic information may either be done through a predefined algorithm in an actuarial way or through the professional insight of the evaluator in an SPJ manner.

2.5.7 Risk factors versus protective factors

Risk assessment measures, even comprehensive ones, have historically been focused predominantly on risk factors. Given the psycholegal context perhaps, this is not surprising as assessors and decision makers are aiming to find out what contributes to dangerousness and investigating deficits seems the most obvious. However, in recent years, clinicians, evaluators, and decision makers have become more aware of the fact that dangerousness may not solely be determined by the presence of risk factors, but also by the absence of strengths or protective factors. In fact, since the early 2000s, understanding has grown regarding the importance of gaining a well-rounded view of the individual as a one-side risk-focused approach may inherently be inaccurate.[106] Scholars are increasingly in agreement that the presence of protective factors is indeed separate from the absence of risk factors and that protective factors should explicitly be evaluated to be able to formulate a clear picture of the individual.[107]

These missing pieces of the risk puzzle have long been ignored or underestimated. One of the first widely used structured risk assessment instruments to incorporate the notion of protective factors, at least to a limited degree, was the SAVRY, an SPJ tool for assessing violence risk for juveniles. Some years later, tools were developed that explicitly incorporate a two-sided view (e.g. START) or even specifically focus on protective factors, in order to complement risk-focus assessment tools (e.g. SAPROF; SAPROF-YV[108]). When interpreting risk assessment results, it should be noted that risk factors and protective factors each provide separate pieces of the risk assessment puzzle, which together provide greater insight into an individual's attitude and behaviour, as well as the supportive elements of their environment. Comprehensive risk assessment that incorporates both risk and protective factors is inherently more accurate and provides more in-depth conclusions regarding dangerousness as well as guidelines for risk management and intervention.[109]

2.5.8 The importance of context

Perhaps the most important protective factor to carefully consider in any risk assessment is context. The protection from situational strengths and limitations is vital to incorporate when evaluating the likelihood of recidivism. For example, an individual who has committed sexual offenses against children in the past who may still have a significant number of risk factors present, nevertheless generally has a 'low' risk of committing new sexual offenses against children while incarcerated or hospitalised, simply because there are no potential victims present. Similarly, an individual with a history of severe intimate partner abuse under the influence of alcohol, might be considered 'low' risk while granted supervised leaves from a forensic hospital, but at the same time be considered 'high' risk for the context of unsupervised leaves to the home environment. These examples highlight the vital importance of considering situation or environmental protection, which may result from legal monitoring, clinical supervision, or social support.

For this exact reason, in many settings, risk assessments are carried out for several contexts at the same time. Especially, dynamic factors that concern an estimation of behaviour in the near future and the final conclusions of a risk assessment regarding future risk are suitable for double rating for multiple contexts simultaneously. For example, if an individual is currently incarcerated, the future-rated factors of the HCR-20^{V3} or the protective factors of the SAPROF can be rated for the in-patient context, but at the same time receive a second set of ratings for the hypothetical context 'what if this individual was released tomorrow'. This comparison within the risk assessment between two different (hypothetical) contexts often provides decision makers with a great deal of insight into the likelihood of recidivism in case certain legal restrictions are dropped or imposed. This way, it can assist in evaluating the necessity of prolonged imposed treatment or probation supervision, or it can provide insight into the expected feasibility of specific interventions or risk management strategies. In forensic clinical practice, sometimes risk assessments are even carried out for three or more different contexts simultaneously, to support decision making regarding the most optimal next step in treatment and supervision. Another area where multiple ratings might be valuable is for pre-trial risk assessments (see paragraph 2.5.9).

2.5.9 Front-end and back-end assessments

Risk assessment is used both at the front end of a forensic trajectory (i.e. pre-court assessments) and at the back end (e.g. assessments preceding leave or discharge from a forensic hospital). The application at the back-end stage is relatively straight forward. First of all, there is more information available at the back end, as the individual has generally been in supervision or treatment for some time and hospital records describe all sorts of observations regarding the individual's behaviour. Secondly, the context for which the assessment is being carried out is generally quite clear and well defined (e.g. unsupervised daytime leaves from the hospital). The better the information and the clearer the context for which the assessment is carried out, the easier and more reliable the assessment. In front-end risk assessments, however, much is often unknown. The information regarding the individual case may be limited, due to incomplete file-information and limited ability for the assessor to speak with the individual and his social network and observe attitudes and behaviours. This may lead to information gaps or one-sided input. An even bigger challenge in pre-court risk assessments concerns the context for which the assessment is carried out. As often, the outcome of the legal decision making is yet unclear to the assessor at the time of the assessment (and sentencing might even be influenced by this assessment), it is complicated for the pre-court assessor to determine the context for which to carry out the assessment. In such a situation, it is often helpful to perform the assessment for different contexts simultaneously (see paragraph 2.5.8), in order to be able to draw conclusions regarding the impact of each of the assessed contexts on the (reduced) likelihood of recidivism. This may help decision makers to oversee the effects of different sentencing decisions and contemplate on the necessity of imposed interventions and/or supervision.

2.5.10 Risk communication and scenarios

Findings from an assessment are often described in a risk assessment report. This report provides an informative narrative for other professionals and decision makers. It is advised to avoid the use of numbers in these assessment reports and instead describe observations and findings in words. Conclusions drawn from assessments in terms of a summarising categorising word (e.g. low/moderate/high) or numerical score (e.g. a risk score of 5) are generally little informative for decision makers as they highly summarise and simplify information and are susceptible to different interpretations. Also, although low-risk individuals are generally the easiest to identify, the implications of low-risk conclusions may be great (i.e. the reduction of supervision or even release) and thus, for assessors, it is more challenging to draw low-risk conclusions than high-risk conclusions. In turn, decision makers sometimes find it difficult to accurately interpret these low/moderate/high-risk outcomes. Thus, there is a need for more informative and effective risk communication.

The newest advancement in risk assessment in recent years has been to describe the conclusions from the assessment in an informative narrative. This narrative provides a short summary that includes the description of the most likely risk scenarios for the individual. Based on previous routes to violence (or other undesirable outcomes, such as criminal behaviour in general) for the individual and current functioning, as well as the anticipated presence of risk and protective factors for the specific assessment context in the near future, the assessor sets out to contemplate on what could happen by asking himself the question: 'based on all the evidence gathered in this assessment regarding the different puzzle pieces for this individual, what am I mostly afraid of in terms of violent behaviour in the near future?'. General questions that can be posed here are 'what type of harmful behaviour is anticipated?', 'who could become victim?', 'how severe would this violence be?', 'how imminent could this take place?', and 'what factors are most likely to enhance or reduce this risk?'. Describing risk scenarios in this manner offers a great deal of insight into the reasoning of the assessor when contemplating on that one final conclusion 'low/moderate/high'. In fact, for one individual, there may be multiple risk scenarios thinkable at the same time, each with a different type of risk, victim, severity, imminence, and precipitating factors.[110] It would be good for decision makers to carefully consider all of the described risk scenarios for an individual when contemplating on the issue of dangerousness and to realise when an assessment does not include these narrative scenarios that the conclusions drawn from the assessment in numbers or in words 'low/moderate/high' compose a very scarce summary of the real estimation of risk that it aims to describe, which isn't nearly as informative for decision making as the more explicit and nuanced description of risk-scenario narratives.

2.5.11 Change over time

As discussed earlier, risk is not a static concept, but inherently changes over time. It is important for decision makers to take the assessment timeframe of specific measures into account. There are measures that assess imminent risk (e.g. DASA[111]), measures that assess risk in the coming weeks to months (e.g. START, HARM[112]), and measures that provide assessment for the more medium term of the coming six months to a year (e.g. HCR-20[V3], SAVRY, and VRS[113]). Thus, different risk assessments also have different 'expiry dates'. Risk far away in time is inevitably more difficult to assess than risk in the near future, as changes in context and individual behaviour may occur. In addition to considering variations in risk between different contexts, it may be useful for the decision maker to take into account changes in risk for an individual over time. This may be informative when aiming to evaluate whether specific interventions result in beneficial risk-reducing effects for the individual and contemplate on possible necessity for alterations in risk management or treatment initiatives.

Measuring change in risk over time, in other words treatment evaluation or routine outcome monitoring, can be accomplished by carrying out repeated assessment with the same measures at different points in time. In an attempt to facilitate this process, some tools have explicitly included a change rating in the assessment procedure (e.g. VRS). By comparing the results from different assessment timepoints, decreases in risk factors and improvements in protective factors can be monitored. It should be noted, however, that when assessments at different timepoints have been caried out for different contexts, it becomes less straight forward to compare the results between different moments in time, as a new context may also bring forth new (risk-enhancing) challenges and new (risk-reducing) protective circumstances. Nevertheless, comparing assessments over time for a given tool provides the decision maker with valuable insight into the improvements an individual is making over time, resulting in risk reduction over time. This may be helpful when deciding on lifting restrictions or allowing specific leaves or ultimately granting discharge. From a clinical perspective, ideally a large database would be created in which data of multiple timepoint assessments are stored for a great number of individuals. This would then facilitate the comparison of change over time of one individual to that of other individuals on similar developmental pathways and with similar psychopathology and initial risk levels, in order to be able to evaluate whether the assessed individual is still on his anticipated change trajectory in comparison to other similar individuals. However, such 'big data' risk assessment databases are not widely available yet, so for now this largely remains an anticipated opportunity to inform decision making in the future.

2.5.12 Generalisability

It should be noted that most risk assessment measures have been developed in Western European or North American contexts. Often, the initial population an assessment tool was developed on predominantly consisted of Caucasian males. Although culturally informed studies attempt to validate widely used risk assessment measures for a range of cultural and ethnic backgrounds, including immigrants and indigenous people,[114] overall the evidence-base for risk assessment measures still varies widely across different groups. Several risk assessment measures have been translated in many different languages and are being applied in a wide range of cultures and countries (e.g. in Japan[115]). Validation studies in these countries often provide comparable results to those found in Western European or North American samples for people from different backgrounds; however; it cannot be assumed that results are universally generalisable across groups before sound validation studies have been carried out. A specifically difficult group to study are immigrants from different countries, as often immigrant groups present in forensic settings represent a large variety of backgrounds, which cannot be grouped together in research and thus complicates validation.

The same may be true for people with varying psychopathologies. While different studies have focused on people with commonly observed psychopathologies in forensic practice, such as psychotic disorders, personality disorders, or substance abuse, less-abundant disorders often remain understudied (e.g. Autism spectrum disorder). As mentioned earlier, it should be noted that the relationship between psychopathology and dangerousness varies greatly between diagnosis and individuals. For example, the relationship between psychotic disorders and violence is generally limited (i.e. most individuals with psychotic symptoms are not violent); however, for the individual case, this relationship can be quite clear.

Finally, risk assessment measures may not generate the same findings for female offenders as for males.[116] For this reason, specific additional measures have been developed that focus on factors which appear more prevalent for women and are valuable to explicitly take into account when doing risk assessment for a female individual (e.g. FAM[117]). In conclusion, risk assessment measures may in practice be applied to people for whom they have not (yet) been properly validated or study results are less convincing. Assessors and decision makers should be aware of this and take this limitation into account when drawing conclusions from assessments carried out for individuals from minority groups in forensic settings.

2.5.13 Age

A related topic that might be relevant for the individual case is the question of age cut-offs for risk assessment measures. Traditionally, adult in risk assessment tools have focused on individuals from the age of 18 upwards, while juvenile risk assessment tools focused on younger individuals between the age of 12 and 17 (e.g. SAVRY, SAPROF-YV, and YLS/CMI[118]). Although in many cultures and jurisdictions, at age 18, an individual is legally regarded as an adult, this artificial cut-off remains quite arbitrary. We do not become altogether different individuals overnight on our 18th birthday, with altogether different risk profiles and assessment needs. Moreover, increasingly, studies of the brain highlight the finding that neurologically young adults are still developing until their mid-twenties.[119] In fact, while the age group of young adults (18–23) shows the highest rates of offending and recidivism,[120] surprisingly few studies focus on risk assessment specifically for this age group. In some legal systems, the notion that this group of young adults may be quite diverse in terms of developmental stage and that the adult sentencing system might not be entirely applicable to these young offenders has led to the development of specific 'adolescent law'. In the Netherlands, sentencing has become flexible in the sense that for young offenders between the age of 17 and 23 either juvenile or adult law can be applied, based on the developmental stage of the individual. Similarly, it would make sense if the application of adult or juvenile risk assessment tools would also be informed by evaluating the young individual's developmental age. If a young adult shows predominantly juvenile like behaviour, such as being in school, living at home, having younger friends, and being dependent on parents or caregivers, then the juvenile risk assessments tools are likely the best suited for assessing the individual. However, if the young adult lives independently, goes to work rather than school and relates mostly to older individuals, then the adult instruments are better suited. While research has shown that at group level, juvenile and adult risk assessment tools perform equally well for young adults at group level,[121] at the individual level it is advised to carefully consider which tools seem most applicable. Similarly, for very young juveniles, it could be considered whether child risk assessment measures (e.g. EARL[122] and SAPROF-CV[123]) might be more appropriate to use than juvenile tools. The decision maker should take note of the fit between the developmental age of the assessed individual and the applied risk assessment measure when drawing conclusions based on the findings in an assessment report.

2.5.14 The certainty of uncertainty

To summarise this contemplation of benefits and limitations of risk assessment in the light of legal decision making, perhaps the most important thing to remember when making use of risk assessment is that whatever measure was used and however results have been reported and interpreted by the assessor, it should be assumed that the assessor has attempted to unravel as many puzzle pieces as possible and from that has drawn conclusions to the best of his ability. Since 'assessment' concerns the future, one thing we know for sure is the certainty of uncertainty. Many seemingly high-risk individuals do not go on to recidivate (false positives), while some individuals who are considered low risk do commit new offenses (false negatives). Predictive validity studies aim to analyse correctly versus incorrectly predicted individuals; however, the question of 'what is considered recidivism?' is also complicated (i.e. what types of offenses are included and within what timeframe after the assessment?). In addition, only a proportion of future crimes lead to convictions. Thus, the balance of correctly identified individuals is a fine one. Societal tolerance for false negatives of serious offenses is limited, while from a legal and ethical perspective, we aim to prevent unnecessary lengthy and costly interventions. From clinical experience, we have learned that gradual community re-integration providing room for learning from mistakes has shown to be the most effective way to prevent future recidivism, which in the end enhances the safety of society as a whole. Risk assessment results should be interpreted in this light by decision makers as well. Generally, personalised interventions and risk-management as offered in a forensic treatment setting are much more effective in terms of recidivism reduction than harsh punishments and lengthy prison sentences. In addition, sometimes slight risks (e.g. granting leaves during prison or hospital stay in order to practice with community re-integration goals) may be acceptable if the anticipated gain is worthwhile (i.e. reduced likelihood of longer-term recidivism) and risks are manageable. In this process, we can only attempt to optimise our assessment of likely future behaviour and from that aim to prevent undesirable outcomes through tailored risk management. Unfortunately, every hint towards certainty in predicting future (criminal) human behaviour is unjustified. Nevertheless, assessors and decision makers should strive for the best possible evaluation of risk and carefully consider the findings from risk assessment when legal decisions are contemplated.

2.6 In sum

In trying to summarise discussions on the current state of knowledge within the psycholegal disciplines and its quality, we realise we may have left the legal decision maker puzzled. But, we feel that transparency about strengths and limitations of forensic assessment eventually enhances the quality of legal decision making based upon it, without mitigating its utility.

In discussing the background of forensic assessment, in what ways the quality of assessment may be judged, and why behavioural assessment in the forensic context is an even more daunting task than in the clinical context, we hope to provide discussions between the disciplines with relevant subject matter to inquire after as well as with appreciation for respective roles and competencies. We have aspired to explain why in general the scientific evidence related to the quality of forensic assessment is hindered by both epistemological and methodological limitations, and why the possibilities for sound, relevant, and universal research on such quality differs enormously per psycholegal concept. Moreover, when the body of knowledge is more vast, for example, regarding risk assessment, it is also because new opportunities present itself to further strengths over limitations, which, however – given also the prospective nature of the endeavor – will never completely be overcome.

In this chapter, we have limited ourselves to three psycholegal concepts relevant for sentencing, as the assessment of other relevant concepts or criteria, for example, related to treatability or the need for treatment, builds on the assessments discussed here. Knowledge on those issues also overlaps with literature from the clinical context or criminology on the effectiveness of interventions, even though such evidence may be less translatable to the forensic context due to the limitations posed by potential legal frameworks.[124]

Indeed, legal decision making on the basis of forensic assessment is a 'puzzling' activity – in more than one meaning – in which some puzzling pieces will always be missing. Nevertheless, we have hoped to provide decision makers with enough guidance on finding pieces of the puzzle to eventually identify the complete picture enough to make a decision with the required certainty, despite remaining uncertainties.

Notes

1 See Meyer, Mihura and Smith, 2005, who performed a meta-analysis of interrater reliability in psychology and medicine to show that clinicians could reliably interpret the Rorschach test.
2 See Cooper, 2008.
3 See for example Halpern, 1980 and Group for the advancement of psychiatry, 1974, regarding legal insanity and competency to stand trial, respectively.
4 Parts of this paragraph are based on Van der Wolf and Van Marle, 2018.
5 McGlen et al., 2015.
6 Cited in Simon and Ahn-Redding, 2006, p. 4.
7 See respectively Walker, 1968 and McGlen et al., 2015.
8 See e.g. Siegel, 1973.
9 Walker, 1968.
10 Robinson, 1996.
11 See for modern influences of Wier and Pinel respectively: Hoorens, 2011 in Dutch, and Weiner, 2010.
12 See Halpern, 1980.
13 Mooij, 1995, in Dutch.
14 See also the Canadian chapter.
15 25% versus 36% respectively, as reported in a questionnaire among Dutch evaluators, Hummelen et al., 2013, in Dutch.
16 As referred to in the English chapter.
17 As for example Van Esch, 2012, in Dutch, found that only a third of the reports in her sample contained an adequate description of the relation between mental disorder and offense – which is the essence of the Dutch concept of criminal responsibility.
18 See for example the country chapters of Germany and the Netherlands.
19 See on a related note; Skeem et al., 2017.
20 Gowensmith et al., 2017a.
21 See Dror, 2016; and Mossman, 2013, specifically for forensic behavioural assessment.
22 Compare Edens and Boccaccini, 2017 and Gowensmith et al., 2017b.
23 See for example Gowensmith, Murrie and Boccaccini, 2013.
24 See Edens and Boccaccini, 2017, in their editorial of a special issue on: Field Reliability and Validity of Forensic Psychological Assessment Instruments and Procedures.
25 See Lamiell, 1998, on how the distinction between the idiographic and nomothetic approach, introduced by the Neo-Kantian philosopher Wilhelm Windelband is used in modern days. In short, the idiographic approach, common in the humanities, is related to the tendency to specify and describes research goals that focus on the individual. The nomothetic approach, common in the natural sciences, is related to the tendency to generalise and fits research goals that focus on generalising individual results to the entire population. Also, in forensic assessment, a combination of these approaches is or should be used to first not omit any relevant generalisable knowledge relevant to the case, while eventually coming to individualised conclusions.
26 See for example the chapter on the Dutch perspective.
27 Felthous, 2012, p. 14.
28 Felthous, 2012, p. 13.
29 See for example Edens and Boccaccini, 2017, and Colins et al., 2017 respectively.
30 See for example Osborne, Davies and Hutchinson, 2017.
31 Bornstein, 2017.
32 Zapf and Dror, 2017.
33 Zapf et al., 2017.
34 Koenraadt and Muller, 2013, in Dutch.
35 See for respective examples Neighbors et al., 2003, and Perrault, Vincent and Guy, 2017.
36 See for an overview of the literature and a conclusion on female retardation Sygel et al., 2015, who found that for people with the diagnosis mental retardation, women found more likely to reoffend.
37 The case in inquisitorial justice systems, see Chapter 10.
38 Zapf and Dror, 2017.
39 See for references the American chapter.
40 Koenraadt and Muller, 2013, mention for example the Horn-effect, the tendency to judge someone (too) negatively and neglect positive traits, and its opposite the Leniency-effect. The Halo-effect and Hawthorne-effect are also relevant in this respect.

41 Zapf and Dror, 2017. As an example of new (and quite opposite) scientific insights they mention the treatability of psychopaths.
42 See for example Bornstein, 2017 and Zapf and Dror, 2017.
43 Most prominently by the French philosopher Foucault, 1978, who has argued that in the nineteenth century, the developing functioning of Western medicine as a public hygiene – often equaling dangerousness with disorder or degeneracy – ensured that safety-measures, especially in continental European jurisdictions, could be used as a 'social defence' against 'non-social' groups in society.
44 See for example Ahonen, 2019.
45 See for example Zsasz, 1960.
46 APA, 2013, there are other systems of classification, like that of the ICD, now up to edition 11.
47 Van Marle and Van der Wolf, 2013, in Dutch.
48 See Ebert and Bär, 2010.
49 Reductionistic, in narrowing the problems of an individual to a certain label. Empiristic, in not incorporating the subjective experience of the person involved. Other common criticism is on the risk of overdiagnosis, possibly in the interest of the pharmaceutical industry.
50 Lane, 2020. As the system is based on cut off scores on longer lists of symptoms, it also allows for very different presentations of mental states under a similar label.
51 See paragraph 2.3 in all the country chapters.
52 See for example the insanity doctrine of Norway for which 'psychosis' is required, which played an important role in the case of the infamous terrorist Breivik, as two teams of experts disagreed on the matter. See Melle, 2013.
53 See also Gowensmith et al., 2017a.
54 See also Rogers et al., 1992.
55 See study in forensic mental health, which found predictive validity (Marin-Avellan et al., 2014), versus a study in prison which did not (Edens et al., 2015), so the type of institution may play a role.
56 See for example Frances, 2016.
57 See for example Maj, 2018.
58 See Chmielewski et al., 2015.
59 For an overview of possible biases especially for the assessment of criminal responsibility, see Meyer and Valença, 2021.
60 See Knoll and Resnick, 2008. See for a Swedish study on the relation between disorder and accountability, Höglund et al., 2009.
61 See Pirelli, Gottdiener and Zapf, 2011.
62 Gowensmith et al., 2017a, p. 697.
63 Van der Wolf, forthcoming.
64 Parts of this paragraph are based on Van der Wolf and Van Marle, 2018.
65 See for example the Dutch and Swedish perspective for deviant doctrines, and Chapter 10 for a comparison.
66 Van der Wolf and Van Marle, 2018.
67 Which is also underlined by prior fault doctrines related to disorders as a consequence of substance use.
68 See for example the American chapter.
69 By changing its qualification to manslaughter. This was derived from the humanitarian approach, originally in Scottish case law, to pardon mentally disordered offenders in capital cases. Walker, 1968.
70 See the chapters of the adversarial countries and Chapter 10.
71 Diamond, 1961.
72 See the Dutch chapter.
73 Compare Halpern, 1980.
74 Knoll and Resnick, 2008. As areas of potential research for evidence-based insanity defense evaluations, they mention studies on threshold criteria for mental disease or defect, malingered insanity (incidence, correlates, and detection methods), and the systematic use of feedback from triers of fact.
75 AAPL, 2002.
76 Rogers and Sewell, 1999.
77 Cai et al., 2014.
78 Meyer et al., 2020.
79 See also Dobbrunz et al., 2020, for a study on criteria used to assess control, related to criminal responsibility, among paraphilic offenders in Germany.
80 Gowensmith, Murrie and Boccaccini, 2013. But when judges disagreed with the majority opinion, they usually did so to find defendants legally sane, rather than insane.

81 See the country chapters of Germany, Sweden and the Netherlands.
82 See for example Guarnera, Murrie and Boccaccini, 2017.
83 Gowensmith, Murrie and Boccaccini, 2013, p. 98.
84 Gowensmith, Sledd and Sessarego, 2014.
85 Acklin, Fuger and Gowensmith, 2015, p. 334. See for an Australian comparison, Large, Nielssen and Elliott, 2009, and for a meta-analysis related to the interrater reliability in competency and insanity cases, Guarnera and Murrie, 2017.
86 Kacperska et al., 2016.
87 Van der Wolf, forthcoming.
88 Hart and Logan, 2011.
89 Andrews and Bonta, 2010.
90 Ward and Brown, 2004.
91 Douglas et al., 2013.
92 Andrews, Bonta and Wormith, 2004.
93 Singh et al., 2013.
94 De Vogel, Van den Broek and De Vries Robbé, 2014.
95 Douglas et al., 2013.
96 Quinsey et al., 1998.
97 Hanson and Thornton, 1999.
98 Fernandez et al., 2012.
99 Douglas et al., 2013.
100 Kropp and Hart, 2000.
101 Borum, Bartel and Forth, 2002.
102 Douglas and Otto, 2021.
103 Webster et al., 2009.
104 De Vogel et al., 2012.
105 See Douglas et al., 2013.
106 Rogers, 2000.
107 De Ruiter and Nicholls, 2011.
108 De Vries Robbé et al., 2015.
109 De Vries Robbé and Willis, 2017.
110 Douglas et al., 2013.
111 Ogloff and Daffern, 2006.
112 Chaimowitz and Mamak, 2011.
113 Wong and Gordon, 2003.
114 Shepherd et al., 2014.
115 Kashiwagi et al., 2018.
116 De Vogel and Nicholls, 2016.
117 De Vogel et al., 2012.
118 Hoge and Andrews, 2006.
119 Diamond, 2002; Steinberg and Icenogle, 2019.
120 Piquero, Farrington and Blumstein, 2007.
121 Kleeven et al., 2020.
122 Augimeri et al., 2001.
123 De Vries Robbé et al., 2021.
124 See also Weisburd, Farrington and Gill, 2016.

References

AAPL (2002). AAPL practice guideline for forensic psychiatric evaluation of defendants raising the insanity defense. American Academy of Psychiatry and the Law. *Journal of the American Academy of Psychiatry and the Law*, 30(2), pp. s3–s40.

Acklin, M.W., Fuger, K., and Gowensmith, W. (2015). Examiner agreement and judicial consensus in forensic mental health evaluations. *Journal of Forensic Psychology Practice*, 15, pp. 318–343.

Ahonen, L. (2019). *Violence and Mental Illness: An Overview*. New York: Springer.

Andrews, D.A., and Bonta, J. (2010). Rehabilitating criminal justice policy and practice. *Psychology Public Policy and Law*, 16(1), pp. 39–55.

Andrews, D.A., Bonta, J., and Wormith, S.J. (2004). *The Level of Service/Case Management Inventory (LS/CMI)*. Toronto, Canada: Multi-Health Systems.

APA (2013). *Diagnostic and Statistical Manual of Mental Disorders* (5th ed.). Washington: APA.

Augimeri, L.K., Koegl, C.J., Webster, C.D., and Levene, K.S. (2001). *Early Assessment Risk List for Boys: EARL-20B, Version 2*. Toronto, Canada: Earlscourt Child and Family Centre.

Bornstein, R.F. (2017). Evidence-based psychological assessment. *Journal of Personality Assessment*, 99, pp. 435–445.

Borum, R., Bartel, P., and Forth, A. (2002). *SAVRY: Manual for the Structured Assessment of Violence Risk in Youth*. Tampa, FL: University of South Florida, Florida Mental Health Institute.

Cai, W., Zhang, Q., Huang, F., Guan, W., Tang, T., and Liu, C. (2014). The reliability and validity of the rating scale of criminal responsibility for mentally disordered offenders. *Forensic Science International*, 2014(236), pp. 146–150.

Chaimowitz, G.A., and Mamak, M. (2011). *Companion Guide to the Aggressive Incidents Scale and the Hamilton Anatomy of Risk Management (HARM)*. Hamilton, Canada: St. Joseph's Healthcare Hamilton.

Chmielewski, M., Clark, L.A., Bagby, R.M., and Watson, D. (2015). Method matters: Understanding diagnostic reliability in DSM-IV and DSM-5. *Journal of Abnormal Psychology*, 124(3), pp. 764–769.

Colins, O.F., Fanti, K.A., Andershed, H., Mulder, E., Salekin, R.T., Blokland, A., and Vermeiren, R.J.M. (2017). Psychometric properties and prognostic usefulness of the youth psychopathic traits inventory (YPI) as a component of a clinical protocol for detained youth: A multiethnic examination. *Psychological Assessment*, 29(6), pp. 740–753.

Cooper, R. (2008). *Psychiatry and Philosophy of Science*. Montreal: McGill-Queen's University Press.

Diamond, B. (1961). Criminal responsibility of the mentally ill. *Stanford Law Review*, 14, pp. 59–86.

Diamond, A. (2002). Normal development of prefrontal cortex from birth to young adulthood: Cognitive functions, anatomy, and biochemistry. In D. Stuss and R. Knight (Eds.), *Principles of Frontal Lobe Function*. New York, NY: Oxford university press, pp. 466–503.

De Ruiter, C., and Nicholls, T.L. (2011). Protective factors in forensic mental health: A new frontier. *International Journal of Forensic Mental Health*, 10, pp. 160–170.

De Vogel, V., De Ruiter, C., Bouman, Y., and De Vries Robbé, M. (2012). *SAPROF. Guidelines for the Assessment of Protective Factors for Violence risk* (2nd ed.). Utrecht, The Netherlands: Van der Hoeven Stichting.

De Vogel, V., De Vries Robbé, M., Van Kalmthout, W., and Place, C. (2012). *Female Additional Manual (FAM). Additional Guidelines to the HCR-20 for Assessing Risk for Violence in Women*. Utrecht, The Netherlands: Van der Hoeven Stichting.

De Vogel, V., Van den Broek, E., and De Vries Robbé, M. (2014). The use of the HCR-20^{V3} in Dutch forensic psychiatric practice. *International Journal of Forensic Mental Health*, 13, pp. 109–121.

De Vogel, V., and Nicholls, T.L. (2016). Gender matters: An introduction to the special issues on women and girls. *International Journal of Forensic Mental Health*, 15(1), pp. 1–25.

De Vries Robbé, M., Geers, M.C.K., Stapel, M., Hilterman, E.L.B., and De Vogel, V. (2015). *SAPROF - Youth Version. Structured Assessment of Protective Factors for Violence Rrisk – Youth Version. Guidelines for the Assessment of Protective Factors for Violence Risk in Juveniles*. Utrecht, The Netherlands: Van der Hoeven Kliniek.

De Vries Robbé, M., Smaragdi, A., Hilterman, E., Walsh, M., and Augimeri, L. (2021, in press). *The Structured Assessment of Protective Factors for violence risk – Child Version (SAPROF-CV)*.

De Vries Robbé, M., and Willis, G. (2017). Assessment of protective factors in clinical practice. *Aggression and Violent Behavior*, 32, pp. 55–63.

Dobbrunz S., Daubmann A., Müller, J.L., and Briken, P. (2020). Predictive validity of operationalized criteria for the assessment of criminal responsibility of sexual offenders with paraphilic disorders: A randomized control trial with mental health and legal professionals. *Frontiers in Psychology*, 11, p. 613081.

Douglas, K.S., Hart, S.D., Webster, C.D., and Belfrage, H. (2013). *HCR-20^{V3} Assessing Risk for Violence. User Guide*. Vancouver, Canada: Mental Health, Law, and Policy Institute, Simon Fraser University.

Douglas, K.S., and Otto, R.K. (Eds.) (2021). *Handbook of Violence Risk Sssessment* (2nd ed.). New York, NY: Routledge.

Dror, I.E. (2016). A hierarchy of expert performance. *Journal of Applied Research in Memory and Cognition*, 5(2), pp. 121–127.

Ebert, E., and Bär, K.-J. (2010). Emil Kraepelin: A pioneer of scientific understanding of psychiatry and psychopharmacology. *Indian Journal of Psychiatry*, 52(2), pp. 191–192.

Edens, J.F., and Boccaccini, M.T. (2017). Taking forensic mental health assessment "Out of the Lab" and into "the Real World": Introduction to the special issue on the field utility of forensic assessment instruments and procedures. *Psychological Assessment*, 29(6), pp. 599–610.

Edens, J.F., Kelley, S.E., Lilienfeld, S.O., Skeem, J.L., and Douglas, K.S. (2015). DSM-5 antisocial personality disorder: Predictive validity in a prison sample. *Law and Human Behavior*, 39(2), pp. 123–129.

Felthous, A. (2012). The diagnosis of psychopathology: Improving reliability and validity in forensic examinations. In T. I. Oei, and M. S. Groenhuijsen (Eds.), *Progression in Forensic Psychiatry*. Deventer: Kluwer, pp. 13–48.

Fernandez, Y., Harris, A.J.R., Hanson, R.K., and Sparks, J. (2012). *STABLE-2007 Coding Manual: Revised 2012*. [unpublished scoring manual]. Ottawa, Canada: Public Safety Canada.

Foucault, M. (1978). About the concept of the 'Dangerous Individual' in 19th-century legal psychiatry. *International Journal of Law and Psychiatry*, 1, pp. 1–18.

Frances, A. (2016). A report card on the utility of psychiatric diagnosis. *World Psychiatry*, 15(1), pp. 32–33.

Gowensmith, W.N., Murrie, D.C., and Boccaccini, M.T. (2013). How reliable are forenisc evaluations of legal insanity? *Law and Human Behavior*, 37(2), pp. 98–106.

Gowensmith, W.N., Sledd, M., and Sessarego, S. (2014). The impact of stringent certification standards on forensic evaluator reliability. *Paper presented at the 122nd annual meeting of the American Psychological Association*, Washington, DC.

Gowensmith, W.N., Sessarego, S.N., McKee, M.K., Horkott, S., MacLean, N., and McCallum, K.E. (2017a). Diagnostic field reliability in forensic mental health evaluations. *Psychological Assessment*, 29(6), pp. 692–700.

Gowensmith, W.N., Murrie, D.C., Boccaccini, M.T., and McNichols, B.J. (2017b). Field reliability influences field validity: Risk assessments of individuals found not guilty by reason of insanity. *Psychological Assessment*, 29(6), pp. 786–794.

Group for the advancement of psychiatry (1974). *Misuse of Psychiatry in the Criminal Courts: Competency to Stand Ttrial*. New York: Group for the advancement of psychiatry.

Guarnera, L.A., and Murrie, D.C. (2017). Field reliability of competency and sanity opinions: A systematic review and meta-analysis. *Psychological Assessment*, 29(6), pp. 795–818.

Guarnera, L.A., Murrie, D.C., and Boccaccini, M.T. (2017). Why do forensic experts disagree? Sources of unreliability and bias in forensic psychology evaluations. *Translational Issues in Psychological Science*, 3(2), pp. 143–152.

Halpern, A.L. (1980). The fiction of legal insanity and the misuse of psychiatry. *Journal of Legal Medicine*, 1(4), pp. 18–74.

Hanson, R.K. and Thorton, D. (1999). *Static-99: Improving Actuarial Risk Assessments for Sex Offenders*. Ottawa, Canada: Department of the Solicitor General of Canada.

Hart, S.D., and Logan, C. (2011). Formulation of violence risk using evidence-based assessments: The structured professional judgment approach. In: P. Sturmey and M. McMurran (eds.), *Forensic Case Formulation*. West Sussex, UK: John Wiley and Sons Ltd., pp. 83–106.

Hoge, R.D., and Andrews, D.A. (2006). *Youth Level of Service / Case Management Inventory (YLS/CMI): User's Manual*. Toronto, Canada: Multi-Health Systems.

Höglund, P., Levander, S., Anckarsäter, H., and Radovic, S. (2009). Accountability and psychiatric disorders: How do forensic psychiatric professionals think? *International Journal of Law and Psychiatry*, 32(6), pp. 355–361.

Hoorens, V. (2011). *Een ketterse arts voor de heksen. Jan Wier (1515-1588)*. Amsterdam: Bert Bakker.

Hummelen, J.W., Van Esch, C.M., Schipaanboord, A.E., and Van der Veer, T.S. (2013). Het inzage- en correctierecht bij gedragsdeskundig onderzoek in strafzaken. *Expertise en Recht*, 2, pp. 44–49.

Kacperska, I., Heitzman, J., Bak, T., Le´sko, A.W., and Opio, M. (2016). Reliability of repeated forensic evaluations of legal sanity. *International Journal of Law and Psychiatry*, 44, pp. 24–29.

Kashiwagi, H., Kikuchi, A., Koyama, M., Saito, D., and Hirabayashi, N. (2018). Strength-based assessment for future violence risk: A retrospective validation study of the Structured Assessment of Protective Factors for violence risk (SAPROF) Japanese version in forensic psychiatric inpatients. *Annals of general psychiatry*, 17(1), pp. 1–8.

Kleeven, A.T.H., De Vries Robbé, M., Mulder, E.A., and Popma, A. (2020). Risk assessment in juvenile and young adult offenders: Predictive validity of the SAVRY and SAPROF-YV. *Assessment*, 29, pp. 1–17.

Knoll, J.L. IV, and Resnick, P.J. (2008). Insanity defense evaluations: Toward a model for evidence-based practice. *Brief Treatment and Crisis Intervention*, 8(1), pp. 92–110.

Koenraadt, F. and Muller, E. (2013). Het psychologisch onderzoek en de daarop gebaseerde rapportage pro justitia. In H.J.C. Van Marle, P.A.M. Mevis and M.J.F. Van der Wolf (Eds.), *Gedragskundige rapportage in het strafrecht, Tweede herziene druk*. Deventer: Kluwer, pp. 269–346.

Kropp, P.R., and Hart, S.D. (2000). The Spousal Assault Risk Assessment (SARA) guide: Reliability and validity in adult male offenders. *Law and Human Behavior*, 24(1), pp. 101–118.

Lamiell, J.T. (1998). 'Nomothetic' and 'Idiographic': Contrasting Windelband's understanding with contemporary usage. *Theory & Psychology*, 8(1), pp. 23–38.

Lane, R. (2020). Expanding boundaries in psychiatry: Uuncertainty in the context of diagnosis-seeking and negotiation. *Sociology of Health and Fitness*, 42(s1), pp. 69–83.

Large, M., Nielssen, O., and Elliott, G. (2009). Reliability of psychiatric evidence in serious criminal matters: Fitness to stand trial and the defence of mental illness. *The Australian and New Zealand Journal of Psychiatry*, 43(5), pp. 446–452.

Maj, M. (2018). Why the clinical utility of diagnostic categories in psychiatry is intrinsically limited and how we can use new approaches to complement them. *World Psychiatry*, 17(2), pp. 121–122.

Marin-Avellan, L.E., McGauley, G.A., Campbell, C.D., and Fonagy, P. (2014). The validity and clinical utility of structural diagnoses of antisocial personality disorder with forensic patients. *Journal of Personality Disorders*, 28(4), pp. 500–517.

McGlen, M., Brown, J., Hughes, N.S., and Crichton, J. (2015). *The Classical Origins of the Insanity Defence (Homicide and Mental Disorder Lecture Series, Book 2)*. Edinburgh: Bahookie Publishers.

Melle, I. (2013). The Breivik case and what psychiatrists can learn from it. *World Psychiatry*, 2013, pp. 16–21.

Meyer, G.J., Mihura, J.L., and Smith, B.L. (2005). The interclinician reliability of Rorschach interpretation in four data sets. *Journal of Personality Assessment*, 84, pp. 296–314.

Meyer, L.F., Leal, C.C.S., Almeida Souza Omena, A. de, Mecler, K., and Valença, A.M. (2020). Criminal responsibility scale: Development and validation of a psychometric tool structured in clinical vignettes for Criminal Responsibility Assessments in Brazil. *Frontiers in Psychiatry*, 11, p. 579243.

Meyer, L.F., and Valença, A.M. (2021). Factors related to bias in forensic psychiatric assessments in criminal matters: A systematic review. *International Journal of Law and Psychiatry*, 75, p. 101681.

Mooij, A.W.M. (1995). TBS en Rapportage pro Justitia. Een historische beschouwing. *Ontmoetingen. Voordrachtenreeks van het Lutje Psychiatrisch-Juridisch Gezelschap*, pp. 21–31.

Mossman, D.M. (2013). When forensic examiners disagree: Bias, or just inaccuracy? *Psychology, Public Policy, and Law*, 19(1), pp. 40–55.

Neighbors, H.W., Trierweiler, S.J., Ford, B.C., and Muroff, J.R. (2003). Racial differences in DSM diagnosis using a semi-structured instrument: The importance of clinical judgment in the diagnosis of African Americans. *Journal of Health and Social Behavior*, 44(3), pp. 237–256.

Ogloff, J.R., and Daffern, M. (2006). The dynamic appraisal of situational aggression: An instrument to assess risk for imminent aggression in psychiatric inpatients. *Behavioral Sciences & the Law*, 24(6), pp. 799–813.

Osborne, D., Davies, P.G., and Hutchinson, S. (2017). Stereotypicality biases and the criminal justice system. In C.G. Sibley and F. K. Barlow (Eds.), *The Cambridge Handbook of the Psychology of Prejudice*. Cambridge: Cambridge University Press, pp. 542–558.

Perrault, R.T., Vincent, G.M., and Guy, L.S. (2017). Are risk assessments racially biased?: Field study of the SAVRY and YLS/CMI in probation. *Psychological Assessment*, 29(6), pp. 664–678.

Piquero, A.R., Farrington, D.P., and Blumstein, A. (2007). *Key Issues in Criminal Career Research: New Analyses of the Cambridge Study in Delinquent Development*. Cambridge, UK: Cambridge University Press.

Pirelli, G., Gottdiener, W.H., and Zapf, P. A. (2011). A meta-analytic review of competency to stand trial research. *Psychology, Public Policy, and Law*, 17(1), pp. 1–53.

Quinsey, V.L., Harris, G.T., Rice, M.E., and Cormier, C.A. (1998). *Violent Offenders: Appraising and Managing Risk*. Washington, DC: American Psychological Association.

Robinson, D. (1996). *Wild Beasts & Idle Humours. The Insanity Defense from Antiquity to the Present.* Cambridge, Massachusetts: Harvard University Press.

Rogers, R. (2000). The uncritical acceptance of risk assessment in forensic practice. *Law and Human Behavior*, 24, pp. 595–605.

Rogers, R., Dion, K.L., and Lynett, E. (1992). Diagnostic validity of antisocial personality disorder: A prototypical analysis. *Law and Human Behavior*, 16(6), pp. 677–689.

Rogers, R., and Sewell, K.W. (1999). The R-CRAS and insanity evaluations: A reexamination of construct validity. *Behavioral Sciences & the Law*, 17(2), pp. 181–194.

Shepherd, S.M., Luebbers, S., Ferguson, M., Ogloff, J.R.P., and Dolan, M. (2014). The utility of the SAVRY across ethnicity in Australian young offenders. *Psychology Public Policy and Law*, 20(1), pp. 31–45.

Siegel, R.E. (1973). Galen on psychology, psychopathology, and function and diseases of the nervous system: An analysis of his doctrines, observations and experiments. In *Galen's System of Physiology and Medicine*. Basel: Karger.

Simon, R.J., and Ahn-Redding, H. (2006). *The Insanity Defense, the World Over*. Lanham: Lexington Books.

Singh, J.P., Yang, S., Bjorkly, S., Boccacini, M.T., Borum, R., Buchanan, A., et al. (2013). *Reporting standards for Risk Assessment Predictive Validity Studies: The Risk Assessment Guidelines for the Evaluation of Efficacy (RAGEE) Statement*. Tampa, FL: University of South Florida.

Skeem, J.L., Kennealy, P.J., Tatar II, J.R., Hernandez, I.R., and Keith, F.A. (2017). How well do juvenile risk assessments measure factors to target in treatment? Examining construct validity. *Psychological Assessment*, 29(6), pp. 679–691.

Steinberg, L., and Icenogle, G. (2019). Using developmental science to distinguish adolescents and adults under the law. *Annual Review of Developmental Psychology*, 1, pp. 21–40.

Sygel, K., Sturup, J., Fors, U., Edberg, H., Gavazzeni, J., Howner, K., Persson, M., and Kristiansson, M. (2015). The effect of gender on the outcome of forensic psychiatric assessment in Sweden: A case vignette study. *Criminal Behavior and Mental Health*, 27(2), pp. 124–135.

Van Esch, C.M. (2012). *Gedragskundigen in strafzaken* (diss. Leiden). Assen: Koninklijke Van Gorcum.

Van Marle, H.J.C., and Van der Wolf, M.J.F. (2013). Forensisch psychiatrische ziekteleer: een inleiding, een handleiding, een handreiking. In H.J.C. Van Marle, P.A.M. Mevis and M.J.F. Van der Wolf (Eds.), *Gedragskundige rapportage in het strafrecht, Tweede herziene druk*. Deventer: Kluwer, pp. 77–130.

Van der Wolf, M.J.F. (forthcoming). The level of agreement between experts in forensic assessment in the Netherlands.

Van der Wolf, M.J.F., and Van Marle, H.J.C. (2018). Legal approaches to criminal responsibility of mentally disordered offenders in Europe. In K. Goethals (Ed.), *Forensic Psychiatry and Psychology in Europe. A Cross-Border Study Guide*. Basel: Springer International Publishing, pp. 31–44.

Walker, N. (1968). *Crime and Insanity in England. Volume One: The Historical Perspective*. Edinburgh: University Press.

Ward, T., and Brown, M. (2004). The good lives model and conceptual issues in offender rehabilitation. *Psychology, Crime and Law*, 10, pp. 243–257.

Webster, C.D., Martin, M.L., Brink, J., Nicholls, T.L. and Desmarais, S.L. (2009). *Short-Term Assessment of Risk and Treatability (START) (Version 1.1)*. Coquitlam, Canada: British Columbia Mental Health and Addiction Services.

Weiner, D.B. (2010). Philippe Pinel in the 21st Century: The myth and the message. In E.R. Wallace, and J. Gach (Eds.), *History of Psychiatry and Medical Psychology*. New York: Springer pp. 305–312.

Weisburd, D., Farrington, D.P., and Gill, C. (Eds) (2016). *What Works in Crime Prevention and Rehabilitation: Lessons from Systematic Reviews*. New York, NY: Springer.

Wong, S., and Gordon, A. (2003). *Violence Risk Scale (VRS)*. Saskatoon, Canada: Regional Psychiatric Centre.

Zapf, P.A., and Dror, I.E. (2017). Understanding and mitigating bias in forensic evaluation: Lessons from forensic science. *International Journal of Forensic Mental Health*, 16(3), pp. 227–238.

Zapf, P.A., Kukucka, J., Kassin, S.M., and Dror, I.E. (2017). Cognitive Bias in forensic mental health assessment: Evaluator beliefs about its nature and scope. *Psychology, Public Policy, and Law*, 24(1), pp. 1–10.

Zsasz, T. (1960). *The Myth of Mental Illness*. New York: HarperCollins.

Chapter 3

An English perspective

Adrian Grounds and Nicola Padfield

3.1 Introduction

3.1.1 The legal system

A key characteristic of the English[1] legal system is often said to be its *adversarialism*, an accusatorial rather than an inquisitorial process. But, this is misleading, since nowadays most people who are prosecuted in the courts plead guilty.[2] Guilty pleas may be made very early in the process, as a sentence discount will be more significant the earlier the guilty plea is registered.

Liaison and diversion schemes provided by the health service aim to identify individuals with mental health, learning disability, substance misuse, or other vulnerabilities when they first come into contact with the police and the courts.[3] The police may ask a doctor or nurse to examine a suspect, and the suspect may be assessed under the Mental Health Act 1983 and diverted into the hospital system, or be referred for other appropriate health or social care. But they may, however, remain within the criminal justice system and be prosecuted. Medical assessments may take place at any stage: decisions on whether the person is fit to be questioned, on charging (where the Crown Prosecution Service will be involved), on bail or remand, and in preparations for trials. A person may be also found to be unfit to plead or not guilty by reason of insanity.

Another key characteristic is said to be the significant *'lay' (non-lawyer) involvement* in criminal justice decision making. There is a sharp division between Magistrates Courts (largely presided over by lay magistrates) and Crown Courts. The Magistrates Courts deal with the majority of criminal prosecutions, but their powers of sentence are now limited to twelve months imprisonment. (The limit was recently increased from six months imprisonment). Serious crime is sent to the Crown Court for trial.

The sharp *distinction between the decision on guilt and the decision on sentence* is also a characteristic of the English legal system. In the Crown Court, this is particularly obvious: where decisions on guilt are made by a jury of 12 lay people, but questions of sentencing are the exclusive preserve of the judge. Unlike many other European jurisdictions, quite different forensic assessments may be required at sentence from those required at trial. Understanding the role of experts at trial involves understanding the complex division of roles between lay jury and judge. There are also subtle changes happening in the relationship between prosecution and defence. A growing concern today is the increasing number of unrepresented defendants.[4] For our purposes, it raises questions about the commissioning of forensic reports. Who commissions reports? Courts or parties? The prosecution is also much more active at the sentencing stage than it was 20 years ago. Then the prosecutor took little interest in sentencing, beyond checking that the judge or magistrates had an up-to-date list of the

DOI: 10.4324/9781351266482-3

An English perspective   35

defendant's previous convictions. Now, there will be an active discussion about the relevant sentencing guidelines[5] and appropriate sentence, and – as further discussed later – appeals against unduly lenient sentences are possible.

It is also worth noting that criminal justice processes are governed by *complex laws, which are frequently changed*. The complex rules of evidence and procedure in England evolved in the nineteenth and twentieth centuries, largely because of the dominant decision-making position of the lay jury. In the last 50 years, there has been an enormous quantity of legislation, which has introduced many more changes, particularly to sentencing law. There have been significant attempts to codify, or at least to consolidate, sentencing provisions, in one statute. The latest attempt, the Sentencing Act 2020, is a consolidation of previous sentencing laws, but excludes, for example, disposals under the Mental Health Act 1983.[6]

Perhaps the most important characteristic of today's criminal justice system is that of a *system under great strain*. The criminal justice process, and its institutions, have seen extraordinarily large cuts in their budgets in the last 10–15 years. These austerity measures have impacted police, Crown Prosecution Service (CPS), courts, prisons, probation – and also forensic science more generally,[7] causing 'serious market instability'.[8] This 'austerity' has been one explanation for the widespread privatisation of services.[9]

3.1.2 The related tradition of forensic assessment

The recognition that an offender with mental derangement may not be culpable was evident in English Common Law for centuries before medical practitioners began to provide expert evidence to criminal courts in the eighteenth century on cases of insanity.[10] Usually, when obvious mental disorder was raised as a defence, the witness testimony would be provided by acquaintances, but from the 1820s onwards medical witnesses appeared with increasing frequency,[11] and they began to claim expertise in identifying and diagnosing forms of insanity that would not be recognised by lay observers.

The role of medical specialists in the criminal courts continued to develop in the nineteenth century. The *M'Naghten Rules* in 1843 formulated criteria for acquittal on the grounds of insanity. Although they soon evoked clinical dissatisfaction and criticism – and proposals for their reform have repeatedly been made[12] – the *Rules* remain the applicable standard. Notwithstanding their limitations, the number of insanity verdicts increased during the late-nineteenth century. Medical assessments became more commonplace when the sanity of those accused of murder was questioned and the consequence of conviction would be capital punishment.[13] For more minor offenders dealt with in the Magistrates Courts, new legal provisions were developed in the early-twentieth century to dismiss criminal charges and to commit those with mental disorders to hospitals or guardianship.[14]

The Homicide Act 1957 introduced a partial defence of diminished responsibility arising from abnormality of mind for individuals charged with murder. The test was considerably broader than the *M'Naghten Rules* and if successful led to a conviction of manslaughter for which a range of sentences, including a hospital order, could be given. Contested cases in which the verdict was decided by a jury provided a further forum for psychiatric evidence in criminal trials, not only on the issue of criminal responsibility but also in relation to sentencing in cases where a medical disposal was recommended.

The increased use of psychiatric evidence for sentencing was a consequence of a major reform of mental health legislation, the Mental Health Act 1959, that introduced the hospital order as a sentencing option for any person charged with an imprisonable offence if medical reports confirmed they were suffering from a form of mental disorder meeting the criteria for inpatient medical treatment. In more serious cases, a Crown Court could add restrictions on the authority of the clinicians to discharge the patient given a hospital order. Increasingly, it was the route to hospital at sentencing stage that became the preferred way of enabling treatment for the seriously mentally ill offender, rather than through seeking to establish unfitness to plead or an insanity defence.

The Mental Health Act 1983[15] maintained the framework of the hospital order and restriction order (under ss. 37 and 41) and introduced additional powers for courts to remand defendants to hospital for psychiatric assessment or treatment. For offenders who could be managed in the community under probation orders, conditions of psychiatric treatment could be added.

Substantial growth in the specialty of forensic psychiatry in the United Kingdom (UK) began after the Butler Committee (1974),[16] which had been established to review the law and services for mentally disordered offenders, recommended that a new type of secure hospital unit should be created in each region of England and Wales. These were regional secure units that would provide an intermediate level of security between the local hospitals and the notoriously overcrowded high security hospitals (such as Broadmoor and Rampton). Over the following decades, the number of forensic psychiatrists in the United Kingdom increased, and their professional work and training focused predominantly on the development and provision of clinical services for mentally disordered offenders. Whilst the provision of reports and testimony for criminal courts was a component of their work, relatively few forensic psychiatrists in the United Kingdom saw their primary professional role and identity as that of an expert witness.

These two features in the development of UK forensic psychiatry – its clinical service identity and a legislative framework that predominantly results in criminal courts using psychiatric evidence for pragmatic purposes of diversion and sentencing – were important for developing a range of specialist treatment and support services, but have resulted in limitations. A notable feature of the provisions in the Mental Health Act 1983 enabling criminal courts to remand or sentence those with mental disorder to hospital is that no such order can be made unless the court has been informed by the relevant clinician or hospital manager that arrangements have been made for the person's admission within a specified period. This has given clinicians a gate-keeping power that can disable a criminal court from making the order that the judge considers to be appropriate. This is arguably contrary to the interests of justice.[17]

A second limitation is that there has probably been insufficient focus on legal and ethical issues in specialty training schemes and research in UK forensic psychiatry. This needs to be addressed if we are to ensure widespread and consistently high competence and reflective practice in the expert witness role. Whilst Rix[18] has contributed excellent and comprehensive guides to the practice of psychiatric expert witness work, principally in England and Wales, it is necessary to turn to literature from the United States for leading analyses of the ethical problems of constructing forensic psychiatric reports and providing expert evidence.[19]

In recent years, the range of clinical research of potential relevance to sentencing has grown. Developments in the fields of risk assessment and of neuroscience are particularly prominent.[20] The application of psychiatric evidence in sentencing decisions has also become more complicated as recent case law and sentencing guidelines have located medical disposal options more firmly within a framework in which determinations of culpability are primary.[21]

As the range of relevant psychological research has grown, expert evidence from clinical and forensic psychology has had an increasingly important role, although its acceptance in the English criminal courts has been a more recent achievement and was initially contested. In *Turner* (1975),[22] the Court of Appeal ruled that expert psychological evidence in a case where there was not a medically diagnosed mental disorder was inadmissible. It was held that the relevant matters concerning the state of mind of the accused could be determined by a jury without the need for expert opinion.

Judicial scepticism continued. It was not until 1991 that the Court of Appeal, when dealing with the issue of disputed confessions in *Silcott, Braithwaite, and Raghip* (1991),[23] broadened the admissibility of psychological evidence to include personality features such as suggestibility. It was a further decade before the House of Lords accepted psychological evidence about the reliability of admissions made in police interviews as the main basis for quashing a conviction in *Pendleton* (2001).[24]

The range of issues on which expert psychological evidence may be relevant includes not only the reliability of admissions and witness testimony but also fitness to stand trial and issues of risk and treatment need in sentencing. In some cases, where there is relevant evidence of both mental disorder and an intellectual impairment, developmental disorder, or personality abnormality, separate psychiatric and psychological assessments may be needed.

3.2 Short overview of the role of assessment in sentencing offenders

3.2.1 Sentences and execution

Sentencing is in the hands of judges (and magistrates), and forensic assessments will rarely be required by the judge. The defence is more likely to seek such reports than the prosecution. We start with a brief review of the available sanctions.

The judges of England and Wales impose life (indeterminate) sentences more frequently than any other European country. On 30 September 2019, there were 9,269 (8,918 male; 351 female) indeterminate sentenced prisoners.[25] There are many routes to a life sentence, including the mandatory life sentence for murder;[26] the automatic life sentence for a second 'listed' offence, created by s. 122 of the Legal Aid, Sentencing and Punishment of Offenders Act 2012;[27] and a discretionary life sentence for serious offences, both under s. 225 of the Criminal Justice Act 2003[28] and under the common law.[29] As a result of many legal changes over the years, there are probably currently people in prison serving 11 different sorts of life sentence.[30]

A semi-indeterminate sentence is the extended sentence, a sentence which is served in custody until some point, followed by an extended supervision period of up to five years for violent offenders and eight years for sexual offenders, with a minimum extension period of one year: introduced in 2012, and now governed by s. 279 of the Sentencing Act 2020. The release rules are particularly complex, having been frequently changed: anyone sentenced after 13 April 2015 will not be released automatically but instead is referred to the Parole Board at the 2/3rds stage and will only be released automatically at the end of the custodial period.

Most prisoners subjected to life or extended sentences will have been deemed 'dangerous' by the sentencing judge. The assessment of 'dangerousness' does not require a professional expert to give evidence. The current version of the definition of dangerousness is that there is '*a significant risk to members of the public of serious harm occasioned by the commission by him of further such [serious] offences*'. Section 308 of the Sentencing Act 2020 provides that in making the assessment of dangerousness, the court (i.e. the sentence)

a   'must take into account all such information as is available to it about the nature and circumstances of the offence,

b   may take into account all such information as is available to it about the nature and circumstances of any other offences of which the offender has been convicted by a court anywhere in the world,

c may take into account any information which is before it about any pattern of behaviour of which any of the offences mentioned in paragraph (a) or (aa) forms part, and

d may take into account any information about the offender which is before it'.

As noted in a recent editorial in the *British Journal of Psychiatry,* there is a lack of good research data providing evidence on optimal practice in the provision of psychiatric evidence for sentencing.[31] An examination of appellate cases suggests great inconsistencies in the use of experts. For example, *Burinskas* (2014),[32] an important appellate case on the interpretation of the 'dangerousness' laws, involved eight quite separate cases. In only two of them had there been psychiatric evidence at the sentencing hearing. In *Thompson* (2018),[33] a case involving four separate appeals: only one involved psychiatric evidence. In this time of 'austerity justice', the Court of Appeal not infrequently discourages the use of experts at sentencing. For example, in *Chall* (2019),[34] the Court of Appeal considered six different cases to give guidance on the proper approach to be taken by a sentencing judge when assessing, for the purposes of a relevant sentencing guideline, whether a victim of crime had suffered severe psychological harm. The Court of Appeal made it clear that they discouraged the use of experts at sentencing. The assessment of whether the level of psychological harm can properly be regarded as severe is for the judge:

> The judicial assessment may in some cases be assisted by expert evidence from a psychologist or psychiatrist. However, we reject the submission that it is always essential for the sentencer to consider expert evidence before deciding whether a victim has suffered severe psychological harm. On the contrary, the judge may make such an assessment, and will usually be able to make such an assessment, without needing to obtain expert evidence.

Thus, a judge may make a finding of 'severe psychological harm' simply on the basis of the contents of what the victim reports in a Victim's Personal Statement (VPS).

A Community Order can be imposed for offences that are serious but not so serious as to warrant custody. It is made up of one or more 'requirements':

- Unpaid work
- Rehabilitation activity
- Programme
- Prohibited activity
- Curfew
- Exclusion
- Residence
- Foreign travel prohibition
- Mental health treatment
- Drug rehabilitation
- Period review of drug rehabilitation
- Alcohol treatment
- Alcohol abstinence and monitoring
- Attendance centre
- Electronic monitoring

None of these formally require an expert's report but it would be unheard of to impose, for example, a mental health treatment requirement without clinical reports. Under this requirement, the 'offender must submit, during a period or periods specified in the order, to treatment by or under the direction of a registered medical practitioner or a registered psychologist'.[35] Similarly, with an alcohol treatment requirement, the court must be satisfied that arrangements have been or can be made for the treatment intended to be specified in the order (including arrangements for the reception of the offender where he is to be required to submit to treatment as a resident).[36]

In addition, a sentencing court has a number of possible mental health 'disposals'. These would not be issued without psychiatric evidence. The most serious is a s. 41 restriction order (all the sections here refer to the Mental Health Act 1983, as amended). This is added to a hospital order, if it is considered necessary for the protection of the public from serious harm. The restriction is without limit of time. A s. 37 hospital order lasts initially for six months but can be renewed for a further six months and then for a year at a time. A hospital order can be discharged by the responsible clinician (RC) or the hospital at any time, but a patient subject to a restriction order can only be released by the Secretary of State (Minister of Justice) or by order of the First Tier Tribunal (Mental Health) in England and the Mental Health Review Tribunal in Wales. Another option in the Crown Court is to make a hospital and limitation direction under s. 45 A of the Mental Health Act 1983, which combines a hospital order (with restriction) and a sentence of imprisonment, and is often known as a hybrid order. This can be done when the Court considers imprisonment to be the appropriate sentence rather than a hospital order for a mentally disordered offender whose condition warrants hospital treatment, and the court directs that instead of being held in prison they are detained in a hospital. In these cases, release will be a matter for the Parole Board and it cannot be ordered by the First Tier Tribunal (Mental Health). Some sentencers may view this as a safeguard for public protection. There is also the possibility of a Guardianship Order (where the local authority or other person receives offender into guardianship), which is rarely used; and a Community Order, with the requirement of psychiatric treatment, which is more commonly used: for example, see *Steward* (2008),[37] a sad case to read. The long delay in bringing the case to court was caused by a detailed investigation as to her fitness to plead, which was eventually confirmed by a consultant forensic psychiatrist at Rampton Hospital. We will return in the following sections to decisions that may be made long before sentencing, but which also can be drawn out over a long period.

Recent case law has clarified how sentencing courts should consider the sentencing options of imprisonment, the hospital and limitation direction, and the hospital order. The judgments in *Vowles* (2015)[38] and *Edwards and others* (2018)[39] challenged the prevailing assumption amongst forensic psychiatrists that a hospital order was an alternative to imprisonment that depended on the person's mental disorder and need for treatment at the point of sentencing, without regard to whether or not the mental disorder affected criminal responsibility. The *Vowles* judgment emphasised that the sentencing court should consider culpability and the option of a prison sentence with a hospital and limitation direction before making a hospital order. The later judgment in *Edwards and others* clarified that the *Vowles* judgment did not provide a 'default' setting of imprisonment. The sentencing judge should first consider whether a hospital order may be appropriate, but before making such an order, the court must consider all the powers at its disposal including a s. 45 A order. A s. 45 A order should be considered first because it includes a penal element and the court must have 'sound reasons' for departing from the usual course of imposing a sentence with a penal element. At para 14, it was stated:

... rehabilitation of offenders is but one of the purposes of sentencing. The punishment of offenders and the protection of the public are also at the heart of the sentencing process. In assessing the seriousness of the offence, s. 143 (1) of the Criminal Justice Act[40] provides that the court must consider the offender's culpability in committing the offence and any harm caused, intended or foreseeable. Hence the structure adopted by the Sentencing Council in the production of its definitive guidelines and the two pillars of sentencing: culpability and harm. Assessing the culpability of an offender who has committed a serious offence but suffers from mental health problems may present a judge with a difficult task but to comply with s.142 and the judgment in *Vowles*, he or she must attempt it.

The *Vowles* and *Edwards* judgments have been the subject of critical commentary[41] and have raised concerns that they could result in more prison sentences and fewer hospital orders for offenders with mental disorder. In 2019, the Sentencing Council issued a draft guideline for sentencing offenders with mental health disorders that reflected the approach of first assessing the degree of culpability of the offender with mental disorder and then including that assessment amongst the matters to be weighed up in determining the sentence.[42] This was then adopted in the definitive *Guideline on Sentencing Offenders with mental disorders, developmental disorders, or neurological impairments,* which became effective from 1 October 2020.[43]

To return to pre-sentence issues: a person who is 'unfit to plead' may simply not be prosecuted and be diverted from the criminal justice process. Where the prosecution does decide to initiate proceedings, a defendant must be 'of sufficient intellect to comprehend the course of the proceedings in the trial so as to make a proper defence, to challenge a juror to whom he might wish to object and comprehend the details of the evidence' (Alderson B in *Pritchard* (1836),[44] where D was deaf and dumb). The test is hardly up to date: defendants rarely get the chance to challenge jurors in England since the abolition of peremptory challenges in 1988, but the principle is that the defendant must be able to plead, and to instruct his lawyers. He need not necessarily be capable of acting in his own best interests. In practice, where there is evidence that he or she is unfit to plead, the court first hears evidence on this issue. If he is fit to plead, then the trial proceeds. If he is not fit to plead, another court then decides if he 'did the act or made the omission charged against him as the offence' (Criminal Procedure (Insanity and Unfitness to Plead) Act 1991, as amended).[45] This is unsatisfactory: a defendant is unfit to plead, but a jury goes on to decide if he did the act charged. There are a number of appellate decisions on this issue, which reveal sad histories.[46] In *John M* (2003),[47] the appellant (who had been found fit to plead) argued that the trial judge had misdirected the jury by setting the test too low. The Court of Appeal, however, endorsed as 'admirable' (para 31) the detailed directions the trial judge had given, explaining in specific terms what each of the relevant criteria meant. These provide a useful guide for clinical report writers. The standing body that oversees law reform, the Law Commission, has recommended reforms that have not been implemented.[48]

A person who is fit to plead, may yet be 'not guilty by reason of insanity'. As noted earlier, rules applying to the insanity verdict are deeply outdated, deriving from the celebrated case of *M'Naghten* (1843) who, in attempting to shoot the Home Secretary, had killed his secretary. After M'Naghten's acquittal by a jury, the judges of the House of Lords were asked to formulate rules for the guidance of juries. Despite some reluctance about answering hypothetical questions on which they had not heard argument, Tindal CJ did report that:

... jurors ought to be told in all cases that every man is to be presumed to be sane, and to possess a sufficient degree of reason to be responsible for his crimes, until the contrary is proved to their satisfaction; and that to establish a defence on the ground of insanity, it must be clearly proved that, at the time of the committing of the act, the party accused was labouring under such a defect of reason, from disease of the mind, as not to know the nature and quality of the act he was doing; or, if he did know it, that he did not know he was doing what was wrong.

This definition is remarkably narrow. For example, someone with delusional beliefs that his actions were right is only legally insane if he did not know that what he did is legally wrong. There are many other difficulties, but despite the excellent discussion paper by the Law Commission (2013), their proposals for reform have not been enacted since their review was completed.[49]

The hospital facilities to which offenders detained under the Mental Health Act 1983 are sent have a range of security. Three high-secure hospitals (Broadmoor, Rampton, and Ashworth Hospitals) together provide about 800 places, with Broadmoor and Ashworth only taking male patients. There are about 3,000 medium-secure hospital beds in units provided both by the NHS and private sector, and a more extensive range of low secure and re-habilitation in-patient units. Many offenders with mental disorder who do not require secure in-patient care will receive assessment and support from community forensic psychiatry teams (which are not uniformly available) or general community mental health teams.

3.2.2 Decisions within sentencing and execution

The execution of a sentence in England, depends on the sentence involved.

i A person who has been sentenced to prison will go there immediately (unless they were made subject to a hospital and limitation direction), even if they are going to appeal. The prison authorities make many decisions in relation to the allocation and categorisation of prisoners. These are significant administrative decisions for the prisoner as they will affect his or her progress through the system. Forensic psychologists are also closely involved in assessing prisoners, particularly with structured risk assessment instruments, and imple-menting offender treatment programmes. Their role in evaluating risk and progress of people in prisons has grown enormously in the last 30 years. Psychiatrists who work in prisons are more rarely involved in providing risk assessment reports: the resources of mental health in-reach teams in the Prison Service are limited in relation to the substantial scale of psychiatric morbidity amongst prisoners, and the clinical staff therefore tend to focus on the psychiatric assessment and care of prisoners with severe mental illness or presenting with other urgent mental health problems and vulnerabilities.[50]

A person sentenced to a life or extended sentence will be released only on the direction of the Parole Board, but the Parole Board is deeply dependant on the reports submitted to them (see later). These may include reports by psychologists and others involved in assessing the prisoners 'risks' and 'needs'. However, psychiatric reports for the Parole Board on prisoners with mental disorder may be less readily available and comprehensive than would normally be the case for offenders in the secure hospital system.

ii A person sentenced to a community order with a mental health treatment requirement will be primarily supervised by an offender manager within the National Probation Service. As noted earlier, the mental health treatment is provided under the direction of a doctor or psychologist. The court making the order will need sufficient information to be satisfied that the offender's mental condition is susceptible to treatment but is not such as to warrant a hospital or guardianship order under the Mental Health Act 1983. During the currency of the treatment requirement, there should be liaison between the supervisor and the clinician. The valuable potential of this framework for managing offenders with mental health needs in the community may have been under-utilised, and one reason for this is the discomfort of some clinicians about participating in breach reporting and enforcement measures against their patients.[51] Long et al. (2018) have described a successful partnership initiative involving the probation service, training for the judiciary, and a mental health service provider with intervention programmes delivered by psychology graduates.[52] The scheme resulted in a significant increase in mental health treatment requirements. The authors reported that the initiative not only led to effective treatment and measurable clinical benefit to the offenders on community orders, but was also associated with a decrease in the number of requests for psychiatric reports 'that are time consuming and do not lead to rapid treatment'.[53]

iii A person detained as an inpatient within the mental health system following sentence is likely to be either under a hospital order[54] with or without an additional restriction order[55], or under a hospital and limitation direction.[56] Sentenced prisoners who need hospital treatment later during sentence can be transferred from prison to hospital and detained with restrictions on their discharge.[57] Release decisions for those given prison sentences and hospital orders are different. The release of sentenced prisoners (who include those on whom the court has made a hospital and limitation direction) is a matter for the Parole Board. The release of patients detained under hospital orders is not. Patients under hospital orders without a restriction order may be given leave and discharged at any time by the responsible clinician, but patients with restriction orders are in a different position. As previously noted, the effect of the restriction order is that their detention is without limit of time, and discharge from hospital can only be directed by the Minister of Justice or by an independent tribunal – the First Tier Tribunal (Mental Health) – chaired by a senior judge. As restricted patients make progress in hospital, decisions about whether they can be granted leave or be transferred to another hospital also require permission by the Ministry of Justice. When those on restriction orders are discharged from hospital, they will usually be subject to conditions for an extended period and be liable to recall. Regular reports on restricted patients also have to be submitted to the Ministry of Justice. The effect of these arrangements is that the reports and assessments made by clinicians need to reflect detailed and extensive clinical risk assessment, often in exhaustive detail, and when clinicians wish to make recommendations for leave, transfer, or discharge, their reports need to be comprehensive, reasoned, and persuasive.

3.2.3 Concepts to be assessed

We have thus seen that there are a number of concepts that may be applied to an offender in sentencing. With regard to the concept of risk, as described earlier, the Criminal Justice Act 2003 set out a definition of the category of 'dangerous offenders' for whom life or extended sentences are appropriate (rules which have been much amended and are now to be found in the Sentencing Act 2020). The law applies to those convicted of specified violent, sexual, or terrorist offences where the court has assessed in the individual case that, '*there is a significant risk to members of the public of serious harm occasioned by the commission by him of further such offences*'. The term 'serious harm' '… *means death or serious personal injury, whether physical or psychological*' (see s. 306(2) of the Sentencing Act 2020). Although these assessments will normally be made by the judge without expert evidence from forensic psychologists and psychiatrists being sought, it is likely that any reports that are already available in the case will form part of the information taken into account by the sentencer. For example, as noted earlier (footnote 29), one of the criteria relevant to a life sentence is whether it appears from a defendant's history *'that he is a person of unstable character likely to commit such offences in the future'*. If a psychiatric report had been prepared for the purpose of assessing the offender's suitability for a medical disposal, it is possible that the content of the report could be used as evidence in relation to the *Hodgson* criterion. Clinical experts (and those who consent to be assessed by them) should be aware that reports prepared for one purpose can be used for others. Clinicians also need to be vigilant about the limitations of risk assessment instruments[58] and the limitations of their expertise in relation to issues such as terrorism risk.[59]

The criteria for unfitness to plead would rarely be relevant in sentencing. As noted earlier, in cases where the issue has been raised (which happens relatively rarely), this will have been before the sentencing stage. If the question arises of whether the accused is 'under disability' in relation to trial, the court can postpone determination of the issue at an early stage if this is in the accused's interests. This can enable a period of psychiatric treatment in the hope that the accused can be remitted for trial later when fit. However, as described earlier, when a court does determine that the individual is 'under disability', the case then proceeds directly to a trial of the facts by a jury who will determine whether the accused committed the act charged against him.[60]

The insanity defence and its criteria as formulated in the *M'Naghten Rules* have been discussed in sections 3.1.2 and 3.2.1, and will be familiar in some other jurisdictions. However, the statutory criteria for a diminished responsibility defence (which applies only in murder charges) merit further discussion here because they pose particular difficulties for the application of psychiatric and psychological evidence. The criteria exemplify how a legal test to which clinical evidence has to be applied can include some concepts that are within the scope of clinical expertise and other concepts that are not.

As previously noted, a person charged with murder may plead guilty to a lesser charge of manslaughter on the basis of mental abnormality that diminished their responsibility. The Coroners and Justice Act 2009, s. 52 specifies:

1   'A person ('D') who kills or is a party to the killing of another is not to be convicted of murder if D was suffering from an abnormality of mental functioning which—

    a   arose from a recognised medical condition,
    b   substantially impaired D's ability to do one or more of the things mentioned in subsection (1 A), and
    c   provides an explanation for D's acts and omissions in doing or being a party to the killing.

1A Those things are –

    a   to understand the nature of D's conduct;
    b   to form a rational judgment;
    c   to exercise self-control.

1B For the purposes of subsection (1)(c), an abnormality of mental functioning provides an explanation for D's conduct if it causes, or is a significant contributory factor in causing, D to carry out that conduct'.

The boundaries of the statutory term 'abnormality of mental functioning' will not be immediately clear to an assessing psychiatrist, but with regard to subsection (1)(a), he/she would have expertise in assessing whether there is a 'recognised medical condition' (although with the proviso that establishing diagnoses at a past point in time may not be straightforward, and co-morbid conditions are common). Criterion (1)(b) should also be within the psychiatrist's expertise, although here two kinds of difficulty can be recognised: first, the practical task of establishing detailed and valid evidence about these abilities, when dependent in large part on the defendant's self-description; and secondly, the uncertainty about what 'substantially' means, and whether or not this is a matter for psychiatric opinion.[61] Criterion (1)(c) is the main problem in relation to psychiatric expertise, and it is perhaps not surprising that a study by Mackay and Mitchell (2017) reported that nearly half the psychiatric reports on diminished responsibility they examined did not refer to the 'explanation' requirement, and over half were silent on the question of the 'causation' requirement.[62] One difficulty here is in the nature of psychiatric explanations. Most psychiatric explanations of abnormal or criminal behaviour are what Walker (1985) termed 'possibility explanations', that is accounts of how it was psychologically possible that D acted as he/she did.[63] It is in the nature of these explanations that plausible alternative accounts are possible. In addition, explanations of behaviour in psychiatry can involve the weighing up of multiple factors with considerable scope for weighing them differently.

When a diminished responsibility verdict is reached, a medical disposal will not necessarily follow. The Sentencing Council (2018) guideline[64] for offences of manslaughter makes clear that with regard to the first step of assessing the offender's level of culpability, the court should determine, in the light of the diminished responsibility finding, what level of responsibility the offender *retained*. For a custodial sentence, the starting point and range will depend on whether the level of responsibility retained is high, medium, or low. After assessing culpability, the court will consider dangerousness and then – if there is medical evidence that the offender is currently suffering from mental disorder and treatment is available – a hospital order can be considered. However, a hospital order will be imposed only after considering all sentencing options and recognising the importance of a penal element that reflects the offender's level of responsibility. Thus, an expert's clinical assessment of the psychological impairments relevant to the diminished responsibility test may set the parameters for the court's assessment of retained 'culpability' responsibility.

The criteria for making a hospital order (or hospital and restriction direction) are set out at ss. 37 and 45 A of the Mental Health Act 1983. The requirements relating to mental disorder are similar to those that apply for detention for treatment under a civil order and are broadly framed. The court must be satisfied on evidence from two registered medical practitioners that the offender is suffering from '… mental disorder … of a nature or degree which makes it appropriate for him to be detained in a hospital for medical treatment', and that, '… appropriate medical treatment is available for him'. The term, 'mental disorder' '… means any disorder or disability of mind' (s. 1(1)), but there are exclusions: dependence on alcohol or drugs (alone) is not considered to be a mental disorder (s. 1(3)). Nor is learning disability unless the disability '… is associated with abnormally aggressive or seriously irresponsible conduct in the individual's case'. The 'nature' of the mental disorder refers essentially to its history over time, including response to treatment; and the 'degree' of the disorder refers to how it is currently manifesting.

The addition by a Crown Court of an order imposing restrictions on discharge (s. 41) is possible if, '…, it appears to the court, having regard to the nature of the offence, the antecedents of the offender, and the risk of his committing further offences if set at large, that it is necessary for the protection of the public from serious harm so to do …' (s. 41(1)).

It is a requirement that one of the two doctors recommending the hospital order has given oral evidence to the court, and this oral evidence should specifically address the question of the offender's risk of serious harm in the future.[65] However, the court is not obliged to accept the medical opinion and a judge has discretion to impose a restriction order even if the medical view is that it is not necessary.[66] The criteria for discharge of a restricted patient from hospital by a First Tier Tribunal (Mental Health) reflect the criteria for detention, although not exactly. The tribunal must order a discharge if it is not satisfied that one (or more) of the following criteria are met: (i) that the patient is suffering from mental disorder of a nature or degree which makes it appropriate for them to be detained in hospital for medical treatment; or (ii) that is it necessary for the health or safety of the patient or the protection of others that they should receive that treatment; or (iii) that appropriate medical treatment is available.

3.2.4 Forensic assessment and procedure

The National Health Service (NHS) in England has responsibilities for commissioning and providing liaison and diversion (L&D) schemes for people with psychosocial vulnerabilities, including mental illness and learning disability, who come into contact with the police and criminal justice system. The purpose of these schemes is to enable early identification, assessment, and intervention, including referral for specialist care. L&D schemes should respond to concerns raised by the police and criminal justice system, and provide clinical advice when needed to inform decisions about charging and sentencing

The schemes have developed slowly but there are plans for NHS England to commission L&D services that are accessible to the whole population.[67] A service specification for these schemes was published in 2019.[68] This states that the L&D services should be available every day in police custody suites, and also comprehensively cover Magistrates Courts, Youth Courts, and specified Crown Courts. One of the service objectives is, 'to provide high quality information to key decision makers in youth and criminal justice agencies, including the police, courts, Crown Prosecution Service (CPS), probation and Youth Offending Teams (YOTs) and youth offending services'.[69] The services should provide written reports to courts that include information on an individual's vulnerabilities (including how those vulnerabilities impact on criminal behaviour) and ability to participate in criminal proceedings. Reports should contain information relevant to case management, remand, and sentencing.[70] The service specification includes a court report template.[71]

A useful summary of good practice guidance for commissioning and providing psychiatric reports for sentencing was published by the Ministry of Justice in 2010.[72] The authors of the guidance conducted a prior research study that identified widespread and substantial barriers to the effective commissioning of reports.[73] These problems included: finding psychiatrists willing to undertake the work; failures to identify the need for reports in some cases; court staff being unfamiliar with the commissioning process; delays in securing funding; lack of detail in letters of instruction; psychiatrists lacking requisite information and knowledge; delays; and failures of liaison and administration. The purpose of the subsequent good practice guidance was to encourage more effective and timely provision of good quality reports.

In theory, the framework of liaison and diversion services should facilitate more extensive provision of relevant clinical information to the criminal courts, and more access to support and treatment for many offenders with mental disorder. However, it is too early to evaluate the extent to which these services – when established for the whole population – will adequately ensure provision of the specialist reports and evidence that sentencing courts require, and in the timely and efficient way outlined in the good practice guidance.[74] Although the sample of interviewees in the research study by McLeod et al. (2010)[75] was relatively small, the fundamental difficulties they reported in the provision of psychiatric reports were extensive and probably long-standing. There should be caution in assuming they will be easily resolved.

Psychiatric and psychological reports for criminal proceedings may be requested directly by the Crown Prosecution Service (CPS), by defence lawyers, and by the courts. The CPS may need information concerning a suspect's mental health in relation to the twofold test for prosecution, namely, whether it is in the public interest and whether there is sufficient evidence for a realistic prospect of conviction.[76]

A defendant's solicitor may also commission a report for sentencing. (However, not all defendants will have legal representation.) The funding of legal representation for defendants with very limited financial resources is usually through Legal Aid. The Legal Aid scheme provides a very limited set fee per case, and solicitors need to make applications for additional funding for unusually complex cases (which may include defendants with mental disorder) and in order to obtain prior authority to instruct experts.[77] In considering whether to fund such reports, the Legal Aid Agency is required to consider fee rates that are specified in regulations.[78] If funding is unavailable, a forensic report is unlikely to be available.

A court may be alerted to the need for a psychiatric report by a Probation Service pre-sentence report. The detailed procedural requirements to be followed when a court requires a medical report for sentencing are set out in the Rule 28(8) of the Criminal Procedure Rules 2020.[79] The court may request a medical examination of the defendant not only when considering a disposal under the Mental Health Act 1983, but also when considering a custodial sentence for a defendant who is, or appears to be, mentally disordered.[80] The court must identify each issue on which expert medical opinion is needed, set a timetable for provision of the report, and may issue directions about how it is to be obtained. The requirements and obligations that apply to expert opinion evidence are set out in Part 19 of the Criminal Procedure Rules and Practice Directions and will be discussed in section 3.3.1.

It is difficult to generalise about the impact of forensic evaluations and empirical research evidence is limited. The influence of reports prepared for sentencing is variable, and judicial decision makers will be more impressed by some reports and some report writers than others. With regard to the use of reports, it is common – particularly in more minor cases and those that do not go to trial – for a single written report to be taken into account in sentencing, particularly for mitigation, without oral evidence being given. In more serious cases and where there is contested expert evidence, the witnesses may be called and cross-examined.

3.3 Safeguards for the quality of forensic assessment

3.3.1 Requirements in law and policy

Legal requirements that apply when a party wishes to introduce expert opinion evidence in the criminal courts of England and Wales, including psychiatric and psychological evidence, are formulated in procedural rules that are periodically updated. The Criminal Procedure Rules (CrimPR) were revised in 2015, with amendments made twice a year, and now (2022) have been re-issued as the Criminal Procedure Rules 2020 (and already amended). Part 19 of these Rules covers expert evidence. These do not prescribe the particular assessment methods and instruments to be used by experts, but they are highly prescriptive and detailed in defining the expert's duty to the court (further discussed later), and in specifying what a report must contain and what must be disclosed. Rule 19(4) specifies that an expert's report must,

a 'give details of the expert's qualifications, relevant experience, and accreditation;
b give details of any literature or other information which the expert has relied on in making the report;
c contain a statement setting out the substance of all facts given to the expert which are material to the opinions expressed in the report, or upon which those opinions are based;

d   make clear which of the facts stated in the report are within the expert's own knowledge;
e   where the expert has based an opinion or inference on a representation of fact or opinion made by another person for the purposes of criminal proceedings (for example, as to the outcome of an examination, measurement, test or experiment)—

   i   identify the person who made that representation to the expert,
   ii   give the qualifications, relevant experience, and any accreditation of that person, and
   iii certify that that person had personal knowledge of the matters stated in that representation;

f   where there is a range of opinion on the matters dealt with in the report—

   i   summarise the range of opinion, and
   ii   give reasons for the expert's own opinion;

g   if the expert is not able to give an opinion without qualification, state the qualification;
h   include such information as the court may need to decide whether the expert's opinion is sufficiently reliable to be admissible as evidence;
i   contain a summary of the conclusions reached;
j   contain a statement that the expert understands an expert's duty to the court, and has complied and will continue to comply with that duty; and
k   contain the same declaration of truth as a witness statement'.

The precise wording of the statement required under (j) and (k) concerning the duty to the court and declaration of truth is not mandatory, but it needs to be extensive. The Criminal Practice Directions at 19B.1 state that it should be in the following terms (or in terms substantially similar):[81]

I (name) DECLARE THAT:

1   I understand that my duty is to help the court to achieve the overriding objective by giving independent assistance by way of objective, unbiased opinion on matters within my expertise, both in preparing reports and giving oral evidence. I understand that this duty overrides any obligation to the party by whom I am engaged or the person who has paid or is liable to pay me. I confirm that I have complied with and will continue to comply with that duty.
2   I confirm that I have not entered into any arrangement where the amount or payment of my fees is in any way dependent on the outcome of the case.
3   I know of no conflict of interest of any kind, other than any which I have disclosed in my report.
4   I do not consider that any interest which I have disclosed affects my suitability as an expert witness on any issues on which I have given evidence.
5   I will advise the party by whom I am instructed if, between the date of my report and the trial, there is any change in circumstances which affect my answers to points 3 and 4 above.
6   I have shown the sources of all information I have used.
7   I have exercised reasonable care and skill in order to be accurate and complete in preparing this report.
8   I have endeavoured to include in my report those matters, of which I have knowledge or of which I have been made aware, that might adversely affect the validity of my opinion. I have clearly stated any qualifications to my opinion.

9 I have not, without forming an independent view, included or excluded anything which has been suggested to me by others including my instructing lawyers.
10 I will notify those instructing me immediately and confirm in writing if for any reason my existing report requires any correction or qualification.
11 I understand that:

    a   my report will form the evidence to be given under oath or affirmation;
    b   the court may at any stage direct a discussion to take place between experts;
    c   the court may direct that, following a discussion between the experts, a statement should be prepared showing those issues which are agreed and those issues which are not agreed, together with the reasons;
    d   I may be required to attend court to be cross-examined on my report by a cross-examiner assisted by an expert.
    e   I am likely to be the subject of public adverse criticism by the judge if the Court concludes that I have not taken reasonable care in trying to meet the standards set out above.

12 I have read Part 19 of the Criminal Procedure Rules and I have complied with its requirements.
13 I confirm that I have acted in accordance with the code of practice or conduct for experts of my discipline, namely *[identify the code]*
14 [For Experts instructed by the Prosecution only] I confirm that I have read guidance contained in a booklet known as *Disclosure: Experts' Evidence and Unused Material* which details my role and documents my responsibilities, in relation to revelation as an expert witness. I have followed the guidance and recognise the continuing nature of my responsibilities of disclosure. In accordance with my duties of disclosure, as documented in the guidance booklet, I confirm that:

    a   I have complied with my duties to record, retain and reveal material in accordance with the Criminal Procedure and Investigations Act 1996, as amended;
    b   I have compiled an Index of all material. I will ensure that the Index is updated in the event I am provided with or generate additional material;
    c   in the event my opinion changes on any material issue, I will inform the investigating officer, as soon as reasonably practicable and give reasons.

I confirm that the contents of this report are true to the best of my knowledge and belief and that I make this report knowing that, if it is tendered in evidence, I would be liable to prosecution if I have wilfully stated anything which I know to be false or that I do not believe to be true.

Although the methods of clinical assessment are not prescribed by the Criminal Procedure Rules or Practice Directions, the records of any clinical examination, test, or investigation carried out in the course of preparing a report and expert opinion have to be disclosed if another party requires to see them (Rule 19(3)(d)).

Within the United Kingdom, the Scottish legal system has a unique and impressive legal and policy framework for risk assessment in sentencing that is not replicated in England and Wales (or Northern Ireland). In 2005, Scotland's Risk Management Authority was established as an independent public body under the Criminal Justice (Scotland) Act 2003. It has statutory duties to set standards and publish guidelines for the assessment and management of risk; and is responsible for the accreditation of practitioners who are authorised to prepare a detailed 'risk assessment report' that has to considered by a High Court Judge before an

Order for Lifelong Restriction can be imposed on a convicted offender assessed to be a danger to the public.[82] These arrangements in Scotland are notable for integrating adherence to research evidence, stringent and consistent assessment standards, and sentencing procedure requirements. Guidelines for Assessors preparing risk assessment reports emphasise a formulation-based approach, based on a review of a comprehensive range of information and evidence. Assessors are expected to select empirically supported risk instruments and other relevant assessment tools that are appropriate to the individual case.[83]

3.3.2 Disciplinary and ethical requirements

Professional requirements and ethical guidance for psychiatrists and psychologists who carry out expert assessments for the courts are set by a range of regulatory bodies and professional organisations.

The regulating body for practitioner psychologists in the United Kingdom is the Health and Care Professions Council (HCPC). The HCPC sets standards for registration of Chartered Psychologists, and maintains a publicly available register.[84] The specialties of practitioner psychologists include the 'protected titles' of Clinical Psychologist and Forensic Psychologist.

The British Psychological Society (BPS), the representative body for UK psychologists, has a Code of Ethics and Conduct that sets the professional standards that BPS members are expected to uphold, based on four ethical principles of respect, competence, responsibility, and integrity.[85] In addition, it publishes detailed practical and ethical guidelines for psychologists acting as expert witnesses.[86] Areas covered in the guidelines include the duty to the court, legal instructions, confidentiality, court testimony, and conflicts of interest. In addition, the BPS has a Directory of Expert Witnesses that Chartered Psychologists can join,[87] and an Expert Witness Advisory Group is available to advise psychologists acting as expert witnesses.[88]

Practising doctors are registered with the General Medical Council (GMC), and those who have completed specialist training (for example, in forensic psychiatry) will be on the relevant specialist register held by the GMC. The GMC also grants the practitioner's current 'licence to practice', which is dependent on periodic revalidation.[89] Courts may have regard to whether an expert witness is on a specialist register when considering their area of expertise.

The GMC also issues ethical guidance to which adherence is expected. The guidance for witnesses in legal proceedings includes requirements of honesty, recognising and working within the limits of one's competence, keeping up to date with relevant law and regulations, and the overriding duty to the court.[90] The application of these principles when acting as an expert witness is set out in detail and particularly emphasises the importance of giving objective, unbiased opinion, and not going outside one's area of expertise.

Professional associations also issue guidance. A recent publication by the Academy of Medical Royal Colleges provides a useful set of guidelines and recommendations that are consistent with those from professional regulatory bodies, other professional organisations, and the Criminal Procedure and Civil Procedure Rules.[91] The guidance provides additional material on the responsibilities experts have as clinicians to maintain continuing professional development, to undertake specific training for being an expert witness, and to have professional indemnity insurance. For those acting as psychiatric expert witnesses, the Royal College of Psychiatrists has published detailed guidance encompassing a range of courts and jurisdictions, and including discussion with reference to case law.[92] The report considers areas of ethical difficulty that are particularly likely to arise in the psychiatry such limitations of confidentiality, and the possibility that the expert's testimony may have negative consequences for the person assessed. The Royal College of Psychiatrists' guidance acknowledges that it is difficult in the context of UK forensic psychiatry to maintain the strict separation between the treating psychiatrist role and the court expert role, a separation that is an accepted principle in other countries (such as the USA). In the United Kingdom, it is not uncommon for psychiatrists to provide expert reports on their patients, notwithstanding the fundamental tension that can arise between the clinical duty of making the care of the patient one's first concern, and the expert's duty to the court that may entail giving objective evidence that could have harmful consequences for the individual they assess, thus breaching the principle of non-maleficence.

One area of assessment in which this dilemma can arise, and the possibility of a harmful outcome is particularly acute, is that of risk. As noted earlier, medical reports addressing the question of risk of serious harm may be needed by sentencers. As medical practitioners, psychiatrists may consider this ethically difficult, and not clearly within their area of expertise, which is the assessment of mental disorder. It may therefore be particularly important to separate the treatment role and the expert witness role in some sentencing cases.

There is no single system of accredited training or qualification specifically for expert witness skills amongst psychologists and psychiatrists. There are membership-based organisations of expert witnesses[93] and independent sources of training.[94] Access to high-quality training and continuing professional development is therefore available for expert witnesses who seek it, but not every expert witness will do so. It is unsatisfactory that there is no single, independent, and regulated register of expert witnesses on which the public can rely. The quality of expert evidence provided to courts is not uniform and can vary from the exemplary to seriously deficient. Whilst the legal requirements and the recommended professional standards for expert evidence are stringent, they are not an effective barrier in every case to poor evidence being admitted, and they are a porous safeguard in practice.

3.3.3 Requirements for the evaluator

From the perspective of the courts, it is important to establish that the evaluator is able to provide expert evidence that is reliable and of good quality. The Law Commission recognised a decade ago that there were insufficient safeguards against unreliable expert evidence coming before the courts:

> The current judicial approach to the admissibility of expert evidence in England and Wales is one of laissez-faire.
>
> Too much expert opinion evidence is admitted without adequate scrutiny because no clear test is being applied to determine whether the evidence is sufficiently reliable to be admitted.[95]

The Law Commission's subsequent report on expert evidence in criminal proceedings proposed a new admissibility test for expert evidence and recommended that it should not be admitted unless it was judged to be sufficiently reliable.[96] The Government declined to act on the Law Commission's proposals at that time but the Criminal Procedure Rules and Criminal Practice Directions were updated so that they incorporated some of the Law Commission's recommendations. In particular, as described earlier, Rule 19(4) lists the matters a report must cover. In addition, the Practice Directions list factors a court may consider in assessing the reliability of expert opinion.

Rule 19(2)(3) of the Criminal Procedure Rules makes clear that the expert's duty to the court includes important obligations to highlight circumstances that could render his/her evidence unreliable. When giving evidence, the expert must draw the court's attention to any question to which the answer would be outside his/her area of expertise. The expert must inform all parties and the court if his/her opinion changes from that given in a statement or report. The expert must also disclose anything that he/she recognises might undermine the reliability of the opinion or detract from their credibility or impartiality.

The Criminal Practice Directions[97] (at 19 A.4) encourage courts 'actively to enquire' into factors that may affect the reliability of an expert's opinion. The factors listed at 19 A.5–19 A.7 merit quoting in full as experts need to be aware of how extensive they are:

19 A.5 ... factors which the court may take into account in determining the reliability of expert opinion, and especially of expert scientific opinion, include:

a the extent and quality of the data on which the expert's opinion is based, and the validity of the methods by which they were obtained;

b if the expert's opinion relies on an inference from any findings, whether the opinion properly explains how safe or unsafe the inference is (whether by reference to statistical significance or in other appropriate terms);

c if the expert's opinion relies on the results of the use of any method (for instance, a test, measurement or survey), whether the opinion takes proper account of matters, such as the degree of precision or margin of uncertainty, affecting the accuracy or reliability of those results;

d the extent to which any material upon which the expert's opinion is based has been reviewed by others with relevant expertise (for instance, in peer-reviewed publications), and the views of those others on that material;

e the extent to which the expert's opinion is based on material falling outside the expert's own field of expertise;

f the completeness of the information which was available to the expert, and whether the expert took account of all relevant information in arriving at the opinion (including information as to the context of any facts to which the opinion relates);

g if there is a range of expert opinion on the matter in question, where in the range the expert's own opinion lies and whether the expert's preference has been properly explained; and

h whether the expert's methods followed established practice in the field and, if they did not, whether the reason for the divergence has been properly explained.

19 A.6 In addition, in considering reliability, and especially the reliability of expert scientific opinion, the court should be astute to identify potential flaws in such opinion which detract from its reliability, such as:

a being based on a hypothesis which has not been subjected to sufficient scrutiny (including, where appropriate, experimental or other testing), or which has failed to stand up to scrutiny;

b being based on an unjustifiable assumption;

c being based on flawed data;

d relying on an examination, technique, method, or process which was not properly carried out or applied, or was not appropriate for use in the particular case; or

e relying on an inference or conclusion which has not been properly reached.

19 A.7 To assist in the assessment described above, CrimPR 19.3(3)(c) requires a party who introduces expert evidence to give notice of anything of which that party is aware which might reasonably be thought capable of undermining the reliability of the expert's opinion,

or detracting from the credibility or impartiality of the expert; and CrimPR 19.2(3)(d) requires the expert to disclose to that party any such matter of which the expert is aware. Examples of matters that should be disclosed pursuant to those rules include (this is not a comprehensive list), both in relation to the expert and in relation to any corporation or other body with which the expert works, as an employee or in any other capacity:

a   any fee arrangement under which the amount or payment of the expert's fees is in any way dependent on the outcome of the case (see also the declaration required by paragraph 19B.1 of these directions);
b   any conflict of interest of any kind, other than a potential conflict disclosed in the expert's report (see also the declaration required by paragraph 19B.1 of these directions);
c   adverse judicial comment;
d   any case in which an appeal has been allowed by reason of a deficiency in the expert's evidence;
e   any adverse finding, disciplinary proceedings, or other criticism by a professional, regulatory or registration body or authority, including the Forensic Science Regulator;
f   any such adverse finding or disciplinary proceedings against, or other such criticism of, others associated with the corporation or other body with which the expert works which calls into question the quality of that corporation's or body's work generally;
g   conviction of a criminal offence in circumstances that suggest:

   i   a lack of respect for, or understanding of, the interests of the criminal justice system (for example, perjury; acts perverting or tending to pervert the course of public justice),
   ii   dishonesty (for example, theft or fraud), or
   iii   a lack of personal integrity (for example, corruption or a sexual offence);

h   lack of an accreditation or other commitment to prescribed standards where that might be expected;
i   a history of failure or poor performance in quality or proficiency assessments;
j   a history of lax or inadequate scientific methods;
k   a history of failure to observe recognised standards in the expert's area of expertise;
l   a history of failure to adhere to the standards expected of an expert witness in the criminal justice system.

At 19 A.9, the Criminal Practice Directions note that the rules 'do not require persistent or disproportionate enquiry' into whether an expert has met his/her disclosure obligations, but if a court becomes aware that there has not been relevant disclosure, the party introducing the evidence '... and the expert, should expect a searching examination of the circumstances by the court ...'

3.3.4 Enforcement of requirements

Although the scrutiny that can be exercised by courts in assessing reliability of expert evidence is formidable, in practice it is unusual for an expert's credentials and methods to be extensively examined. (It is perhaps more common for experts to experience on entering the witness box a formulaic preliminary invitation to list their qualifications, and then to hear uncomfortably courteous references to being 'distinguished' or 'highly experienced' before the court proceeds to substantive testing of their evidence.) On occasions, however, the expert's qualifications and methods will be sharply tested in cross-examination or by a judge.

There can be serious consequences if a failure to meet requirements becomes manifest and is then pursued. Alleged breaches of good medical practice standards and misconduct may be investigated by the General Medical Council and can result in erasure from the medical register, or findings of impaired fitness to practice. The Royal College of Psychiatrists report by Rix et al. (2015) noted two examples.

In *KumarvGeneral Medical Council* (2012),[98] a consultant psychiatrist appealed unsuccessfully against a decision of the GMC to suspend his registration for four months after finding his fitness to practice was impaired by misconduct. The misconduct related to evidence he gave in a murder trial in 2009. The outline of facts in the 2012 appeal judgement records (at para 2) that when Dr Kumar gave evidence at the murder trial:

> He found that a difficult experience. The multiplicity of deficiencies in his expertise, experience, preparation, diagnosis ... his obligations of the disclosure to the court and in his understanding of the legal framework for diminished responsibility were laid bare. ... After the verdict, the trial judge ... summarised the defects in Dr Kumar's work and referred him to the GMC, with a view to his undertaking training on the role of an expert in criminal trials: he thought that Dr Kumar had at times shown an embarrassing lack of professionalism.

The GMC Fitness to Practice Panel found that there had been conduct that was misleading and reckless, and that the doctor had acted below the standard of a reasonably competent psychiatrist acting as an expert witness.

In *PoolvGeneral Medical Council* (2014),[99] a psychiatrist appealed unsuccessfully against a finding of misconduct by the Medical Practitioners Tribunal Service and GMC that resulted in a condition on his registration. The condition restricted him in accepting expert witness instructions for a three-month period. Dr Pool was on the GMC specialist register for the psychiatry of learning disabilities, and in preparing his psychiatric report (relating to the fitness to practice of a paramedic), he did not make clear that he was not an expert in the field of adult general psychiatry, and the GMC found he had not confined his opinion to areas in which he had expert knowledge and competence.

However, the practice of reports being provided by psychiatrists who arguably are not the appropriate specialists may not be uncommon. In a study of psychiatric reports on juvenile perpetrators of homicide, Rodway et al. (2011) found that only a fifth of reports were prepared by consultants in child and adolescent forensic psychiatry.[100] Over half were prepared by consultants in adult psychiatry (of whom most were forensic psychiatrists but some were general adult psychiatrists). The reports prepared by those who were not child and adolescent psychiatrists had less information on developmental, educational, and child care history, and more information on matters relevant to older offenders (such as relationship history). With respect to the expectations of the Criminal Procedure Rules and Criminal Practice Directions, the findings were troubling, as was the fact that the authors had to conclude:

> We believe for the court to determine the most appropriate outcome for juvenile homicide perpetrators, more efforts should be made to ensure that the commissioned psychiatrist possesses the appropriate expertise to provide a thorough assessment of the juvenile and their mental state at the time of the offence (p. 902)

In *JonesvKaney* (2011),[101] the Supreme Court concluded that expert witnesses do not have immunity from being sued for negligence in the performance of their expert witness duties.

This was a majority (5:2) decision that reversed a longstanding tradition of immunity for expert witnesses that protected them from retaliatory action by disappointed civil litigants or criminal defendants. The judgment arose from a case of personal injury proceedings in which there was contested expert clinical opinion, and a clinical psychologist who had prepared a report on behalf of the injured individual subsequently agreed a joint statement with the other expert to the effect the injured individual's condition was less serious and genuine than had been stated in the psychologist's first report. In consequence, the injured individual's financial claim was settled at a lower level. The judgment does not imply that experts can not change their opinions: they may need to do so when there are good reasons. The point is that there should be a remedy for the assessed individual in the event that the expert acts negligently.

3.4 Safeguards 'against' the limited quality of forensic assessment

3.4.1 Questioning the assessment by the defence

When psychiatric or psychological reports are prepared for sentencing, they will often have been instructed by defence lawyers. If reports are introduced by the prosecution, or commissioned by the court, it will be open to the defence to challenge them. In the adversarial context of criminal proceedings, the procedural rules do not provide for the court to instruct opposing experts to produce a joint statement (as may be done in civil proceedings).

After conviction and sentence, appeals against sentence are rarely successful – the trial judge is allowed a wide margin of discretion and the Court of Appeal will only interfere if the sentence was 'manifestly excessive or wrong in principle'. A person wishing to appeal needs leave to do so, and this will not be given unless there is an arguable basis. An appeal from a case in the Magistrates Court is by way of rehearing in Crown Court; and where leave is granted to appeal against a sentence passed in the Crown Court, the matter is considered by the Court of Appeal. Statutory provisions for appeal against sentence are set out at ss. 9–11 Criminal Appeal Act 1968.

After the appeal process is exhausted, it is possible to apply to the Criminal Cases Review Commission (CCRC) for a review of a conviction or sentence, and after reviewing a case the CCRC may refer the case to the Court of Appeal if there is 'a real possibility' the conviction or sentence would be overturned if it was referred. This will normally have to be based on new evidence, information, or argument that was not put forward at trial or appeal.[102] Fewer than 3% of CCRC applications result in referral to the Court of Appeal.[103]

If, after sentence, new clinical information emerges that indicates mental disorder was not fully or correctly assessed in the trial proceedings, this will not necessarily enable a successful appeal. Whilst the Court of Appeal has a wide discretion to admit fresh evidence, if it is in the interests of justice in a particular case,[104] it was stated in *R v Erskine and Williams* (2009)[105] at para 39:

> ... it is well understood that, save exceptionally, if the defendant is allowed to advance on appeal a defence and/or evidence which could and should have been but were not put before the jury, our trial process would be subverted. Therefore if they were not deployed when they were available to be deployed, or the issues could have been but were not raised at trial, it is clear from the statutory structure ... that unless a reasonable and persuasive explanation for one or other of these omissions is offered, it is highly unlikely that the 'interests of justice' test will be satisfied.

The Court of Appeal will need to be satisfied that there are reasons to regard a case as 'exceptional' before allowing an appeal. In granting leave to admit new psychiatric evidence in *Foy* (2019),[106] the Court stated (at para 26):

> We ... wish to make clear we are not giving a general licence to defendants to come to this court after conviction with 'better' psychiatric evidence advancing a different defence, or evidence that is an improved version of a failed diminished responsibility defence. For the reasons we have given they are likely to be given short shrift. Our decision is specific to the facts of this case; the decision whether to permit an appeal to go forward on the basis of fresh evidence is always fact dependent.

This underlines the importance of ensuring as far as possible that clinical evidence at the trial is correct. It may not be possible to review it on appeal.

3.4.2 Questioning the assessment by the court

Courts may test assessments made in reports prepared for sentencing by questioning the report writers if they attend hearings to give evidence, but, in many cases, written reports are considered without additional oral evidence. There appears to have been limited research examining the extent to which courts accept the opinions and recommendations of psychiatric and psychological reports in sentencing. A study in the 1990s by Hosty and Cope (1996) reviewed the outcomes of a consecutive series of referrals for court reports to a forensic psychiatry service in the West Midlands.[107] Recommendations were rejected (in the sense that sentencing outcomes were more punitive than the recommended disposals) in just over a quarter of cases (27%). Psychiatric reports commissioned by defence solicitors had a higher likelihood of rejection than reports commissioned by courts; and more punitive disposals also appeared to be more likely for graver categories of offence. It is not clear whether similar findings would apply to contemporary practice. It may be speculated that for serious offences, hospital orders may now be less likely and prison sentences more likely as a result of the Criminal Justice Act 2003 and the principles reflected in Sentencing Council guidelines. (It is notable that in Hosty and Cope's series there was 97% agreement when a hospital order was recommended, and only one case in which a prison sentence was made instead of a recommended hospital order.)

3.4.3 Other questioning of the assessment

The opportunities for the defence to question assessments prior to sentencing, and to appeal after sentence, are summarised in section 3.4.1. If the prosecution considers that a sentence should be challenged after it has been passed, there is provision for appeals against 'unduly lenient sentences' made in the Crown Courts. The power to ask the Court of Appeal for leave to refer a sentence for review resides with the Attorney General (a Government law officer),[108] and the Crown Prosecution Service may submit a case to the Attorney General to consider. (A victim or member of the public can also ask the Attorney General to consider referring a sentence.) A sentence is unduly lenient,

> ... where it falls outside the range of sentences which the judge, applying his mind to all the relevant factors, could reasonably consider appropriate. In that connection, regard must of course be had to reported cases and in particular to the guidance given by this Court from time to time in the so-called guideline cases.[109]

The Court of Appeal may increase such a sentence.

Sentencing and criminal appeal proceedings that depend on evaluating psychiatric or psychological evidence will normally only include the parties in the case.

In the civil arena, there is provision to permit a relevant organisation that is not a party to an appeal to be an 'intervener' in judicial review proceedings when the issues in the case may have a wider public impact. For example, the charities Medical Justice and MIND were interveners in a case challenging the immigration detention of a woman with serious mental illness.[110] Permission may also be given by the UK Supreme Court for interveners to make submissions when this will assist the court in dealing with a matter of general public importance.[111] For example, the General Medical Council was in intervenor in a medical negligence case in which the Court was ask to reconsider the duty of a doctor to a patient in relation to advice about treatment.[112]

However, we are not aware of any appeals relating to clinical assessments for sentencing that have included relevant third-party organisations in the appeal proceedings.

3.5 Safeguarding the quality of decision making when confronted with disagreement between experts

3.5.1 Dealing with disagreement

Disagreement can be particularly prominent in murder trials in which a defence of diminished responsibility is pleaded by the defendant but not accepted by the prosecution. The contested clinical evidence will be heard before a jury. As previously noted, the disagreement is tested and adjudicated through an adversarial process, and the formal procedures that can be used in civil cases to narrow areas of conflict and direct joint statements do not apply. It would also be unusual for a third report to be commissioned in the event of experts disagreeing at a trial.

The adversarial process of examination and cross-examination, supplemented by questioning by the judge, in criminal proceedings can enable rigorous and meticulous testing of clinical opinion, particularly with regard to its basis, consistency, logic, and reasoning. It is well recognised that an expert's evidence should be correspondingly thorough, accurate, honest, objective, and be presented in a clear, understandable way.

The context of adversarial criminal proceedings can add heavily to the burden of dealing with disagreement. Expert witnesses need the psychological ability constantly to perceive questioning and cross-examination as a search for truth and not experience it as attack or personal criticism. They also need constantly to respect the human tragedies that lie behind criminal trials, and not be invested in winning a contest.

Professional peer group training, mentoring, and discussion are therefore important for developing both the quality of expert evidence, and the practitioner's ability to work effectively and reflectively.

3.5.2 Best practices

The observations on best practice that follow are more aspirational than established.

First, the importance of peer-group work for reviewing the quality and soundness of expert witness opinion could be more widely recognised. Whilst many practitioners implement peer review in a structured way, some clinicians conduct their personal expert witness work in a more isolated manner.

Secondly, in the context of clinical work, the approach to dealing with uncertainty and differing views about assessment, diagnosis, and treatment should be collaborative.[113] Clinical practitioners should assist each other in trying to reach agreed, evidence-based conclusions, and should continue to be open to revising these conclusions in the light of new evidence. A primarily adversarial approach would be fundamentally inimical to these norms of clinical work. For the purpose of seeking to achieve correct clinical assessments for courts, sharing of information and opinions between clinical experts will therefore often be useful, and should be encouraged to the extent that it is appropriate and possible in the context of criminal proceedings.

Thirdly, a relevant issue is the style adopted by judges and advocates in court when contested expert evidence has to be tested. The approach needs to be optimal for the purposes of revealing (and enabling witnesses to acknowledge) the strengths and weaknesses of their evidence.

Lastly, in recent years, there has been recognition of the need to help the judiciary be better informed about areas of scientific knowledge relevant to expert evidence. A 'judicial primers project' was established as a collaboration between the judiciary, the Royal Society, and the Royal Society of Edinburgh.[114] The project resulted in two peer-reviewed primers for the judiciary in 2017 (on forensic DNA analysis and forensic gait analysis), written by leading scientists.[115] Whilst no plans are evident for primers in the neuroscience or mental health fields, the collaborative initiative was an imaginative development.

3.6 Critical reflections

We have posed a number of questions – explicitly or implicitly – in this review. Will liaison and diversion schemes be fully effective in identifying mental health problems and enabling care provision? Does current sentencing and mental health law ensure appropriate sentences are achieved for offenders with mental disorder? Does the current framework of professional regulation and criminal procedure ensure that courts receive only good-quality expert evidence when it is needed for sentencing?

We doubt that these questions can be answered affirmatively. They will need continuing scrutiny.

Notes

1 This chapter focuses on the English and Welsh legal system, though we make some references to practice in Scotland and Northern Ireland.
2 Around 68% plead guilty to all counts in the Crown Court (though the percentage is much lower for sexual offences, and higher for theft and drugs offences): see annual criminal court statistics at https://assets.publishing.service.gov.uk/government/uploads/system/uploads/attachment_data/file/851932/ccsq-bulletin-q3–2019.pdf
3 https://www.england.nhs.uk/commissioning/health-just/liaison-and-diversion/about/
4 Even in hearings before the Court of Appeal, some prisoners are not represented, or are represented by a lawyer *pro bono* (*Lyne* [2019] EWCA Crim 1313 is a sad example of a mentally ill defendant who does not get legal aid).
5 Further information about sentencing guidelines is available on the website of the Sentencing Council for England and Wales: https://www.sentencingcouncil.org.uk/sentencing-and-the-council/about-sentencing-guidelines/
6 An unsuccessful attempt at codification was the Powers of the Criminal Courts (Sentencing) Act 2000. More recently, the Law Commission undertook a major project to put sentencing law in one 'Code': see Law Commission, *The Sentencing Code*, 2018, HC 1724: https://s3-eu-west-2.amazonaws.com/lawcom-prod-storage-11jsxou24uy7q/uploads/2018/11/Sentencing-Code-report-Web-version-1.pdf. The Sentencing Act 2020, which came into force in December 2020, is a consolidation of much previous legislation, but by no means all.
7 House of Lords Science Committee, 2019.

8 House of Commons Science and Technology Committee, 2011, p. 3.
9 See, amongst many things, House of Commons Health and Social Care Committee, 2018; Padfield, 2017.
10 Walker, 1968; Eigen, 1984.
11 Eigen and Andoll, 1986.
12 Law Commission, 2013.
13 Loughnan and Ward, 2014.
14 Walker and McCabe, 1973; Loughnan and Ward, 2014.
15 In January 2021 the Government published proposals for reform of the Mental Health Act 1983, https://www.gov.uk/government/consultations/reforming-the-mental-health-act/reforming-the-mental-health-act

At the time of completing this chapter (July 2021), these proposals remain under consultation and subject to future funding decisions, and a timetable for legislative change is awaited. Although significant reform of the criteria for civil detention were proposed, these were not applied to Part III of the Act governing patients in criminal proceedings. Changes to the existing criteria for detention under Part III of the Act (including for hospital and restriction orders) were not recommended, but more frequent referrals to tribunals for subsequent reviews of liability to detention were proposed.
16 Butler, 1974; Butler, 1975.
17 Grounds, 2019.
18 Rix, 2011; Rix et al., 2020.
19 Candilis, Weinstock and Martinez, 2007; Buchanan and Norko, 2011.
20 Royal Society, 2011; Jones et al., 2013.
21 Sentencing Council, 2020. See also Peay, 2016.
22 *Turner* [1975] 1 All ER 70. See Colman and Mackay, 1994.
23 *Silcott, Braithwaite and Raghip*, The Times, 9 December 1991.
24 *Pendleton* [2001] UKHL 66; see Gudjonsson, 2003.
25 https://assets.publishing.service.gov.uk/government/uploads/system/uploads/attachment_data/file/842590/OMSQ_2019_Q2.pdf
26 Known as 'Detention during Her Majesty's Pleasure' for those convicted of a murder committed as a child.
27 This section of the 2012 Act added a new section 224 A into the Criminal Justice Act 2003. It has now been replaced by s. 283 of the Sentencing Act 2020. As we have seen, a characteristic of sentencing law in England is it complexity.
28 Now repealed, but many people are in prison sentenced under this provision.
29 Applying the *Hodgson* (1967) 52 Cr App R 113 criteria:

When the following conditions are satisfied, a sentence of life imprisonment is in our opinion justified: (1) where the offence or offences are in themselves grave enough to require a very long sentence; (2) where it appears from the nature of the offences or from the defendant's history that he is a person of unstable character likely to commit such offences in the future; and (3) where if the offences are committed the consequences to others may be specially injurious, as in the case of sexual offences or crimes of violence.
30 Padfield, 2016.
31 Taylor et al., 2021.
32 *Burinskas* [2014] EWCA Crim 334.
33 *Thompson* [2018] EWCA Crim 639.
34 *Chall* (2019) EWCA Crim 865.
35 Paragraph 16(1) of Schedule 9 to the Sentencing Act 2020.
36 Paragraph 24(3) of Schedule 9 to the Sentencing Act 2020.
37 *Steward* [2008] EWCA Crim 1255.
38 *Vowles* [2015] EWCA Crim 45; see also *Nelson* [2020] EWCA Crim 1615.
39 *Edwards and others* [2018] EWCA Crim 595.
40 s. 143(1) of the Criminal Justice Act 2003 requires the sentencing court to consider the offender's culpability when considering the seriousness of their offence.
41 Ashworth and Mackay, 2015.
42 Sentencing Council, 2019. There are other relevant decisions of the Court of Appeal, and this Guideline remains a draft: this is an area, which at the time of writing, appears quite fluid.
43 Sentencing Council, 2020.
44 Pritchard (1836) 7 C & P 303.

An English perspective 59

45 The legal provisions concerning unfitness to plead are set out in the Criminal Procedure (Insanity and Unfitness to Plead) Act 1964, as amended by the Criminal Procedure (Insanity and Unfitness to Plead) Act 1991, and ss. 22 and 24–26 of the Domestic Violence, Crime and Victims Act 2004.
46 See for example *Wells, Kail, Hone, Masud* (2015) EWCA Crim 2; *Roberts* [2019] EWCA Crim 1270.
47 *John M* [2003] EWCA Crim 3452.
48 Law Commission, 2016.
49 Law Commission, 2013.
50 National Audit Office, 2017.
51 Scott and Moffatt, 2012.
52 Long, Dolley and Hollin, 2018.
53 At page 215.
54 S. 37 Mental Health Act 1983.
55 S. 41 Mental Health Act 1983.
56 S. 45 A Mental Health Act 1983.
57 Under ss. 47 and 49 Mental Health Act 1983.
58 Buchanan et al., 2012.
59 Dernevik et al., 2009.
60 S.4 A Criminal Procedure (Insanity and Unfitness to Plead) Act 1964.
61 The UK Supreme Court considered how the test 'substantially impaired' should be approached in *Golds* [2016] UKSC 61.
62 Mackay and Mitchell, 2017.
63 Walker, 1985.
64 The specific guideline for diminished responsibility manslaughter is at: https://www.sentencingcouncil. org.uk/offences/crown-court/item/manslaughter-by-reason-of-diminished-responsibility/
65 *Chalk* [2002] EWCA Crim 2435 M.H.L.R 430 (para 34). Cited in: Jones et al., 2013, p. 294.
66 *Birch* (1989) 11 Cr App R (S) 202.
67 NHS England, 2016.
68 NHS England and NHS Improvement, 2019.
69 NHS England and NHS Improvement, 2019, para 2.1, p. 7.
70 NHS England and NHS Improvement, 2019, para 2.7.6, p. 15.
71 NHS England and NHS Improvement, 2019, Appendix 1, pp. 34–36.
72 Ministry of Justice, 2010.
73 McLeod, Sweeting and Evans, 2010.
74 See Ministry of Justice, 2010, at footnote 69.
75 McLeod, Sweeting and Evans, 2010.
76 Crown Prosecution Service, 2019.
77 Legal Aid Agency, 2020.
78 The Criminal Aid (Remuneration) Regulations 2013, Schedule 5.
    http://www.legislation.gov.uk/uksi/2013/435/schedule/5
79 The Criminal Procedure Rules 2020: https://www.legislation.gov.uk/uksi/2020/759/contents/made
80 S. 157 Criminal Justice Act 2003.
81 Criminal Practice Directions 2015 (consolidated with amendments 2016–2019). Available at: https:// www.judiciary.uk/wp-content/uploads/2019/03/crim-pd-amendment-no-8-consolidated-mar2019.pdf
82 For more information about the work of the Risk Management Authority in Scotland and its publications, see: https://www.rma.scot/about/
83 Risk Management Authority, 2018.
84 The HCPC register is available at: https://www.hcpc-uk.org
85 British Psychological Society, 2018b.
86 British Psychological Society, 2017.
87 See: https://www.bps.org.uk/lists/EWT
88 See also British Psychological Society, 2018a.
89 The medical register is publicly available at: https://www.gmc-uk.org/registration-and-licensing/the-medical-register
90 General Medical Council, 2013.
91 Academy of Medical Royal Colleges, 2019.
92 Rix, Eastman and Adshead, 2015.
93 Examples are:

The Academy of Experts. http://www.academyofexperts.org/about-tae
The Expert Witness Institute https://www.ewi.org.uk/home/
The UK Register of Expert Witnesses https://www.jspubs.com
The Society of Expert Witnesses https://www.sew.org.uk/about/index.cfm

94 An example is the legal training company Bond Solon. https://www.bondsolon.com
95 The quotation is from the Law Commission's summary of the problem leading to their project, at: https://www.lawcom.gov.uk/project/expert-evidence-in-criminal-proceedings/
96 Law Commission, 2011.
97 Criminal Practice Directions 2015 (consolidated with amendments 2016–2019). Available at: https://www.judiciary.uk/wp-content/uploads/2019/03/crim-pd-amendment-no-8-consolidated-mar2019.pdf
98 *Kumar* v *General Medical Council* [2012] EWHC 2688 (Admin).
99 *Pool* v *General Medical Council* [2014] EWHC 3791 (Admin).
100 Rodway et al., 2011).
101 *Jones* v *Kaney* [2011] UKSC 13.
102 S.13 Criminal Appeal Act 1995.
103 For information on the work of the CCRC ,see: https://ccrc.gov.uk
104 S. 23 Criminal Appeal Act 1968, as amended by the Criminal Appeal Act 1995, sets out criteria considered by the Court of Appeal in deciding whether to receive new evidence.
105 *Erskine and Williams* [2009] EWCA Crim 142.
106 *Foy* [2019] EWCA Crim 1156.
107 Hosty and Cope, 1996.
108 The relevant statutory provisions are: ss.35–36 Criminal Justice Act 1988.
109 AG's Ref. No. 4 of 1989 (Brunt) (1989) 11 Cr.App.R.(S) 517.
110 *R (Das) v Secretary of State for the Home Department* [2014] EWCA Civ 45.
111 UK Supreme Court Practice Direction 8.8. Available at: https://www.supremecourt.uk/docs/practice-direction-08.pdf
112 *Montgomery v Lanarkshire Heath Board* [2015] UKSC 11.
113 The GMC guidance 'Good Medical Practice' indicates this is obligatory in stating at para 35:
'You must work collaboratively with colleagues, respecting their skills and contributions'
https://www.gmc-uk.org/ethical-guidance/ethical-guidance-for-doctors/good-medical-practice/domain-3---communication-partnership-and-teamwork#paragraph-35
114 The Royal Societies are independent academies of exceptionally distinguished scientists.
115 See: https://royalsociety.org/about-us/programmes/science-and-law/

References

Academy of Medical Royal Colleges (2019). *Acting as an Expert or Professional Witness. Guidance for Healthcare Professionals*. London: Academy of Medical Royal Colleges.

Ashworth, A. and Mackay, R. (2015). Case comment. R v Vowles (Lucinda). *Criminal Law Review*, 7, pp. 542–548.

Baird, C (2009). *A Question of Evidence: A Critique of Risk Assessment Models Used in the Justice System*. Oakland, California:National Council of Crime and Delinquency.

British Psychological Society (2017). *Psychologists as Expert Witnesses: Guidelines and Procedure* (4th edition). Leicester: British Psychological Society.

British Psychological Society (2018a). *Ethical Guidelines for Applied Psychological Practice in the Field of Extremism, File Event Extremism and Terrorism*. Leicester: British Psychological Society.

British Psychological Society (2018b). *Code of Ethics and Conduct*. Leicester: British Psychological Society.

Buchanan, A. and Norko, M. (2011). *The Psychiatric Report. Principles and Practice of Forensic Writing*. Cambridge: Cambridge University Press.

Buchanan A., Binder, R., Norko, M., and Swartz, M. (2012). Resource document on psychiatric violence risk assessment. *American Journal of Psychiatry*, 169(3), data supplement.

Butler, Lord R.A. (Chairman) (1974). *Interim Report of the Committee on Mentally Abnormal Offenders*. Cmnd. 5698. London: HMSO.

Butler, Lord R.A. (Chairman). (1975). *Report of the Committee on Mentally Abnormal Offenders*. Cmnd. 6244. London: HMSO.

Candilis, P., Weinstock, R., and Martinez, R. (2007). *Forensic Ethics and the Expert Witness*. New York: Springer.

Coid, J., Yang, M., Ullrich, S., Zhang, T., Roberts, A., Roberts, C., Rogers, R., and Farrington, D. (2007). *Predicting and Understanding Risk of Reoffending: The Prisoner Cohort Study*. London: Ministry of Justice (Research Summary No. 6).

Colman A. and Mackay R. (1994). Psychological evidence in court: Legal developments in England and the United States. *Psychology, Crime and Law*, 1(3), pp. 261–268.

Crown Prosecution Service (2019). *Mental health: Suspects and defendants with mental health conditions or disorders*. (Legal guidance 14 October 2019). https://www.cps.gov.uk/legal-guidance/mental-health-suspects-and-defendants-mental-health-conditions-or-disorders

Dernevik, M., Beck, A., Grann, M., Hogue, T., and McGuire, J. (2009). The use of psychiatric and psychological evidence in the assessment of terrorist offenders. *The Journal of Forensic Psychiatry and Psychology*, 20(4), pp. 508–515.

Eigen, J. (1984). Historical developments in psychiatric forensic evidence: The British experience. *International Journal of Law and Psychiatry*, 6(3-4), pp. 423–429.

Eigen, J. and Andoll, G. (1986). From mad-doctor to forensic witness: The evolution of early English court psychiatry. *International Journal of Law and Psychiatry*, 9(2), pp. 159–169.

Fowles, T. and Wilson, D. (2011). Psychiatric reports and sentencing. *Howard Journal of Criminal Justice*, 50(1), pp. 111–113.

General Medical Council (2013). *Acting as a Witness in Legal Proceedings*. London: General Medical Council.

Grounds A. (2019). Discrimination against offenders with mental disorder. *Criminal Behaviour and Mental Health*, 29(4), pp. 247–255.

Gudjonsson, G. (2003). Psychology brings justice: The science of forensic psychology. *Criminal Behaviour and Mental Health*, 13, pp. 159–167.

Hosty, G. and Cope, R. (1996). The outcome of psychiatric recommendations to courts. *Medicine, Science and the Law*, 36(2), pp. 163–166.

House of Commons Health and Social Care Committee (2018). *Prison Health. Twelfth Report of Session 2017–19*. HC 963. London: House of Commons.

House of Commons Science and Technology Committee (2011). *The Forensic Science Service* (Seventh Report, Session 2010–12, HC 855). London: The Stationary Office Limited.

House of Lords Science Committee (2019). *Forensic science and the criminal justice system: A blueprint for change*, https://publications.parliament.uk/pa/ld201719/ldselect/ldsctech/333/333.pdf

Jones, O., Wagner, A., Faigman, D., and Raichle, M. (2013). Neuroscientists in court. *Nature Reviews: Neuroscience*, 14(10), pp. 730–736.

Law Commission (2011). *Expert Evidence in Criminal Proceedings in England and Wales* (Law Com No 325). HC 829. London: The Stationary Office.

Law Commission (2013). *Criminal liability: Insanity and automatism. A discussion paper*. https://s3-eu-west-2.amazonaws.com/lawcom-prod-storage-11jsxou24uy7q/uploads/2015/06/insanity_discussion.pdf

Law Commission (2016). *Unfitness to Plead: Report No 364*, HC 714-1. https://s3-eu-west-2.amazonaws.com/lawcom-prod-storage-11jsxou24uy7q/uploads/2016/01/lc364_unfitness_vol-1.pdf

Legal Aid Agency (2020). *Criminal Legal Aid Manual (v.20)*. https://assets.publishing.service.gov.uk/government/uploads/system/uploads/attachment_data/file/858742/criminal-legal-aid-manual_January_2020.pdf

Long, C., Dolley, O., and Hollin, C. (2018). The use of the mental health treatment requirement (MHTR): Clinical outcomes at one year of a collaboration. *Journal of Criminal Psychology*, 8(3), pp. 215–233.

Loughnan, A. and Ward, T. (2014). Emergent authority and expert knowledge: Psychiatry and criminal responsibility in the UK. *International Journal of Law and Psychiatry*, 37(1), pp. 25–36.

Mackay, R. and Mitchell, B. (2017). The new diminished responsibility plea in operation: Some initial findings. *Criminal Law Review*, 1, pp. 18–35.

McLeod, R., Sweeting, A., and Evans, R. (2010). *Improving the Structure and Content of Psychiatric Reports for Sentencing: Research to Develop Good Practice Guidance*. Liverpool: John Moores University. http://www.ohrn.nhs.uk/resource/policy/ImprovingPsychiatricReports.pdf

Ministry of Justice (2010). *Good Practice Guidance: Commissioning, Administering and Producing Psychiatric Reports for Sentencing. Prepared for: Her Majesty's Court Service*. London: Ministry of Justice. http://www.ohrn.nhs.uk/resource/policy/GoodPracticeGuidePsychReports.pdf

National Audit Office (2017). *Mental Health in Prisons*. HC 42. London: NAO.

NHS England (2016). *Strategic Direction for Health Services in the Justice System: 2016–2020*. https://www.england.nhs.uk/wp-content/uploads/2016/10/hlth-justice-directions-v11.pdf

NHS England and NHS Improvement (2019). *Liaison and Diversion Standard Service Specification 2019*. https://www.england.nhs.uk/wp-content/uploads/2019/12/national-liaison-and-diversion-service-specification-2019.pdf

Oosterhuis, H. and Loughnan, A. (2014). Madness and crime: Historical perspectives on forensic psychiatry. *International Journal of Law and Psychiatry*, 37(1), pp. 1–16.

Padfield, N. (2016). Justifying indeterminate detention – on what grounds? *Criminal Law Review*, 11, pp. 795–820.

Padfield, N. (2017). Preventive sentencing. In K. Kemshall and K. McCartan (Eds.), *Contemporary Sex Offender Risk Management*. Palgrave Macmillan, pp. 89–114.

Peay, J. (2016). Responsibility, culpability and the sentencing of mentally disordered offenders: objectives in conflict. *Criminal Law Review,* 11(3), pp. 152–164.

Risk Management Authority (2018). *Standards and Guidelines. Risk Assessment Report Writing*. Paisley: Risk Management Authority.

Rix, K. (2011). *Expert Psychiatric Evidence*. London: Royal College of Psychiatrists.

Rix, K., Eastman, N., and Adshead, G. (2015). *Responsibilities of Psychiatrists Who Provide Expert Opinion to Courts and Tribunals*. College Report CR 193. London: Royal College of Psychiatrists.

Rix, K., Mynors-Wallis, L., and Craven, C. (2020). *Rix's Expert Psychiatric Evidence* (2nd ed.). Cambridge: Cambridge University Press.

Rodway, C., Norrington-Moore, V., Appleby, L., and Shaw, J. (2011). An examination of the quality of psychiatric court reports for juvenile perpetrators of homicide. *Journal of Forensic Psychiatry and Psychology*, 22(6), pp. 895–904.

Royal Society (2011). *Neuroscience and the law (RS Policy document 05/11)*. London: The Royal Society. https://royalsociety.org/~/media/Royal_Society_Content/policy/projects/brain-waves/Brain-Waves-4.pdf

Scott, G., and Moffatt S. (2012). *The mental health treatment requirement. Realising a better future*. London: Centre for Mental Health.

Sentencing Council (2018). *Manslaughter. Definitive guideline*. London: Sentencing Council.

Sentencing Council (2019). *Sentencing offenders with mental health conditions or disorders: Draft guideline*. https://www.sentencingcouncil.org.uk/offences/magistrates-court/item/sentencing-offenders-with-mental-health-conditions-or-disorders-for-consultation-only/

Sentencing Council (2020). *Sentencing offenders with mental disorders, developmental disorders, or neurological impairments*. https://www.sentencingcouncil.org.uk/overarching-guides/magistrates-court/item/sentencing-offenders-with-mental-disorders-developmental-disorders-or-neurological-impairments/

Taylor, P., Eastman, N., Latham, R., and Holloway, J. (2021). Sentencing offenders with mental disorders, developmental disorders or neurological impairments: What does the new *Sentencing Council Guideline* mean for psychiatrists? *The British Journal of Psychiatry*, 218(6), pp. 299–301.

Walker, N. (1968). *Crime and insanity in England. Vol 1, The Historical Perspective*. Edinburgh: Edinburgh University Press.

Walker, N. (1985). Psychiatric explanations as excuses. In M. Roth and R. Bluglass (Eds.), *Psychiatry, Human Rights and the Law*. Cambridge: Cambridge University Press, pp. 96–113.

Walker, N., and McCabe, S. (1973). *Crime and Insanity in England. Vol 2, New Solutions and new Problems*. Edinburgh: Edinburgh University Press.

Chapter 4

An American perspective

Christopher M. King, Sharon Kelley, Lauren Grove, and Brooke Stettler

4.1 Introduction

The United States of America (USA) is an important country for consideration in evaluating forensic evaluations for sentencing from an international perspective. This is becuase the USA has the largest adult criminal and juvenile justice populations per capita in the world.[1] In addition, there are a variety of sentencing-related issues in the USA involving psycholegal factors, which has produced much forensic mental health and legal scholarship.

In this chapter, we review the history and status of forensic evaluations for informing criminal sentencing and other related dispositions in the USA. We focus specifically on (1) adult criminal sentencing, both non-capital and capital; and (2) dispositions for juveniles who are adjudicated delinquent. We also attend to certain civil law matters that are so closely related to sentencing that, to omit them, would neglect large areas of forensic assessment practice with criminal defendants: dispositions following an (3) insanity acquittal or (4) designation as a sexually dangerous or violent person or predator. Forensic evaluations in such cases always involve assessment of one or more of general crime (*criminogenic*) or violence risk (e.g. dangerousness to the public); criminogenic needs (e.g. substance misuse); response-to-treatment (*responsivity*) factors (e.g. incorrigibility and developmental maturity); and non-criminogenic needs (including mental health issues without a functional relationship to offending).[2] For forensic evaluation information about dangerousness, rehabilitation potential, and other case management issues, such as emotional distress and other mental health problems, variously inform aspects of the typical sentencing and disposition rationales in the USA – namely, retribution, deterrence, incapacitation, and rehabilitation.[3]

4.1.1 The legal system

The USA has both national (federal) and localised units of governments (states, territories, and Native American tribes), and the complex interplay among the federal and local governments is known at federalism.[4] As there can be much legal variation across jurisdictions within the country, we include references to various federal and state legal authorities throughout this chapter to serve as examples of interjurisdictional trends, or to highlight discrepancies across jurisdictions. Furthermore, the law in the USA, at both the national and local levels, is organised around three branches of government – legislative, executive, and judicial – which were designed to both limit and complement one another. The three governmental branches have numerous responsibilities, both distinct and interrelated.[5]

The legislative branch is comprised of legislators, the legislative bodies to which they belong, and assistive legislative agencies. This branch has primary responsibility for enacting constitutional and statuary laws. Relevant examples include constitutional rights to due process of law,

DOI: 10.4324/9781351266482-4

criminal defendants' constitutional freedoms from compelled self-incrimination, and cruel and unusual punishment and criminal defendants' guarantee of effective assistance of counsel. They also include statutory rules of evidence and direction for the development and utilisation of sentencing guidelines.[6]

The executive branch is largely comprised of executives, such as the President of the United States and state governors; and their agencies, such as a justice department with subunits that include policing, prosecutions, community corrections, and custodial corrections. A great many administrative functions are within the province of the executive branch, including issuance of regulations that clarify how statutory laws will be implemented. A relevant example is prosecuting violations of crime statutes, which often includes sentencing arguments that may be informed by a forensic evaluation conducted by a prosecution-retained expert witness. Another example is supervising justice-involved persons in confinement or the community by a department of corrections, parole, or probation, which may include post-sentencing decision-making authority concerning adjustment to supervision intensity – such as early release to the community or modification of community supervision requirements.[7]

Finally, the judicial branch resolves disputes between legal parties, be they individuals, organisations, or units of government. While the resolution of disputes may just hinge on facts (termed *questions of fact*), courts are also empowered to determine what constitutional, statutory, and administrative laws, and their interrelationships, mean when disputes resolve around interpretations of law (termed *questions of law*). In both the federal and state systems, there are trial and appeals courts. The resolution of factual matters and initial answers to questions of law are the province of trial courts. Appellate courts may reconsider lower rulings – by trial courts or intermediate appellate courts – about questions of law, but reviewing courts are very deferential to lower courts on questions of fact. Relevant judicial branch examples include interpretations by the Supreme Court of the United States (SCOTUS) of some federal (and nationally applicable) constitutional rights in the context of forensic evaluation evidence.[8] Other examples include evidentiary rules concerning trial judges' determinations of the admissibility of expert witness evidence and the significant deference that appellate courts must pay to those decisions.[9]

Courts in the USA essentially break out into criminal courts and non-criminal courts. The latter system hears cases concerning a great many topics, including civil lawsuits and family law matters. While they are generally distinct, the criminal and non-criminal legal systems can and do intersect. For one, conduct can sometimes give rise to both criminal and civil cases, which can yield different results and consequences. For example, for criminal responsibility and punishment, on the one hand, and civil liability and financial responsibility for various forms of damage, on the other. When it comes to children and adolescents – often legally termed *juveniles* – alleged to have engaged in illicit conduct, legal responses were traditionally distinguished from that of a criminal case. Today, cases involving justice-involved youth can involve non-criminal adjudication and disposition within the juvenile justice system, criminal conviction and sentencing within the criminal justice system, or a blending of the two, depending on the jurisdiction and legal procedures employed in the individual case.[10] In addition, criminal cases involving individuals with mental illness sometimes produce hybrid criminal and civil outcomes with respect to indefinite civil confinement in lieu of or following criminal conviction and sanctioning.[11]

The three branches of government often interrelate. A relevant example is sentencing guidelines, the development of which may be delegated by statute to a judicial agency known as a sentencing commission. Pursuant to statutes, issued sentencing guidelines are then to be considered in individual cases by judges before meting out sentences. Sentencing guidelines factors are informed by case-specific details, which may include criminogenic risk and other forensic evaluation results – in some locales reported in part by probation officers from the executive branch.[12]

Judicial proceedings in the USA are adversarial in nature.[13] The two sides in a trial or hearing engage in polar argumentation about facts at issue, for decision by the factfinder – a jury or judge, depending – and often also present different interpretations of pure issues of law, for decision by a judge.

The USA also affords many legal rights to citizens and other persons within the country vis-à-vis the government. For instance, adult criminal defendants generally have a right to a trial by jury for the factual determination of culpability. However, this right does not apply to misdemeanor cases with particularly short maximum possible custodial sentences, and jurisdictions vary as to whether the right extends to juvenile cases and civil commitment proceedings. Moreover, the right to a jury trial can also generally be waived by a criminal defendant to enable a judge to determine guilt.[14]

Culpability and sentencing decisions are generally bifurcated in the USA, such that the latter is addressed separately from the former, though not necessarily for juvenile cases in all locales.[15] Sentences and dispositions are typically the prerogative of a judge rather than a jury, although there are some exceptions for severe sentences, such as capital punishment and other 'enhanced' sentences that require certain proofs akin to those for culpability.[16] Some jurisdictions may also utilise juries for civil commitment decisions.[17]

There are two types of witnesses of note for sentencing and disposition matters. The first are lay or fact witnesses, who are primarily permitted to testify only about what they perceived through their senses. However, there is some latitude granted for non-expert opinion testimony to the extent that the opinions are rationally related to the witnesses' perceptions, and helpful to clarify their testimony or determine a fact at issue.[18] Expert witnesses, in contrast, are provided broad leeway to testify about their opinions.[19] Either side in a criminal case can hire a witness to serve as an expert, and a judge can also appoint an expert witness.[20] Expert witnesses must be qualified as such, by virtue of their education, training, experience, knowledge, or skill, in the opinion of the judge, before providing evidence.[21] Psychiatrists and psychologists tend to be the types of professionals who report and testify about forensic evaluation information bearing on culpability – for example, to inform mental state defenses such as insanity and diminished capacity – and sentencing and dispositions.[22] However, community or custodial corrections workers may also report and testify about some such information for sentencing and disposition hearings.[23]

At trials – for determining culpability, for instance – witnesses qualified as experts may testify about their opinions and related matters if certain criteria are met. Specifically, if their testimony is the result of use of reliable principles and methods, which have been applied reliably to sufficient facts or data, such that the witnesses' scientific, technical, or other specialised knowledge will help the judge or jury to understand other evidence or determine a fact in question.[24] While the law often uses the term *reliability* concerning the admissibility of expert testimony, both reliability and validity are contemplated. A litigant can challenge the admissibility of expert evidence on the ground that an expert's method is unreliable. In most jurisdictions, when such a challenge is made, the judge evaluates the theory or technique via a flexible inquiry that may include consideration of whether it can and has been tested, has been peer reviewed and published, has a known or potential error rate, has standardisation procedures, and has garnered widespread acceptance by the relevant professional community.[25]

With some jurisdiction- and issue-specific exceptions, expert witnesses' trial testimony may generally go so far as to include an opinion about the ultimate legal issue or issues in the case,[26] such as whether someone ought to be found to be a sexually dangerous person.

However, some scholars have cautioned against this practice.[27] Also, although there is some jurisdictional variability, expert witnesses in many locales may base their opinions on facts or data that may typically be inadmissible – such as collateral reports contributing to forensic evaluations that may constitute hearsay – if other experts in their field would likewise reasonably rely on such information to form an opinion on the matter.[28] They can also generally testify about their opinions and the reasons for them without first testifying about the underlying facts or data, although a judge may order that the facts or data be disclosed, or the information may be elicited during cross-examination.[29] Facts or data that would typically be inadmissible, though, may only be disclosed if the prejudicial effect of the disclosure to the other side is substantially outweighed by the probative value of such information for helping the judge or jury to evaluate the opinion.[30]

Notable, however, is that the more stringent rules of evidence for trials typically do not apply to adult sentencing or juvenile disposition hearings.[31] In contrast, they do often apply to civil commitment hearings in many locales.[32] But, even when trial-type admissibility rules are not operable, judges are still tasked with considering the sufficiency of indicators of the reliability and probable accuracy of relevant information before factoring such information into their sentencing or disposition decisions.[33] Moreover, when expert evidence is admitted or considered, the weight to be afforded it by the judge or jury can often still be challenged via adversarial procedures, such as cross-examination and opposing expert testimony.[34] So too might some jurists implicitly refer to trial-admissibility criteria to inform their weighing of the reliability of more relaxedly introduced evidence during sentencing and disposition hearings.[35]

4.1.2 The related tradition of forensic assessment

Historically, forensic psychiatry in the USA traces back to the first third of the nineteenth century, a period marked by governmental interests in sanity in civil and criminal matters.[36] Early examples of forensic psychology, in turn, can be found in the first decade of the twentieth century, including a psychology clinic serving the country's first juvenile court.[37] The parallel recognition of the expertise of psychologists vis-à-vis psychiatrists in sanity matters, though, continued to develop throughout the first half of the twentieth century. The 1962 federal appellate court case of *Jenkins v. United States*, in which it was held that psychologists could be qualified to testify about mental disorders in insanity cases, is regarded as a watershed decision that ushered in the now widespread legal acceptance of forensic psychologists.[38] Case law mentions of psychiatrists and psychologists offering expert opinions in juvenile commitment and sexually dangerous persons matters trace back to at least the 1950s and 1960s.[39] In addition to psychiatry and psychology, the twenty-first century has seen increasing involvement of probation and parole officers and other corrections staff in criminogenic risk and needs assessments.[40]

Also of historical note are descriptions of four generations of criminogenic risk assessment.[41] The first generation, evident throughout the first two thirds of the twentieth century, consisted of unstructured professional judgment about risk based on training and experience.[42] Scholars and professional organisations came to express concerns about the reliability and validity of this approach for long-term risk predictions.[43]

SCOTUS took note of these critiques in several cases in the 1970s and 1980s that challenged Texas's capital sentencing system, which directed that dangerousness be considered in the decision whether to impose a death sentence. However, SCOTUS ultimately declined the invitations to disallow dangerousness determinations and related expert evidence. The Court reasoned that risk-related decision making was ubiquitous throughout the legal system, that it was preferable that all potentially relevant information be available to decision makers, and that allowance of expert risk assessment evidence did not prohibit jurors from also hearing critiques of such evidence. SCOTUS disagreed with arguments that expert risk assessment evidence was so unreliable and unduly persuasive that it should be categorically banned, noting that there was no universal professional consensus against risk assessment. Moreover, the Court held that expert risk assessment evidence need not be based on personal examination of a defendant but could instead take the form of opinions in response to hypothetical questions.[44]

Notwithstanding SCOTUS's allowance for risk assessment evidence based on the first-generation approach, scholars continued to investigate methods that could yield more reliable and valid predictions and advocated for more nuanced thinking about violence and criminogenic risk.[45] The second generation of risk assessment, which gradually began to supplant the first generation over the course of the 1970s and 1980s, was marked by greater use of actuarial – that is, systematic and statistical – risk assessment methods.[46] Second-generation approaches came to be critiqued for their over-reliance on atheoretical and historical/immutable predictor variables, which hampered explanations of risk, and legal decisions that might contemplate changes in risk.[47] Notwithstanding limitations, the second generation of risk assessment did offer utility to the legal system and expert testimony that incorporates second-generation tools continues to this day.[48]

Somewhat parallel to the rise of the second generation of risk assessment was a third generation, being distinguished by its focus on methods that incorporated both static and dynamic covariates of future illicit conduct.[49] More recently, the fourth generation of risk assessment has built upon the third by incorporating information relevant to risk management beyond just risk factors. Examples include correctional treatment needs that are generally unrelated to risk for violent or criminal conduct, such as mental illness, and systematic frameworks for assigning offenders to interventions and levels of supervision and custody.[50] These latter generations also facilitated more theoretical and contextualised conceptualisations of risk – that is, risk appraisals – beyond balder predictions.[51] Thus, third- and fourth-generation approaches offered utility for legal decisions concerned with both risk prediction and risk management. Accordingly, use of third- and fourth-generation risk assessment tools can be seen for probation and parole decisions about adjusting juvenile and adult sentences, and indeterminate commitments of insanity acquittees and sexually dangerous persons, based on demonstrated reductions in risk.[52]

The scientific merits of evidence-based risk assessment – that is, second- through fourth-generation approaches – have resulted in increased use of criminogenic and violence risk assessment tools throughout the legal system.[53] However, courts have long recognised mental health professionals as experts, including their unstructured clinical evaluations and judgments. The greater empirical transparency of risk assessment tools, in comparison, makes more discernible their limitations. This transparency about both strengths and weaknesses, in turn, may make forensic evaluations involving risk assessment tools more susceptible to admissibility or weight/persuasiveness challenges than first-generation approaches.[54] Something similar can be said for forensic evaluations that incorporate any psychological testing – for example, concerning mental health symptoms, deviant sexual preferences, or developmental maturity – versus reliance on just a clinical interview and collateral information.[55]

4.2 Short overview of the role of assessment in sentencing offenders

4.2.1 Sentences and execution

4.2.1.1 Overview of types of sentences and dispositions and related forensic assessments

Adult sentencing commences following a guilty conviction in criminal court. A verdict of guilt can be returned by the factfinder – be it a jury or judge – at the conclusion of a trial.

However, most defendants plead guilty before trial as part of a bargaining process with prosecutors.[56] In general, prosecutors agree to allow defendants to plead guilty to less-severe charges – when charges of differing levels of severity would each encompass the alleged illicit conduct – with lesser potential penalties associated with them. Or else prosecutors agree to recommend a more lenient sentence to the extent that sentencing discretion is available.[57] Judges have an incentive to generally honour such arrangements, as the plea-bargaining process aids in the efficient processing of criminal cases.[58] Lawyers sometimes utilise criminogenic risk assessment evidence in negotiating pleas with defendants.[59]

Depending on the jurisdiction, dangerousness considerations may play a role at the frontend or backend of a sentence. Such considerations may also play a role prior to adjudication, regarding whether pretrial detention will be ordered by a judge.[60] Criminogenic and violence risk assessment evidence is often considered to aid dangerousness determinations. Although unless mandated by a jurisdiction – which is more common in backend decision making concerning adjustments to probation and parole – such evidence is not technically required for a legal finding of dangerousness. For instance, other indicators in the case can be utilised, such as a history of prior offending. Moreover, expert evidence of dangerousness might also be disallowed in some contexts and locales, in contrast to other indicators – such as prosecutor statements based on non-expert evidence. For example, in capital sentencing in California.[61]

Non-penal civil dispositions can also result in criminal cases in two notable ways. First, if a defendant pleads and is found not guilty by reason of insanity – which in the classical tradition excuses the defendant from criminal responsibility and hence punishment – the person will likely be indeterminately remanded for secure hospitalisation.[62] A judge will continue to monitor the case for readiness for release to the community and eventual discharge from court supervision. Civil commitment – be it of a non-justice-involved person in the community, a defendant found not guilty by reason of insanity, or a convicted person in a penal facility facing a prison-to-hospital transfer – requires both an initial and continued finding of mental illness (besides antisocial personality disorder) and dangerousness.[63] However, dangerousness can be established simply by virtue of having been found not guilty by reason of insanity.[64]

Second, a defendant convicted of sex crimes may also be found to be a sexually dangerous person (jurisdictions that have this option use a few variations of the term). Such a determination is made circa initial sentencing or else sometime during the serving of the criminal sentence, depending on the jurisdiction. After a person is found to be a sexually dangerous person, they will be indeterminately remanded to a specialty secure facility for the purpose of treatment or incapacitation following completion of the criminal sentence, or else placed on long-term community supervision. Like an insanity acquittee, the committed sexually dangerous person will receive ongoing judicial monitoring for readiness for release.[65]

In both insanity and sexually dangerous person dispositions, abnormal mental functioning and dangerousness always play a role at both the frontend and backend of detention. And expert violence or sexual criminogenic risk assessment evidence, while not technically required, is almost always presented, toward the government meetings its burden to satisfy the standard of proof necessary for commitment. The standard for commitment is at least 'clear and convincing' evidence, or approximately 75% persuasiveness – though jurisdictions may opt for a higher standard of 'beyond a reasonable doubt', or approximately 95% convincingness. A lower standard, a 'preponderance' of the evidence – regarded as evidentiary weight of at least 51% – may be used for release decisions, and the burden may be shifted to the committed person in some locales.[66]

Most juvenile justice cases – that is, the cases of persons under the age of majority, age 18 – are processed in juvenile court. However, some juveniles are prosecuted in criminal court and legally treated like adults, sometimes in part due to dangerousness determinations, in addition to other juvenile transfer factors.[67] The juvenile justice system utilises different parlance in line with its historical philosophical differences with the adult criminal justice system.[68] Practically speaking, though, the functions of the procedures are similar, and dangerousness considerations may be involved similarly to adult sentencing. However, owing to the philosophical distinctions of the juvenile justice system, youth disposition decisions tend to readily incorporate more holistic forensic evaluation information, including non-criminogenic needs and responsivity factors, like mental health, developmental maturity, and treatment amenability.[69]

4.2.1.2 Capital sentencing of adults

For adult offenders, a slight majority of states and the federal government permit capital sentencing. The death penalty is generally reserved for severe homicide cases.[70] Defendants who were juveniles at the time of the homicide, or adult defendants who have an intellectual disability, are ineligible for the death penalty.[71] Persons sentenced to death are typically not executed until many years later, owing to criminal appeals and civil claims about unlawful detention.[72] And if they become legally incompetent while awaiting the carrying out of the sentence – due to the effects of mental illness, for instance – an execution cannot occur unless and until competence is regained.[73]

The USA's constitutional ban on cruel and unusual punishment has been interpreted to require that a capital defendant be distinguished from the typical serious offender, in a manner that avoids arbitrary and capricious imposition of the death penalty.[74] This is accomplished via a requirement that a jury find that at least one statutorily specified aggravating factor has been proven beyond a reasonable doubt – that is, a death-eligibility determination.[75] Then, a jury – or judge or judges in a small number of locales – will decide whether to recommend or impose the death penalty on an eligible defendant after considering both evidence of additional aggravating factors and evidence that might tend to mitigate against such a sentence. This has been termed the death-selection determination.[76]

A few jurisdictions statutorily specify dangerousness as an aggravating factor for the death-selection decision, and in those that do not, courts typically still allow for it to be considered as a non-statutory aggravating factor.[77] In contrast, any relevant mitigating evidence can be argued and considered in death selection, such as psychological problems, youth adversities, and environmental disadvantages.[78] Mitigation evidence may include risk assessment evidence indicating that the defendant presents a low risk for institutional violence during life imprisonment – the typical alternative sentence to that of death. However, some courts have held that testimony specifically about the risk-reducing effects of secure prison conditions is excludable as irrelevant to mitigation and for rebutting aggravating evidence of future dangerousness, reasoning that future dangerousness focuses on inclination rather than opportunity, and contemplates risk both in prison and the community.[79]

Jurisdictions vary as to whether the sentencer is given explicit instructions about how to weigh aggravating and mitigating evidence.[80] But a defendant's right to have a jury meaningfully consider all relevant mitigating evidence is impermissibly infringed when the jury is directed, via judicial instruction, to contextualise mitigating evidence as yes-or-no answers to two aggravating factors: (1) offense deliberateness and foreseeability of victim death, and (2) future dangerousness.[81] When a defendant's future dangerousness is argued in support of death selection, and the only alternative sentence available is life without parole, the defendant has a due process right to inform the jury that no parole is possible.[82] The prosecution, however, can request that the judge instruct the jury that a defendant sentenced to life without parole could still conceivably be released via executive clemency powers.[83]

70 Christopher M. King et al.

In capital sentencing, risk reduction in a case is achieved via incapacitation or specific deterrence, in the form of death or life imprisonment. Arguments for and against general deterrence effects on other prospective capital offenders have also been advanced.[84] Rehabilitation for prisoners sentenced to die is arguably irrelevant, besides the rationale that a death row inmate might refrain from institutional misconduct to atone in preparation for meeting their maker.[85] Death-sentenced prisoners are housed in special highly secured units in prisons with execution chambers (known as *death rows*).

4.2.1.3 Non-capital sentencing of adults

In non-capital cases, sentencing options can be classified as custodial (e.g. incarceration in jail or prison facilities, depending on duration); community-based (e.g. probation, community service, home confinement, electronic monitoring); and economic (e.g. fines and restitution). A sequential blend of custodial and non-custodial sentence components is often ordered. Jurisdictions vary as to how and by whom sentencing discretion is exercised – involving an interplay of legislatures, sentencing commissions, prosecutors, judges, and correctional decision-makers, especially parole boards. Sentencing regimes can roughly be categorised, given the potential for overlap, as those that are predominantly indeterminate and those that are predominantly determinate. Indeterminate sentencing systems involve discretion at both the frontend and backend of sentencing, whereas determinate systems exclusively involve frontend discretion. Mechanisms by which discretion is limited or otherwise channeled can be found in both systems, including prosecutorial and sentencing guidelines, and mandatory minimum sentences (e.g. for repeat offenders).[86]

In indeterminate sentencing systems, judges exercise discretion to individualise a sentence based on considerations of the circumstances of the offense and the defendant's background and character, as informed by evidence presented during a sentencing hearing. Allowable ranges – minimum and maximum endpoints of a sentence – are set by a legislature and sometimes further delineated by a sentencing commission. Once a ranged sentenced is decided by a judge, authority is transferred to corrections professionals – often parole boards, which may utilise parole-granting guidelines – to release prisoners after completion of the minimum sentence duration but before reaching the maximum sentence date. Prior-to-max release may be decided, for instance, upon demonstration of rehabilitation. Once popular among states, indeterminate sentencing systems are no longer the norm, owing to concerns about sentencing and release disparities and limitations of rehabilitation, and shifts to more retributive thinking and expectations that longer prison sentences would curb crime.[87]

In determinate sentencing, legislatures or sentencing commissions prescribe for a given crime a specific fixed sentence or, more typically, a permissible durational range from which to select a fixed sentence. If the latter, a judge decides a fixed sentence duration within the allowable range, and in some locales, this decision is informed by an initial presumptive fixed sentence determined by a legislature or sentencing commission.[88] When statutes mandate a sentence be enhanced beyond the standard range due to the presence of additional facts or aggravating factors, defendants are entitled to have juries decide whether such facts or factors have been proven beyond a reasonable doubt.[89]

The major difference between indeterminate and determinate sentencing regimes is that in the latter, the penalty duration is set permanently at the time of sentencing – a correctional agency has no authority to reduce it based on rehabilitation or other considerations.[90] However, prisoners who receive determinate sentences may still be released early through a credit system for time spent incarcerated pretrial and while awaiting sentencing, for refraining from custodial misconduct, and for participation in rehabilitation activities, such as educational, vocational, and therapeutic programming.[91]

Sentencing guidelines, where they exist, vary in their complexity and systemic effects. Judicial sentencing commissions draft and revise such guidelines while monitoring their effects on criminal justice system objectives. They operate within the bounds of sentence ranges authorised by statute for different crimes, and often go into effect only after the legislature has approved of them.

Presumptive or mandatory guidelines facilitate sentence calculations based on, for example, offense type and criminal history. They may yield presumptive custodial or stayed custodial (i.e. community-based) sentences. Judges might depart from a presumptive dispositional (custodial or non-custodial) or durational (longer or shorter) sentence when aggravating or mitigating factors are appropriately proven.

Advisory sentencing guidelines, in contrast, afford judges more discretion in sentencing, and more deference during appellate review. Advisory calculated sentence ranges serve as a starting point, a generalised recommendation, and sentences that deviate from them are not to be presumed unreasonable.[92] Federal trial judges, for instance, consider a variety of sentencing policies and objectives, including whether a departure upward or downward from an advisory guideline sentence range is justified based on atypical aggravating or mitigating factors, and whether statutorily delineated factors justify an upward or downward variance from the advisory guideline sentence. Some of these delineated factors include protection of the public from future crime by the defendant, and the defendant's need for educational or vocational training, correctional treatment, or medical care.[93]

Judges are often authorised by statute to impose community-based sanctions as an alternative to incarceration or are otherwise afforded the discretion to stay or suspend a custodial sentence and impose a community-based one. A jurisdiction's sentencing guidelines may or may not afford judges as much guidance in the imposition of community-based sentences as they do for custodial sentences.[94] Defendants must comply with the conditions of their probation. For example, regularly scheduled meetings with their probation officer, random drug screening, not possessing a firearm, and not associating with persons with a known history of felony convictions. Or else their probation may be revoked, and they may be ordered to serve all or part of their custodial sentence.[95]

Depending on the jurisdiction, forensic evaluations may be introduced as aggravating or mitigating evidence in frontend judicial sentencing decisions, to inform decisions about whether to impose a custodial sentence, and which conditions ought to be included if opting for a community-based sentence. They may also be used by custodial and community correctional authorities on the backend of a sentence to inform initial and ongoing offender classification in terms of security and rehabilitative service needs, and to inform release, reentry, and similar decisions by parole boards, prison authorities, or probation departments.

Given the range of sentencing options that may be implemented with adult defendants, risk management and reduction may be achieved via some combination of deterrence (e.g. community-based monitoring), temporary incapacitation (e.g. imprisonment, levels of secure custody), and rehabilitation (e.g. rehabilitative programming). Rights to or the provision of assorted assistive and rehabilitation services may arise from state constitutions or federal or state statutes and regulations.[96] Offenders may generally decline to participate in such services, although this may variously prove to their detriment.[97] A notable exception to the right to refuse treatment pertains to prisoners who are severely disturbed and dangerous to themselves or others, and for whom the proposed treatment is in their medical interest.[98]

4.2.1.4 Insanity acquittee and sexually dangerous person commitments

Although an insanity acquittal does not involve a determination of dangerousness – but rather legally specific functional impairments stemming from mental illness at the time of the offense[99] – the subsequent disposition of the case does. A defendant found not guilty by reason of insanity may be automatically or else discretionarily remanded by a judge to a secure psychiatric facility for treatment, a commitment which the judge will continue to monitor with periodic progress hearings.[100] The requirements for civil commitment – mental illness and dangerousness – can be presumed in an insanity acquittal.[101] However, ongoing civil commitment requires continued evidence of both mental illness and dangerousness.[102]

Thus, forensic evaluations informing an insanity defense focus on mental illness and its effects circa the time of the crime, whereas forensic evaluations informing initial and subsequent commitment decisions of insanity acquittees focus on both mental illness and dangerousness. Risk reduction is achieved via rehabilitation or else risk is managed via incapacitation. The general trend among courts is to acknowledge that civilly committed persons have some federal constitutional or statutory rights to rehabilitation in the least restrictive alternative setting.[103] Conversely, courts have recognised a right for civilly committed persons to refuse certain treatment, such as psychiatric medications, absent an emergency or court determination that a proposed treatment is in the best medical interests of the patient, and no less intrusive or restrictive alternative is available.[104] So too is a determination of a serious threat of harm to self or others likely required in transferring a sentenced prisoner to inpatient psychiatric treatment.[105]

Also of note are other mental state defenses, and particularly that of diminished capacity. Jurisdictions vary with respect to recognising this claim and in which form. It is distinct from an insanity defense, which typically excuses a defendant from any criminal punishment whatsoever. Instead, a diminished capacity claim – sometimes referred to as a 'heat of passion' defense given one of its forms – may serve to negate the precise *mens rea* element of an offense, such as specific intent. Or it may serve to otherwise reduce the defendant's level of culpability, such that they are convicted of a lesser offense. In either form, the reduction in culpability stems from evidence of the effects of mental illness or emotional disturbance at the time of the offense. But owing to oftentimes more general mental-state requirements of lesser offenses applicable to the same illicit conduct, a claim of diminished capacity rarely results in a defendant escaping punishment altogether.[106]

The import of diminished capacity for sentencing is that the defendant may be convicted of a lesser offense than that originally charged – for example, second-degree homicide or reckless homicide/manslaughter, rather than first-degree murder – with less severe potential sentences possible for it. Moreover, a judge might incorporate the idea of diminished capacity at sentencing by considering evidence of mental illness or emotional distress – presented either at trial or a sentencing hearing – as mitigating the warranted punishment.[107]

Another option available in some jurisdictions is a verdict of guilty but mentally ill.[108] As contrasted with a verdict of not guilty by reason of insanity, a defendant found guilty but mentally ill is still sentenced to a custodial or community-based punishment. The defendant's sentence just includes provisions for treatment during that sentence – for example, transfer to and from a mental health facility and prison, or treatment as a condition of probation or parole[109] – thereby achieving risk management and reduction via deterrence, incapacitation and rehabilitation. The front-end factfinder in a case resulting in a verdict of guilty but mentally ill will typically have considered forensic evaluation evidence for an insanity defense – that is, a forensic evaluation focused on mental illness. Criminogenic and violence risk assessment, in turn, tends to inform backend release decision-making evidence in jurisdictions that have this verdict option.

Many jurisdictions also have laws for designating persons convicted of sexual offenses as sexually dangerous persons or analogous legal terms. Like ordinary civil commitment, sexually dangerous persons statutes require a finding of both mental illness – typically more broadly defined than in traditional civil commitment, to include, for example, paraphilic disorders – and dangerousness – including a finding of serious difficulty controlling one's behaviour.[110] Persons so classified become eligible for specialised civil commitment, which often takes the form of custodial care in specialised sexually dangerous person facilities, although community-based commitments can also be ordered.[111] As is the case with ordinary civil commitment, release decision-making is based chiefly on demonstrated reduction in sexual criminogenic risk.[112]

Sexual criminogenic risk assessment is thus a frontend and backend issue with sexually dangerous person commitments, and forensic evaluations in these cases must also attend to issues of mental illness. Regarding risk management and reduction, sexually dangerous person laws are not exclusively justified by a rehabilitation objective – incapacitation is also a legitimate state interest for such respondents.[113] It is also worth noting that jurisdictions may utilise sexual criminogenic risk assessments for varying purposes in their sex offender registration and notification laws, although they do not appear required to do so.[114]

4.2.1.5 Juvenile dispositions

Depending on the jurisdiction, through various mechanisms – including some that may utilise forensic evaluation evidence, such as judicial waiver of juvenile court jurisdiction – some juveniles may be prosecuted as adults in criminal court.[115] If so, these youths will be eligible for adult sanctions, or different forms of blended adult sanctions and juvenile dispositions.[116] A few notable limits for adult-like sentences imposed on youth include that a juvenile cannot be sentenced to death nor mandatorily (versus discretionarily) sentenced to life without the possibility of parole.[117] States also vary in their responsiveness to federal laws aimed at keeping detained youth separate from adult inmates.[118]

Most juvenile defendants' cases, though, are processed in juvenile court.[119] Different terminology tends to be used in the juvenile justice system owing to its historically rehabilitative philosophy.[120] Examples include *delinquency* instead of *crime*, *adjudication* instead of *conviction*, *disposition* instead of *sentence*, *detention* instead of *jail,* and *residential placement* or *training school* instead of *prison*. In addition, certain problematic conduct that is not illegal for adults can nevertheless bring a youth within the jurisdiction of a juvenile court – referred to as *status offenses*.[121] Furthermore, the jurisdiction of the juvenile justice system is generally limited to childhood and adolescence – though it sometimes extends into young adulthood in some locales – such that the time at which point a juvenile would age out of the system represents the maximum limit on the duration of a disposition.[122]

Notwithstanding these and other distinctive elements of the juvenile justice system, in practice, it shares many parallels with its adult counterpart – especially as the juvenile justice system developed to incorporate non-rehabilitative objectives, such as accountability. Accordingly, juveniles are afforded most, although not all, of the procedural due process rights in juvenile court that adult defendants enjoy in criminal court.[123] So too do the dispositional options available to juvenile court judges generally mirror those discussed for non-capital adult sentencing, except that juvenile probation caseloads and custodial facilities will be populated by juveniles instead of adults.[124] Insanity defenses may be available to youth processed as juveniles, and sexually dangerous person statutes often include older juveniles within their reach.[125]

However, given the historically greater emphasis on rehabilitation by the juvenile justice system, juveniles' rights to rehabilitation may be more often or broadly acknowledged by courts.[126] Dispositions will tend to be responsive to youths' developmental needs.[127] More restorative justice programs may be available for juvenile offenders, and juvenile judges might also dispose of some cases by referral to a community agency or other provider for treatment.[128] As is the case with adults, both frontend and backend applications of forensic evaluation evidence can be seen in juvenile justice, and the range of dispositional options available for youth reflect deterrence, incapacitation, and rehabilitation approaches to risk management and reduction.

4.2.2 Decisions within sentencing and execution

Throughout the USA, dangerousness is involved, in one way or another, in both frontend and backend sentencing and disposition decisions. This includes decisions about whether to impose certain sentences. For example, some jurisdictions' adoption of 'evidence-based sentencing' – that is, criminogenic risk and needs assessment – to determine whether to impose a community-based punishment, and the conditions of that probation. It also includes decisions about whether to effectuate previously suspended sentences. For example, some jurisdictions' use of risk and needs assessment in probation revocation hearings, which may result in the violator being remanded to a jail or prison. Furthermore, it includes decisions about whether to prolong or abbreviate sentences. For instance, some jurisdictions' use of risk and needs assessment to facilitate early reentry to the community from prisons.[129]

Similar examples as to imposition and execution, suspension, prolongation, and termination could likewise be offered for civil commitments and juvenile dispositions. Though in the case of civil commitment, forensic evaluation evidence concerning mental health functioning plays a prominent role in addition to forensic evaluation evidence about dangerousness. And, in general, forensic evaluation evidence concerning developmental maturity and treatment amenability tend to play a more prominent role for youth dispositions relative to adult sentencing.

4.2.3 Concepts to be assessed

Legal standards that may invoke assessment of criminogenic or violence risk, needs, and responsivity factors vary according to the referral issue.[130] For instance, with respect to risk, statutes, regulations, case law, and other legal sources must be reviewed to determine nuanced parameters of the relevant target behaviour given vague statutory references to dangerousness, harm, safety, or protection of the community, serious misconduct, and other such legal terminology.[131] As an example, the outcome criteria used in mandated federal probation and prison risk assessment tools is general and violent recidivism.[132] As another example, forensic evaluators often consider contextual/environmental factors in their risk assessments. Yet in the capital sentencing context, a jurisdiction's case law may indicate that expert testimony about the risk-reducing effects of the prison environment is irrelevant both as mitigation evidence and to rebut evidence of dangerousness as an aggravating factor, owing to the jurisdiction's focus on a defendant's personal disposition if, hypothetically, divorced from situational effects, both in prison and the community.[133]

In general, though, the criminal justice system tends to be interested in long-term violence risk in the capital sentencing context. For non-capital criminal sentencing and delinquency dispositions, the focus tends to be on intermediate-term criminogenic or violence recidivism risk. For civil commitment of insanity acquittees, the focus is typically imminent violence risk to self or others (although the SCOTUS case of *Jones v United States* referred to criminogenic recidivism risk for the initial commitment of insanity acquittees).[134] And for civil commitment of sexually dangerous persons, the focus tends to be on long-term sexual criminogenic risk.[135]

In different sentencing and disposition contexts, other criteria besides dangerousness are virtually always also relevant. And these factors too often present definitional challenges. In capital and non-capital adult sentencing and juvenile dispositions, numerous aggravating, mitigating, and other factors will be considered in deciding on a sentence or disposition.[136] For inpatient civil commitment of insanity acquittees and sexually dangerous persons, an initial and ongoing finding of mental illness, variously defined, is also required.[137] So too is a finding of volitional impairment, variously defined, required for sexually dangerous person commitments.[138] Amenability to treatment – and relatedly, for youth, developmental maturity – might also be relevant in some contexts. For example, for specialised treatment-oriented sentencing of sex offenders, and youth dispositions.[139]

Race is an impermissible factor for criminogenic risk assessment and sentencing in general.[140] However, scholars have raised concerns that reliance on other risk factors may implicate race or otherwise produce racially disparate effects.[141] The law is newly developing concerning the permissibility or not of using gender as a criminogenic risk factor in sentencing, considering constitutional guarantees of due process and equal protection.[142]

In the face of the typical legal vagueness as to many psycholegal factors often relevant for sentencing and disposition, the Risk-Need-Responsivity (RNR) model has proven very influential for experts' conceptualisation of forensic mental health information in such cases.[143] Legal professionals are becoming more educated about this conceptual framework as well.[144]

Forensic evaluations are highly prevalent across sentencing and disposition matters, even if they are not often required. For example, lay witnesses can testify about their observations of an individual, including recent instances of violent or threatening behaviour that can persuade legal decision-makers of dangerousness.[145] Nevertheless, the expertise of forensic mental health professionals is generally expected and sometimes mandated across different sentencing and dispositions contexts. Such experts may be private practitioners who are attorney retained or court appointed, or else state-employed evaluators may be court appointed, for capital and non-capital adult sentencing, juvenile dispositions, and insanity acquittee and sexually dangerous person commitments. Assessments bearing on some forensic mental health issues, such as criminogenic risk, may also be conducted by community or correctional staff persons in probation, parole, and other frontend or backend level-of-supervision decisional scenarios.

Owing to the adversarial nature of the USA legal system, opposing experts are often involved in sentencing and disposition matters. The prosecution will retain one or more experts, and one or more other experts will be retained by an attorney or appointed by the court for the defense – or the *respondent* in technically civil matters, such as sexually dangerous person commitments. So too might several independent evaluators be appointed by the state pursuant to its sexually dangerous person procedural scheme.[146] Thus, in many sentencing and disposition scenarios, a forensic dialogue is facilitated via opposing testimony at a sentencing or disposition hearing, or an evaluator's review of an independent professional's assessment prior to such a hearing.

4.2.4 Forensic assessment and procedure

4.2.4.1 The division of evaluator and decision-maker provinces

Forensic evaluators must be qualified as experts to report and testify about their evaluations. A judge or sometimes a jury, in turn, decides all sentencing and disposition questions, and in doing so, the legal factfinder has the general prerogative to weigh the evidence in making such judgments. Their decisions are subject only to certain standards upon review by higher authorities – in the event of an appeal, for instance. Because legal decision-makers alone are so empowered, and because their judgments often include additional considerations beyond which forensic evaluators have expertise, such as the interest of the public, some scholars caution against practitioners offering opinions on ultimate legal issues.[147]

In some sentencing and disposition scenarios, like probation supervision and ongoing civil commitment, forensic evaluator opinions about changes in criminogenic or violence risk or mental health status may prompt petitions for judicial determinations of readiness for modifications to level of supervision or discharge from inpatient care, respectively. Similarly, periodic forensic evaluations might prompt the sharing of updated risk management and reduction information with parole boards or other correctional releasing authorities.[148]

4.2.4.2 The impact of forensic assessments on decisions

Research on the impact of criminogenic and violence risk assessment information on clinical and legal decision-making suggests that such information does influence professional and lay judgments related to sentencing and dispositions, and that how risk is communicated produces differential effects.[149] Relatedly, forensic evaluation evidence of psychopathic traits has also been found to influence attitudes in the direction of more punitive sanctions, including for youth defendants.[150] Jurors in sexually dangerous person cases have reported viewing forensic evaluators as honest and helpful, the use of sexual criminogenic risk assessment instruments by experts as increasing perceived predictive credibility, and regarding disagreement among experts as reflecting case complexity and increasing skepticism about experts' predictive capabilities.[151] Jurors in such cases have also generally reported that risk assessment evidence was less influential on their decisions than other offender, offense, and testimony characteristics; but jurors who were influenced by the risk assessment evidence were particularly likely to regard the respondent as being high risk.[152] Courts in one state frequently made decisions consistent with expert evaluator opinions in sexually dangerous person cases, especially when evaluators' opinions were supportive of sexually dangerous person commitment.[153]

4.2.4.3 How a forensic assessment may be processed

Since rules of evidence for trials generally do not apply at sentencing and disposition hearings, judges have especially wide latitude to consider forensic evaluation evidence. An expert can be appointed by the court to conduct and testify about a criminogenic risk assessment.[154] Case law also indicates that sentencing judges are further empowered to compel advanced notification to the other side regarding defense-retained experts who will be utilised at a hearing, and to overcome assertions of attorney-client privilege for defense-retained experts, allowing access to that expert's information for use by the prosecution and judge.[155]

Stricter trial-type rules of evidence do, however, often apply at civil commitment proceedings.[156] Thus, evidentiary admissibility rules may play more of a role in insanity acquittee and sexually dangerous person commitments. And there may be a stronger argument for deference to attorney-client privilege in these contexts. For example, that the prosecution should be blocked from accessing a respondent-retained expert who yielded unfavorable opinions for the respondent and was discarded. However, the law is not clear on this point.[157] Nevertheless, the effect of stricter admissibility rules may be that potentially more expert evidence is excluded from consideration in civil commitment proceedings.

4.3 Safeguards for the quality of forensic assessment

4.3.1 Requirements in law and policy

There are few legal rules or formal policies in place for forensic evaluations. In the capital sentencing context, a defendant's rights against compelled self-incrimination and assistance of counsel require that the defendant be warned about his right to not participate in a court-appointed evaluation reaching the issue of dangerousness, and that the defense attorney be given advanced notice about the purpose of such an evaluation.[158] Such may also be the case for non-capital sentencing and juvenile dispositions, although not in civil commitments owing to the non-criminal nature of such cases.[159] Also, while not the norm, some jurisdictions mandate that certain risk assessment tools be used in certain sentencing contexts. Examples include criminogenic and violence risk assessment tools developed by the federal government for use in federal jurisdiction probation and prison decision making, and Virginia's requirement that a particular sexual criminogenic risk assessment tool be used in the screening of sexually dangerous persons.[160]

4.3.2 Disciplinary and ethical requirements

Licensing statutes and regulations include similar provisions to ethical codes issued by professional societies, as discussed later, and some states specifically incorporate a professional society's ethical codes or guidelines, giving such the force of law.[161] Licensees who run afoul of licensing law provisions may have complaints filed against them – by forensic examinees or attorneys, for instance – with their state licensing authority, which results in an administrative investigation and disposition. If the licensee is found to have violated one or more of the applicable licensing laws, the licensee can be disciplined in the form of fines, restrictions of practice areas, temporary practice suspension, or permanent revocation of the privilege to practice. Professionals who are found to have engaged in substandard practice may also confront challenges with maintaining professional liability insurance coverage.[162]

While uncommon, a civil malpractice lawsuit can also be filed against a professional, typically based on a negligence theory for engaging in conduct that is below the minimal standard of care.[163] However, court-appointed evaluators typically have absolute immunity from liability for damages connected to their forensic evaluations and testimony.[164] So too do evaluators employed by the government, such as those working for a state correctional or mental health agency, often have qualified immunity against claims of civil rights violations. This defense is applicable when such persons do not violate clearly established rights of which the reasonable professional would have known.[165] Moreover, evaluators retained by the prosecution or defense, rather than appointed by a judge, also enjoy absolute immunity from civil liability connected to their court testimony.[166] However, jurisdictions may recognise immunity for forensic reports and testimony, while still allowing for potential liability for negligence in the actual conducting of a forensic evaluation.[167] And the costs of defending against such lawsuits, regardless of whether a plaintiff's suit is likely to succeed, serve as a practical deterrent to mental health professionals from engaging in subpar practices.[168] In addition, certain egregious forms of unprofessional conduct, such as perjured testimony, can give rise to criminal prosecution of a professional.[169]

Apart from licensing board complaints and malpractice lawsuits, professional societies, such as the American Psychological Association, American Psychiatric Association, and American Academy of Psychiatry and the Law, also issue ethical codes and guidelines to regulate the general practices of their members, including in specialty areas like forensic psychology and forensic psychiatry.[170] Members who violate ethical standards in areas such as competence, informed consent, and conducting assessments can be sanctioned, up to and including being expelled from the organisation.[171] However, unlike potential discipline by a jurisdiction's licensing authority, sanctions issued by professional societies do not restrict one from practicing.

4.3.3 Requirements for the evaluator

The professions typically permitted or recognised as experts to conduct forensic evaluations relevant to sentencing and dispositions are doctoral-level providers (i.e. psychiatry and psychology). Although certain master's-level providers (e.g. social workers) may also be allowed to engage in forensic practice in some locales.[172] Moreover, probation and other court or corrections workers, who typically have at least a four-year college degree in a social science field or social work, have, with on-the-job training, become increasingly involved in criminogenic risk and needs assessment.[173]

Traditional mental health professionals – for example, psychologists, psychiatrists, and clinical social workers – must be licensed in the jurisdictions in which they practice, or otherwise satisfy a jurisdiction's temporary-practice provisions.[174] Some states also require that mental health professionals acquire special certifications to engage in forensic work.[175] A judge ultimately decides whether a professional, proffered as an expert witness, is so qualified given the professional's education, training, experience, knowledge, or skill.[176]

4.3.4 Enforcement of requirements

Attorneys help to safeguard forensic evaluation quality through challenges to forensic evaluators as being unqualified to function as expert witnesses, or challenges to the admissibility of their opinions as being the product of insufficient information or unreliable methods. They also challenge admitted expert testimony via cross-examination and the presentation of opposing expert testimony.[177] So too might they offer nominations for candidate mental health professionals to be appointed by the court.[178]

Judges, in turn, decide whether to admit proffered expert testimony and the legal factfinder decides the weight to assign to that testimony. An administrative agency may require that mental health professionals be certified to engage in forensic work, maintaining a list of duly certified practitioners for use by courts and attorneys.[179] Licensing authorities review and respond to complaints filed against licensees, and attorney general offices may prosecute professionals whose practice violated criminal laws. Jurisdiction-specific or national professional societies review ethics complaints and may sanction members with organisational expulsion and revocation of organisation-issued certifications of expertise.

The application of varying rules of evidence in sentencing and disposition matters may result in a judge deciding that a proffered forensic evaluator is not qualified to testify as an expert, or that an otherwise qualified expert's assessment methods are insufficiently reliable for admissibility. Furthermore, a legal factfinder has the prerogative to find admitted expert testimony to be lowly credible and unpersuasive. Beyond rules of evidence, evaluators who are not certificated to perform forensic work in jurisdictions that require such certification may be disqualified from testifying as an expert.[180] In addition, professionals who engage in ethically or legally substandard practice may be sanctioned by professional organisations and licensing authorities, sued for malpractice, or prosecuted for criminal conduct.

As an example, the prosecution-retained psychiatrist in *Barefoot v. Estelle* (1983), Dr. James Grigson, had ethics complaints filed against him with the American Psychiatric Association and Texas Society of Psychiatric Physicians. Both professional organisations ultimately expelled him for testifying as to diagnoses without personally examining defendants and asserting that he could predict with 100% certainty that examinees would go on to engage in violent conduct.[181] However, he was never stripped of his license to practice in Texas, and he focused the remainder of his later career on civil forensic work.[182]

4.4 Safeguards 'against' the limited quality of forensic assessment

4.4.1 Questioning the assessment by the defense

4.4.1.1 Legal procedures requiring or allowing for contesting assessments

Defendants are typically permitted to present evidence in sentencing and disposition matters. However, SCOTUS, and most other courts that have confronted the issue, have denied a constitutional right – rooted in either the federal constitutional right to confront adverse witnesses at trial or due process – to confront and cross-examine all adverse witnesses at sentencing hearings, even in capital cases.[183] Courts have similarly denied a constitutional right for confrontation of witnesses in juvenile dispositions, although some jurisdictions allow for it.[184] Furthermore, prisoners have very little in the way of due process rights connected to parole or other release decision making.[185]

The right to respond to and challenge evidence is, however, typically afforded in civil commitment hearings.[186] Moreover, SCOTUS has held that capital defendants have a due process right to access and deny or explain all information in a pre-sentence investigation report. No assertions or their source contained therein can be withheld from a capital defendant as confidential.[187] This includes allegedly sensitive forensic evaluation information that could conceivably hinder future rehabilitation efforts, which SCOTUS regarded as a weak justification in general, and an irrelevant concern on the part of the prosecution in the specific context of capital sentencing.

Criminogenic risk and needs assessments may be included in pre-sentencing or pre-disposition investigation reports in adult and juvenile cases.[188] Although challenges may occur relatively infrequently across sentencing and disposition hearings, challenges to risk and needs assessments might involve their admissibility or weight due to concerns about non-standard administration, proper interpretation, psychometric properties, fit with the defendant or legal question, helpfulness, and probativeness and prejudicialness.[189] However, a state supreme court has upheld the denial of a defendant's request to review the underlying details of a proprietary risk assessment tool used at sentencing.[190]

4.4.1.2 Contesting forensic assessments during hearings and via appeal

Forensic evaluation evidence appears to generally be admissible for sentencing and dispositions, although whether such evidence should be considered at all can be challenged concerning insufficient evaluator expertise, methodological reliability or validity, or relevance to specific legal questions. In addition, the weight that the factfinder will ultimately assign such evidence may properly vary.[191] To attack the credibility of such evidence, defendants can often utilise cross-examination and contrary expert opinions.[192]

Adult and juvenile defendants can also typically appeal sentences or dispositions, although they may generally waive this right if they pled guilty prior to sentencing.[193] So too can respondents subjected to civil commitment typically appeal that decision.[194] Once all other routes for relief have been exhausted, defendants and respondents can also file a civil petition for a writ of *habeas corpus*, arguing that they are being unlawfully detained.[195] The grounds for an appeal or *habeaus corpus* petition can be arguments – of the sort that may be raised during the original hearing – about a forensic evaluator or evaluation that informed the sentence or disposition.[196]

4.4.1.3 Legal aid for indigent defendants

All criminal defendants have a right to the effective assistance of counsel at initial sentencing hearings.[197] If they cannot afford to hire an attorney, indigent defendants have the right to appointed counsel in all felony cases and in misdemeanor cases when they are sentenced to incarceration or when such a custodial sentence is suspended.[198] Accordingly, most criminal defendants will be assisted by counsel in contesting assessments conducted by prosecution-retained experts via utilisation of procedural due process safeguards, which may vary depending on whether the assessment bears upon a trial issue or a sentencing matter. Moreover, in capital cases, the federal constitutional guarantee of effective assistance of counsel includes that defense counsel conduct a thorough investigation for all potentially mitigating evidence, even when the defendant and their family suggest that there is no such evidence.[199] Jurisdictions also provide for appointed counsel for civil commitment and juvenile disposition hearings.[200]

There are indications from SCOTUS that the admissibility of forensic evaluation evidence bearing on dangerousness is justified in part by the possibility for challenging such evidence via opposing expert testimony.[201] And, this possibility does not hinge on the ability to pay for an expert, at least in the capital sentencing context. SCOTUS has held that when the prosecution presents expert forensic evidence of future dangerousness as an aggravating factor for capital sentencing, an indigent defendant has a due process right to a court-appointed mental health expert for assistance in responding to it.[202] And, the right to effective assistance of counsel can be violated when a defense attorney unreasonably fails to secure adequate court funding for a sufficiently persuasive expert.[203] Indigent defendants may not, however, enjoy the benefit of attorney–client privilege with court-appointed experts, such that the results of the evaluation cannot be kept from the prosecution even if unfavourable to the defendant.[204]

4.4.1.4 How challenges to an assessment are dealt with in practice

There are a few different strategies for challenging a forensic evaluation. Of course, if the expert was privately retained, the attorney has the option of not disclosing the results of the assessment if it is unhelpful to the defense's case. But, in other cases, experts might be court appointed, or the proceedings otherwise require experts to submit their assessments to all concerned parties: the prosecution, defense, and court.

In these cases, the first opportunity to challenge an adverse assessment may be at an admissibility hearing, based on the argument that the expert's procedures do not satisfy the jurisdiction's admissibility standard. However, this admissibility procedure, applicable to trials, may not be required for many sentencing and disposition matters, although their spirit may be incorporated by judges in individual cases. Thus, attorneys in sentencing and disposition matters will rely chiefly on two strategies at the primary sentencing or disposition hearing to attempt to persuade the decision maker to not to give the adverse expert's opinions much weight. The first is cross-examination of the adverse expert by the attorney, potentially informed ahead of time by a retained expert consultant's review of the adverse testifying expert's work. The second is the presentation of countervailing expert evidence and testimony from a retained evaluating expert, or a non-evaluating expert on the generally applicable science.

Challenges to forensic evaluations can also be raised via argumentation on appeal or petitions for *habeas corpus* relief. However, since SCOTUS's decision in *Barefoot v Estelle*, courts have generally been reluctant to deem criminogenic and violence risk assessments inadmissible.[205] For instance, in *Coble v State*, the trial court admitted expert testimony on violence risk assessment despite the expert's acknowledgement that he used 'his own personal methodology' and '[did] not know whether others rely upon this method, and he [did] not know of any psychiatric or psychology books or articles that use his factors'.[206] Although the Court of Criminal Appeals of Texas later held that the expert's testimony should have been ruled inadmissible, it also decided that the testimony did not have a 'substantial or injurious' effect on the jury's deliberations and declined to grant relief.[207]

Aside from these legal challenge avenues, aggrieved parties have the option – even if infrequently utilised – of filing a complaint against an expert with a state licensing board or professional society. An opposing forensic evaluator can do so as well if they believe their colleague acted unethically or in a manner inconsistent with standards of practice. The American Psychological Association's ethics code directs psychologists to first confront their colleague prior to making a professional complaint, and some scholars have offered guidance on how to do so tactfully.[208] Moreover, the American Psychological Association directs that ethics complaints against a licensed psychologist who is a member of the organisation first be directed to the applicable state psychology licensing authority, in part because professional societies have no direct legal authority over the practice of their members.[209]

4.4.2 Questioning the assessment by the court

Scholarly resources are available to assist legal professionals with more critically appraising and challenging forensic evaluations and related expert mental health testimony.[210] However, available case law evidence suggests that legal decision makers are generally uncritical of structured criminogenic and violence risk assessment tools and unstructured risk assessment testimony.[211] Research conducted in one state also suggests a fair degree of concordance between evaluator opinions and court decisions in sexually dangerous person commitments.[212]

4.4.3 Other questioning of the assessment

.Professional societies and other groups may submit *amicus curiae* (non-party informational) briefs in appellate case that raise significant issues about forensic evaluation, especially dangerousness assessments.[213] Such filings by mental health professional groups have tended to call for respect for scientifically supported risk assessment practices, including an appreciation for the limits of the state of the science.[214] Interestingly, though, courts have generally upheld or mandated risk assessment practices beyond the scientific limits that have been suggested in such filings.[215]

4.5 Safeguarding the quality of decision making when confronted with disagreement between experts

4.5.1 Dealing with disagreement

4.5.1.1 Decisions that especially evoke disagreement

Given the involved stakes, capital sentencing and sexually dangerous person commitment are the most hotly contested types of sentencing and disposition matters. This is suggested, for instance, by the number of SCOTUS decisions and *amicus curiae* briefs these types of cases have generated. And experts' criminogenic and violence risk assessments are often the most contentious issues within such cases.

Frontend criminogenic risk assessment to inform sentencing is also a current practice or proposal in several jurisdictions subject to active debate, especially given questions that have been raised about multicultural generalisability issues in risk assessment.[216] The field reliability of risk assessment tools, and adversarial allegiance/partisan potential of evaluators that can manifest in the scoring of risk assessment tools, have also been a recent focus of researchers.[217]

4.5.1.2 Formal options for facilitating optimal decisions

To facilitate an optimal decision about psycholegal issues involved in sentencing and dispositions, the legal system generally makes use of multiple forensic evaluators. Often, by practice or by law, decisions concerning criminogenic and violence risk – especially high stakes decisions in capital cases or sexually dangerous person commitment proceedings – involve two evaluators, one retained by or appointed for each party.[218] Although the two-evaluator system is ripe for leading to expert disagreement, it is consistent with the USA's adversarial system. In theory, the legal system arrives at optimal decisions by allowing litigants to make their best arguments – sometimes in part through expert witnesses – with the legal decision maker considering both sides' arguments and then arriving at a final decision.

There are, however, jurisdictions that involve three forensic evaluators as a matter of course, or processes whereby courts can sometimes appoint a third evaluator if the judge so chooses. Hawaii, for example, historically used a three-evaluator model for evaluations of competence to stand trial, mental state at the time of the offense, and insanity acquittee conditional release. Other states allow for the appointment of multiple evaluators in more serious cases.[219]

Another option available in the federal system and at least some states is for the court to appoint its own expert. However, judges seem to rarely exercise this option.[220] Although resistance to the notion of the court appointing a neutral expert, particularly in criminal cases, is multifaceted, it often boils down to a perception that doing so runs counter to the adversarial system.[221] For instance, based on surveys and interviews conducted with federal district court judges, it was concluded, in part, that '[j]udges view the appointment of an expert as an extraordinary activity that is appropriate only in rare instances in which the traditional adversarial process has failed to permit an informed assessment of the facts'.[222]

There is no standard process for deliberation among forensic evaluators. In cases with multiple evaluators, depending on the jurisdiction and type of case, laws may either prohibit or permit consultation between the experts. For example, in the context of competence to stand trial evaluations, a review of states' practices revealed that, of the states that routinely assigned multiple evaluators to the same case, over 80% allowed the evaluators to communicate about their findings and opinions.[223] In contrast, in Virginia insanity acquittee conditional release evaluations, which are performed by one psychiatrist and one clinical psychologist, the experts are instructed to 'conduct their examinations and report their findings separately'.[224]

There is also no formal system for concurrent expert evidence, a practice developed in Australia and colloquially referred to as 'hot tubbing'. In this model, experts testify at the same time, instead of sequentially, allowing them to explicitly address one another's approach and findings. Although not expressly provided for, legal frameworks in the USA do not explicitly prohibit this approach either. Some federal courts have occasionally directed for concurrent testimony in civil litigation.[225]

Legal scholars have observed variability in how courts have implemented this practice, ranging from using the concurrent approach exclusively, or implementing it after the traditional, sequential presentation of expert evidence.[226] Some scholars have noted that concurrent expert evidence might be at odds with defendants' constitutional rights in criminal proceedings. For instance, in such a procedure, defendants would be put in the position of presenting substantive evidence before the prosecution has met its evidentiary proof burden.[227] Yet, the somewhat relaxed procedural requirements for many sentencing and disposition matters may cut against such arguments. Nevertheless, we are not aware of any courts that have used this approach to resolve expert disagreement about dangerousness and other sentencing and disposition referral questions.

4.5.1.3 How disagreement between experts is dealt with in practice

Disagreement between experts, particularly in the context of criminogenic and violence risk assessment, is common. Indeed, a growing body of literature has documented the field reliability of forensic evaluators — that is, agreement among clinicians under routine practice conditions, rather than well-controlled studies — both in terms of experts' scores on forensically relevant assessments instruments and their opinions.[228] Findings from this body of research include relatively low agreement for scores on risk assessment instruments when experts use them in adversarial proceedings.[229] Similarly, research suggests that experts disagree in about half of insanity acquittee conditional release cases, and similarly modest rates of agreement have been observed in studies investigating experts' commitment recommendations in sexually dangerous person cases.[230]

There are a multitude of reasons for expert disagreement, and some are more easily resolvable than others. One core issue is the complexity and difficulty of forming a forensic opinion. Experts are tasked with reviewing and synthesising often limited and contradictory information to draw conclusions about psychological functioning and future behaviour — an inherently challenging undertaking. Other potential explanations for disagreement include the following. First, limitations of professionals, such as those stemming from training deficits, the potential for use of unstandardised methods, and individual evaluator differences. Second, experts' reliance on different information or procedures, such as when experts are given access to different records or use different evaluation procedures in the same case. Third, biases in the selection of experts, such as when attorneys select experts likely to provide a favourable opinion. Fourth, biases brought about by the adversarial system, including adversarial allegiance, or the tendency for evaluators' opinions to drift towards findings that support the retaining party.[231]

In practice, it is relatively uncommon for courts to carefully explore the precise reasons for expert disagreement and generate novel solutions. Courts are likely unsurprised by expert disagreement, as legal scholars have long lamented that experts — particularly medical experts — may be biased towards the party that retained them.[232] So too do courts anticipate expert disagreement to be drawn out by attorneys using the traditional adversarial tools of cross-examination and opposing testimony. In some contexts, such as sexually dangerous person commitment proceedings, a hearing featuring testimony from opposing experts is the norm.[233] Similarly, given the gravity of capital proceedings, opinions from opposing experts about dangerousness — even if the two opinions overlap substantially — typically result in rigorous cross-examination and conflicting expert testimony.

In other scenarios, however, courts opt to resolve expert disagreement without expert testimony, and rely only on attorneys' arguments, their own reading of the experts' reports, or their own judgments based on other evidence. For instance, at least in some states, insanity acquittee commitment proceedings do not regularly require expert evidence. And when faced with conflicting expert evidence, some scholars suggest that courts tend to resolve disagreements by selecting the more conservative choice, such as ordering sexually dangerous person commitment rather than conditional release.[234]

Overall, forensic mental health expert disagreement is quite common, and not at all surprising to courts. In practice, courts will consider what opposing experts reported and testified about, the experts' responses when cross-examined by attorneys, and ultimately, their own judgements about the experts' convincingness and the non-expert evidence bearing on the psycholegal factors at issue. Although courts generally have the discretion and prerogative to implement other solutions for managing disagreement among experts – such as appointing a third expert or arranging for concurrent presentation of expert evidence – scholars suggests that courts do not regularly employ these less-traditional options.

4.5.1.4 Roles of professional organisations and licensing authorities

Professional societies can issue ethical codes and practice guidelines for specialty areas, such as forensic psychology, related to those general codes. And, they can sanction members up to expulsion from the organisation for violations of ethical standards. They can also advocate with mental health professionals and courts via mechanisms such as policy-oriented research reviews – such as those issued by the American Psychology–Law Society's Scientific Review Paper Committee – and *amicus curiae* briefs submitted to courts.[235]

State licensing authorities, in turn, promulgate administrative regulations that implement state statutes in more detail to direct acceptable practice, and sanction licensees for deficient practice. This includes up to stripping them of the privilege to engage in forensic work, or their profession at all. Anecdotally, however, state licensing authorities tend to be more concerned about forensic practice in family law cases than sentencing or disposition matters.[236]

4.5.1.5 Training exchanges among involved disciplines

Cross-training of the involved disciplines – that is, training forensic evaluators about law, and legal professionals about forensic evaluation – can play a significant role in improving decision making in cases that feature forensic evaluations. As a guiding principle, all forensic evaluators should have some training in the law to be properly grounded in work that will be used to inform legal decision makers. For without an appropriate grounding in the law, evaluators are at risk of misunderstanding their roles or providing information that is irrelevant to legitimate psycholegal questions. Similarly, legal professionals who receive training about forensic evaluation are positioned to be much savvier consumers. Solid training in basic principles of forensic evaluation can empower lawyers and judges to discriminate between cases where reasonable professionals might disagree and cases where there is disagreement because one or both experts did not follow standard or best practices.

Whether and how forensic evaluators and legal professionals receive relevant cross-disciplinary training varies tremendously. Regarding training of evaluators, some clinicians receive this education during their graduate training or at the postdoctoral fellowship level, while others seek out training later in their careers if they become interested in transitioning to forensic work.[237] Some states have instituted statewide training requirements as a prerequisite to mental health professionals completing certain forensic evaluations, including some involving risk assessments. For example, in Virginia, to participate in insanity acquittee conditional release cases, evaluators must be 'skilled in the diagnosis of mental illness and intellectual disability and qualified by training and experience to perform such evaluations'.[238] The necessary

An American perspective 85

training is overseen by the state's Office of Forensic Services in the Department of Behavioral Health and Developmental Services. Similarly, in Washington State, the Office of Forensic Mental Health Services, part of the Department of Social and Health Services, has implemented a statewide, comprehensive forensic mental health services training program.[239] These types of training programs include, as a foundation, the law applicable to different types of forensic evaluations.

Importantly, though, many statewide training programs, and the state statutes or regulations that require them, pertain primarily to competence to stand trial and mental state at the time of the offense evaluations.[240] They do not necessarily extend to forensic evaluations for sentencing or dispositions. And while evaluator certification programs are becoming increasingly common, at least for evaluations such as competence to stand trial, most states do not have any such mandatory training requirements.[241]

Training of judges and lawyers about the principles of forensic evaluation, and criminogenic and violence risk assessment specifically, is neither standardised nor systematic. Judges certainly receive training in expert testimony and rules of evidence (e.g. through the National Judicial College), but they do not necessarily have opportunities to attend trainings about forensic evaluation for sentencing and disposition matters. The same is true for attorneys. While lawyers might happen across workshops or seminars about forensic evaluations generally, or risk assessment specifically, this type of training generally is generally not afforded in a systematic fashion.

Forensic mental health scholars may publish articles in outlets (e.g. *Court Review*, the journal of the American Judges Association), or issue reports that are intended for legal audiences.[242] Similarly, multidisciplinary panels of experts might issue reports through professional organisations, such as the American Bar Association's *Criminal Justice Standards on Mental Health*.[243] So too do forensic mental health professionals offer educational lectures for legal professionals, and vice versa.[244]

4.5.2 Best practices

All said, there are relatively few processes for resolving expert disagreement. Nonetheless, courts generally are empowered to implement creative solutions, and forensic researchers and scholars have identified some such potential solutions to further facilitate optimal decision making. Some practices are relevant to cases involving disagreement between experts, whereas others are designed to reduce the likelihood of disagreement from the outset.

One cause of disagreement involves forensic evaluators considering different information. This might be the product of experts having access to different records or other informational sources concerning the examinee, or eliciting different statements, reactions, or behaviours from the examinee during interviews or testing. Similarly, if experts use different evaluation procedures, it is not particularly surprising that they may arrive at different conclusions. Disagreements that arise from use of different information or procedures could be resolved by greater utilisation of legal procedures (e.g. judicial orders) to ensure that experts are given access to the same information and follow the same basic procedures. Although, given the nature of the USA's adversarial system, it can be expected that some attorneys would dispute such developments. Additionally, recording evaluations – while not often required in any jurisdiction – can be a way for mental health and legal professionals to see for themselves how a particular expert's questions and evaluation procedures may have led to the expert's particular opinions. Thus, judges have occasionally required experts to record evaluations in highly contested cases.

Forensic evaluator transparency is a crucial component for understanding and resolving expert disagreement. Thus, evaluators should be transparent about their sources of information and employed procedures, and how they arrived at their conclusions. Of course, testimony and cross-examination can also draw out these matters to highlight and elucidate reasons for disagreement – allowing the legal decision maker to give greater weight to the opinion that was based on better data, procedures, and reasoning. Concurrent expert evidence also has the potential to efficiently clarify the reasons for expert disagreement by requiring experts to respond to one another in real time. However, this process is rarely used and might not be feasible in criminal proceedings given certain due process rights enjoyed by defendants.

Other options involve restructuring the assessment process to reduce the odds of expert disagreement from the outset. Given the research on adversarial allegiance, or the tendency for experts to drift towards supporting the side that retained them, courts and attorneys might consider the use of 'blinded' experts – that is, experts who do not know which party retained their services. One model for blinded experts has been described for civil legal questions, and it is possible that some offices employing several forensic evaluators could implement blinding via an intermediary staff member who interacts with the referring party and passes on only relevant case information to the evaluators.[245] The use of blinded experts does, however, pose a host of challenges in many forensic evaluation contexts, and requires courts and attorneys to see value in the novel solution.

Somewhat like the model of a court-appointed expert, attorneys could also consider the distinctive solution of mutual referral to a single evaluator. This approach would help ensure that an evaluator is given access to all relevant information, as determined by both parties. Such a solution is thus free, in theory, from the drift that may occur due to adversarial allegiance.

4.6 Critical reflections

A review of forensic evaluations for sentencing and dispositions in the USA is a complex task, both by virtue of the complex federalism presented by the USA's legal system, and the range of sentencing and disposition legal questions involving psycholegal factors. Moreover, the law has not yet provided clear answers to several subtopics we have described. Entire texts have been devoted to some of this complexity.[246] Indeed, the international comparative law approach used by this book could just as fruitfully be applied to the numerous jurisdictions within the USA. Nonetheless, a few concluding remarks can be made.

In many ways, forensic evaluations and dangerousness determinations are regarded as so firmly rooted in the legal system that they are beyond reproach.[247] However, jurisdictions have proceeded more cautiously with certain other risk assessment applications, especially when it comes to incorporating criminogenic risk assessments into 'pure' frontend sentencing decisions – often termed *evidence-based sentencing*. Increased attention is also being paid to the field reliability of risk assessment, and evaluator biases and debiasing strategies. As the state of the science of the assessment of risk, needs, responsivity factors, and noncriminogenic needs – psychological constructs relevant to the different psycholegal factors that may be involved in various sentencing and disposition matters – has progressed, so too has the legal system learned of some of these advancements and limitations through the educational advocacy efforts of professional organisations and scholars, and the testimony of experts in individual cases.

Today, lawyers, judges, legislators, and other professionals involved with the legal system have generally come to expect better-quality forensic evaluations, which they consider with a more critical eye. But progress has been slow. Sentencing and disposition decisions implicate bedrock American principles such as liberty and equal protection of laws. The reciprocal spurring of the disciplines that conduct forensic evaluations or make legal decisions regarding dangerousness and other psycholegal factors – to continue to refine practices and policies, with sensitivity to fairness and systemic effects – are desirable pressures and aspirations.

Notes

1 Hazel, 2008; World Prison Brief, n.d.
2 Roesch and Zapf, 2013; Bonta and Andrews, 2017.
3 Branham, 2017.
4 May, Ides and Grossi, 2019.
5 Chemerinsky, 2019.
6 Branham, 2017; Dressler, 2018; Giannelli, 2018.
7 Wachter, 2015; Probation and Pretrial Services Office, 2018; Office of the Attorney General, 2020.
8 *Jurek v Texas*, 1976; *Estelle v Smith*, 1981; *Barefoot v Estelle*, 1983; *Satterwhite v Texas*, 1988; *Buck v Davis*, 2017.
9 *Daubert v Merrell Dow Pharmaceuticals Inc*, 1993; *Kumho Tire Co v Carmichael*, 1999.
10 Heilbrun, et al., 2017.
11 Myers, 2019.
12 Ostrom, et al., 2002; Va Code Ann § 19.2-298.01.
13 Kagan, 2019.
14 Hamilton, 2011; Dressler, 2018; Gardner, 2018; Perlin, 2021.
15 Heilbrun, et al., 2017.
16 Branham, 2017.
17 DeMatteo, et al., 2015; Perlin, 2021.
18 Giannelli, 2018.
19 Giannelli, 2018.
20 Fed R Evid 706.
21 Fed R Evid 702.
22 *Whatley v State*, 2010; Vitacco, et al., 2012; DeMatteo, et al., 2014b; Urquhart and Viljoen, 2014; *Lawlor v Zook*, 2018; *United States v Souders*, 2018.
23 In re *Isaac D*, 2012; Fed R Crim Proc 32.
24 Fed R Evid 702.
25 *Daubert v Merrell Dow Pharmaceuticals Inc*, 1993; Morgenstern, 2020.
26 Fed R Evid 704.
27 Heilbrun, Grisso and Goldstein, 2009.
28 Heilbrun, et al., 2015; Giannelli, 2018.
29 Fed R Evid 705.
30 Fed R Evid 703.
31 US Sentencing Guidelines Manual § 6A1.3, 2018; Davis, 2021.
32 Hamilton, 2011.
33 Heilbrun, et al., 2017; US Sentencing Guidelines Manual § 6A1.3, 2018.
34 *Barefoot v Estelle*, 1983; Davis, 2021.
35 Burke, 2020.
36 Mohr, 1997.
37 Grisso, 2018.
38 Grisso, 2018.
39 In re *Weintraub*, 1950; *People v Capoldi*, 1957; In re *Williams*, 1967.
40 Probation and Pretrial Services Office, 2018; Office of the Attorney General, 2020.
41 Andrews, Bonta and Wormith, 2006.
42 Bureau of Justice Assistance, n.d.
43 Monahan, 1981; Brief Amicus Curiae for the American Psychiatric Association, 1983.
44 *Jurek v Texas*, 1976; *Estelle v Smith*, 1981; *Barefoot v Estelle*, 1983.
45 Monahan, 1984.
46 Probation and Pretrial Services Office, 2018.
47 Bonta and Andrews, 2007.
48 Heilbrun, 1997; Neal, et al., 2019.
49 Heilbrun, 1997; Bonta and Andrews, 2007.
50 Bonta and Andrews, 2007.

51 Hart and Logan, 2011.
52 Urquhart & Viljoen, 2014; *United States v Hinckley*, 2016; Probation and Pretrial Services Office, 2018; Office of the Attorney General, 2020.
53 King, et al., 2017.
54 Slobogin, 2007.
55 Neal, et al., 2019.
56 Devers, 2011; Gramlich, 2019.
57 Dressler and Michaels, 2015.
58 Redlich, et al., 2017
59 Monahan, et al., 2020.
60 Dressler and Michaels, 2015.
61 *People v Murtishaw*, 2003.
62 National District Attorneys Association, 2010.
63 *O'Connor v Donaldson*, 1975; *Vitek v Jones*, 1980; *Foucha v Louisiana*, 1992.
64 *Jones v United States*, 1983.
65 *Kansas v Hendricks*, 1997; DeMatteo, et al., 2015.
66 *Addington v Texas*, 1979; National District Attorneys Association, 2010; 2012.
67 Heilbrun, et al., 2017.
68 Heilbrun, et al., 2017.
69 Salekin, 2015; Melton, et al., 2018.
70 Carter, Kreitzberg and Howe, 2018.
71 *Atkins v Virginia*, 2002; *Roper v Simmons*, 2005.
72 Death Penalty Information Center, n.d.b.
73 *Ford v Wainwright*, 1986; *Panetti v Quarterman*, 2007.
74 *Furman v Georgia*, 1972; *Gregg v Georgia*, 1976.
75 *Ring v Arizona*, 2002; Carter, Kreitzberg and Howe, 2018.
76 Carter, Kreitzberg and Howe, 2018.
77 Death Penalty Information Center, n.d.b.; *United States v LeCroy*, 2006; *Commonwealth v Smith*, 2010; *Whatley v State*, 2010; but cf. *Fletcher v State*, 2015.
78 *Lockett v Ohio*, 1978; *Eddings v Oklahoma*, 1982; Roesch and Zapf, 2013.
79 *Lawlor v Commonwealth*, 2013.
80 Carter, Kreitzberg and Howe, 2018.
81 *Abdul-Kabir v Quarterman*, 2007.
82 *Simmons v South Carolina*, 1994; *Shafter v South Carolina*, 2001.
83 *California v Ramos*, 1983.
84 Carter, Kreitzberg and Howe, 2018; *Ring v Arizona*, 2008.
85 *Ford v Wainwright*, 1986; *Ring v Arizona*, 2002.
86 Branham, 2017.
87 Dressler, 2018.
88 Branham, 2017.
89 *Apprendi v New Jersey*, 2000; *Blakely v Washington*, 2004; *United States v Booker*, 2005.
90 Dressler, 2018.
91 Branham, 2017.
92 *Gall v United States*, 2007; *Rita v United States*, 2007.
93 Branham, 2017.
94 Branham, 2017.
95 Dressler, 2018.
96 Rotman, 1986; Palmer, 2015.
97 *McKune v Lile*, 2002; Palmer, 2015.
98 *Washington v Harper*, 1990.
99 *Kahler v Kansas*, 2020.
100 Dressler, 2018.
101 *Jones v United States*, 1983.
102 *Foucha v Louisiana*, 1992.
103 *Rouse v Cameron*, 1967; *Wyatt v Stickney*, 1971; *Youngberg v Romeo*, 1982; *Olmstead v L C*, 1999.
104 Myers, 2019.
105 Comapre *Vitek v Jones*, 1980, with *Foucha v Louisiana*, 1992.
106 Dressler, 2018.

107 Dressler, 2018.
108 Palmer and Hazelrigg, 2000.
109 Mich Comp Laws § 768.36.
110 *Kansas v Hendricks*, 1997; *Kansas v Crane*, 2002; Weaver and Meyer, 2019.
111 Meyer, et al., 2003.
112 Roesch and Zapf, 2013; DeMatteo, et al., 2015.
113 *Kansas v Hendricks*, 1997.
114 *Connecticut Dept of Public Safety v Doe*, 2003; Weaver and Meyer, 2019.
115 Heilbrun, et al., 2017.
116 Gardner, 2018.
117 *Roper v Simmons*, 2005; *Montgomery v Louisiana*, 2016; Kavanaugh and Grisso, 2021.
118 Lahey, 2016.
119 Hockenberry and Puzzanchera, 2020.
120 Heilbrun, et al., 2017.
121 Hockenberry and Puzzanchera, 2020.
122 Heilbrun, et al., 2017.
123 *Kent v United States*, 1966; In re *Gault*, 1967; McKeiver *v Pennsylvania*, 1971; Heilbrun, et al., 2017.
124 Gardner, 2018.
125 Rogers and Myers, 2013; DeMatteo, et al., 2015.
126 Gardner, 2018; cf. Palmer, 2015.
127 E.g. NJ Rev Stat § 2 A:4A-43.
128 Wilson, Olaghere and Kimbrell, 2017; Office of Juvenile Justice and Delinquency Prevention, 2020.
129 Vitacco et al., 2012; Elek, Warren and Casey, 2015; Office of the Attorney General, 2020.
130 Slobogin, 2007; Roesch and Zapf, 2013.
131 Roesch and Zapf, 2013.
132 Probation and Pretrial Services Office, 2018; Office of the Attorney General, 2020.
133 *Lawlor v. Commonwealth*, 2013.
134 *Jones v United States*, 1983.
135 Roesch and Zapf, 2013.
136 Branham, 2017; Heilbrun, et al., 2017.
137 *Foucha v Louisiana*, 1992; Weaver and Meyer, 2019; see Myers, 2019, regarding more lax requirements that may be in place for outpatient commitments.
138 DeMatteo, et al., 2015.
139 Roesch and Zapf, 2013; Melton, et al., 2018.
140 *Buck v Davis*, 2017.
141 Harcourt, 2015; Picard, et al., 2019; Skeem and Lowenkamp, 2016.
142 *State v Loomis*, 2016; *King v Nevada*, 2019.
143 Roesch and Zapf, 2013; Bonta and Andrews, 2017.
144 Burke, 2020.
145 Myers, 2019.
146 Miller, et al., 2012.
147 Heilbrun, et al., 2009.
148 18 USC § 3624; Mich Comp Laws § 768.36.
149 Singh, Bjørkly and Fazel, 2016; Krauss, Cook and Klapatch, 2018; Batastini, et al., 2019a; 2019b; Kamorowski, et al., 2020.
150 Edens et al., 2017; Kelley et al., 2019; Berryessa & Wohlstetter, 2019.
151 Boccaccini, Murrie and Turner, 2014.
152 Turner, Boccaccini and Murrie, 2015.
153 Elmwood, 2019.
154 *United States v DM*, 2013.
155 *United States v Catalan-Roman*, 2005; *State ex rel Gabrielle M v Janes*, 2016.
156 Myers, 2019; National District Attorneys Association, 2012.
157 United *States v Alvarez*, 1975; *United States* ex rel *Edney v Smith*, 1976; *Buchanan v Kentucky*, 1987; *Kansas v* Cheever, 2013.
158 *Estelle v Smith*, 1981; *Satterwhite v Texas*, 1988.
159 In re *Gault*, 1967; *Allen v. Illinois*, 1986; *Mitchell v United States*, 1999.
160 Joint Legislative Audit Review Committee, 2012; Probation and Pretrial Services Office, 2018; Office of the Attorney General, 2020.

161 E.g. 49 Pa Code §41.61; see also Heilbrun, et al., 2008.
162 Melton, et al., 2018.
163 Heilbrun, et al., 2008.
164 Myers, 2019.
165 Myers, 2019.
166 *Briscoe v LaHue*, 1983.
167 Appelbaum, 2001.
168 Appelbaum, 2001.
169 Appelbaum, 2001; Melton, et al., 2018.
170 American Academy of Psychiatry and the Law, 2005; American Psychiatric Association, 2013; American Psychological Association, 2013; American Psychological Association, 2017.
171 American Psychological Association, 2008; Ethics Committee of the American Psychological Association, 2018.
172 Frost, de Camara and Earl, 2006; DeMatteo, et al., 2014b.
173 Austin, 2003; Baglivio, Greenwald and Russell, 2014; Cohen, Lowenkamp and Robinson 2018; Singh, Bjørkly and Fazel, 2016; US Bureau of Labor Statistics, 2021.
174 Heilbrun, et al., 2008.
175 Frost, de Camara and Earl, 2006.
176 Fed R Evid 702.
177 Neal, et al., 2019.
178 Fed R Evid 706.
179 E.g. Or Admin R 309-090-0000.
180 Melton, et al., 2018.
181 *Gardner v Johnson*, 2001.
182 Tran, 2020.
183 *Williams v New York*, 1949; Branham, 2017.
184 Heilbrun, et al., 2017.
185 Branham, 2017.
186 Weaver and Meyer, 2019.
187 *Gardner v Florida*, 1977.
188 Center for Sentencing Initiatives, n.d.; Heilbrun, et al., 2017.
189 Neal, et al., 2019.
190 *State v Loomis*, 2016.
191 E.g. *Barefoot v Estelle*, 1983.
192 Myers, 2019; Neal, et al., 2019.
193 Branham, 2017; Heilbrun, et al., 2017; Carter, Kreitzberg and Howe, 2018.
194 National District Attorneys Association, 2010; 2012.
195 Branham, 2017.
196 E.g. *Barefoot v Estelle*, 1983.
197 *Mempa v Rhay*, 1967.
198 *Scott v Illinois*, 1979; *Alabama v Shelton*, 2002.
199 *Wiggins v Smith*, 2003; *Rompilla v Beard*, 2005.
200 Heilbrun, et al., 2017; Myers, 2019.
201 *Barefoot v Estelle*, 1983.
202 *Ake v Oklahoma*, 1986.
203 *Hinton v Alabama*, 2014.
204 Melton, et al., 2018.
205 *Barefoot v Estelle*, 1983.
206 *Coble v State*, 2010, p. 271.
207 *Coble v State*, 2010, p. 287.
208 Brodsky and McKinzey, 2002.
209 American Psychological Association, 2008.
210 E.g. Faust, 2012.
211 *Barefoot v. Estelle*, 1983; DeMatteo, et al., 2014a; Neal, et al., 2019.
212 Elmwood, 2019.
213 E.g. Brief for Amici Curiae, American Psychological Association and Texas Psychological Association, 2011.

214 Brief Amicus Curiae for the American Psychiatric Association, 2013; Motion of American Psychiatric Association et al., for Leave to File Brief Amicus Curiae and Brief Amicus Curiae in Support of Petition for Rehearing, 1975.
215 *Tarasoff v Regents of University of California*, 1976; *Barefoot v Estelle*, 1983.
216 Monahan and Skeem, 2016; Hamilton, 2020.
217 Murrie and Boccaccini, 2015; Edens and Boccaccini, 2017; Gowensmith, et al., 2017.
218 E.g. Va Code Ann §§ 37.2-904, 37.2-907.
219 Gowensmith, Pinals and Karas, 2015; Gowensmith, et al., 2017.
220 Posner, 2016.
221 Cecil and Willging, 1993; Posner, 2016.
222 Cecil and Willging, 1993, p. 5.
223 Gowensmith, Pinals and Karas, 2015.
224 Va Code Ann § 19.2-182.2.
225 Butt, 2017.
226 Butt, 2017.
227 Krauss, et al., 2017.
228 Murrie, et al., 2008; Edens, Boccaccini and Johnson, 2010; Gowensmith, et al., 2017.
229 Murrie, et al., 2008; Miller, et al., 2012.
230 Levenson, 2004; Guarnera and Murrie, 2017.
231 Guarnera, Murrie and Boccaccini, 2017.
232 Hand, 1901; Wigmore, 1923.
233 E.g. Va Code Ann § 37.2-908.
234 Elmwood, 2019.
235 American Psychology–Law Society, 2014; see also Dvoskin, et al., 2011.
236 E.g. NJ Admin Code tit 13, ch 42, subch 12.
237 DeMatteo, et al., 2016.
238 Va Code Ann § 19.2-182.2.
239 Washington State Department of Social and Health Services, n.d.
240 Gowensmith, Pinals and Karas, 2015.
241 Gowensmith, Pinals and Karas, 2015.
242 E.g. Vincent, Guy and Grisso, 2013.
243 American Bar Association, 2016.
244 CONCEPT Professional Training, n.d.; Global Institute of Forensic Research, n.d.; Mental Disability Law and Policy Associates, n.d.
245 Robertson, 2010.
246 Monahan, 1981; Slobogin, 2007; Heilbrun, 2009; Faust, 2012; Roesch and Zapf, 2013; Melton, et al., 2018.
247 *Jurek v Texas*, 1976; *Barefoot v Estelle*, 1983; Slobogin, 2007.

References

American Academy of Psychiatry and the Law (2005). *Ethics Guidelines for the Practice of Forensic Psychiatry.* Bloomfield, CT: American Academy of Psychiatry and the Law. [online] Available at: https://www.aapl. org/ethics.htm [Accessed 30 June 2021].

American Bar Association (2016). *Criminal Justice Standards on Mental Health.* Chicago, IL: American Bar Association. [pdf] Available at: https://www.americanbar.org/content/dam/aba/publications/criminal_ justice_standards/mental_health_standards_2016.authcheckdam.pdf [Accessed 30 June 2021].

American Psychiatric Association (1983). *The Principles of Medical Ethics With Annotations Especially Applicable to Psychiatry, 2013 Edition.* Washington DC: American Psychiatric Association. [pdf] Available at: https:// www.psychiatry.org/File%20Library/Psychiatrists/Practice/Ethics/principles-medical-ethics.pdf [Accessed 30 June 2021].

American Psychological Association (2008). *Complaints regarding APA members.* [online] Available at: https:// www.apa.org/ethics/complaint [Accessed 30 June 2021].

American Psychological Association (2013). Specialty guidelines for forensic psychology. *American Psychologist*, 68(1), pp. 7–19. 10.1037/a0029889

American Psychological Association (2017). *Ethical Principles of Psychologists and Conduct of Conduct.* Washington DC: American Psychological Association. [pdf] Available at: https://www.apa.org/ethics/code/ethics-code-2017.pdf [Accessed 30 June 2021].

American Psychology–Law Society (2014). *Committee terms of reference.* [online] Available at: https://www.apadivisions.org/division-41/leadership/committees/reference [Accessed 30 June 2021].

Andrews, D.A., Bonta, J., and Wormith, J.S. (2006). The recent past and near future of risk and/or need assessment. *Crime & Delinquency*, 52(1), pp. 7–27. 10.1177/0011128705281756

Appelbaum, P.S. (2001). Law and psychiatry: Liability for forensic evaluators: A word of caution. *Psychiatric Services*, 52(7), pp. 885–886. 10.1176/appi.ps.52.7.885

Austin, J. (2003). Findings in prison classification and risk assessment. *National Institute of Corrections, Prisons Division - Issues in Brief.* Washington DC: US Department of Justice. [pdf] Available at: https://s3.amazonaws.com/static.nicic.gov/Library/018888.pdf [Accessed 30 June 2021].

Baglivio, M.T., Greenwald, M.A., and Russell, M. (2014). Assessing the implications of a structured decision-making tool for recidivism in a statewide analysis. *Criminology & Public Policy*, 14(1), pp. 5–49. 10.1111/1745-9133.12108

Batastini, A.B., Hoeffner, C.E., Vitacco, M.J., Morgan, R.D., Coaker, L.C., and Lester, M.E. (2019a). Does the format of the message affect what is heard? A two-part study on the communication of violence risk assessment data. *Journal of Forensic Psychology Research and Practice*, 19(1), pp. 44–71. 10.1080/24732850.2018.1538474

Batastini, A.B., Vitacco, M.J., Coaker, L.C., and Lester, M.E. (2019b). Communicating violence risk during testimony: Do different formats lead to different perceptions among jurors? *Psychology, Public Policy, and Law*, 25(2), pp. 92–106. 10.1037/law0000196

Berryessa, C. M. and Wohlstetter, B. (2019). The psychopathic "label" and effects on punishment outcomes: A meta-analysis. *Law and Human Behavior*, 43(1), pp. 9–25. 10.1037/lhb0000317

Boccaccini, M.T., Murrie, D.C., and Turner, D.B. (2014). Jurors' views on the value and objectivity of mental health experts testifying in sexually violent predator trials. *Behavioral Sciences & the Law*, 32(4), pp. 483–495. 10.1002/bsl.2129

Bonta, J. and Andrews, D.A. (2007). *Risk-Need-Responsivity Model for Offender Assessment and Rehabilitation.* Ottawa, Canada: Public Safety Canada. [pdf] Available at: https://www.publicsafety.gc.ca/cnt/rsrcs/pblctns/rsk-nd-rspnsvty/rsk-nd-rspnsvty-eng.pdf [Accessed 30 June 2021].

Bonta, J., and Andrews, D.A. (2017). *The Psychology of Criminal Conduct.* 6th ed. New York, NY: Routledge.

Branham, L.S. (2017). *The Law and Policy of Sentencing and Corrections.* 10th ed. St. Paul, MN: West Academic.

Brief Amicus Curiae for the American Psychiatric Association, *Barefoot v Estelle* 463 US 880 (1983). (No 82–6080), https://www.psychiatry.org/File%20Library/Psychiatrists/Directories/Library-and-Archive/amicus-briefs/amicus-1982-barefoot.pdf

Brief for Amici Curiae, American Psychological Association and Texas Psychological Association, in Support of Petition for a Writ of Certiorari, *Coble v Texas* 131 S Ct 3030 (2011). (No 10–1271), https://www.apa.org/about/offices/ogc/amicus/coble.pdf

Brodsky, S.L., and McKinzey, R.K. (2002). The ethical confrontation of the unethical forensic colleague. *Professional Psychology: Research and Practice*, 33(3), pp. 307–309. 10.1037/0735-7028.33.3.307

Bureau of Justice Assistance (n.d.). *History of risk assessment.* [online] Available at: https://bja.ojp.gov/program/psrac/basics/history-risk-assessment [Accessed 30 June 2021].

Burke, K.S. (2020). Evidence-based sentencing. In P. Hora, B. MacKenzie, T. Stalcup, and D. Wallace (Eds.), *Science Bench Book for Judges.* (2nd ed.). Reno, NV: National Judicial College. Ch.10. Available at: https://www.judges.org/wp-content/uploads/2021/01/Science-Bench-Book-2nd-Ed.pdf [Accessed 30 June 2021].

Butt, A. (2017). Concurrent expert evidence in U.S. toxic harms cases and civil cases more generally: Is there proper role for hot tubbing. *Houston Journal of International Law*, 40(1), pp. 1–104.

Carter, L.E., Kreitzberg, E.S., and Howe, S.E. (2018). *Understanding capital punishment law.* 4th ed. Durham, NC: Carolina Academic Press.

Cecil, J.S. and Willging, T.E. (1993). *Court-appointed experts: Defining the role of experts appointed under Federal Rule of Evidence 706.* Washington DC: Federal Judicial Center. [pdf] Available at: https://www.fjc.gov/sites/default/files/2012/Experts.pdf [Accessed 30 June 2021].

Center for Sentencing Initiatives (n.d.). *State policies and legislation*. [online] Available at: https://www.ncsc.org/csi/in-the-states/state-activities/state-policies-and-legislation [Accessed 30 June 2021].

Chemerinsky, E. (2010). *Constitutional Law: Principles and Policies*. 6th ed. New York, NY: Wolters Kluwer.

Cohen, T.H., Lowenkamp, C.T., and Robinson, C. (2018). The federal post-conviction risk assessment instrument: A tool for predicting recidivism for offenders on federal supervision. In J.P. Singh, D.G. Kroner, J.S. Wormith, S.L. Desmarais, and Z. Hamilton, (Eds.), *Handbook of Recidivism Risk/Needs Assessment Tools*. Hoboken, NJ: John Wiley & Sons. Ch.4.

CONCEPT Professional Training (n.d.). *Explore CONCEPT course offerings*. [online] Available at: https://concept.paloaltou.edu/ [Accessed 30 June 2021].

Davis, S.M. (2021). *Rights of Juveniles 2d: The Juvenile Justice System*. New York, NY: Clark Boardman Callaghan.

Death Penalty Information Center (n.d.a.). *Aggravating Factors by State*. Washington DC: Death Penalty Information Center. [online] Available at: https://deathpenaltyinfo.org/facts-and-research/crimes-punishable-by-death/aggravating-factors-by-state [Accessed 30 June 2021].

Death Penalty Information Center (n.d.b.). *Time on Death Row*. Washington DC: Death Penalty Information Center. [online] Available at: https://deathpenaltyinfo.org/death-row/death-row-time-on-death-row [Accessed 30 June 2021].

DeMatteo, D., Burl, J., Filone, S., and Heilbrun, K. (2016). Training in forensic assessment and intervention: Implications for principle-based models. In R. Jackson and R. Roesch (Eds.), *Learning Forensic Assessment: Research and Practice*. New York, NY: Routledge. Ch.1.

DeMatteo, D., Edens, J.F., Galloway, M., Cox, J., Smith, S.T., and Formon, D. (2014a). The role and reliability of the Psychopathy Checklist—Revised in U.S. sexually violent predator evaluations: A case law survey. *Law and Human Behavior*, 38(3), pp. 248–255. 10.1037/lhb0000059

DeMatteo, D., Edens, J.F., Galloway, M., Cox, J., Smith, S.T., Koller, J.P., and Bersoff, B. (2014b). Investigating the role of the Psychopathy Checklist–Revised in United States case law. *Psychology, Public Policy, and Law*, 20(1), pp. 96–107. 10.1037/a0035452

DeMatteo, D., Murphy, M., Galloway, M., and Krauss, D.A. (2015). A national survey of United States sexually violent person legislation: Policy, procedures, and practice. *International Journal of Forensic Mental Health Volume*, 14(4), pp. 245–266. 10.1080/14999013.2015.1110847

Devers, L. (2011). *Plea and Charge Bargaining: Research Summary*. Arlington, VA: Bureau of Justice Assistance. [pdf] Available at: https://bja.ojp.gov/sites/g/files/xyckuh186/files/media/document/PleaBargaining ResearchSummary.pdf [Accessed 30 June 2021].

Dressler, J. (2018). *Understanding Criminal Law*. 8th ed. Durham, NC: Carolina Academic Press.

Dressler, J. and Michaels, A.C. (2015). *Understanding Criminal Procedure, Volume 2: Adjudication*. 4th ed. Durham, NC: Carolina Academic Press.

Dvoskin, J.A., Skeem, J.L., Novaco, R.W., and Douglas, K.S. (Eds.) (2011). *Using Social Science to Reduce Violent Offending*. New York, NY: Oxford University Press.

Edens, J.F. and Boccaccini, M.T. (2017). Taking forensic mental health assessment "out of the lab" and into "the real world": Introduction to the special issue on the field utility of forensic assessment instruments and procedures. *Psychological Assessment*, 29(6), pp. 599–610. 10.1037/pas0000475

Edens, J.F., Boccaccini, M.T., and Johnson, D.W. (2010). Inter-rater reliability of the PCL-R total and factor scores among psychopathic sex offenders: Are personality features more prone to disagreement than behavioral features? *Behavioral Science and the Law*, 28(1), pp. 106–119. 10.1002/bsl.918

Edens, J.F., Mowle, E.N., Clark, J.W., and Magyar, M.S. (2017). "A psychopath by any other name?": Juror perceptions of the DSM-5 "Limited Prosocial Emotions" specifier. *Journal of Personality Disorders*, 31(1), pp. 90–109. 10.1521/pedi_2016_30_239

Elek, J.K., Warren, R.K., and Casey, P.M. (2015). *Using Risk and Needs Assessment Information at Sentencing: Observations From Ten Jurisdictions*. Williamsburg, VA: National Center for State Courts. [pdf] Available at: https://www.ncsc.org/__data/assets/pdf_file/0020/19127/rna-guide-final.pdf [Accessed 30 June 2021].

Elmwood, R.W. (2019). Agreement between courts and SVP evaluators in the state of Wisconsin. *Criminal Justice and Behavior*, 46(6), pp. 853–865. 10.1177/0093854819839746

Ethics Committee of the American Psychological Association (2018). *Rules and Procedures*. Washington DC: American Psychological Association. [pdf] Available at: https://www.apa.org/ethics/committee-rules-procedures-2018.pdf [Accessed 30 June 2021].

Faust, D. (Ed.) (2012). *Coping With Psychiatric and Psychological Testimony*. 6th ed. New York, NY: Oxford University Press.

Frost, L.E., de Camara, R.L., and Earl, T.R. (2006). Training, certification, and regulation of forensic evaluators. *Journal of Forensic Psychology Practice*, 6(2), pp. 77–91. 10.1300/J158v06n02_06

Gardner, M. (2018). *Understanding Juvenile Law*. 5th ed. Durham, NC: Carolina Academic Press.

Giannelli, P.C. (2018). *Understanding Evidence*. 5th ed. Durham, NC: Carolina Academic Press.

Global Institute of Forensic Research (n.d.). *All Trainings*. [online] Available at: https://www.gifrinc.com/all/ [Accessed 30 June 2021].

Gowensmith, W.N., Murrie, D.C., Boccaccini, M.T., and McNichols, B.J. (2017). Field reliability influences field validity: Risk assessments of individuals found not guilty by reason of insanity. *Psychological Assessment*, 29(6), pp. 786–794. 10.1037/pas0000376

Gowensmith, W.N., Pinals, D.A., and Karas, A.C. (2015). States' standards for training and certifying evaluators of competency to stand trial. *Journal of Forensic Psychology Practice*, 15(4), pp. 295–317. 10.1080/15228932.2015.1046798

Gardner, M.R. (2018). *Understanding Juvenile Law*. 5th ed. Durham, NC: Carolina Academic Press.

Gramlich, J. (2019). *Only 2% of Federal Criminal Defendants Go to Trial, and Most Who Do Are Found Guilty*. Washington DC: Pew Research Center. [online] Available at: https://www.pewresearch.org/fact-tank/2019/06/11/only-2-of-federal-criminal-defendants-go-to-trial-and-most-who-do-are-found-guilty/ [Accessed 30 June 2021].

Grisso, T. (2018). The evolution of psychology and law. In T. Grisso and S.L. Brodsky (Eds.), *The Roots of Modern Psychology and Law: A Narrative History*. New York, NY: Oxford University Press. Ch. 1.

Guarnera, L.A. and Murrie, D.C. (2017). Field reliability of competency and sanity opinion: A systematic review and meta-analysis. *Psychological Assessment*, 29(6), pp. 795–818. 10.1037/pas0000388

Guarnera, L.A., Murrie, D.C., and Boccaccini, M.T. (2017). Why do forensic experts disagree? Sources of unreliability and bias in forensic psychology evaluations. *Translational Issues in Psychological Science*, 3(2), pp. 143–152. 10.1037/tps0000114

Hamilton, M. (2011). Public safety, individual liberty, and suspect science: Future dangerousness assessments and sex offender laws. *Temple Law Review*, 83(3), pp. 697–756.

Hamilton, M. (2020). Judicial gatekeeping on scientific validity with risk assessment tools. [online] *Behavioral Sciences and the Law*, 38(3), pp. 226–245. 10.1002/bsl.2456

Hand, L. (1901). Historical and practical considerations regarding expert testimony. *Harvard Law Review*, 15, pp. 40–58. 10.2307/1322532

Hart, S.D., and Logan, C. (2011). Formulation of violence risk using evidence-based assessments: The structured professional judgment approach. In P. Sturmey and M. McMurran (Eds.), *Forensic Case Formulation*. Chichester, UK: John Wiley & Sons. Ch. 4.

Harcourt, B.E. (2015). Risk as a proxy for race: The dangers of risk assessment. *Federal Sentencing Reporter*, 27(4), pp. 237–243. 10.1525/fsr.2015.27.4.237

Hazel, N. (2008). *Cross-National Comparison of Youth Justice*. London, UK: Youth Justice Board. [pdf] Available at: https://dera.ioe.ac.uk/7996/1/Cross_national_final.pdf [Accessed 30 June 2021].

Heilbrun, K. (1997). Prediction versus management models relevant to risk assessment: The importance of legal decision-making context. *Law and Human Behavior*, 21(4), pp. 347–359. 10.1023/A:1024851017947

Heilbrun, K. (2009). *Evaluation for Risk of Violence in Adults*. New York, NY: Oxford University Press.

Heilbrun, K., DeMatteo, D., King, C., and Filone, S. (2017). *Evaluating Juvenile Transfer and Disposition: Law, Science, and Practice*. New York, NY: Routledge.

Heilbrun, K., DeMatteo, D., Marczyk, G., and Goldstein, A.M. (2008). Standards of practice and care in forensic mental health assessment: Legal, professional, and principles-based consideration. *Psychology, Public Policy, and Law*, 14(1), p. 126. 10.1037/1076-8971.14.1.1

Heilbrun, K., Grisso, T., and Goldstein, A.M. (2009). *Foundations of Forensic Mental Health Assessment*. New York, NY: Oxford University Press.

Heilbrun, K., NeMoyer, A., King, C., and Galloway, M. (2015). Using third-party information in forensic mental-health assessment: A critical review. *Court Review*, 51(1), pp. 16–35.

Hockenberry, S., and Puzzanchera, C. (2020). *Juvenile Court Statistics 2018*. Pittsburg, PA: National Center for Juvenile Justice. [pdf] Available at: https://ojjdp.ojp.gov/sites/g/files/xyckuh176/files/media/document/juvenile-court-statistics-2018.pdf [Accessed 30 June 2021].

Joint Legislative Audit Review Committee (2012). *Review of the civil commitment of sexually violent predators*. Richmond, VA: Joint Legislative Audit and Review Commission. [pdf] Available at: http://jlarc.virginia.gov/pdfs/reports/Rpt423.pdf [Accessed 30 June 2021].

Kamorowski, J., Ask, K., Schreuder, M., Jelícic, M., and de Ruiter, C. (2021). 'He seems odd': the effects of risk-irrelevant information and actuarial risk estimates on mock jurors' perceptions of sexual recidivism risk. [online] *Psychology, Crime & Law*, 28(4), pp. 342–371. 10.1080/1068316X.2021.1909016

Kelley, S.E., Edens, J.F., Mowle, E.N., Penson, B.N., and Rulseh, A. (2019). Dangerous, depraved, and death-worthy: A meta-analysis of the correlates of perceived psychopathy in jury simulation studies. *Journal of Clinical Psychology*, 75(4), pp. 627–643. 10.1002/jclp.22726

Krauss, D.A., Cook, G.I., and Klapatch, L. (2018). Risk assessment communication difficulties: An empirical examination of the effects of categorical versus probabilistic risk communication in sexually violent predator decisions. *Behavioral Sciences & the Law*, 36(5), pp. 532–553. 10.1002/bsl.2379

Krauss, D.A., Gongola, J., Scurich, N., and Busch, B. (2017). Mental state at time of offense in the hot tub: An empirical examination of concurrent expert testimony in an insanity case. *Behavioral Science and the Law*, 36(3), pp. 358–372. 10.1002/bsl.2348

Kagan, R.A. (2019). *Adversarial Legalism: The American Way of Law*. 2nd ed. Cambridge, MA: Harvard University Press.

Kavanaugh, A. and Grisso, T. (2021). *Evaluations for Sentencing of Juveniles in Criminal Court*. New York, NY: Oxford University Press.

King, C., Wade, N., and Tillson, J. (2017). Case law references as a big-picture snapshot of psychological test use in forensic mental health assessment. In American Psychology-Law Society Annual Conference, Seattle, WA, 16–18 March 2017. Washington DC: American Psychology-Law Society.

Lahey, J. (2016). The steep costs of keeping juveniles in adult prisons. *The Atlantic*, [online] 8 January. Available at: https://www.theatlantic.com/education/archive/2016/01/the-cost-of-keeping-juveniles-in-adult-prisons/423201/ [Accessed 30 June 2021].

Levenson, J.S. (2004). Reliability of sexually violent predator civil commitment criteria in Florida. *Law and Human Behavior*, 28(4), pp. 357–368. 10.1023/B:LAHU.0000039330.22347.ad

May, C.N., Ides, A., and Grossi, S. (2019). *Constitutional Law: National Power and Federalism*. 8th ed. New York, NY: Wolters Kluwer.

Melton, G.B., Petrila, J., Poythress, N.G., Slobogin, C., Otto, R.K., Mossman, D., and Condie, L.O. (2018). *Psychological Evaluations for the Courts: A Handbook for Mental Health Professionals and Lawyers*. 4th ed. New York, NY: Guilford Press.

Mental Disability Law and Policy Associates (n.d.). *Services*. [online] Available at: http://www.mdlpa.net/services [Accessed 30 June 2021].

Meyer, W.J., Molett, M., Richards, C.D., Arnold, L., and Latham, J. (2003). Outpatient civil commitment in Texas for management and treatment of sexually violent predators: A preliminary report. *International Journal of Offender Therapy and Comparative Criminology*, 47(4), pp. 396–406. 10.1177/0306624X03253846

Miller, C.S., Kimonis, E.R., Otto, R.K., Kline, S.M., and Wasserman, A.L. (2012). Reliability of risk assessment measures used in sexually violent predator proceedings. *Psychological Assessment*, 24(4), pp. 944–953. 10.1037/a0028411

Mohr, J.C. (1997). The origins of forensic psychiatry in the United States and the great nineteenth century crisis over the adjudication of wills. *Journal of the American Academy of Psychiatry and the Law*, 25(3), pp. 273–284.

Monahan, J. (1981). *The Clinical Prediction of Violent Behavior*. Rockville, MD: National Institute of Mental Health.

Monahan, J. (1984). The prediction of violent behavior: Toward a second generation of theory and policy. *American Journal of Psychiatry*, 141(1), pp. 10–15. 10.1176/ajp.141.1.10

Monahan, J., Metz, A., Garrett, B.L., and Jakubow, A. (2020). Risk assessment in sentencing and plea bargaining: The roles of prosecutors and defense attorneys. *Behavioral Sciences & the Law*, 38(1), pp. 1–11. 10.1002/bsl.2435

Monahan, J. and Skeem, J.L. (2016). Risk assessment in criminal sentencing. *Annual Review of Clinical Psychology*, 12, pp. 489–513. 10.1146/annurev-clinpsy-021815-092945

Morgenstern, M. (2020). *Daubert v. Frye – A state-by-state comparison*. [online] Available at: https://www.expertinstitute.com/resources/insights/daubert-v-frye-a-state-by-state-comparison/ [Accessed 30 June 2021].

Motion of American Psychiatric Association, Area VI of the Assembly of the American Psychiatric Association, Northern California Psychiatric Society, California State Psychological Association, San Francisco Psychoanalytic Institute and Society, California Society for Clinical Social Work, National Association of Social Workers, Golden Gate Chapter, and California Hospital Association for Leave to File Brief Amicus Curiae and Brief Amicus Curiae in Support of Petition for Rehearing, *Tarasoff v Regents of the University of California* 529 P2d 553 (Cal 1974) (No 405694), https://www.psychiatry.org/File%20Library/Psychiatrists/Directories/Library-and-Archive/amicus-briefs/amicus-1975-Tarasoff.pdf

Myers, J.E.B. (2019). *Mental Health Law in a Nutshell*. 2nd ed. St. Paul, MN: West Academic.

Murrie, D.C. and Boccaccini, M.T. (2015). Adversarial allegiance among expert witnesses. *Annual Review of Law and Social Science*, 11, pp. 37–55. 10.1146/annurev-lawsocsci-120814-121714

Murrie, D.C., Boccaccini, M.T., Johnson, J.T., and Janke, C. (2008). Does interrater (dis)agreement on psychopathy checklist scores in sexually violent predator trials suggest partisan allegiance in forensic evaluations? *Law and Human Behavior*, 32(4), pp. 352–362. 10.1007/s10979-007-9097-5

National District Attorneys Association (2010). *Involuntary Civil Commitment Related to Criminal Offenses*. Arlington, VA: National District Attorneys Association. [pdf] Available at: https://ndaa.org/wp-content/uploads/ncpca_statute_Civil-Commitment-Statutes2010.pdf [Accessed 30 June 2021].

National District Attorneys Association (2012). *Civil Commitment of Sex Offenders*. Arlington, VA: National District Attorneys Association. [pdf] Available at: https://ndaa.org/wp-content/uploads/Sex-Offender-Civil-Commitment-April-2012.pdf [Accessed 30 June 2021].

Neal, T.M.S., Slobogin, C., Saks, M.J., Faigman, D.L., and Geisinger, K.F. (2019). Psychological assessments in legal contexts: Are courts keeping "junk science" out of the courtroom? *Psychological Science in the Public Interest*, 20(3), pp. 135–164. 10.1177/1529100619888860

Office of Juvenile Justice and Delinquency Prevention (2020). *Statistical Briefing Book*. [online] Available at: https://www.ojjdp.gov/OJSTATBB/court/qa06501.asp?qaDate=2018 [Accessed 30 June 2021].

Office of the Attorney General (2020). *The First Step Act of 2018: Risk and Needs Assessment System – UPDATE*. Washington DC: US Department of Justice. [pdf] Available at: https://www.bop.gov/inmates/fsa/docs/the-first-step-act-of-2018-risk-and-needs-assessment-system-updated.pdf [Accessed 30June2021].

Ostrom, B.J., Kleiman, M., Cheesman, F., Hansen, R.M., and Kauder, N.B. (2002). *Offender Risk Assessment in Virginia: A Three-Stage Evaluation*. Williamsburg, VA: National Center for State Courts and Virginia Criminal Sentencing Commission. [pdf] Available at: http://www.vcsc.virginia.gov/risk_off_rpt.pdf [Accessed 30 June 2021].

Palmer, C.A. and Hazelrigg, M. (2000). The guilty but mentally ill verdict: A review and conceptual analysis of intent and impact. *Journal of the American Academy of Psychiatry and the Law*, 28(1), pp. 47–54.

Palmer, J.W. (2015). *Constitutional Rights of Prisoners*. 9th ed. New York, NY: Routledge.

Perlin, M.L. (2021). *Advanced Introduction to Mental Health Law*. Cheltenham, UK: Edward Elgar Publishing.

Picard, S., Watkins, M., Rempel, M., and Kerodal, A.G. (2019). *Beyond the Algorithm: Pretrial Reform, Risk Assessment, and Racial Fairness*. New York, NY: Center for Court Innovation. [pdf] Available at: https://www.courtinnovation.org/sites/default/files/media/document/2019/Beyond_The_Algorithm.pdf [Accessed 30 June 2021].

Posner, R.A. (2016). What is obviously wrong with the federal judiciary, yet eminently curable: Part I. *Green Bag*, 19, pp. 187–201.

Probation and Pretrial Services Office (2018). *An overview of the Federal Post Conviction Risk Assessment*. Washington DC: Administrative Office of the United States Courts. [pdf] Available at: https://www.uscourts.gov/sites/default/files/overview_of_the_post_conviction_risk_assessment_0.pdf [Accessed 30June2021].

Redlich, A.D., Bibas, S., Edkins, V.A., and Madon, S. (2017). The psychology of defendant plea decision making. *American Psychologist*, 72(4), pp. 339–352. 10.1037/a0040436

Robertson, C.T. (2010). Blind expertise. *New York University Law Review*, 85, pp. 174–257.

Roesch, R. and Zapf, P.A. (Eds.) (2013). *Forensic Assessments in Criminal and Civil Law: A Handbook for Lawyers*. New York, NY: Oxford University Press.

Rogers, J.E. and Myers, W.C. (2013). The insanity defense and youths in juvenile court. *Journal of the American Academy of Psychiatry and the Law*, 41(4), pp. 496–500.

Rotman, E. (1987). Do criminal offenders have a constitutional right to rehabilitation. *Journal of Criminal Law and Criminology*, 77(4), pp. 1023–1068. 10.2307/1143667

Salekin, R. (2015). *Forensic Evaluation and Treatment of Juveniles: Innovation and Best Practices*. Washington DC: American Psychological Association.

Singh, J.P., Bjørkly, S., and Fazel, S. (Eds.) (2016). *Interpersonal Perspectives on Violence Risk Assessment*. New York, NY: Oxford University Press.

Skeem, J.L. and Lowenkamp, C.T. (2016). Risk, race, and recidivism: Predictive bias and disparate impact. *Criminology: An Interdisciplinary Journal*, 54(4), pp. 680–712. 10.1111/1745-9125.12123

Slobogin, C. (2007). *Proving the Unprovable: The Role of Law, Science, and Speculation in Adjudicating Culpability and Dangerousness*. New York, NY: Oxford University Press.

Tran, K. (2020). *Grigson, James Paul, Jr. (1932–2004)*. In Texas State Historical Association (Ed.), *Handbook of Texas*. Austin, TX: Texas State Historical Association. [online] Available at: http://www.tshaonline.org/handbook/online/articles/fgrjp [Accessed 30 June 2021].

Turner, D.B., Boccaccini, M.T., and Murrie, D.C. (2015). Jurors report that risk measure scores matter in sexually violent predator trials, but that other factors matter more. *Behavioral Sciences & the Law*, 33(1), pp. 56–73. 10.1002/bsl.2154

Urquhart, T.A., and Viljoen, J.L. (2014). The use of the SAVRY and YLS/CMI in adolescent court proceedings: A case law review. *The International Journal of Forensic Mental Health*, 13(1), pp. 47–61. 10.1080/14999013.2014.885470

US Bureau of Labor Statistics (2021). *How to become a probation officer or correctional treatment specialist*. [online] Available at: https://www.bls.gov/OOH/community-and-social-service/probation-officers-and-correctional-treatment-specialists.htm#tab-4 [Accessed 30June2021].

Vincent, G.M., Guy, L.S., and Grisso, T. (2012). *Risk Assessment in Juvenile Justice: A Guidebook for Implementation*. Chicago: John D. and Catherine T. MacArthur Foundation. [pdf] Available at: https://escholarship.umassmed.edu/cgi/viewcontent.cgi?article=1601&context=psych_cmhsr [Accessed 30 June 2021].

Vitacco, M.J., Erickson, S.K., Kurus, S., and Apple, B.N. (2012). The role of the violence risk appraisal guide and historical, clinical, risk-20 in U.S. courts: A case law survey. *Psychology, Public Policy, and Law*, 18(3), pp. 361–391. 10.1037/a0025834

Wachter, A. (2015). *Statewide Risk Assessment in Juvenile Probation*. Pittsburg, PA: National Center for Juvenile Justice. [pdf] Available at: http://www.ncjj.org/pdf/JJGPS%20StateScan/JJGPS_StateScan_Statewide_Risk%20Assessment_2014_2.pdf [Accessed 30 June 2021].

Washington State Department of Social and Health Services (n.d.). *Office of Forensic Mental Health Services*. [online] Available at: https://www.dshs.wa.gov/bha/office-forensic-mental-health-services [Accessed 30 June 2021].

Weaver, C.M. and Meyer, R.G. (2019). *Law and Mental Health: A Case-Based Approach*. 2nd ed. New York, NY: Guilford Press.

Wilson, D.B., Olaghere, A., and Kimbrell, C.S. (2017). *Effectiveness of Restorative Justice Principles in Juvenile Justice: A Meta-Analysis*. Washington DC: Office of Juvenile Justice and Delinquency Prevention. [pdf] Available at: https://www.ncjrs.gov/pdffiles1/ojjdp/grants/250872.pdf [Accessed 30 June 2021].

Wigmore, J. (1923). *A Treatise on the Anglo-American System of Evidence in Trials at Common Law Including the Statutes and Judicial Decisions of All Jurisdictions of the United States and Canada*. Boston, MA: Little, Brown, and Company.

World Prison Brief (n.d.). *Highest to lowest - Prison population total*. [online] Available at: https://www.prisonstudies.org/highest-to-lowest/prison-population-total?field_region_taxonomy_tid=All [Accessed 30 June 2021].

Chapter 5

A Canadian perspective

Michelle S. Lawrence and David W. Morgan

5.1 Introduction

The complexity of Canadian law and practice in the sentencing of violent offenders cannot easily be captured in a short chapter. What follows is the authors' best attempt at summarising the salient aspects of the topic, in the hope that the content assists in a productive comparative analysis between the experiences of our country and those of our counterparts around the world. There is much that Canada can contribute to the global conversation on this topic and, as set out herein, much we might yet improve.

5.1.1 The legal system

Canada's legal system is based on common law and civil law traditions and is inclusive of Indigenous legal orders and treaty rights. In that way, our legal system reflects the region's unique history and the constellation of peoples who have inhabited this part of North America over centuries.

The modern nation of Canada was constituted in 1867 on the passage by the British Parliament of the *British North America Act*.[1] That Act united British colonies into a single confederation. It established two levels of government – a federal government and a provincial government – and it distributed specific legislative powers to each.

The sentencing of offenders engages both federal and provincial legislative powers. The *British North America Act* assigned the federal government jurisdiction over matters of criminal law and procedure (s. 91(27)) and the management of penitentiaries (s. 91(28)). It gave the provincial government authority over prisons (s. 92(6)) and the administration of courts of criminal jurisdiction (s. 92(14)). Moreover, significant to cases involving the prosecution and sentencing of accused persons with mental disorders, it assigned provincial government jurisdiction over hospitals and asylums (s. 92(7)).

Pursuant to its jurisdiction over criminal law and procedure, the Canadian federal government enacted the *Criminal Code*[2] and the *Youth Criminal Justice Act*.[3] The *Criminal Code* includes principles and rules for the sentencing of adult offenders (Part XXIII). It also includes a preventive detention regime for the designation of offenders as dangerous or long-term offenders and for the imposition of extended sentences in those cases (Part XXIV). The *Youth Criminal Justice Act* includes specific principles and rules to be applied in cases involving young persons. In Canada, for sentencing purposes, a 'young person' is defined in the *Youth Criminal Justice Act* to mean 'a person who is, or in the absence of evidence to the contrary, appears to be twelve years old or older, but less than eighteen years old …' and includes any person charged with an offence committed while in that particular age range (s. 2(1)).

DOI: 10.4324/9781351266482-5

Criminal prosecutions are conducted by federal and provincial prosecution services. Prosecutors are referred to as Crown Counsel, though they are expected to operate independently from the political branches of government. Prosecutions generally proceed in criminal courts situated at or near the place where the offence was committed. These courts are administered by provincial governments, pursuant to the authority vested to them by section 92(14) of the *British North America Act*.

Canada has three territories in its northern region, each with its own government. Territorial governments operate with the delegated authority of the federal government. They do not have the same constitutional standing as provincial governments. In Canada's territories, courts of criminal jurisdiction are administered by the federal government and prosecutions are run by federal prosecutors.

As a result, the process and practice for sentencing offenders vary somewhat between regions. Notably, in some regions, there are specialised courts dedicated to the management of cases involving Indigenous accused persons and offenders. In other regions, the courts integrate Indigenous practices, such as sentencing circles, into their process.

Notwithstanding these regional variations, all courts of criminal jurisdiction – wherever situated in Canada – are required to follow the rules of criminal procedure stipulated in the *Criminal Code*. These rules are premised on the adversarial model. In this model, the Crown represents the public interest. Generally speaking, to secure a conviction the Crown must prove all elements of the offence and the absence of a viable defence to the standard of proof beyond a reasonable doubt. The accused has a right to remain silent. Accordingly, the accused is not required to give testimony and may elect not to introduce any evidence by way of defence. Victims are not parties and, with limited exception, do not have formal standing in criminal proceedings.

Trial proceedings may proceed before a judge and jury or before a judge alone. There are specific rules in the *Criminal Code* that stipulate how a particular case can proceed. By contrast, sentencing hearings always proceed before a judge alone. In the sentencing phase of a criminal prosecution, judges serve as both the triers of fact and of law. In relation to the latter, in accordance with Canada's common law traditions, they must apply the doctrine of *stare decisis*. In the interpretation and application of legislation, and in their exercise of their discretion generally, they are governed by the decisions of any superior court, including the appellate courts within their province or territory. The Supreme Court of Canada is the highest court in Canada. Its decisions bind all lower courts throughout the country.

It is important to note that all governments and courts in Canada are subject to the *Canadian Charter of Rights and Freedoms*.[4] The *Charter* is a constitutional document and is considered to be the supreme law of Canada. It contains fundamental freedoms and rights, including legal rights applicable to criminal prosecutions. Among these legal rights is the right not to be subject to any cruel and unusual treatment or punishment (s. 12). Any law found by the courts to violate a *Charter* right or freedom – including, for example legislation that imposes a grossly disproportionate mandatory minimum sentence – may be struck down (s. 52(1)).[5]

5.1.2 The related tradition of forensic assessment

The term *forensic* can be described as relating to, or dealing with, the application of scientific knowledge to legal problems. In Canada, as elsewhere, a forensic psychiatric assessment is therefore only undertaken pursuant to a request or order from a third party, such as a lawyer, a court or a review board, and the sole purpose is to address a legal issue.

A clinical assessment is usually undertaken in order to reach a diagnosis, formulate a treatment plan and identify the means to deliver treatment, with the intention of alleviating the patient's clinical distress and improving their level of functioning. The medical concept of mental disorder is utilised, and is defined in the DSM-5-TR as a 'syndrome characterized by clinically significant disturbance in an individual's cognition, emotion regulation, or behavior that reflects a dysfunction in the psychological, biological, or developmental processes underlying mental functioning'.[6] In undertaking a clinical assessment, the forensic psychiatrist is acting in a treatment role, has a fiduciary duty to the patient and, as such, is ethically bound to act in the best interests of the patient at all times.[7]

It follows that the approach taken in a forensic assessment differs from a clinical assessment. In undertaking a forensic assessment, the role of the forensic psychiatrist is that of an expert witness whose duties flow not to the patient but to the court. There are also other important ethical differences between forensic and clinical assessments which will be explored later. As detailed below, the definition of mental disorder for legal purposes also is defined in materially different ways. Moreover, whether a particular condition constitutes a mental disorder by law is a matter for the court alone to decide.

In Canada, forensic assessments can be ordered by the court under specific provisions of the *Criminal Code* and *Youth Criminal Justice Act*. These are described below. It is important to note that, while the focus of this chapter is on the sentencing of offenders in the criminal justice system, forensic assessments are not limited purely to the criminal, but can also encompass civil tort actions, issues of professional regulation, malpractice, and disability.

The professions able to undertake court-ordered assessments are designated by the relevant Provincial Minister of Justice, and across Canada, psychiatrists are universally so designated. With regard to forensic psychiatry, in particular, the Royal College of Physicians and Surgeons of Canada (RCPSC) is the recognised national body which sets standards for the training, education, and maintenance of certification for all specialist physicians and surgeons. The RCPSC was established in 1929 by a special act of Parliament to oversee the medical education of specialists in Canada, and as such is neither a licensing nor disciplinary body. Its remit is instead to set national standards for medical education and continuing professional development in Canada for 67 specialties and subspecialties. Forensic psychiatry is recognised as a subspecialty by the RCPSC.[8] It requires an additional year of subspecialty training, which is undertaken subsequent to the completion of a five-year psychiatry residency and the successful completion of the FRCPC examinations. In Canada, entry is competitive. Forensic psychiatry subspecialty training has a defined academic curriculum, together with prescribed periods of training and numbers of assessments in adult forensic criminal psychiatry and electives in, for example, youth forensic criminal psychiatry, correctional psychiatry and civil forensic psychiatry. There is a subspecialty written examination at the end of the PGY-6, and on passing this the individual is recognised as a subspecialist forensic psychiatrist. The Royal College is responsible for the standards and accreditation of all postgraduate subspecialty academic training schemes in forensic psychiatry in Canada, such as those at the Universities of Toronto, Ottawa, McMaster, Alberta, and British Columbia, and at the University level training is overseen by a training programme director.

The Canadian Academy of Psychiatry and the Law (CAPL) is the national body representing forensic psychiatrists, and its members include faculty at various academic institutions across the country. The mission statement of CAPL includes the development of professional standards of practice, the advancement of continuing education, and the stimulation and encouragement of research. CAPL holds an annual scientific and education conference and the executive meets twice yearly. Provincial chapters exist in Québec and British Columbia.

Psychologists also often undertake forensic assessments in Canada, both in criminal and civil matters. Criminal forensic psychology doctoral programmes are offered at a number of

Canadian universities, and entry to these programmes is competitive. Licensure is regulated at a provincial level, and the relevant standards of each province are consistent with the standards of the Canadian Psychological Association (CPA), the national association for psychology in Canada. Forensic psychology is not recognised as a subspecialty by the licensing provinces or by the CPA. In order to become a member of the CPA, an individual must possess a master's or doctoral degree in psychology, conferred by a university of recognised standing. The CPA does have a section for criminal justice psychology, for members who undertake work in a variety of criminal justice and forensic settings, and it organises workshops, symposia, and discussions at the annual CPA convention.

Beyond its tradition of rigorous training of mental health professionals, Canada has a long and distinguished history in the development of psychological instruments for the risk assessment of violence and sexual violence, particularly in the provinces of Ontario and British Columbia. Instruments developed by Canadian academics for use in adults include actuarial tools, such as the VRAG and SORAG,[9] Static 99 R,[10] and PCL-R,[11] and structured professional judgements, such as the HCR-20,[12] RSVP,[13] START,[14] eHARM,[15] and SARA.[16] Risk assessment tools for adolescents developed in Canada include the PCL-YV,[17] SAVRY,[18] and START-AV[19] for violence and the ERASOR[20] for sexual violence. For further details regarding the specific instruments, their validity and reliability, the reader is directed to the *Handbook of Violence Risk Assessment*.[21] Close relationships between academic institutions and provincial forensic psychiatric services in Canada have facilitated the development of these instruments, and have led to their use being widely embedded in practice.

5.2 Short overview of the role of assessment in sentencing offenders

5.2.1 Sentences and execution

The *Criminal Code* stipulates maximum custodial sentences for particular offences, and for some offences it also includes mandatory minimum sentences. There is no provision in the *Criminal Code* for the death penalty. For the offence of first-degree murder, which is considered the most serious form of homicide in Canadian law, the mandatory minimum sentence is life imprisonment without eligibility for parole for a period of 25 years (s. 235(1)).

It is also possible in Canada for a sentence to run for an indeterminate period. As noted above, Part XXIV of the *Criminal Code* includes a preventive detention regime. This regime is based on an assessment of the offender's likelihood to commit offences in the future. It is often engaged in cases where there is evidence of a long-standing pattern of the offender being unable to withhold deviant impulses, resulting in chronic offending that causes noxious harm and poses a significant and ongoing risk to the public. In such cases, the sentencing court may designate an offender as a "dangerous offender" or a "long-term offender". The latter designation may result in a long-term supervision order for a period of up to ten years beyond whatever sentence was imposed for the index offence (s. 753.1(3)). The former designation may result in an order of confinement in a federal penitentiary for an indeterminate period (s. 753(4)(a)).

In the provinces, if an accused is convicted and sentenced to a custodial term of less than two years, then the offender will be required to serve that sentence in a provincial prison. These institutions typically offer mental health and psychiatry in reach services, and a limited choice of rehabilitative programmes, such as those to address substance use. If a mentally disordered offender requires transfer to a hospital for inpatient psychiatric treatment, then the region's provincial or territorial mental health legislation is used. The exact mechanism for the transfer depends on the arrangements in place in that region. Offenders typically serve short sentences in provincial prisons and are released to community supervision. Once in the community they are usually required to serve a term of community supervision under a probation order and may be able to access community forensic psychiatric services, which can range in the services they can offer.

If the sentence is for a term of incarceration of two years or more, the offender must serve the sentence in a federal penitentiary. Naturally, by reason of the lengthy nature of their sentences, long-term and dangerous offenders are housed in federal facilities. These facilities are located throughout Canada and are managed by the Correctional Service of Canada (CSC). CSC is organised on a regional basis, and each region provides a range of different security establishments. Before being classified and placed in a particular facility, offenders are first evaluated in a Regional Reception and Assessment Centre (RRAC) where assessments of the risk of violence and institutional adjustment are undertaken, and psychological instruments, such as the PCL-R and HCR-20, are used. The federal correctional system offers a wide variety of different rehabilitative programmes for violent offenders, sexual offenders, and Indigenous offenders. When providing treatment, the Risk-Needs-Responsivity model[22] dictates that treatment should incorporate various learning strategies, and be tailored to the offender's particular learning style; this is applied in the federal system. The federal system also offers an entirely integrated psychiatric hospital system, where offenders can be admitted under the relevant provincial or territorial mental health legislation for treatment. When a federal offender is granted parole by the Parole Board, there then follows a period of community supervision. During this time, CSC contracts with psychiatrists in the community to provide ongoing psychiatric care. Parole officers maintain supervision, challenge antisocial attitudes and undertake maintenance programming.

Custodial sentences are rarely imposed on young offenders. The *Youth Criminal Justice Act* includes provisions that significantly restrict the ability of a sentencing court to imprison a young offender (s. 39). Likewise, for adult offenders, the *Criminal Code* articulates a principle of restraint in sentencing. The *Criminal Code* includes provisions that discourage the use of incarceration and promote non-custodial sentencing options (ss. 718(c), 718.2(d), 718.2(e)). It allows some sentences to be served in the community on what is called a conditional sentence order (s. 742). It permits in some cases non-custodial options such as fines (s. 716, 734), probation (s. 731(1)) and discharges (s. 717). It provides also for the granting of a variety of ancillary orders, including weapons prohibitions (ss. 490(9), 491), sex offender registration requirements (ss. 490.011–490.32), and orders that compel the offender to submit a DNA sample to a national repository used by law enforcement for investigative purposes (s. 487.051).

Part XX.1 of the *Criminal Code* creates a separate disposition regime for accused persons who are found to be not criminally responsible by reason of a mental disorder (NCRMD). In such cases, the trial court may craft its own disposition, or it may defer the issue to the relevant provincial or territorial Review Board. The court or Review Board may order that the accused be detained in a psychiatric hospital (s. 672.54(c)) or discharged into the community on conditions (s. 672.54(b)). Either way, pursuant to section 672.54(a) of the *Criminal Code,* an NCR accused person is entitled to be absolutely discharged unless he is found to constitute a significant threat to public safety.

Part XX.1 of the *Criminal Code* was amended recently on the passage of the *Not Criminally Responsible Reform Act.*[23] This Act introduced new provisions whereby the court could designate an NCR accused person as a 'high-risk accused'. The high-risk accused designation is similar in some ways to a dangerous offender designation in the sense that it may be based on evidence that shows a pattern of grave offending. It also is particularly onerous in that it significantly limits the remedies and privileges otherwise available to the NCR accused.

The impact of these amendments has yet to be fully realised, though they are expected to affect a large number of NCR accused persons in Canada.[24] Arguably, however, some aspects of those amendments are constitutionally infirm and might yet be struck down if they are found in a future case to violate the *Charter*.[25]

There is no provision in the *Criminal Code* for the imposition of treatment without the consent of the offender.[26] Pursuant to section 742.3(2)(e) of the *Criminal Code,* as part of probation or as a condition of discharge, sentencing courts may require that an offender attend a treatment programme. This provision does not authorise a further requirement that the offender takes medication. The sole exception to the general prohibition on compelled treatment in Canadian criminal law is for cases where the accused is found unfit to stand trial by reason of mental disorder. Section 672.58 of the *Criminal Code* provides that a court may direct the treatment of an unfit accused person for the purpose of making that person fit to stand trial. Even then, the *Criminal Code* stipulates strict preconditions and limitations for such an order (ss. 672.59–672.62).

Otherwise, in Canada, any physician who seeks to administer treatment without the consent of the patient – whether that patient is an NCR accused person or an offender subject to a sentence in a prison or penitentiary – must comply with the strict requirements of the applicable provincial or territorial mental health legislation. These requirements vary between regions.[27] For example in the province of Ontario, medication cannot be administered without the prior consent of the patient given while competent, or the consent of the patient's substitute decision-maker.[28] By contrast, in the province of British Columbia, a patient's consent may be deemed by operation of statute. Section 31(1) of the *Mental Health Act*[29] stipulates that treatment authorised by the director of a mental health facility is deemed to be given with the consent of the patient.

5.2.2 Decisions within sentencing and execution

5.2.2.1 Decisions concerning fitness to stand trial

It is a fundamental principle of Canadian law that an accused person is entitled to be present throughout his trial. That entitlement extends through to the sentencing hearing.[30] The concept of presence includes not only physical presence but also mental presence. In Canada, by operation of section 672.22 of the *Criminal Code,* an accused is presumed fit to stand trial. However, where there are reasonable grounds to believe that the accused is unfit on account of mental disorder, the court may direct that the issue of fitness be tried (s. 672.23). If the court decides that the accused is in fact unfit to stand trial, then the criminal prosecution is postponed until such time as the accused becomes fit, or until some other disposition can properly be made.

An accused who is found to be unfit is managed in the forensic mental health system subject to the terms of disposition in section 672.54 of the *Criminal Code*. These are described below.

5.2.2.2 Decisions on the sentencing of adult offenders

On the conviction of an adult offender, the court must decide what sentence to impose by way of punishment. This decision necessarily involves the identification of those sentencing options permitted under the *Criminal Code*. The sentencing court is bound by whatever restrictions are specified in the governing legislation. It otherwise falls to the sentencing court to exercise judicial discretion in the selection of sentence.

In deciding how to exercise its discretion on sentencing, the sentencing court is guided by case law and by the principles of sentencing articulated in Part XXIII of the *Criminal Code*. These principles are important to the determination of what constitutes a fit sentence in Canadian law. Others have written extensively on the topic.[31] Significant for the purposes of this chapter is the fundamental principle of sentencing articulated in section 718.1 of the *Criminal Code,* that being the principle that '[a] sentence must be proportionate to the gravity of the offence and the degree of responsibility of the offender'.

In some cases, the application of the proportionality principle requires that the sentencing court determine whether an offender's moral blameworthiness was impacted by mental disorder. Forensic assessment can help the sentencing court understand the extent to which an accused's capacity to exercise rational choice was constrained by mental disorder, and whether the degree of responsibility attributable to the accused was diminished as a result. In such cases, assessments may focus on any mental disorders present, and their relationship to the offending behaviour. The essence of a forensic assessment, after all, is to analyse and understand the mental factors and processes driving the behaviour in question. These assessments may also include risk assessments and speak to the question of how various clinical factors – including treatment potential – interplay to increase or mitigate the individual's risk of future violence. Evidence of this nature is not strictly required, but it is useful to the sentencing court as it relates to the potential manageability of the individual in a community setting. Naturally, in such cases, it is important to consider adverse childhood experiences, and any particular relevant considerations such as stalking, domestic violence or fixated threat. Comparable assessments undertaken on adolescents add developmental complexity, be that physical, sexual, cognitive, emotional, moral, or interpersonal.[32]

Whatever the outcome of sentencing, the court cannot direct that the offender serves the sentence at a particular institution or facility. As noted earlier, adult offenders with custodial sentences of two years or more are housed and managed by the Correctional Service of Canada (CSC). Sentences of less than two years are served in provincial jails. In all cases, however, risk assessments may be undertaken by forensic psychiatrists or psychologists during the offender's tenure in the correctional institution. In the federal system, risk assessments are initially undertaken at the time of entry and are used to determine the level of security required for the offender. As noted earlier, they are also considered when an offender applies for parole.

5.2.2.3 Decisions on the sentencing of young offenders

In Canada, young people may be held criminally responsible for offences committed at 12 years of age. However, in the criminal justice process, they are dealt with very differently than adults. In sentencing adults (aged 18 years or older), the court must craft a sentence that takes into account, among other objectives, the goals of denunciation, deterrence and rehabilitation. By contrast, in dealing with youth who commit offences, the paramount consideration is the objective of rehabilitation. Courts prefer to use custodial sentences as a last resort, and instead look to maximise community resources so as to minimise any disruption. The principles set out in section 3 of the *Youth Criminal Justice Act* aim to hold the young person accountable for their actions through appropriate and proportionate sanctions, with the intention of promoting their rehabilitation and reintegration into the community. The Act specifically provides for young people to be referred to community programmes or agencies to help them address the circumstances underlying their offending behaviour, and thus supports the prevention of crime. Such programmes or agencies are delegated to a provincial level and vary considerably across Canada.

In sentencing young offenders, the *Youth Criminal Justice Act* permits various assessments to be ordered by the court. These are most commonly pre-sentence reports which provide the court with an assessment of the young person's background, development, functioning, strengths and clinical needs relevant to their offending behaviour. In cases involving adolescents, particular attention should be given to cognitive, emotional, interpersonal, and moral development, and the effect of any abuse, neglect, or other adverse childhood experiences. Personality traits may become clearer as a youth gets older, but significant caution should be exercised before diagnosing a personality disorder. Psychological assessments of intelligence and academic achievement, state and trait anger, and emotional functioning can be of significant assistance in the forensic assessment of adolescents, as can specific risk assessments for violence (SAVRY) and sexual violence (ERASOR).

In addition, the Act provides for assessments in cases involving applications in particularly serious cases to transfer the matter to adult court. In cases involving youth, there is a statutory presumption of reduced moral culpability and immaturity, and if this presumption can be rebutted by Crown Counsel then the young offender can be raised to adult court for sentencing.

5.2.2.4 Decisions on applications for preventive detention

In cases where Crown Counsel seek to invoke the preventive detention provisions of the *Criminal Code*, the sentencing court must decide whether to designate the offender as a dangerous or long-term offender and it must determine the appropriate disposition.

The criteria for designation are set out in sections 753 and 753.1 of the *Criminal Code*. Pursuant to section 753, the court shall designate an offender to be a dangerous offender in two possible scenarios. A dangerous offender designation may be made if the court is satisfied that the offence for which the offender is convicted is a serious personal injury offence that involves the use or attempted use of violence, and the offender constitutes a threat to the life, safety, or physical or mental well-being of other persons as assessed on the basis of the pattern and nature of the offender's past behaviour. Alternatively, the court may designate the offender as a dangerous offender if the offender is convicted of sexual assault and his conduct in any sexual matter has shown a failure to control sexual impulses and the likelihood of causing harm to another person through failure in the future to control those impulses.

Pursuant to section 753.1 of the *Criminal Code*, the court may designate an offender a long-term offender if it is satisfied that the current offence warrants a sentence of imprisonment of two years or more, that there is a substantial risk the offender will re-offend, and there is a reasonable possibility of eventual control of that risk in the community. Section 751.1(2) includes a non-exhaustive list of circumstances the court may consider when deciding whether the offender is at substantial risk of re-offending, including the nature and pattern of behaviours that show a likelihood of future harm.

On the designation of an offender as a dangerous offender or a long-term offender, in accordance with section 751(4) of the *Criminal Code*, the sentencing court must then determine the appropriate disposition. Its options for the sentencing of dangerous and long-term offenders are listed, respectively, in sections 753(3) and 753.1(3) of the *Criminal Code*. Pursuant to section 753(4.1), on the designation of an offender as a dangerous offender, the court is obliged to impose a sentence of detention in a penitentiary for an indeterminate period unless it is satisfied that there is a reasonable expectation that a lesser measure will adequately protect the public from a future act of murder or another serious personal injury offence.

5.2.2.5 Decisions in cases of NCR accused persons

On an application for a declaration of NCRMD, the trial court must decide whether the requirements of section 16 of the *Criminal Code* are established to the standard of proof on a balance of probabilities. The threshold question in such cases is whether the accused was suffering from a mental disorder at the material time of the offence. The court otherwise must decide whether, by reason of that mental disorder, the accused was incapable either of appreciating the nature and quality of his acts, or of knowing they were morally wrong. Forensic assessment in NCRMD cases therefore involves a careful retrospective re-construction of the accused's mental state at the material time of the offence.

On the declaration of an accused as NCRMD, or on the declaration that an accused is unfit to stand trial, the courts typically refer the determination of disposition to the provincial or territorial Review Board. In such cases, the Review Board first must decide if the NCR accused person poses a significant threat to public safety. If not, pursuant to section 672.54(a) of the *Criminal Code,* the NCR accused is entitled to be absolutely discharged. Otherwise, the Review Board must determine whether the individual should be detained in custody in a hospital (s. 672.54(c)) or discharged to the community subject to conditions (s. 672.54(b)). The disposition that it selects must be the least restrictive and least onerous in the circumstances of the case and must take into account the paramount consideration of public safety, as well as the NCR accused person's rehabilitation, reintegration into the community and other needs.

Forensic assessments inform these decisions. The Review Board may be provided with reports from psychiatrists, psychologists, psychiatric nurses, occupational therapists, and social workers. In such cases, the treating forensic psychiatrist is placed in a difficult position with regard to dual agency, as they are required to step out of the treatment role temporarily and into the forensic assessment role. As described earlier, there are very different ethical prin-ciples underpinning each of these different roles, which can lead to conflict. Regardless, the precise nature of the reports prepared by these professionals varies according to jurisdiction. The reports should contain an actuarial or structured professional judgement risk assessment, or sometimes both. The history of the development of forensic risk assessment highlights the deficiencies of using an individual idiosyncratic approach and the benefit of using evidence-based risk assessment instruments.[33]

The period of time between Review Board hearings varies, but they are typically held on an annual basis. In addition to furnishing the Review Board with a written report and risk assessment, the forensic psychiatrist will also be expected to provide *viva voce* evidence. Other members of the NCR accused persons' treatment team may also attend Review Board hearings to provide additional *viva voce* evidence. Disposition is rendered on the basis of the evidence. Any conditions imposed by the Review Board in the disposition order cannot be punitive in nature.

5.2.3 Concepts to be assessed

In criminal proceedings in Canada, the forensic assessment may assist a trier of fact to decide any matter where the accused's mental condition is at issue. Its potential use is not limited to sentencing and may extend to decisions on criminal liability. For example, in cases involving the defence of self-defence, a forensic assessment may assist the court in understanding whether a perception of imminent harm was reasonable.[34] Forensic assessments may be si-milarly useful in any case where mental capacity is an issue, including cases where the defence of intoxication is raised. That said, as discussed next, forensic assessments are most often tendered to assist the court in deciding whether the offender was suffering from a mental disorder, the nature of any consequent cognitive or volitional impairment, and the nature of any future risk that the individual poses to the public.

5.2.3.1 Mental disorder

In cases involving consideration of fitness to stand trial, and on application under section 16 of the *Criminal Code* for declarations of NCRMD, the threshold question for the court is the question of whether the accused's mental state constitutes a 'mental disorder' for criminal law purposes. In Canada, the term is defined in section 2 to mean a 'disease of the mind'. In the seminal case of *R v Cooper* (1980),[35] the Supreme Court of Canada described 'disease of the mind' as a broad concept and one that includes 'any illness, disorder or abnormal condition which impairs the human mind and its function, excluding however, self-induced states caused by alcohol or drugs, as well as transitory mental states such as hysteria or concussion' (p. 1159). As noted earlier, this definition is materially different from that prescribed in the DSM-5-TR for clinical assessment and treatment purposes.

Naturally, forensic assessments can include a formal diagnosis of any psychiatric illness or medical condition that the accused might have. However, that diagnosis is not determinative. It is well-established in Canadian law that the 'disease of the mind' concept is a legal concept and not a medical concept. In Canada, it falls to the trier of law to decide whether a particular condition constitutes a 'mental disorder' within the meaning of section 2 of the *Criminal Code*, and to the trier of fact to determine whether the accused was experiencing symptoms of that mental disorder at the relevant time.[36] Assessors therefore must be careful in their reports not to usurp decision-making authority of the court. Their role is to assist the decision-maker, not be the decision-maker.

5.2.3.2 Unfit to stand trial

The concept of 'unfit to stand trial' is defined in section 2 of the *Criminal Code* to mean:

> ... unable on account of mental disorder to conduct a defence at any stage of the proceedings before a verdict is rendered or to instruct counsel to do so, and, in particular, unable on account of mental disorder to

> a   understand the nature or object of the proceedings,
> b   understand the possible consequences of the proceedings, or
> c   communicate with counsel.

The remaining parts of the section 2 definition of 'unfit to stand trial' have been narrowly construed by Canadian courts as a test of limited cognitive capacity.[37] The central question in this test – and the central question for which forensic assessment might therefore be required – is whether the accused has sufficient mental capacity to understand the process and communicate with counsel. It is not necessary that the accused person also is capable of making rational decisions beneficial to his own interests, or that he is capable of sound analytical reasoning when deciding whether to accept the advice of counsel.

In such cases, the assessor must consider whether a mental disorder is currently present and active, and how that disorder impacts the accused's ability to meaningfully participate in proceedings. Such an assessment usually comes about when an accused person appears to be suffering from a mental disorder which is impacting their ability to participate in court proceedings, usually their ability to communicate with defence counsel. Generally, mental disorders which commonly interfere with an accused's fitness to stand trial include severe mood disorders, severe psychotic disorders and developmental and intellectual disabilities. The bar for fitness to stand trial in Canada is low.

Indeed, it has been argued that the test for fitness in Canada is unduly low.[38] Reform may yet be required to fairly accommodate circumstances where an accused may be capable of communication with counsel but where that communication is superficial. The accused in the relatively recent case of *R v John* (2019)[39] was unable to convey the facts required to seek and receive legal advice about the prospect of establishing a particular defence. He was charged with second-degree murder and attempted murder. If convicted, he would receive a significant custodial sentence. In her decision on fitness, Madam Justice Warren of the British Columbia Supreme Court described in paragraph 144 the ability of the accused to assess this defence as 'crucial to the proceedings' and 'vital to [the accused's] meaningful participation'. She concluded that the accused was unfit to stand trial as a result but she was required to apply a generous interpretation of the fitness test – arguably one that goes beyond the parameters set by the Supreme Court of Canada in the *Taylor* case – to achieve that result. As noted, the *John* decision is relatively recent, and it remains to be seen whether Madam Justice Warren's expansion of the fitness test will be adopted by other courts in future cases.

5.2.3.3 Not criminally responsible by reason of mental disorder

Pursuant to section 16 of the *Criminal Code,* in any prosecution, it is open to either Crown Counsel or the accused to apply for a declaration that the accused is 'NCRMD'. In practice, an assessment for NCRMD is usually raised by the defence. To succeed in such an application, the applicant must establish on a balance of probabilities that the accused was suffering from a 'mental disorder' at the time of the offence, and that the accused was incapable as a result of that mental disorder of either 'appreciating the nature and quality of the act or omission or of knowing that it was wrong'.

The term 'mental disorder' is defined in section 2 and has been described earlier. Otherwise, the concept of 'appreciating the nature and quality of the act or omission' has been interpreted by the courts to require that the accused know the nature of the act (or omission) and the physical consequences.[40] In Canada, it is not necessary that the accused also appreciate the emotional or penal consequences of the act or omission. The concept of 'knowing that it was wrong' has been broadly interpreted to mean either legally or morally wrong in the circumstances according to the standards of the ordinary person.[41]

The starting point in an NCRMD assessment is the legal presumption, articulated in section 16(3) of the *Criminal Code,* that the accused person does not suffer from a mental disorder. The bar for a finding of NCRMD is high. The assessor must first consider whether a mental disorder was present and whether it was active at the material time of the alleged offence. The examiner must next consider whether the mental disorder, if active, was so severe so as to deprive the accused of the mental capacity to appreciate the nature and quality of their actions or know that they were legally or morally wrong. The test thus contains two different limbs, with different cognitive tests – appreciate versus know. As noted earlier, forensic assessment is in these cases a retrospective reconstruction of the accused's mental state at the material time. This necessarily requires careful consideration of whatever contemporaneous records might be available and is informed by the outcome of multiple interviews with the accused. Though there is potential for considerable variation in practice, a relatively recent trajectory study of NCRMD cases in certain provinces identified relative consistency of assessment approaches between Ontario and British Columbia.[42]

The language of section 16 of the *Criminal Code* clearly contemplates cognitive impairment. It is important to note that, by operation of common law, the NCRMD defence is also available to accused persons whose mental disorder produced volitional impairment. In the case of *R v Stone* (1999),[43] the Supreme Court of Canada held that declarations of NCRMD should be made in cases where the accused's mental disorder produced automatism, and where the accused's actions were not voluntary as a result. These cases are relatively rare. Moreover, in the relatively recent case of *R v Bouchard-Lebrun* (2011),[44] the Court suggested *obiter dictum* that the NCRMD defence might be extended in future cases of co-occurring mental disorder and substance use. The Court endorsed the use of a 'more holistic approach' test in such cases, and suggested that an accused might be declared NCRMD if he is at risk of relapse to psychosis by reason of a dependency on psychoactive substances.[45]

5.2.3.4 Future risk to public safety

Risk has been defined as a hazard which is incompletely understood, and thus can only be forecast with uncertainty.[46] In dangerous offender hearings the court must consider whether the offender 'constitutes a threat to the life, safety or mental well-being of other persons',[47] whereas in dealing with an NCRMD accused the Review Board must determine whether the NCR accused poses a 'significant threat to the public safety'.[48]

For the purposes of the preventive detention regime in Part XXIV of the *Criminal Code,* the designation and disposition of an offender require a prospective assessment of risk. These decisions engage questions of whether the accused is likely to re-offend, and whether that risk can somehow be managed safely in the community. That determination necessarily includes consideration of whether the accused's condition is likely to be responsive to treatment.[49] It has to be established whether a mental disorder is present. For example in the case of sexual offenders, the usual drivers of sexual offending are an antisocial personality structure and paraphilic disorders.[50] Paraphilic disorders can be treated with medications and psychological treatments, but interventions for paraphilic disorders and antisocial individuals are quite different.[51] Both actuarial and SPJ approaches have a part to play in the risk assessment, and the risk assessment should help inform the targets for treatment.

For the purposes of the disposition of unfit and NCR accused persons under Part XX.1 of the *Criminal Code*, concepts of risk inform the question of whether the accused poses a significant threat to public safety. That term is defined in section 672.5401 of the *Criminal Code* and has been interpreted by the courts to mean a real risk of serious physical or psychological harm to members of the public resulting from conduct that is criminal in nature but not necessarily violent.[52] This concept also informs the question of which disposition is necessary and appropriate taking into account, among other factors, the safety of the public.

In undertaking a risk assessment for violence or sexual violence, the focus depends on the nature of the legal question to be identified. Generally, when undertaking a risk assessment an assessor should be trying to answer the following questions: what behaviour is the individual likely to engage in, who are the most likely victims, how serious could the potential physical and psychological harm to a victim be, in which environment is this most likely to happen, and how immediately could this happen. Scenario planning is often used. In addition to risk assessment instruments relevant to these questions, there are also protective factors and the strengths of the individual to consider. The SAPROF[53] is one such instrument for considering this. Whilst there are no legal requirements regarding the forensic methodology employed in undertaking a risk assessment, professional standards of practice are developed by professional associations such as CAPL.

5.2.4 Forensic assessment and procedure

Court assessment orders are directed at provincial forensic psychiatric services, to whom many forensic psychiatrists contract their services, and are strictly time-limited. They are made pursuant to the powers vested in the court in section 672.11 of the *Criminal Code,* and therefore relate largely to fitness issues and criminal responsibility issues under section 16.

It is also open to the court, defence or prosecutor to retain their own expert independently, and this is often required where no statutory provision to order an assessment exists. Some provinces, such as British Columbia, have made specific arrangements with local forensic psychiatric services for dangerous offender assessments and pre-sentence reports,[54] whereas other provinces have not. Otherwise, in relation to any issue where mental state is in question, ranging from bail assessments to mental disorder defences to sentencing, a private expert may be retained.

When undertaking a forensic psychiatric assessment, good practice dictates that the examiner generally needs to ascertain (i) whether there is a mental disorder present, and the broad definition of mental disorder, together with the diagnostic criteria provided in the DSM-5-TR; (ii) whether that mental disorder was active at the material time of the alleged offence, what symptomatology was present and how severe it was – the assessor should in particular be interested in the cognitive, emotional, and interpersonal psychopathology and processes which arise as a result of the mental disorder; (iii) how these potentially impacted or will impact behaviour; (iv) what treatment has previously been attempted and with what results; and (v) how severe the mental disorder presently is.

In undertaking a forensic assessment, there are various stages. The first of these is the identification of the legal issue to be addressed, together with any relevant statutes and legal authorities. These are described earlier. The second stage is the identification of the information required to address the legal issue, and the collection of this; such information could include, but is not limited to, written legal depositions, records relating to previous offending and community supervision, medical records, school records, employment records, video footage, and collateral interviews with informants. The assessor also should collect and review as much potentially relevant collateral information as can be obtained. If further information beyond what has been provided is required, then a request should be directed to the referring agency. Some forensic psychiatrists will review the collateral information in detail prior to interviewing the examinee, whereas others prefer to interview first and review collateral information later. Both approaches attempt to limit bias, and there is no accepted professional consensus at this time.

The third stage is the synthesis of this information and the formation of a clinical opinion, and finally the fourth stage involves the preparation of the written report.

The forensic approach throughout these stages is of critical importance and differs significantly from a clinical assessment. The forensic assessor must obtain valid, informed consent from the individual being assessed, who must be informed as to the nature and purpose of the assessment, the independent status and duty of the assessor to the court, any limits regarding confidentiality, and the individual's right to withhold information. Strict confidentiality must be maintained, and the assessor may be bound by solicitor–client privilege if privately retained. The assessor is ethically bound to strive for honesty, objectivity, and truth. They must identify any sources of potential bias and take steps to minimise it. The minimisation of bias is of critical importance as regards the admissibility of expert evidence in court, and knowledge and awareness of the different types of bias on the part of the examiner is critical. A request for a forensic assessment when one has already been in a treatment relationship with a patient should not be accepted or should be undertaken only in highly extenuating circumstances, given the potential for dual agency bias. Guidelines for the forensic assessment are published in scholarly journals by relevant North American professional organisations[55] and should be adhered to. When assessing adolescents, developmental issues relating to maturity and culpability demand extra attention.[56]

5.3 Safeguards for the quality of forensic assessment

5.3.1 Requirements in law and policy

In Canada, the law of evidence serves as the primary safeguard for the quality and reliability of forensic assessments that may be considered by the trier of fact. It provides that opinion evidence – in the form of a forensic assessment or otherwise – is not admissible unless it satisfies certain conditions. These conditions have been refined and reformulated by Canadian courts on several occasions. They were first enunciated in the decision of the Supreme Court of Canada in the seminal case of *R v Mohan* (1994),[57] and were recently refined and reformulated by the Supreme Court of Canada in the case of *White Burgess Langille Inman v Abbott and Haliburton Co* (2015)[58] (*White Burgess*).

In *White Burgess,* the Court endorsed a two-step framework for the admissibility of opinion evidence. In the first step, the trial court must be persuaded that the opinion evidence satisfies four strict preconditions. These preconditions are derived from the *Mohan* decision and are referred to as *Mohan* criteria. First, the opinion evidence must be logically relevant to an issue in the proceeding. Second, the opinion evidence must be necessary because it concerns matters that are likely to be outside the experience and knowledge of the trier of fact. Third, the opinion evidence itself cannot run afoul of any other rule of evidence. It cannot, for example, contain inadmissible hearing evidence or constitute impermissible oath-helping. Fourth, and significantly, the individual proffering the opinion evidence must be a properly qualified expert. They must have the requisite knowledge, training, and expertise. The particular professional qualifications of forensic psychiatrists and forensic psychologists are prescribed by the Royal College of Physicians and Surgeons and the Canadian Psychological Association, respectively, and are described above. In addition, the proposed expert must be fair, objective and non-partisan. The Supreme Court of Canada made clear in the *White Burgess* case that the duty of an expert witness is to the court and not to any particular party.

In the second step of the *White Burgess* framework, the trial judge must decide whether the proposed opinion evidence is sufficiently beneficial to the trial process to warrant its admission despite the potential harm to the trial process that may flow from its admission. This involves a cost-benefit analysis. The court may consider on the one hand the probative value of the opinion evidence and the significance of the issue to which the opinion evidence relates and on the other hand the risks that admission will compromise the trial process by introducing time, prejudice, and confusion. At the heart of the analysis is the fundamental question of the quality and reliability of the opinion.

Canadian courts impose such strict limitations on the admissibility of opinion evidence owing to underlying concerns about the perceived dangers attached to such evidence, not least of which is the fear that an expert witness may usurp the role of the trier of fact. There can be little doubt that the Canadian justice system is vulnerable to flawed forensic science. There are many documented cases in Canada of miscarriages of justice arising from the misplaced reliance on problematic expert evidence. Significant among these are multiple wrongful convictions for child homicides – in some cases of parents for the deaths of their own children – recently found to be attributable to the flawed assessments of a forensic pathologist in Ontario named Dr. Charles Smith.[59] These cases serve as a reminder of the particular need in Canada for strict adherence to the *White Burgess* requirements.

5.3.2 Disciplinary and ethical requirements

For physicians and psychologists, professional regulatory oversight occurs at the provincial and territorial level through their respective College of Physicians and Surgeons and College of Psychologists. Professional and ethical practice standards are prescribed in relevant codes of conduct. To fall afoul of these professional standards in the preparation and provision of substandard forensic assessments, however, would seem to require relatively egregious conduct. The more likely outcome in any given case would be a court ruling on the application of the *White Burgess* test that the assessment itself is inadmissible due to a lack of qualifications on the part of the assessor or the poor quality of the assessment itself. Alternatively, an assessment might be admitted in evidence but be dismissed by the court on its merits. Either way, the reputation of the forensic assessor might be adversely impacted. The court may generate a written decision on the issue. That decision would be available to the public. In Canada, decisions of this nature are of interest to professional colleagues, and sometimes even attract media attention.

5.3.3 Requirements for the evaluator

Arguably, beyond the strict legal requirements for the admissibility of expert opinion evidence, the main safeguard for the quality of the forensic assessment is the high quality of postgraduate training that forensic mental health professionals receive in Canada, coupled with ongoing requirements of Canadian governing regulatory bodies for continuing professional development.

As described earlier, in Canada, subspecialty training in forensic psychiatry is undertaken following successful completion of the RCPSC psychiatry Fellowship examination. The PGY-6 forensic psychiatry subspecialty year is intense, and during this time the resident is progressively exposed to more challenging cases. The theoretical and ethical aspects of practice are covered in a series of academic lectures. In the near future, postgraduate training will change to Competence By Design. This will involve more of a mentorship model and the development of specific competencies in forensic psychiatry.

There is a responsibility incumbent on all physicians to complete adequate continuing professional development, and the RCPSC maintenance of the certification programme is compulsory. This requires the completion of 400 hours of professional academic development over a 5-year cycle, with at least 40 hours in any one year. These hours include a compulsory peer review element, and attendance at professional conferences count towards total hours. For psychologists, the CPA offers a number of educational opportunities, but specific continuing professional development requirements are set by the provincial licensing bodies, and therefore vary. Psychologists are generally required to complete around 50 hours every two years.

5.3.4 Enforcement of requirements

Provincial licensing and regulatory bodies supervise and enforce their codes of conduct and their requirements for education and training. They may hold disciplinary hearings and impose regulatory sanctions on findings of fault. These sanctions can range from mandatory training requirements to the suspension of an individual's license and right to practice in the profession.

Otherwise, in the application of the *White Burgess* test for expert evidence, Canadian courts rely on the mechanics of the adversarial process to bring to light any instances where proposed expert evidence falls short of that required for admissibility. It is expected in the Canadian system that parties who are adverse in interest will be sufficiently motivated to expose any gaps in the expert's qualifications, to effectively test evidence through skilled cross-examination, and bring to the attention of the court any contrary opinion evidence through the use of independent experts. The ability of the parties and the courts to question evidence in this way is discussed in greater detail in the next part.

5.4 Safeguards 'against' the limited quality of forensic assessment

5.4.1 Questioning the assessment by the defense

In criminal litigation, parties may challenge a forensic assessment in two main ways. First, they may oppose the admissibility of the assessment on the grounds that the evidence does not satisfy the *Mohan* criteria in the first step of the *White Burgess* test, or on the ground that the potential costs of admission outweigh any potential benefits under the second step of that test. Second, if the forensic assessment is admitted into evidence, they may call into doubt the quality and reliability of that assessment through skilled cross-examination of the expert witness or through the introduction of contrary independent evidence from their own expert. In some cases, counsel may elect to do both. Either way, their objective is to draw out the evidentiary foundation necessary to support their argument that the trier of fact should assign little to no weight to the forensic assessment.

Not surprisingly, the ability of defence counsel to marshal contrary independent evidence depends in many cases on the provision of legal aid funding. Mentally disordered individuals accused of a crime cannot necessarily be expected to have the personal resources or family support required to fund a robust legal defence.[60] The amount of public funding available to defence counsel in such cases depends on the tariffs and guidelines in place in each region, and in some cases appears to be wholly inadequate in terms of both the rates of pay and the scope of compensable work. The situation in British Columbia was described by one lawyer as 'scandalous'.[61] It perhaps goes now without saying that, in Canada, the reported lack of funding for accused persons with mental disorders represents a significant barrier to access to justice for this community.

This concern is particularly acute given the limited ability of an accused person or offender to appeal from questions of fact. In Canada, the admissibility of evidence is a question of law, and any party to the proceedings may advance an appeal on the basis of an alleged error of law. However, the decision to accept or reject the evidence itself, in whole or in part, is a question of fact. As set out in section 675 of the *Criminal Code,* an appeal on such a question may only be brought by an accused person with leave of the court. Moreover, the threshold for appellate interference in findings of fact is high. An appellate court will not intervene in such cases if the verdict rendered is one that a properly instructed jury acting judicially could reasonably have rendered.[62]

5.4.2 Questioning the assessment by the court

In criminal proceedings, it is open to a court to ask questions of an expert witness. However, many judges incline against an activist approach. Instead, they rely on counsel in the discharge of their duties in the adversarial process to conduct the necessary questioning and bring to the court's attention any frailties in that evidence.

In some cases, the court may opt to appoint an *amicus curiae* to participate in the case, if and as necessary, to ensure a fair process. This might be appropriate where, for example, an accused person has elected to proceed without legal representation. Among the roles that might be assigned to an *amicus curiae* is the cross-examination of an expert witness.

5.4.3 Other questioning of the assessment

As noted earlier, in legal practice, criminal prosecutions proceed in Canada in the adversarial tradition. Judges generally rely on the parties to challenge expert evidence through cross-examination and through the introduction of contrary independent evidence. Of course, the adversarial model works best when the parties are equally equipped and resourced for the litigation. Unfortunately, as noted above, legal aid funding cannot necessarily be relied on to adequately support all accused persons and offenders. To some extent, resource inequities between the prosecution and defence might be remedied through greater judicial engagement in the questioning of forensic assessments. Even then, however, the potential for miscarriages of justice remains of concern and necessitates strict adherence to the restrictions stipulated in the *White Burgess* case for the admission of expert evidence.

That concern is less grave in proceedings before Review Boards, and the restrictions on the admission of expert evidence are more relaxed in that setting as a result. This is in part attributable to the inquisitorial nature of the Review Board process and in part a reflection of the expert nature of Review Boards. Section 672.39 of the *Criminal Code* requires that Review Boards include members with expertise and experience in psychiatry and mental health training. These members are well-equipped to critically engage with information presented in forensic assessments and to question the assessor directly in the course of Review Board hearings.[63] If they find that the evidence falls short, they may order the production of additional evidence, including further assessments.

The relatively recent case of *Ewert v Canada*[64] brought to the fore the important issue of the need to validate actuarial risk assessment instruments, including the PCL-R, for use in cases involving Indigenous offenders.[65] Some research has already been undertaken on this topic,[66] and the issue is under consideration in other jurisdictions as well.[67] For now, in appropriate cases, concerns regarding the use of actuarial risk assessment instruments for Indigenous persons might be addressed by using a Structured Professional Judgement.

5.5 Safeguarding the quality of decision-making when confronted with disagreement between experts

Individuals commonly disagree with the opinions other generate, particularly when those opinions relate to matters as subjective as psychiatry. Canadian courts are accustomed to disagreements between expert witnesses and are generally well-equipped to deal with them provided the expert witnesses are themselves honest, accurate in the presentation of their evidence, and otherwise fair, objective and non-partisan.

5.5.1 Dealing with disagreement

In certain circumstances, a court or Review Board may order an assessment into the mental condition of an accused person where it has reasonable grounds to believe that such evidence is necessary.[68] These circumstances are stipulated in the *Criminal Code* and include cases where fitness to stand trial is an issue. Beyond that, however, there are no formal options or alternate bodies for the resolution of disagreement between experts.

Instead, in the Canadian criminal justice process, the trier of fact is expected to render an independent decision on the basis of the totality of the evidence before it in any given proceeding. It must weigh the relative merits of the evidence and apply the relevant standard of proof, whether that be proof beyond a reasonable doubt or the balance of probabilities standard. However, in doing so, the trier of fact need not actually resolve a disagreement between witnesses. It is permitted to reject or accept evidence in whole or in part, based on its own assessment of the strength and probative value of the evidence. As a result, in cases where the experts disagree, the trier of fact may simply prefer one expert's assessment over another expert's assessment, or adopt parts of each. In connection with forensic assessments, in particular, they may be influenced by the relative expertise of the assessor as well as their demeanour and conduct in the courtroom, particularly when under cross-examination.

5.5.2 Best practices

In 2007, in the aftermath of the Chief Coroner's review of Dr. Charles Smith's work and the child homicide cases in which he was involved, the Government of Ontario appointed Justice Goudge to lead a public inquiry into the oversight of the paediatric forensic pathology system. At the conclusion of that inquiry, Justice Goudge issued a series of recommendations, including recommendations for best practices in the presentation of forensic pathology evidence in criminal proceedings. He articulated basic principles which, although focused on the practice of forensic pathology, are equally applicable to other forensic disciplines and are commended to readers for further study.[69]

Significantly, Justice Goudge's recommendations speak to the need for forensic professionals to be independent and evidence-based in their work, and to present their findings in ways that are transparent and open to effective external review. They speak also to the important role of the court in protecting the legal system against the potentially devastating effects of expert evidence that is not only flawed in substance but also misleading in its presentation. Justice Goudge noted on page 48 that '[n]o justice system can be immunized against the risk of flawed scientific opinion evidence. But with vigilance and care, we can move toward that goal'.

Of particular interest for practitioners of forensic psychiatry, Justice Goudge cautioned against language in expert reports that overstates the expert's level of confidence. He described forensic pathology as an 'interpretative discipline in which degrees of certainty are not easily quantified or may not even be scientifically supportable' (p. 413). Similar observations might be made with respect to forensic psychiatry. To that end, future best practices might include – as Justice Goudge recommends for forensic pathology – the development of uniform language to describe the level of confidence that the expert has, and which makes plain the extent of any doubt that they might hold with respect to their conclusions. In the same vein, experts should make full and proper disclosure of alternate diagnoses, and readily disclose for the benefit of the trier of fact not only the limitations in their own expertise but also controversies and uncertainties in the science on which they rely.

Also of note, with regard to scientific research, *The National Trajectory Project of Individuals Found Not Criminally Responsible on Account of Mental Disorder*[70] generated several valuable papers, including research examining the use of the NCRMD verdict in Canada.[71] Among other things, that research showed that Québec courts produced many more NCRMD verdicts than the courts of Ontario or British Columbia, with differences in psychopathology at the material time of the index offence.[72] It also demonstrated significant interprovincial differences regarding initial dispositions, legal representation at Review Board hearings and duration of Review Board supervision.[73]

5.6 Critical reflection

It should be apparent from the information included in this chapter that, in Canada, the quality of forensic assessments is generally the product of two measures. The first measure concerns the quality of the expert and the expert's work product. The second measure relates to the quality of the justice system itself.

For the most part, Canada is relatively strong on both fronts. Canada has rigorous standards for the education and training of its forensic psychiatrists. Forensic methodology – including the knowledge of, and adherence to, the ethical principles of assessment, the minimisation of bias, honesty and the application of evidence-based risk assessments and the evidence underpinning these – is addressed through subspecialist training in forensic psychiatry and continuing professional development. In addition, although shortfalls in legal aid funding are of concern, Canadian courts appear to make effective use of the adversarial system to bring to light shortcomings in expert opinion evidence. Canadian law includes strict conditions for the admission of expert opinion evidence, and Canadian legal process facilitates the testing of that evidence through cross-examination.

It cannot be said with confidence, however, that these two measures alone can fully safeguard against error. For the reasons explained in this chapter, there remains a very real risk of miscarriages of justice. The risk of wrongful outcomes is exacerbated in the current era by shortfalls in legal aid funding. Arguably, however, that same risk might be mitigated, at least in some part, through the maintenance of high standards in the quality of forensic assessment. As noted herein, in this regard, Canada can be proud of its contributions to the development of evidence-based risk assessments for violence and sexual violence. This work is set to continue, and it will contribute further to the quality of our assessment practices.

Notes

1 *British North America Act,* 1867, 30–31 Vict., c 3.
2 *Criminal Code,* R.S.C. 1985, c C-46.
3 *Youth Criminal Justice Act,* S.C. 2002, c. 1. The *Criminal Code, supra,* and the *Youth Criminal Justice Act* are the primary – but not the only – statutes enacted pursuant to the federal jurisdiction over criminal law. See also, *inter alia,* the *Controlled Drugs and Substances Act,* S.C. 1996, c 19, which sets out offences and sentencing provisions for drug offences.
4 *Canadian Charter of Rights and Freedoms,* s 7, Part 1 of the *Constitution Act,* 1982, being Schedule B to the *Canada Act 1982* (UK), 1982, c 11.
5 See *R v Lloyd* 2016 SCC 13.
6 DSM-5-TR, 2022.
7 CMA, 2018.
8 Bourget and Chaimowitz, 2010; RCPSC, 2020.
9 Quinsey et al., 2006.
10 Harris, Phenix and Williams, n.d.
11 Hare, 1980.
12 Douglas et al., 2013.
13 Hart et al., 2003.
14 Nicholls et al., 2009.
15 Mullally et al., 2018.
16 Kropp and Hart, 2015.
17 Forth et al., 2003.
18 Borum et al., 2006.

19 Viljoen et al., 2010.
20 Worling and Curwen, 2001.
21 Otto and Douglas, 2010.
22 Andrews et al., 1990.
23 *Not Criminally Responsible Reform Act* SC 2014, c 6.
24 Goosens et al., 2019.
25 Lacroix et al., 2017.
26 Verdun-Jones and Lawrence, 2013.
27 Shone, Liddle and Gray, 2008; Verdun-Jones and Lawrence, 2013.
28 *Mental Health Act,* RSO 1990, c M.7; *Health Care Consent Act, 1996,* SO 1996, c 2.
29 *Mental Health Act,* RSBC 1996, c 288.
30 *R v Jaser,* 2015 ONSC 4729.
31 See Ruby et al., 2017 and Manson, 2001.
32 Grisso, 2013.
33 Dolan and Doyle, 2018
34 See *R v Lavallee* [1990] 1 SCR 852.
35 *R v Cooper* [1980] 1 SCR 1149.
36 *R v Simpson* (1977) 16 O.R. (2d) 129 (CA).
37 *R v Taylor* [1992] 11 OR (3d) 323 (CA); *R v Whittle* [1994] 2 SCR 914.
38 See, *inter alia,* Schneider and Bloom, 1995–96.
39 *R v John* 2019 BCSC 1600.
40 *R v Kjeldsen* [1981] 2 SCR 627; *R v Abbey* (1981) 29 BCLR 212 (CA).
41 *R v Chaulk* [1990] 3 SCR 1303; *R v Oommen* [1994] 2 SCR 507.
42 Crocker et al., 2015b.
43 *R v Stone* [1999] 2 SCR 290.
44 *R v Bouchard-Lebrun* 2011 SCC 58.
45 Lawrence, 2016.
46 Douglas et al., 2013.
47 *Criminal Code,* s 753.1
48 *Criminal Code,* s 672.54.
49 *R v Boutilier* 2017 SCC 64.
50 Hanson and Morton-Bourgon, 2004.
51 Thibaut et al., 2010; Bonta et al., 2010.
52 *Winko v British Columbia Forensic Psychiatric Institute* [1999] 2 SCR 625.
53 Vogel et al., 2009.
54 Lovett and Westmacott, 2011.
55 Glancy et al., 2015; CAPL, 2018.
56 Grisso, 2013
57 *R v Mohan* [1994] 2 SCR 9.
58 *White Burgess Langille Inman v Abbott and Haliburton Co* 2015 SCC 23.
59 Goudge, 2008.
60 Lawrence and Verdun-Jones, 2015 at 7–9.
61 Lawrence and Verdun-Jones, 2015 at 9.
62 *R v Biniaris* 2000 SCC 15.
63 Research by Crocker et al appears to bear this out. However, there are also cases in which the appellate courts have overturned the findings of Review Boards, including findings on risk. See, for example *Re Wall* 2017 ONCA 713 and *Re Pellett* 2017 ONCA 753.
64 *Ewert v Canada,* 2018 SCC 30.
65 Hart, 2016.
66 Babischin et al., 2012.
67 Shepherd et al., 2014.
68 See, for example *Criminal Code,* ss 672.12, 672.121.
69 Goudge, Chapters 15 & 16.
70 Crocker et al., 2015a.
71 Crocker et al., 2015b.
72 Crocker et al., 2015c.
73 Crocker et al., 2015d.

References

American Psychiatric Association (2022). *DSM-5-TR: Diagnostic and Statistical Manual of Mental Disorders* (5th, ed., Text Revision). Washington, DC: American Psychiatric Association.

Andrews, D.A., Bonta, J., and Hoge, R.D. (1990). Classification for effective rehabilitation. *Criminal Justice and Behaviour*, 17(1), pp. 19–52.

Babischin, K.M., Blais, J., and Helmus, L. (2012). Do static risk factors predict differently for Aboriginal sex offenders? A multi-site comparison using the original and revised Static 99 and Static 2002 Scales. *Canadian Journal of Criminology and Criminal Justice*, 54, pp. 1–43.

Bloom, H., and Schneider, R.D. (2013). *Law and Mental Disorder. A Comprehensive and Practical Approach.* Toronto, ON: Irwin Law.

Bonta, J., Bourgon, G., Rugge, T., Scott T., Yessine, A.K., Gutierrez, L., and Li, J. (2010). *The Strategic Training Initiative in Community Supervision: Risk-need-responsivity in the Real World 2010-11. Corrections Research Users Report.* Ottawa, ON: Public Safety and Emergency Preparedness Canada.

Borum, R., Bartel, P., and Forth, A. (2006). *Manual for the Structured Assessment of Violence Risk in Youth* (SAVRY). Odessa, FL: Psychological Assessment Resources.

Bourget, D., and Chaimowitz, G.A. (2010). Forensic psychiatry in Canada: A journey on the road to specialty. *JAAPL*, 38(2), pp. 158–162.

Canadian Medical Association (CMA) (2018). *CMA Code of Ethics and Professionalism.* Ottawa, ON: CMA. Available through: https://policybase.cma.ca/documents/policypdf/PD19-03.pdf [Accessed April 10, 2020].

Canadian Academic of Psychiatry and the Law (2019). *Ethical Guidelines for Canadian Forensic Psychiatrists.* Available through: http://www.capl-acpd.org/wp-content/uploads/2019/06/CAPL-Ethics-FIN-Rev2019-EN.pdf [Accessed April 10, 2020].

Candilis, P.J., Weinstock, R., and Martinez, R. (2007). *Forensic Ethics and the Expert Witness.* New York: Springer.

Charette, Y., Crocker, A.G., Seto, M.C., Salem L., Nicholls, T.L., and Caulet, M. (2015). The national trajectory project of individuals found not criminally responsible on account of mental disorder in Canada. Part 4: Criminal recidivism. *Canadian Journal of Psychiatry*, 60(3), pp. 127–134.

Crocker, A.G., Nicholls, T.L., Charette, Y., and Seto, M.C. (2014). Dynamic and static factors associated with discharge dispositions: The national trajectory project of individuals found not criminally responsible on account of mental disorder in Canada. *Behavioural Science and the Law*, 32(5), pp. 577–595.

Crocker, A.G., Nicholls, T.L., Seto, M.C., and Cote, G. (2015a). The national trajectory project of individuals found not criminally responsible on account of mental disorder. *Canadian Journal of Psychiatry*, 60(3), pp. 96–97.

Crocker, A.G., Nicholls, T.L., Seto, M.C., Cote, G., Charette, Y., and Caulet, M. (2015b). The national trajectory project of individuals found not criminally responsible on account of mental disorder in Canada. Part 1: Context and methods. *Canadian Journal of Psychiatry*, 60(3), pp. 98–105.

Crocker, A.G., Nicholls, T.L., Seto, M.C., Charette, Y., Cote, G., and Caulet, M. (2015c). The national trajectory project of individuals found not criminally responsible on account of mental disorder in Canada. Part 2: The people behind the label. *Canadian Journal of Psychiatry*, 60(3), pp. 106–116.

Crocker, A.G., Charette, Y., Seto, M.C., Nicholls, T.L., Cote, G., and Caulet, M. (2015d). Dynamic and static factors associated with discharge dispositions: The national trajectory project of individuals found not criminally responsible on account of mental disorder in Canada. Part 3: Trajectories and outcomes through the forensic system. *Canadian Journal of Psychiatry*, 60(3), pp. 117–126.

Dolan M. and Doyle M. (2018). Violence risk prediction: Clinical and actuarial measures and the role of the psychopathy checklist, *British Journal of Psychiatry*, 177(4), pp. 303–311.

Douglas, K.S., Hart, S.D., Webster, C.D., and Belfrage, G. (2013). *HCR20-V3: Assessing risk of violence – User Guide.* Burnaby, BC: Mental Health, Law and Policy Institute, Simon Fraser University.

Forth, A.E., Kosson, D., and Hare, R.D. (2003). *The Hare PCL: Youth Version*, Toronto, ON: Multi-Health Systems.

Glancy, G.D., Ash, P., Bath, E.P., Buchanan, A., Fedoroff, P., Frierson, R.L., Harris, V.L., Hatters Friedman, S.J., Hauser, M.J., Knoll, J., Norko, M., Pinals, D., Price, M., Recupero, P., Scott, C.L., and Zonana, H.V. (2015). AAPL practice guideline for the forensic assessment. *JAAPL*, 43(2), pp. S3–S53.

Goosens, I., Nicholls, T.L., Wilson, C., Charette, Y., Seto, M.C., and Crocker, A.G. (2019). Examining the high-risk accused designation for individuals found not criminally responsible on account of mental disorder. *Canadian Psychology*, 60(2), pp. 102–114.

Goudge, S.T. (2008). *Inquiry into Pediatric Forensic Pathology in Ontario*. Toronto, ON: Ontario Ministry of the Attorney General.

Grisso, T. (2013). *Forensic Evaluation of Juveniles*. Sarasota, FL: Professional Resource Press.

Hanson, R.K., and Morton-Bourgon, K.E. (2004). *Predictors of Sexual Recidivism: An Updated Meta-analysis, Corrections Research Users Report 2004-02*. Ottawa, ON: Public Safety and Emergency Preparedness Canada. Available through: http://www.static99.org/pdfdocs/hansonandmortonbourgon2004.pdf [Accessed April 10, 2020].

Hanson, R.K., and Morton-Bourgon, K.E. (2009). The accuracy of recidivism risk assessments for sexual offenders: A meta-analysis of 118 prediction studies. *Psychological Assessment*, 21, pp. 1–21.

Hare, R.D. (1980). A research scale for the assessment of psychopathy in criminal populations. *Personality and Individual Differences*, 1(2), pp. 111–119.

Harris, A.J.R., Phenix, A., and Williams, K.M. (n.d). *Static 99 Clearinghouse*. Available through: http://www.static99.org [Accessed 10 April 2020].

Hart, S.D. (2016). Culture and violence risk assessment: The case of *Ewert v. Canada*. *Journal of Threat Assessment and Management*, 3(2), pp. 76–96.

Hart, S.D., Kropp, R.K., Laws, R.L., Klaver, J., Logan, C., and Watt, K.A. (2003). *The Risk for Sexual Violence Protocol (RSVP): Structured Professional Guidelines for Assessing Risk of Sexual Violence*. Burnaby, Canada: Mental Health, Law and Policy Institute, Simon Fraser University.

Kropp, R., and Hart, S.D. (2015). *SARA V3: User Manual for Version 3 of the Spousal Assault Risk Assessment Guide*. Vancouver, BC: Protect International Risk and Safety Services.

Kropp, R., Hart, S.D., and Lyon, D.R. (2008). *Guidelines for Stalking Assessment and Management (SAM)*. Vancouver, BC: Protect International Risk and Safety Services.

Lacroix, R., O'Shaughnessy, R., McNeil, D., and Binder, R.L. (2017). Controversies concerning the Canadian Not Criminally Responsible Reform Act. *JAAPL*, 45(1), pp. 44–51.

Lawrence, M. (2016). Drug-Induced psychosis: Overlooked obiter dicta in *Bouchard-Lebrun*. *Criminal Reports*, 32, pp. 151–154.

Lawrence, M., and Verdun-Jones, S.N. (2015). Delusions of justice: Results of qualitative research on the management in British Columbia of cases involving allegations of substance-induced psychosis. *Criminal Law Quarterly*, 62, pp. 475–502.

Lovett, D.K., and Westmacott, A.R. (2011). *Criminal Code* Court ordered psychiatric and psychological assessments and the role of the Forensic Psychiatric Services Commission. *The Advocate*, 69(5), pp. 663–673.

Manson, A. (2001). *The Law of Sentencing*. Toronto, ON: Irwin Law.

Mullally, K., Mamak, M., and Chaimovitz, G.A. (2018). The next generation of risk assessment and management: Introducing the eHARM. *International Journal of Risk and Recovery*, 1(1), pp. 21–25.

Nicholls, T.L., Brink, J., Desmarais, S., Webster, C.D., and Martin, M. (2009). *The Short Term Assessment of Risk and Treatability (START)*. Vancouver, BC: British Columbia Mental Health and Substance Use Services.

Olver, M.E., Neumann C.S., Sewall L.A., Lewis K., Hare R.D., and Wong S.C.P. (2018). A comprehensive evaluation of the Hare Psychopathy Checklist – Revised in a Canadian multisite sample of indigenous and nonindigenous offenders. *Psychological assessment*, 30(6), pp. 779–792

Otto, R.K., and Douglas, K.S. (Eds.) (2010). *International Perspectives on Forensic Mental Health: Handbook of Violence Risk Assessment*. New York: Routledge/Taylor & Francis Group.

Quinsey, V.L., Harris, G.T., Rice M.E., and Cormier, C.A. (2006). *Violent Offenders. Appraising and Managing Risk*, (2nd ed.). Washington DC: American Psychological Association.

Rix, K. (2011). *Expert Psychiatric Evidence*. London, UK: Royal College of Psychiatrists.

Royal College of Physicians and Surgeons of Canada (RCPSC) (2020). *Information by Discipline*. Available through: http://www.royalcollege.ca/rcsite/ibd-search-e?N=10000033+10000034+4294967070 [Accessed April 10, 2020].

Ruby, C., Chan, G., Hasan, N.R., and Enenajor, A. (2017). *Sentencing* (9th ed.). Markham, ON: LexisNexis Canada.

Salem, L., Crocker, A.G., Charette, Y., Earls, C.M., Nicholls, T.L., and Seto, M.C. (2016). Housing trajectories of forensic psychiatric patients. *Behavioural Sciences and the Law*, 34(3), pp. 352–365.

Schneider, R.D., and Bloom, H. (1995–96). *R. v. Taylor.* A decision not in the best interest of some mentally ill accused. *Criminal Law Quarterly*, 38, pp. 186–205.

Shepherd, S.M., McEntyre, E., Adams, Y., and Walker, R. (2014). Violence risk assessment in Australian Aboriginal offender populations: A review of the literature. *Psychology, Public Policy and Law*, 20(3), pp. 281–293.

Shone, M.A., Liddle, P.F., and Gray, J.E. (2008). *Canadian Mental Health Law and Policy* (2nd ed.). Markham, ON: Lexis Nexis Canada.

Thibaut, F., De La Barra, F., Gordon, H., Cosyns, P., and Bradford, J.M. (2010). The World Federation of Societies of Biological Psychiatry (WFSBP) Guidelines for the biological treatment of paraphilias. *World Journal of Biological Psychiatry*, 11(4), pp. 604–655.

Verdun-Jones, S.N., and Lawrence, M. (2013). The *Charter* right to refuse psychiatric treatment: A comparative analysis of the laws of Ontario and British Columbia concerning the right of mental-health patients to refuse psychiatric treatment. *UBC Law Review*, 46(2), pp. 489–527.

Viljoen, J., Nicholls, T.L., Cruise, K., Desmarais, S., and Webster, C.D. (2010). *START-AV*. Vancouver, BC: Protect International Risk and Safety Services.

Vogel, V., Ruiter, C., Bouman, Y., and Vries Robbe, M. (2009). *SAPROF Guidelines for the Aassessment of Protective Factors for Violence Risk, English Version*. Utrecht, The Netherlands: Forum Educatief.

Worling, J.R., and Curwen, T. (2001). Estimate of risk of adolescent sexual offence recividism (Version 2.0: The 'ERASOR'). In M.C. Calder, *Juveniles Who Sexually Abuse: Frameworks for Assessment*. Lyme Regis, Dorset, UK: Russell House Publishing.

Chapter 6

An Australian perspective

Jamie Walvisch and Andrew Carroll

6.1 Introduction

6.1.1 The legal system

In Australia, people with mental health problems 'comprise a disproportionate number of people who are arrested, who come before the courts and who are imprisoned'.[1] As Australia has a federal criminal law system, with nine different jurisdictions,[2] the precise effect that an individual's mental health problems will have on their journey through the criminal justice process will depend (to some extent) on their location. In broad strokes, however, it may:

- affect the ways in which the police are allowed to pursue their investigation[3];
- affect police or prosecutorial charging decisions[4];
- influence a judge's decision about whether to grant them bail[5];
- provide a reason for diverting them away from the traditional trial processes[6];
- result in them being found unfit to stand trial[7];
- lead to any confessions or admissions they make being held inadmissible in court[8];
- prevent them from giving evidence at their trial, or require a jury warning to be given about the potential unreliability of their evidence[9];
- negate the prosecution's case that they acted voluntarily or with the requisite mental state[10];
- provide the basis for a mental state defense such as insanity[11] or diminished responsibility[12];
- affect the way a judge sentences them if they are convicted of an offence[13];
- influence the decision about whether to release them from prison on parole[14]; or
- provide a reason for continuing to supervise or detain them upon the expiry of their sentence.[15]

Forensic mental health assessments are required by statute for some of these determinations: unfitness to stand trial, the defense of insanity (referred to by various names in Australian law, such as the defense of mental impairment)[16], and detention in custody (or imposition of other conditions) after the expiry of a sentence for high-risk offenders.[17] Even where such assessments are not required by law, they will frequently be conducted and will influence the relevant decisions. It is thus critical that adequate safeguards are in place when the courts rely on such evidence.

Limited public information is available about the way in which forensic mental health assessments are used in the parole and post-sentence contexts. By contrast, there is a vast jurisprudence concerning the use of these assessments at the sentencing stage. Consequently, the focus of this chapter is on the sentencing of convicted offenders.

DOI: 10.4324/9781351266482-6

The sentencing process occurs after an offender pleads guilty to an offence or is convicted at trial.[18] The jury plays no role in determining an offender's sentence: it is a single sentencing judge or magistrate who determines an appropriate sanction, after consideration of all relevant matters.[19] A sentencing hearing is held to allow the judge to gather the necessary information. While the precise nature of the information that is considered relevant will differ from case to case, it will usually relate to the circumstances of the offence and the offender, and the impact the offence has had on the victim. This information may be provided orally or in written form by the prosecution, the defense, or the victim. While judges do not have an inquisitorial role, they can seek further details, especially if some essential fact is missing.[20]

While Australia's federal criminal law system precludes discussion of an 'Australian' approach to the way mental health problems are taken into account in the sentencing process, in recent years there has been a convergence of the law in this area, with all jurisdictions adopting the approach taken by the Victorian Court of Appeal in the landmark case of *R v Verdins* (see section 6.2).[21] Victorian courts have also taken a leading role in attempting to enhance the quality and reliability of forensic mental health evidence that is relied on in sentencing hearings, issuing Australia's first court Practice Note that specifically address this issue (see section 6.3).[22] For these reasons, in this chapter we focus on Victorian law and practice.

6.1.2 The tradition of forensic assessment

The past 30 years have seen the progressive redevelopment and reconfiguration of forensic mental health services in Victoria. Historically, treatment for people with mental health problems who were incarcerated after encountering the criminal justice system was provided by small, low prestige services without affiliation to broader academic or clinical structures.[23] The courts were reliant on evidence provided by a very small number of forensic mental health experts, who generally worked within those services.[24] Nowadays, however, nearly all treatment for such people is carried out by the Victorian Institute of Forensic Mental Health (VIFMH or *Forensicare*): a large and expanding service that includes a 124-bed secure hospital (Thomas Embling Hospital),[25] various prisons and court-based services and a community-based arm. VIFMH is integrated within the broader Victorian public mental health system and has various academic linkages, most notably to the 'Centre for Forensic Behavioural Science' (CFBS) at Swinburne University of Technology.

This revolution in the provision of forensic mental health treatment services has facilitated parallel developments in the delivery of forensic mental health evidence to the criminal courts. Under the leadership of world-class clinical academics Paul Mullen and James Ogloff, specialised training structures were established[26]; more importantly, a practice culture developed, that greatly increased the availability of properly trained psychiatrists and psychologists to provide the courts with high-quality forensic assessments. Academic training for forensic experts is now based at CFBS, which also supports a range of research activities on topics relevant to forensic court assessment work. Many experts providing assessment reports for the courts in Victoria have past or current clinical experience with VIFMH. A significant number also have honorary or substantive academic positions at CFBS.[27]

An important transdisciplinary development has been the establishment and growth of the Australian and New Zealand Association for Psychiatry, Psychology and Law (ANZAPPL). This is an Australasian entity with local branches, of which the Victorian branch has been particularly active. ANZAPPL organises professional development events, including evening seminars and conferences, at local, binational (Australia and New Zealand), and international levels. The philosophy of ANZAPPL is inclusive, encouraging a membership that includes psychiatrists, psychologists, lawyers, and people from other disciplines working in the forensic field. ANZAPPL events are often organised in conjunction with the Royal Australian and New Zealand College of Psychiatrists (RANZCP) and the Australian Psychological Society (APS). Other transdisciplinary developments have included the regular involvement of forensic mental health experts in training programmes targeted at judges and magistrates.

6.2 Overview of the role of assessment in sentencing offenders

6.2.1 Sentences and execution

Sentencing in Victoria is largely governed by the *Sentencing Act 1991* (Vic) (the '*Sentencing Act*'). This Act sets out the different sanctions a judge may impose on an offender, as well as the principles that should guide the sentencing determination. Common sanctions for adults include imprisonment, Drug and Alcohol Treatment Orders,[28] Community Correction Orders (CCOs)[29] and fines. It is possible to combine a short term of imprisonment (less than one year) with a CCO.[30] Custodial sanctions will be served in prison, although prisoners may be temporarily transferred to a mental health facility (usually Thomas Embling Hospital) under mental health legislation as a 'security patient' if they have a mental illness and require immediate treatment to prevent a serious deterioration in their health, or serious harm to themselves or another.[31] There are also specific sanctions for minors,[32] including detention in a youth justice centre or youth residential centre, and Youth Supervision Orders.[33] As the sentencing practice and principles surrounding young and adult offenders differ significantly, this chapter solely focuses on adult offenders.

On the surface, there appears to be one sentencing sanction which is particularly relevant to convicted offenders with mental health problems: the Court Secure Treatment Order (CSTO).[34] This is a 'hybrid order', which involves the imposition of a determinate custodial sentence, but orders that the offender be detained and treated in a designated mental health facility rather than prison. If their mental health recovers during the period of the order, the offender must then be transferred to prison for the remainder of the term.[35] To impose a CSTO, the judge needs to be satisfied that the offender has a mental illness at the time of sentencing and that they need treatment to prevent their mental or physical health from seriously deteriorating, or to prevent serious harm being caused to the offender or another person.

Whilst such circumstances are not uncommon, the imposition of a CSTO also requires that a mental health facility be available and willing to provide the offender's treatment subject to a CSTO. The imperative for appropriate security means that the facility in question would generally be Thomas Embling Hospital; at its current state of development, however, Thomas Embling Hospital usually has insufficient resources to enable care to offenders under a CSTO. In practice, therefore, the CSTO has very rarely been utilised in Victoria. Sentenced or remanded offenders with acute mental health needs do, however, receive intensive mental health care either on a voluntary basis within dedicated mental health units inside the prisons or on an involuntary basis by way of transfer to Thomas Embling Hospital as a 'security patient'.

Therefore, at the point of sentencing, judges generally rely on the ordinary sentencing options contained in the *Sentencing Act,* imposing appropriately moderated CCOs and/or terms of imprisonment on offenders with mental health problems. CCOs may (and often do) contain a condition that the offender undergoes mental health assessment and treatment, including psychological or psychiatric treatment.[36] The judge's selection of sanction and sentencing conditions will be influenced by any forensic mental health evidence that is provided in the sentencing hearing (see below).

6.2.2 Decisions within sentencing and execution

Most criminal offences in Victoria are statutory, with the relevant statute specifying the maximum penalty an individual may be given if he or she is convicted of the offence. This usually sets the upper bounds of the sentence that may be imposed by a sentencing judge, although in some circumstances a judge may be permitted to hand down an indefinite sentence (see section 6.2.2.3). Imposition of the maximum penalty is rare, being reserved for the worst examples of the offence that are likely to be encountered in practice.[37] In other cases, a judge will generally have some discretion about the type and length of sentence that may be given, and the conditions that may be imposed.[38] In addition to specifying the maximum period for which the sentence may be imposed, judges must usually fix a 'non-parole period', during which the offender is not eligible to be released on parole.[39]

The *Sentencing Act* sets out the principles that should guide the sentencing determination. Of central importance is section 5(1), which states that sentences may *only* be imposed for the purposes of just punishment, deterrence, rehabilitation, denunciation or community protection. Ordinarily, there is no *primary* sentencing rationale: instead, it is for the judge to decide which of the listed purposes should predominate in the particular case.[40] The decision about which purpose, or synthesis of purposes, is the most appropriate is seen to be a 'matter of judicial sentencing discretion based upon experience and intuition'.[41] However, in some circumstances a judge is directed to treat one of the sentencing objectives as the principal objective. For example adult offenders who are convicted of certain specified arson, drug, violent or sexual offences, and who have been sentenced to a term of imprisonment, will be classified as 'serious offenders'.[42] This classification is not contingent upon any expert opinion regarding the risk of re-offending. When sentencing a 'serious offender', the court must regard the protection of the community from the offender as the principal purpose.[43]

The risk that any offender is seen to pose to the community will be relevant to a judge's assessment of the weight to be given to the various sentencing objectives. Where the offender is seen to pose a high risk of re-offending, a judge is likely to give greater weight to the principles of community protection and specific deterrence.[44] By contrast, where the risk of re-offending is lower a rehabilitative sentence may be considered more appropriate. In determining the level of risk, a judge will be guided by factors such as the nature of the offence committed, the offender's prior criminal history, their attitude towards their offending behaviour and any relevant mental health problems (discussed later). No specific form of risk assessment is mandated for the purposes of sentencing. The courts, however, are particularly assisted by mental health expert evidence that delineates specific evidence-based risk factors and protective factors and utilises structured professional judgement approaches.

The *Sentencing Act* also lists a number of factors to which a judge must have regard when sentencing an offender, such as the nature and gravity of the offence, the offender's culpability and the presence of any aggravating or mitigating factors.[45] The Act reinforces the common law principle of parsimony by prohibiting a judge from imposing a sentence that is more severe than necessary to achieve the purposes for which the sentence is imposed.[46]

Australian Courts have struggled with the ways in which offenders' mental health problems should be taken into account under this framework. Originally, they focused on the conflict between the fact that an offender's culpability may be reduced due to their mental health problems (suggesting a need for the penalty to be reduced), and the possibility that the offender may pose a greater danger to the community due to those problems (suggesting a need for the penalty to be increased). For example in *Channon v R*, Brennan J stated that

> *Psychiatric abnormality falling short of insanity is frequently found to be a cause of, or a factor contributing to, criminal conduct. The sentencing of an offender in cases of that kind is inevitably difficult. The difficulty arises in part because the factors which affect the sentence give differing significance to an offender's psychiatric abnormality. An abnormality may reduce the moral culpability of the offender and the deliberation which attended his criminal conduct; yet it may mark him as a more intractable subject for reform than one who is not so affected, or even as one who is so likely to offend again that he should be removed from society for a lengthy or indeterminate period. The abnormality may seem, on one view, to lead towards a lenient sentence, and on another to a sentence which is severe.[47]*

In these early cases, the courts made it clear that judges could not impose disproportionately long sentences on offenders for the purposes of community protection or rehabilitation.[48] However, they provided little guidance about how judges *should* determine a proportionate sentence given this tension. It was left up to judges to strike an appropriate balance between these conflicting principles.

Over the following years, several disparate decisions focused on other ways in which offenders' mental health problems may affect their sentences, including the effect it may have on the principles of general and specific deterrence, and the impact it may have on their experience of imprisonment.[49] In 2007, these principles were brought together by the Victorian Court of Appeal in the leading case of *R v Verdins* ('*Verdins*').[50]

6.2.2.1 The Verdins principles

In *Verdins*, the Victorian Court of Appeal identified six ways in which an offender's mental health problems may be relevant to the sentencing process. Such problems may

1 reduce the offender's moral culpability, thereby affecting the punishment that is just in the circumstances and the importance of denunciation as a sentencing consideration;
2 influence the kind of sentence that should be imposed, or the conditions under which it should be served;
3 moderate or eliminate the need for general deterrence as a sentencing consideration;
4 moderate or eliminate the need for specific deterrence as a sentencing consideration;
5 make a sentence weigh more heavily on the offender than on a person in normal health, thereby affecting the determination of a proportionate sentence; or
6 create a serious risk of imprisonment having a significant adverse effect on the offender's mental health, suggesting the need to reduce the sanction.[51]

These '*Verdins* principles' have been held to apply to any proceeding in which the ruling body has disciplinary powers,[52] and where

> *the offender is shown to have been suffering at the time of the offence (and/or to be suffering at the time of sentencing) from a mental disorder or abnormality or an impairment of mental function, whether or not the condition in question would properly be described as a (serious) mental illness.[53]*

The courts have emphasised that the *Verdins* principles should be regarded as exceptional and should not be invoked in 'routine cases'.[54] They have held that the principles should only be applied 'after careful scrutiny and assessment, based on cogent evidence, of the relationship between the mental disorder and the offence and other matters'.[55]

6.2.2.2 Conditions covered by the Verdins principles

Prior to *Verdins*, it had been suggested that the principles concerning the sentencing of offenders with mental health problems only applied to offenders who had a 'serious psychiatric illness' at the time of the offence, or who were likely to experience such an illness during the course of their sentence.[56] However, in *Verdins* the Court of Appeal made it clear that there is no need for an offender to have a diagnosable mental illness, or for that condition to be of a particular level of gravity, for the principles to apply.[57] The offender's mental health problems also do not need to be permanent.[58] What matters is 'what the evidence shows about the nature, extent and effect of the mental impairment experienced by the offender at the relevant time'.[59] In particular, sentencing courts need to consider 'how the particular condition (is likely to have) affected the mental functioning of the particular offender in the particular circumstances – that is, at the time of the offence or in the lead-up to it—or is likely to affect him/her in the future'.[60]

In describing the conditions covered by the *Verdins* principles, the court used the phrase 'mental disorder or abnormality or impairment of mental functioning'.[61] It intended that this phrase be interpreted broadly, to cover a wide range of conditions. In subsequent cases, the courts have accepted that the *Verdins* principles may apply in cases where the offender experiences the following conditions: acquired brain injury,[62] adjustment disorder,[63]; anxiety disorders,[64] attention deficit hyperactivity disorder (ADHD),[65] autism spectrum disorders (including Asperger's syndrome),[66] bereavement disorder,[67] bipolar disorder,[68] conversion disorder,[69] dementia,[70] depression,[71] dysthymia,[72] eating disorders (including anorexia and bulimia),[73] hypoglycemia,[74] intellectual disability,[75] obsessive-compulsive disorder,[76] postnatal depression,[77] post-traumatic stress disorder (PTSD),[78] schizophrenia,[79] and schizoid personality disorder.[80]

In some cases, the court has been willing to apply the *Verdins* principles even without a specific diagnosis. For example in *R v Hill* the judge noted that although there was 'difficulty in establishing a firm diagnosis' in relation to the offender's mental health, it was clear that the condition 'has had an impact' on his behaviour. The offender therefore should 'not be sentenced as someone who functions well in the world'.[81]

For a time, personality disorders were excluded from the scope of the principles, on the basis that they do not constitute 'impairments of mental functioning'.[82] This decision was strongly criticised for being inconsistent with contemporary scientific understandings of such disorders[83] and was subsequently overturned. It is now accepted that personality disorders may in fact lead to severe functional impairment and should therefore be treated no differently from other mental health problems.[84]

The courts have, however, placed some limits on the scope of the *Verdins* principles. For example they have been held not to cover impairments that arise from the ordinary pressures of daily life (such as work, financial, and marital pressures),[85] emotional immaturity or volatility,[86] paedophilia, or sexual sadism.[87] They also do not cover substance-related disorders, which are addressed by separate legal principles.[88]

6.2.2.3 Factors not addressed in Verdins

It has become apparent from the cases following *Verdins* that the six principles identified by the Court of Appeal do not cover the field: there are other ways in which mental health problems can affect sentencing. Such problems can affect the offender's prospects for rehabilitation[89] and the need for community protection.[90] They may also provide grounds for the judicial exercise of mercy.[91]

In addition, the existence of mental health problems may be relevant to a judge's determination of whether to impose an indefinite term of imprisonment on an offender. A judge may impose such a sentence if they are satisfied, to a high degree of probability, that the offender poses a serious danger to the community because of their character, past history, age, *health or mental condition*; the nature and gravity of the offence; and any other special circumstances.[92] In determining whether this requirement is met, the court must focus on the danger the offender poses to the community at the time of sentencing (not at the time of his or her anticipated release).[93]

In practice, sentences of indefinite imprisonment are rarely imposed, even where an offender has severe mental health problems. This is because, to impose such a sentence, the judge must be 'clearly satisfied by cogent evidence that the convicted person is a constant danger to the community'.[94] There are no legislative requirements concerning the form that this evidence must take or the grounds on which it must be based. In practice, however, it would be provided by a forensic mental health expert, such as a forensic psychiatrist, psychologist or neuropsychologist, using whatever tools they consider most appropriate in the circumstances. The courts have emphasised that the cases in which this evidentiary threshold will be met are exceptional and that this sentencing option should be used sparingly.[95] There have only been three reported instances when a term of indefinite imprisonment has been imposed in Victoria.

6.2.2.4 Rehabilitative interventions

In a recent ruling, the Victorian Court of Appeal noted

> It is a catchcry of modern governments that 'the safety of the community is our first priority'. Accepting that to be so, the protection of the community—to which the Director quite properly directed our attention—requires that offenders ... be given access to the support services and specialised treatment on which their rehabilitation depends ... He must, of course, remain ready to engage with treatment but the responsibility rests on the State, which controls his incarceration, to ensure that it is made available.[96]

An important aspect of the Australian criminal justice system is that, for incarcerated offenders, 'support services and specialised treatment' (offence-based rehabilitation) are delivered under the auspices of correctional services. Although the court sets an earliest release date for the purposes of parole, decisions regarding which rehabilitative interventions are made available to a prisoner, and the actual date of release after the minimum term has been served, are made independently of the sentencing court by the Adult Parole Board.[97] The Board is at liberty to source expert forensic mental health assessments (generally provided by experts at VIFMH) to assist with this process. It will also take note of expert forensic mental health expert evidence that was endorsed by the sentencing judge in his or her published reasons for sentence. Evidence-based offender rehabilitation is delivered by a specific service within 'Corrections Victoria', and outcomes from such interventions for each offender are fed back to the Adult Parole Board to assist with its deliberations. Community leave for rehabilitative purposes is strictly limited and eligibility is determined entirely by Corrections Victoria.

Treatment of mental disorders for prisoners is delivered at arm's length from Corrections Victoria, by a small number of independent healthcare providers (including but not limited to VIFMH). There is generally rather minimal mutual information exchange between these healthcare providers and the Adult Parole Board, which at times can lead to poorly co-ordinated release planning for offenders with mental disorders.

6.2.3 Concepts to be assessed

When sentencing an offender with mental health problems, the key decisions to be made by a sentencer relate to (i) the type of sanction to be imposed (e.g. imprisonment or a community correction order); (ii) the length of the sentence; and (iii) the nature of any conditions to be imposed on the offender. In determining an appropriate sanction, the judge must take into account the *Verdins* principles (where relevant), as well as general sentencing principles relating to matters such as rehabilitation, community protection, and mercy.

None of the *Verdins* sentencing considerations can apply in the absence of specific expert evidence about the nature, extent, and effects of the offender's mental health problems.[98] This evidence will help the judge to

- determine whether the *Verdins* principles apply, by addressing the nature and severity of the offender's mental health condition;
- assess the offender's culpability for the offence, by addressing the ways in which the offender's mental health condition contributed to their offending behaviour;
- decide whether the offender's sanction should be reduced, by addressing the ways in which the offender's mental health condition is likely to affect their experience of punishment or the likelihood of their mental health deteriorating during their term of imprisonment;
- determine the offender's prospects for rehabilitation (including treatability of any underlying mental disorders) or future risk of re-offending,[99] and hence the need for the community to be protected from the offender, by addressing the offender's treatment prospects and prognosis;
- formulate the conditions to be imposed on the offender, by addressing available services and treatment options.

It is important to note that while mental health evidence may *assist* the judge to determine these matters, all sentencing decisions are for the judge to make. Sentencing judges may choose to accept or reject any evidence given by mental health experts, even if it is un-challenged. Such evidence must be thoroughly scrutinised, having regard to matters such as the witness's expertise and the information upon which it was based.[100]

6.2.4 Forensic assessment and procedure

If a party wishes the judge to take any matter (including the offender's mental health) into account in the sentencing process, it is up to that party to bring the matter to the attention of the judge.[101] This will usually be done by tendering a report written by a relevant mental health expert and calling the expert to give oral evidence. In practice, it is almost invariably the defense that chooses to commission such evidence. It is surprisingly rare for the Office of Public Prosecutions (OPP) in Victoria to call its own expert evidence for purposes of sentencing hearings, even in high-profile cases of considerable gravity.[102] Witnesses may be cross-examined by the other party. The burden of proof depends on the matter that is raised. If it is an aggravating factor (that will increase the penalty), it must be established by the prosecution beyond reasonable doubt. If it is a mitigating factor (that will reduce the penalty), it must be established by the defense on the balance of probabilities.[103]

Judges may also order the Secretary to the Department of Justice to prepare a 'pre-sentence report' to help them to determine an appropriate sentence.[104] The report may set out a wide range of matters, including the offender's medical history, psychiatric history, and history of drug and alcohol use.[105] The report may address the offender's suitability for the particular type of sentence being considered, the existence of any necessary facilities for carrying out that sentence, or the types of conditions it may be appropriate to attach to a CCO. In Victoria, such reports are usually written by a psychiatrist or psychologist at VIFMH. The appropriateness or otherwise of CCOs and of Drug and Alcohol Treatment Orders are established by way of assessors working for 'Community Corrections' or the 'Drug Court', respectively.

The task of determining an appropriate sentence has often been conceptualised as a balancing process, with judges performing an 'instinctive synthesis of all the various aspects involved in the punitive process':[106]

> Sentencing is not a mechanical process. It requires the exercise of a discretion. There is no single 'right' answer which can be determined by the application of principle. Different minds will attribute different weight to various facts in arriving at the 'instinctive synthesis' which takes account of the various purposes for which sentences are imposed—just punishment, deterrence, rehabilitation, denunciation, protection of the community—and which pays due regard to principles of totality, parity, parsimony and the like.[107]

However, some limits are placed on the sentencing judge's discretion. For example in determining an appropriate sanction judges must take into account any guideline judgements that have been issued by the Court of Appeal,[108] as well as current sentencing practices.[109] When imposing a sentence, judges must state their reasons for deciding on the sentence given.[110]

6.3 Safeguards for the quality of forensic assessment

6.3.1 Requirements in law and policy

Sentencing hearings are not subject to the same rules of evidence that govern a trial: judges may consider any evidence they consider to be of assistance to the sentencing task. However, since 2017, Victorian Courts have had a specific 'Practice Note' (Supreme Court of Victoria Practice Note SC CR 7: *Sentencing Hearings: Expert Reports on Mental Functioning of Offenders*) that governs the use of expert mental health evidence in sentencing hearings.[111] Lawyers must comply with the terms of the Practice Note unless directed otherwise, and expert witnesses are expected to be familiar with its content.

The stated purposes of the Practice Note is

> to enhance the quality and reliability of expert evidence relied on in sentencing hearings in connection with questions of the mental functioning of persons who are to be sentenced; and

> to improve the utility of such evidence by ensuring that opinions expressed are within the scope of the expert's specialised knowledge, and are supported by clearly-identified facts and reasoning.[112]

The Practice Note seeks to achieve these objectives by defining the appropriate boundaries of expert opinion, specifying the type of matters that should be included in the substance of an expert report, and highlighting the importance of expert witnesses being impartial participants in the process.

6.3.1.1 Boundaries and substance of the report

A high-quality forensic mental health expert opinion needs to be

- *helpful*: it must say something in the form of a concluded opinion that will assist the court and which the court otherwise would not have been able to conclude based on mere 'common sense';
- *appropriately constrained*: it must be confined to matters within the expert's areas of medical expertise, and must not opine on legal matters;
- *clear and comprehensible*: it must make sense to laypeople without specific mental health training; and
- *logical*: the opinions expressed must be based on clearly articulated facts, and must demonstrate a clear path of reasoning, linking those facts to the concluded opinions. It is important to note however that it is possible for there to be a diversity of logical opinions based on the same set of facts. In such a value-laden and complex field, it is not uncommon for experts to legitimately advance differing but equally high-quality opinions from the same set of agreed facts.

All of these requirements are addressed by the Practice Note, which starts by pointing out that '[t]he scope and purpose of an expert report is defined by the needs of the sentencing judge. Axiomatically, the function of an expert witness is to assist the Court…'.[113] The Note goes on to outline the appropriate division of labour between the judge, commissioning party, and expert witness.

- It is the responsibility of the party commissioning the report to ensure that the report's purpose is clearly defined and that the opinions sought and expressed are relevant to that purpose.[114]
- It is the expert's responsibility to assist the judge to understand the offender's mental functioning at relevant times before, during and/or after the offence.[115]
- It is the judge's responsibility to make decisions about sentencing.

The Practice Note further clarifies the distinct roles of judges and experts by noting that it is the role of the sentencing judge to decide, for example whether the *Verdins* principles apply, and that it is 'beyond the scope of an expert report to express an opinion on whether any of those considerations is applicable to the exercise of the sentencing discretion'.[116] This reflects the case law in the area, which has repeatedly emphasised that mental health experts should not comment on matters such as moral culpability or the relative burden of imprisonment, as these are legal issues.[117] They should confine their evidence to the nature, extent, and effects of the offender's mental health condition.

The Note also delineates the specific matters that the courts expect to comprise the substance of a mental health expert report. Of particular importance is the following provision, which sets out the key issues to be addressed

> *The expert report should state the expert's opinion as to the following matters, so far as applicable*

- *the nature, extent and effect of the condition experienced by the subject at the time of the offence and/or at the time of sentence;*
- *how the condition affected or is likely to have affected, the mental functioning of the subject at the time of the offence or in the lead up to it;*

An Australian perspective 131

- *how the condition is likely to affect the subject in the future and whether this has implications for the type of sentence that the judge should consider;*
- *whether the condition would be likely:*

  i   *to affect adversely the ability of the subject to cope with imprisonment; and/or*
  ii *to deteriorate as a result of the subject being imprisoned.*[118]

In addressing these issues, the expert must not simply rely on diagnostic labels or simply record their opinion or conclusions.[119] They must articulate the facts on which their opinion is based and the reasons for the opinion.[120] In this regard, it is notable that the courts in Victoria are increasingly concerning themselves with the minutiae of psychiatric phenomenology, including the specific contents of delusional beliefs and the subjective moral evaluations that flow from such beliefs.[121] The implication of this is that the substance of an opinion ought to go well beyond merely commenting on the presence or absence of psychotic symptoms, for example. Similarly, the courts have become increasingly critical of reports that merely transcribe a psychosocial history in the expectation that this may garner some degree of mitigation[122]: judges expect the expert to analyse and interpret such data to yield a cogent opinion of substance.

To assist expert witnesses with this process, the Practice Note explicitly outlines certain matters that must be addressed, depending on the specific case. For example if the expert is of the view that the offender's mental health condition contributed to the offending behaviour, they 'must state, as precisely as possible, how the particular condition was (or is likely to have been) operative at the time and how it was (or is likely to have been) connected with the offence'.[123] Similarly, where the opinion concerns the likely impact of the offender's condition on the experience of punishment, or the likely impact of imprisonment on their condition, 'the report must state as precisely as possible the basis for each such opinion'.[124]

The Practice Note also addresses the matter of 'remorse'. This is a contentious issue, with some clinicians arguing that the experts' role in this area should be strongly constrained: that they should be limited to opining on the potential impact of diagnosable mental health conditions (such as the negative symptoms of schizophrenia) on the emotional concomitants of remorse. However, other clinicians argue that mental health experts have specific expertise in detecting the 'genuineness' of remorse, and so should be allowed to give evidence on this issue. Ultimately, the Practice Note allows for expert opinion to be expressed but urges caution:

> *Any opinion expressed with respect to the subject's remorse, or lack of remorse, must state as comprehensively as possible the basis of the opinion. If the expert concludes that a lack of remorse is the result of the condition, this should be pointed out.*[125]

The vexed issue of risk assessment is also addressed in the Practice Note. If an opinion on matters of future risk is sought by the commissioning party, the mental health expert is encouraged to consider how a sentence might be suitably shaped by mental health expertise in order to optimise rehabilitation and thereby reduce future endangerment to the public.[126] Risk factors relevant to mental health are particularly emphasised: the expert is *not* expected to always provide an 'actuarial' categorical opinion regarding likelihood of re-offending. Evidence-based risk assessment tools are frequently used by experts, especially in cases involving sexual offending, but no specific tool is mandated by the Practice Note.

After the Practice Note was published, Victoria Legal Aid, with the assistance of the RANZCP Faculty of Forensic Psychiatry, developed a set of questions that mental health experts will generally be asked to address in sentencing cases (see Table 6.1). It is not

Table 6.1 Victoria Legal Aid's Standard Questions for Mental Health Experts in Sentencing Cases

- Any psychiatric conditions my client has or had when the offending behaviour occurred, how long he has had the condition and whether the condition is of a temporary or permanent nature.
- The nature, extent and effect of the condition experienced by my client at the time.
- What, if any, is the relationship between my client's condition and the offence.
- How is the condition likely to affect my client in the future.
- Whether the condition would be likely to affect adversely the ability of my client to cope with imprisonment.
- Whether the condition would be likely to deteriorate as a result of my client being imprisoned.
- Treatment of the condition currently or previously undertaken and its effectiveness.
- In relation to my client's prospects of rehabilitation:
  o whether there are any aspects of his/her mental functioning which may impede rehabilitation;
  o whether there are any implications of the condition(s) for the risk of future offending and if so how might these best be managed.
- My client's response to the offences and any psychiatric factors relevant to remorse.
- Any other matters you consider relevant.

mandatory for instructing lawyers to use this set of questions, but in practice, it has been found to be very helpful in both ensuring that the substance of an opinion is appropriate and that the boundaries of expertise are not transgressed.

6.3.1.2 Impartiality

It is axiomatic that judges are less likely to be persuaded by experts who they consider to be unduly influenced by their affiliation with the aims of the legal team by whom they have been briefed. The 'fake and partisan hired gun are the favourite bogymen of lawyers' stories about experts in court',[127] and a perception that an expert witness is advocating for the instructing party can readily result in their evidence being disregarded. While this bias may sometimes be overt, in other cases it may be more subtle: an 'unwitting lack of neutrality'.[128]

The Practice Note makes the importance of impartiality abundantly clear, noting that 'the function of an expert witness is to assist the court, not to advocate for the interests of a party',[129] and that an expert 'has an overriding duty to assist the court impartially, by giving an objective, unbiased opinion on matters within the expert's specialised knowledge. This duty overrides any obligation to the commissioning party or to the person by whom the expert is paid'.[130]

In addition to these statements of general principles, there are various other provisions in the Practice Note that address concerns about partiality. One such issue relates to the permissibility of instructing lawyers making amendments to an experts' report to suit their needs. In developing the Practice Note (see section 6.6), some lawyers assertively argued that minor changes to reports ought to be permitted without further comment. However, this position was ultimately rejected, with the Practice Note disallowing any degree of 'settling' of reports

> *An expert must never alter a report or an opinion at the request of the commissioning party. If factual clarification is requested, or additional information is provided, a supplementary report must be prepared which clearly identifies the nature of any change of fact or opinion.*[131]

The long-recognised risk that dogmatic experts may seek to deny the 'plural nature of scientific enquiry'[132] is also addressed, with experts being strongly encouraged to consider opposing schools of thought when appropriate:

Where an expert is aware of any significant and recognised disagreement or controversy within the relevant field of specialised knowledge, which is directly relevant to the expert's ability, technique or opinion, the expert must disclose the existence and nature of that disagreement or controversy.[133]

The Practice Note also obliges experts to fully disclose all relevant facts, with expert reports required to include 'a declaration that the expert has made all the inquiries and considered all the issues which the expert believes are desirable and appropriate, and that no matters of significance which the expert regards as relevant have, to the knowledge of the expert, been withheld'.[134] Importantly, this extends to the results of psychometric assessments, with authors prevented from 'cherry-picking' test data that favour their concluded opinion:

When an expert conducts a psychometric assessment for the purposes of preparing a report, the expert should ensure that … all measures administered are reported appropriately.[135]

A further concern addressed by the Practice Note is the possibility that forensic assessors may naïvely rely solely on self-reports by the offender. This issue was the subject of detailed discussion during the development of the Practice Note. On the one hand, appropriately robust scepticism was felt to be an important attribute of the expert assessor; on the other hand, mental health experts were keen to disavow any notion that they can function as 'truth detectors'. A compromise position was ultimately reached

When a report includes matters reported by the subject, the expert should comment on the clinical plausibility of the self-report; and any discrepancies between the self-report and other information available to the expert.[136]

The Practice Note also addresses concerns about impartiality that arise when a practitioner provides an opinion to the court on matters pertaining to a patient under their clinical care. Interestingly, there remains a diversity of opinions within the psychiatric profession regarding the legitimacy of this practice.[137] In Victoria, it is certainly not uncommon at the Magistrate's Court level for treating clinicians to be asked to provide 'forensic' opinions on people being sentenced for less serious summary matters. The Practice Note, however, makes it clear that the opinions of treating clinicians must be significantly constrained

A report prepared by the subject's treating practitioner should be confined to information relevant to treatment provided to the subject (e.g. presenting signs and symptoms, diagnosis, clinical formulation, treatment, treatment response and treatment needs).[138]

6.3.2 Disciplinary and ethical requirements

At the court level, in addition to the Practice Note discussed above, the higher Victorian courts have Expert Witness Codes of Conduct which set out the general duties (including the ethical duties) of experts who provide reports or give evidence in court.[139] These Codes note that expert witnesses have a paramount duty to assist the court impartially, and must not be an advocate for a party. They also set out some basic requirements that must be complied with in reports, such as providing the expert's qualifications, specifying the assumptions and material facts on which each opinion is based, identifying the reasoning in support of the opinion, and outlining any qualifications or concerns that the expert has about the opinion. Legal practitioners have an obligation to provide a copy of the relevant Code to an expert as soon as practicable after their engagement, and the expert must acknowledge that he or she has read and complied with the Code in the preparation of the report.[140]

In recent years, relevant professional bodies have increasingly concerned themselves with the subspecialty of 'forensic' expert evidence, providing formal training and accreditation. For psychiatrists, post-graduate training in forensic psychiatry can be carried out in parallel with, or subsequent to, the obtaining of the general qualification as a Consultant Psychiatrist (FRANZCP: Fellowship of The Royal Australian and New Zealand College of Psychiatrists). This involves demonstrating a range of relevant competencies, which are developed in a supervisory relationship with a properly accredited forensic psychiatrist within a formal training programme. This Advanced Training in forensic psychiatry ultimately results in the award of a Certificate with associated postnominals and 'Accredited Membership' of the RANZCP Faculty of Forensic Psychiatry. Psychiatrists with other appropriate forensic experience and training may also become Accredited Members of the Faculty. As well as accrediting formal training programmes, the RANZCP publishes guidelines regarding ethical and pragmatic matters pertaining to medicolegal work,[141] which are regularly reviewed and updated. The guidelines cover, amongst other things, matters of impartiality, boundaries and substance of opinions.

For psychologists, legal use of the title 'forensic psychologist' is only allowed by those who have an 'area of practice endorsement' in forensic psychology with the Psychology Board of Australia. In order to get this one must undertake accredited post-graduate training in forensic psychology involving both academic study and supervised practice. The Australian Psychological Society has published guidelines for psychological practice in forensic contexts, which clarify the application of its code of ethics to psychological practice in forensic contexts.

While no formal training and accreditation are available to neuropsychologists working in the forensic arena, there is a thriving local culture, with a number of experts in forensic neuropsychology regularly providing evidence to the courts.

It is important to note that expert witnesses are not required to have a formal 'forensic' qualification in order to be able to give evidence at trial or in a sentencing hearing. As discussed in the next section, it is generally sufficient that they be a specialist in the relevant mental health discipline. However, these specialisations can help to establish the quality of the witness and may assist a decision-maker in determining the weight to give to their evidence.

6.3.3 Requirements for the evaluator

To be allowed to give evidence during a *trial*, an expert witness must have specialised knowledge based on his or her training, study or experience.[142] The same restrictions do not exist at the *sentencing* stage, unless in a specific case the court chooses to direct that they apply.[143] Consequently, sentencing judges can technically accept mental health evidence from anyone they deem fit, including psychiatrists, psychologists, neuropsychologists, and General Practitioners.

In practice, however, courts will generally require expert witnesses to have specialised knowledge, and the Practice Note states that expert reports should be commissioned and prepared on this basis.[144] Furthermore, the increasing quantity and, arguably, complexity of work conducted by forensic mental health experts has led to a growth in the number of experts who work predominantly or even exclusively within the medicolegal arena. Whereas historically the 'phenomenon of the expert functioning principally as a forensic expert'[145] was frowned upon by both judges[146] and clinicians,[147] this approach to sub-specialisation no longer receives the level of opprobrium that it once did.[148]

This shift has been assisted by the increasing focus by relevant professional bodies on the subspecialty of forensic expert evidence (see section 6.3.2). Psychiatrists and psychologists who complete the relevant training obtain formal endorsement from their respective associations. This is recognised by the courts as being a marker of special expertise in forensic work.

Although it is certainly still possible (and not uncommon) for mental health experts who give evidence in sentencing hearings to lack specific forensic accreditation, judges are increasingly becoming aware of the importance of training and ongoing professional development in the area. This can result in greater weight being given to evidence provided by appropriately accredited experts. The Practice Note includes two Schedules to assist judges to assess the qualifications of psychiatrists and psychologists, and to determine the validity of claimed expertise.[149] The Schedules address matters such as the roles of the different professional organisations working in the area, and the meaning of the various titles, qualifications and endorsements a judge may encounter.

The RANZCP also oversees peer review programmes, in which specific cases (suitably anonymised) and matters arising from forensic work are discussed with a small group of similarly skilled and experienced colleagues. In practice, the importance of such discussions as a component of a forensic expert's ongoing professional development cannot be overemphasised.

More informal discussions between colleagues, often across the disciplines of psychiatry, psychology, neuropsychology and law, are also an important informal mechanism in enhancing the quality of forensic expertise provided to the courts in Victoria. Such interprofessional dialogue is strongly promoted by ANZAPPL. In recent times, peer to peer discussions have been further enhanced by the utilisation of the secure encrypted social media platform WhatsApp: several closed confidential groups have been established, enabling judicious discussion of matters (suitably de-identified) pertaining to forensic mental health expertise in a more informal online environment. These structures also mean that professionals new to the field of forensic work in Victoria can find ample support from more experienced colleagues who will provide appropriate mentoring and support.

6.3.4 Enforcement of requirements

If a judge is not satisfied that an expert's opinion is based, wholly or substantially, on specialised knowledge, they can refuse to admit the evidence into court.[150] The court can also refuse to accept evidence that does not comply with the requirements of the Practice Note or the Expert Witness Codes of Conduct or to give such evidence limited weight in reaching their determination. This provides substantial safeguards against poor quality reports proffered by experts who deliberately or unwittingly fail to comply with the strictures of those Notes and Codes.

In addition, when imposing a sentence, judges must state their reasons for the decision.[151] The regular publication online of judges' sentencing comments is an important source of feedback, and hence quality assurance, for mental health experts. Robust opinions provided by judges regarding the quality, or lack thereof, of evidence provided by specific experts are routinely published and are thereby available in the public domain. As well as providing guidance as to what kinds of evidence are deemed to be more or less influential in a judge's sentencing decision, sentencing comments can also flag new emerging issues for consideration by the expert witness. For example in recent times, two Victorian Court of Appeal cases have highlighted the importance of providing both detailed phenomenology of offenders' states of mind at times of offence (including the form, nature and intensity of psychotic symptoms), and of outlining the underlying motivations for offenders' usage of psychotogenic illicit substances.[152] Such judicial commentary will influence how mental health experts go about their work in future.

It should also be emphasised that the extent to which judges publicly approve of, and are influenced by, a particular expert's opinions, will be noted by lawyers who are looking to brief an expert in the future. In short, reputation matters, and judicial comments contribute to a process of natural selection wherein poorer quality expert evidence is likely to result in fewer future referrals for the expert involved. This quality assurance mechanism for expert evidence, although rarely commented upon,[153] may in practice be the most important of all. No single centralised database of mental health experts exists: solicitors are free to commission from whomsoever they see fit and referral decisions are influenced by perceived quality as well as availability.

Neither the RANZCP nor the APS has any role in overseeing the quality of expert work or in enforcing adherence to their guidelines, and expert witnesses in Australia are generally immune from being civilly sued in relation to evidence that is connected to court proceedings.[154] It is, however, open to judges, lawyers or indeed offenders or their relatives to complain directly about an expert psychiatrist or psychologist to the national registration board (the Australian Health Practitioner Regulation Agency). This Agency oversees registered health practitioners and has the ability to cancel their registration or impose conditions on them. In practice, this appears to be a rare event.

6.4 Safeguards 'against' the limited quality of forensic assessment

6.4.1 Questioning the assessment by the defense

As noted above, decisions about the ways in which an offender's mental health should be taken into account in the sentencing process occur after a sentencing hearing. This is an adversarial process, in which the prosecution and defense are both free to tender reports, call witnesses and cross-examine the other party's witnesses. Consequently, where the prosecution tenders adverse evidence about the offender's mental health at a sentencing hearing, the defense can contest that evidence either by cross-examining the prosecution witness, or by tendering their own report and calling their own witness(es) to rebut the prosecution's case. As noted, however, in practice the Victorian Office of Public Prosecutions rarely calls a mental health expert[155]; similarly, the court itself only occasionally uses its powers to seek an independent mental health report. In the vast majority of cases therefore there is a single expert, briefed by the defense.

Ordinarily, the offender must bear the costs of commissioning an expert to write a report or appear in court. However, where they lack the means to fund an expert's involvement in their case, they may call on financial support from Victoria Legal Aid. The grant of such funding is contingent on the representing lawyer demonstrating legitimate grounds for the need for mental health expertise in order to assist the courts. In practice, a significant proportion of mental health evaluations are funded in this way.

6.4.2 Questioning the assessment by the court

It is for the sentencing judge to determine the ways in which an offender's mental health problems should be taken into account in sentencing. In making this decision, judges are in no way bound to accept mental health evidence provided by expert witnesses, even if that evidence is uncontested. On the contrary, the courts have emphasised the importance of only applying the *Verdins* principles 'after careful scrutiny and assessment, based on cogent evidence, of the relationship between the mental disorder and the offence and other matters'.[156]

The need for judges to critically assess the forensic mental health evidence presented at a sentencing plea is also implicit in the Practice Note, which states that '[i]n order to evaluate what reliance to place on an expert report, the sentencing judge needs to know the purpose of the report, the relevant qualifications and expertise of the expert, the expert's opinions and the factual foundation of each opinion'.[157] This provision indicates that the weight to be given to any mental health assessment should be critically determined by the judge in all cases, paying particular regard to the nature of the evidence and the witnesses' expertise.

For Magistrates' Court matters, experts are virtually never called for cross-examination and reports are simply submitted by the relevant lawyer. For more serious matters, experts may be called to give oral evidence at the request of either party or by the court itself.

6.4.3 Other questioning of the assessment

While it would be theoretically possible for an organisation such as the RANZCP or APS to intervene in a sentencing hearing as an *amicus curia*, in practice this does not occur. Courts rarely grant permission for third parties to intervene in sentencing hearings: to date, this has only occurred in cases which involve broad issues of principle. To the authors' knowledge, no mental health organisation has ever sought to be involved in a Victorian sentencing matter in this capacity.

6.5 Safeguarding the quality of decision-making when confronted with disagreement between experts

6.5.1 Dealing with disagreement

As noted above, in most Victorian sentencing cases only one expert witness (the defense expert) is relied on. Consequently, there is rarely a need to deal with the issue of disagreement between witnesses. However, if experts do appear before the courts with contrasting opinions, robust cross-examination can be expected. It will be for the sentencing judge to make a final determination on the relevant issues, after considering all of the evidence presented.

Although this issue seldom arises, the Practice Note does contain three procedural provisions that can help resolve any disagreements which do occur. First, the courts have the power to direct the experts to discuss the expert issues in the proceeding in advance of the sentencing hearing, and to 'prepare a statement for the court of the matters on which they agree and disagree, giving their reasons'.[158] The content of the experts' discussion may not be referred to at the sentencing hearing without the court's permission.[159] If an expert fails to comply with this direction, their evidence may not be introduced.[160]

Second, the courts may convene a special 'pre-hearing' prior to the sentencing hearing.[161] At this pre-hearing, the court or any other party to the hearing may seek clarification of any aspect of the expert evidence. The court may also direct the experts to identify and narrow the areas of disagreement. Once again, if the expert does not comply with the court's direction in this regard, their evidence will be inadmissible.[162]

Third, the courts have the power to vary the order in which evidence is given in the sentencing hearing. Ordinarily, the defense and prosecution will call all of their witnesses (including any mental health experts) in turn. Depending on the number of witnesses to be called, this can lead to a significant delay in hearing from conflicting experts. To overcome this problem, the courts have the power to order that the experts give their evidence consecutively.[163] Alternatively, they can order them to give their evidence concurrently, colloquially known as 'hot tubbing'.[164] This can only be done with the agreement of the parties, who it is expected will confer in advance and attempt to agree on the procedure to be adopted. To date, the use of this power has been very limited in the criminal law context.

In addition, courts do have the capacity to commission independent forensic mental health reports from VIFMH if required.

6.5.2 Best practices

In our view, the Practice Note articulates best practices concerning the ways in which areas of disagreement between experts should be addressed (see section 6.5.1). In appropriate cases, experts should be required to discuss the issues in advance of the sentencing hearing, and to advise the court of areas of agreement and disagreement. Courts should be proactive in seeking clarification of expert reports and narrowing down the contentious issues. Conflicting witnesses should be subjected to robust cross-examination, to highlight the relative strengths and weaknesses in their differing positions.

By contrast, we do not believe that it is best practice for courts to rely solely on defense-appointed mental health experts, as is ordinarily the case in Victoria. While we appreciate that this practice reflects the pragmatic trade-off between the thoroughness and robustness of evidence versus the cost implications (in terms of both time delays and finances) of having experts also called by the prosecution or appointed by the court itself, any single expert will inevitably have certain inclinations of thought (sometimes amounting to frank biases) and a particular set of strengths and weaknesses that they bring to bear on the forensic opinion that they deliver. This is particularly the case with forensic mental health work, given the complex, value-laden nature of the terrain. In our view, best practice would instead generally require, at least at the level of the Supreme Court, that where the defense has sought to rely upon evidence from a mental health expert, evidence to also be called from a mental health expert appointed by the Office of Public Prosecutions or the court.

The Victorian system beyond the point of sentencing falls some way short of best practice. The lack of sufficient forensic mental health beds[165] means that the key sentencing aims of rehabilitation and community protection are often not adequately achieved for offenders with serious mental disorders. This problem is compounded by the suboptimal coordination between parole processes and clinical mental health treatment services for prisoners. Further aggravating this issue is the difficulty that most male prisoners in Victoria face in accessing non-pharmacological therapies for mental disorders; despite the high prevalence of conditions requiring such care, current resource constraints result in substantial unmet needs.

6.6 Critical reflections

The quality of a forensic mental health assessment is contingent on the degree to which relevant expertise (knowledge, training and experience) is fairly and appropriately brought to bear on assisting the court with whatever its task may be. Given that the admissibility and use of opinion evidence is ultimately determined by judges, it is especially useful to consider judicial opinions regarding the quality of expertise. An important questionnaire study of Australian judges reported that decision-makers

> need to look for touchstones of reliability, indicia including the experts being impartial, a disinclination by the expert to step beyond their limits of expertise, and the familiarity on the part of the expert with the relevant facts. In short, the decision maker needs to feel secure that their application of an expert opinion to facts in dispute is truly fair and reasonable. In turn, this will be a function of their perception of the quality of the evidence before them.[166]

The study also found judges to be

> *concerned to reduce what they identify as a culture of inadequate objectivity by many doctors, accountants, scientists and psychologists, to improve the performance of experts and advocates alike and to explore means of bringing information before the courts in a form which is both clear and amenable to sophisticated and cost-efficient assessment.*[167]

These findings indicate that there are three distinct but overlapping domains of quality in relation to forensic mental health evidence: impartiality; substance; and boundaries. To properly safeguard the quality of such evidence, it is crucial that each of these issues be clearly addressed by a jurisdiction's laws or practice rules.

Within Australia, Victoria is a clear leader in this regard, explicitly addressing each of these issues in its Practice Note. The means by which this Practice Note was developed was somewhat unusual and may be instructive for other jurisdictions. Following the expression of dissatisfaction with the quality of some forensic mental health evidence by the judiciary,[168] the President of the Victorian Court of Appeal (Maxwell P) convened the 'Forensic Evidence Working Group' (FEWG) – a committee of senior representatives from relevant bodies – with the aim of developing a Practice Note to enhance the quality of forensic mental health evidence in sentencing hearings. The stakeholders represented on the FEWG included all relevant legal and mental health bodies, including

- The Supreme and County Court Judiciary
- The Criminal Bar Association
- Victoria Legal Aid
- The Office of Public Prosecutions
- The Faculty of Forensic Psychiatry of the RANZCP
- The Forensic College of the APS
- The VIFMH

Assistance to the FEWG was also provided by a legal academic with particular expertise and knowledge in sentencing and mental health.[169]

The members of the FEWG initially consulted with members of their respective bodies to ascertain the key issues which should be included in the Practice Note. Once these were agreed upon, President Maxwell, as Chair of the FEWG, produced a draft for circulation. This was progressively refined with feedback from the relevant stakeholders. Following the publication of the Practice Note by the Supreme and County Courts in March 2017, the FEWG has continued to meet periodically in order to review its functioning and the possible need for refinement.

The fact that this process involved input from multiple stakeholders, including experienced mental health experts and legal practitioners, rather than being an *ex cathedra* proclamation handed down by the judiciary, ensured that the Note covered all key areas and established a best practice framework. In this regard, the importance of a healthy dialectic between different fields of expertise cannot be overemphasised.[170] This interdisciplinary, ground-up approach has also ensured buy-in from the relevant stakeholders, helping to ensure that the Practice Note is used in the way intended. This is helping to improve the quality and reliability of expert mental health evidence relied on sentencing hearings and ensuring that such evidence is properly fit for purpose.

Notes

1 Senate Select Committee on Mental Health, 2006, para 13.1.
2 Each of Australia's six states (New South Wales, Queensland, South Australia, Tasmania, Victoria and Western Australia) and two territories (Australian Capital Territory and Northern Territory) has its own criminal laws, policies and procedures. There is also a Commonwealth criminal law, however, it is somewhat restricted in scope.
3 For example an individual who is suffering from mental health problems may not be fit to be interviewed by the police: see, for example Department of Health and Human Services, 2016.
4 For example a suspect's mental health problems may be regarded as a reason for discontinuing a prosecution: see, for example Director of Public Prosecutions for Victoria, 2019.
5 Bail legislation typically requires judges to refuse to grant bail where they believe there is an unacceptable risk that the accused person will fail to attend court or will commit further offences while on bail: see, for example *Bail Act 1977* (Vic) *Bail Act 1977* (Vic) s 4E. Judges will often believe this to be the case where the accused has a mental health problem.
6 See, for example Richardson and McSherry, 2010.
7 See, for example *Crimes (Mental Impairment and Unfitness to be Tried) Act 1997* (Vic) s 6(1).
8 See, for example *Evidence Act 2008* (Vic) s 85.
9 See, for example ibid. ss 13, 165.
10 See, for example *R v Falconer* (1990) 171 CLR 30.
11 See, for example *Crimes (Mental Impairment and Unfitness to be Tried) Act 1997* (Vic) s 20.
12 See, for example *Crimes Act 1900* (NSW) s 23 A.
13 See, for example *R v Verdins* (2007) 16 VR 269.
14 See, for example Adult Parole Board of Victoria, 2018.
15 See, for example *Serious Offenders Act 2018* (Vic).
16 See https://www.legalaid.vic.gov.au/about-us/news/explainer-crimes-mental-impairment-and-unfitness-to-be-tried-act for a detailed description of the regime regarding both unfitness to stand trial and the defense of mental impairment in the Australian State of Victoria.
17 See https://www.corrections.vic.gov.au/parole/detention-and-supervision-orders for a detailed description of the regime regarding post-sentence regimes for serious offenders in the Australian State of Victoria.
18 As individuals who are found not guilty because of mental impairment (i.e. 'insane') are not *convicted*, they do not face the sentencing process. Instead, the judge will need to determine whether to impose a custodial or non-custodial supervision order on the individual or release them unconditionally. Custodial supervision orders involve mandatory detention; for individuals with mental illness, this almost invariably involves care and treatment in a secure forensic mental health facility. Non-custodial supervision orders allow the affected individual to be supported and supervised while living in the community. Supervision orders are made for an indefinite period of time but must be periodically reviewed by the court. There is a legislated process that facilitates the transition from Custodial Supervision Orders, to Non-custodial Orders and eventual revocation of the Order, contingent on acceptable risk to self and the general community.
19 Magistrates are judicial officers who operate at the lowest level of the court hierarchy. They act within the same general sentencing framework as judges but are more limited in the sanctions available to them. For the sake of linguistic simplicity, the remainder of this chapter will only refer to judges.
20 *Chow v DPP (NSW)* (1992) 28 NSWLR 593.
21 (2007) 16 VR 269. On the consistent adoption of the *Verdins* principles by intermediate appellate courts around Australia, and the High Court of Australia's apparent acceptance of those principles, see *R v Guode* (2020) 267 CLR 141 n 6.
22 Supreme Court of Victoria, 2017. This Practice Note is designed for use in matters heard in the Supreme Court, Victoria's highest Court. It has been replicated for matters that are heard in the County Court of Victoria, which hears less serious matters: see County Court of Victoria, 2017b.
23 Mullen et al., 2000.
24 Bartholomew, 1986.
25 Substantial expansion in the form of a further 82 beds was announced in 2021 following a review of Victoria's mental health system.
26 See section 6.3.2.
27 One of the authors of this article, Associate Professor Andrew Carroll, has such an appointment.

An Australian perspective   141

28 A Drug and Alcohol Treatment Order can only be given by the Victorian Drug Court. The court imposes a sentence of up to two years' imprisonment, which is suspended while the offender undergoes treatment and supervision. Offenders will only have to serve the specified term of imprisonment if they fail to abide by the conditions of the order. See *Sentencing Act 1991* (Vic) ss 18X-18ZT.

29 A Community Correction Order is a non-custodial sanction that can be imposed with or without conviction. It includes mandatory terms and must contain at least one condition. Conditions are chosen based on the circumstances of the offender and the offence. See ibid. Part 3 A.

30 Ibid. s 44.

31 *Mental Health Act 2014* (Vic) Division 4.

32 Victorian law distinguishes between 'children' and 'young offenders'. 'Children' are aged between 10 and 17 at the time of the offence, and are under 19 when the criminal proceedings begin: *Children, Youth and Families Act 2005* (Vic) s 3. 'Young offenders' are aged under 21 at the time of sentencing: *Sentencing Act 1991* (Vic) s 3.

33 Youth justice centre and youth residential centre orders are sentences of detention for children and young offenders. The difference between the orders is that children aged 15 to 20 are detained in youth justice centres, while children aged under 15 are detained in youth residential centres. See *Sentencing Act 1991* (Vic) s 32. Youth supervision order may be imposed on children, and require them to report to a youth justice unit, undertake supervised community work if directed, and satisfy any other conditions imposed: *Children, Youth and Families Act 2005* (Vic) Division 7.

34 *Sentencing Act 1991* (Vic) ss 94A-94C. As a sentencing sanction, this disposition is limited to convicted offenders. It does not apply to those found not guilty because of mental impairment, who will generally be made subject to custodial or non-custodial supervision orders: see in note 18 above. A CSTO may not be combined with any other sentencing sanction.

35 If the offender's mental health does not recover during the period of the order, the offender must be released from the mental health facility upon its expiry, unless the Mental Health Tribunal makes a civil Inpatient Treatment Order under the *Mental Health Act 2014* (Vic).

36 Ibid. s 48D. See for example *Williams v R* [2018] VSCA 171.

37 See, for example *R v Ibbs* (1987) 163 CLR 447.

38 In some cases, a mandatory minimum penalty will limit the judge's discretion. However, judges retain a certain level of discretion even where a mandatory minimum sentence has been set. For example while they may be prohibited from giving a lesser sentence than that set down by the statute, they will generally be permitted to impose a more severe sentence.

39 The 'non-parole period' must be at least six months less than the maximum term of the sentence. There are some limited circumstances in which the court does not need to set a non-parole period: see *Sentencing Act 1991* (Vic) s 11.

40 *R v Dixon* (1975) 22 ACTR 13, 17–18.

41 Judicial College of Victoria, 2020, para 7.1.2.

42 *Sentencing Act 1991* (Vic) ss 6A-C. The determination of an offender's status as a 'serious offender' depends solely on the nature of the offence for which they have been convicted and the sanction imposed. No risk assessment process is undertaken.

43 Ibid. s 6D(a).

44 A person is punished for the purpose of 'specific' deterrence when the sentence aims to deter him or her from re-offending. A person is punished for the purpose of 'general' deterrence when the aim of the sentence is to induce other people who might be tempted to commit a crime to desist out of fear of the penalty.

45 *Sentencing Act 1991* (Vic) ss 5(2)-(7).

46 Ibid. s 5(3).

47 *Channon v R* (1978) 20 ALR 1, 4–5.

48 Ibid. 10–11; *Veen v R [No.1]* (1979) 143 CLR 458; *Veen v R [No.2]* (1988) 164 CLR 465.

49 For an overview of the development of the law in this area, see Walvisch, Carroll and Marsh, 2021.

50 (2007) 16 VR 269.

51 For a detailed analysis of the *Verdins* principles, see Walvisch, 2010.

52 *Quinn v Law Institute of Victoria Ltd* (2007) 27 VAR 18.

53 *R v Verdins* (2007) 16 VR 269, 271.

54 *R v Vuadreu* [2009] VSCA 262, [37]; *Charles v R* (2011) 34 VR 41.

55 *Mune v R* [2011] VSCA 231, [31].

56 See, for example *R v Tsiaras* (1996) 1 VR 398, 400.

57 *R v Verdins* (2007) 16 VR 269, 271.

58 Ibid. 276.
59 Ibid. 271.
60 Ibid. 272.
61 Ibid. 271.
62 See, for example *R v Koelman* [2010] VSC 561.
63 See, for example *DPP v Dimitrakis* [2010] VSC 614.
64 See, for example *R v Prideaux* [2009] VSCA 193.
65 See, for example *Londrigan v R* [2010] VSCA 81.
66 See, for example *Hladik v R* [2015] VSCA 149.
67 See, for example *Pantazis v R* (2012) 38 VR 446.
68 See, for example *R v Zander* [2009] VSCA 10.
69 See, for example *R v RLP* (2009) 213 A Crim R 461.
70 See, for example *Kavanagh v R* [2011] VSCA 234.
71 See, for example *R v Tresize* [2008] VSCA 8.
72 See, for example *R v Svetina* [2011] VSC 392.
73 See, for example *R v Epshtein* [2011] VSC 8.
74 See, for example *R v Lubik* [2011] VSC 137.
75 See, for example *Ashe v R* [2010] VSCA 119.
76 See, for example *R v Pyrczak* [2011] VSC 219.
77 See, for example *DPP v Felsbourg* [2008] VSC 20.
78 See, for example *Myers v R* [2011] VSCA 271.
79 See, for example *DPP v Maxfield* [2015] VSCA 95.
80 See, for example *R v Cheney* [2009] VSC 154.
81 *R v Hill* [2012] VSC 353, [39].
82 *DPP (Vic) v O'Neill* (2015) 47 VR 395.
83 See Walvisch and Carroll, 2017.
84 *Brown v R* [2020] VSCA 212, [6].
85 *R v Margach* [2008] VSC 255.
86 *Anh-Tuan Tran v R* [2011] VSCA 252; *Kells v R* [2013] VSCA 7.
87 *Reid (a Pseudonym) v R* [2014] VSCA 145.
88 For an overview of the legal principles concerning substance-related disorders, see Walvisch, forth-coming. See Walvisch, 2017 and Walvisch, 2018 for a discussion of the difficulties that arise when defining the concept of 'mental disorder' for legal purposes.
89 See, for example *DPP v Weidlich* [2008] VSCA 203.
90 See, for example *Wright v R* [2015] VSCA 88.
91 See, for example *Seddon v R* [2011] VSCA 375.
92 *Sentencing Act 1991* (Vic) ss 18A–B. A person who is serving an indefinite sentence is not eligible to be released on parole, and a judge who imposes an indefinite sentence must not fix a non-parole period.
93 *R v Carr* [1996] 1 VR 585.
94 *Chester v R* (1988) 165 CLR 611, 618–9.
95 See, for example *R v Davies* (2005) 11 VR 314.
96 *DPP v Herrmann* [2021] VSCA 160.
97 See https://www.adultparoleboard.vic.gov.au/board-decisions for details.
98 *O'Connor v R* [2014] VSCA 108, [65].
99 See *DPP v Dolheguy* [2020] VSC 704 for a recent homicide case in which treatability and risk in the context of a severe personality disorder were explored at length at the sentencing hearing.
100 *Ross v R* [2015] VSCA 302. If a judge is considering rejecting unchallenged evidence, they should provide the defence with a chance to address their concerns. They must also provide reasons for their decision.
101 *R v Olbrich* (1999) 199 CLR 270.
102 See, for example *R v Singh* [2021] VSC 182. This was a very high-profile case of culpable driving that led to the deaths of four police officers on duty. Despite the presence of a range of complex psychiatric issues, only a single (defence) expert was commissioned.
103 Ibid.
104 *Sentencing Act 1991* (Vic) s 8 A.
105 Ibid. s 8B.
106 *R v Williscroft* [1975] VR 292, 300.
107 *R v Storey* [1998] 1 VR 359, 366.

108 *Sentencing Act 1991 (Vic)* Part 2AA. No guideline judgements have yet been issued concerning the sentencing of offenders with mental health problems.

109 Ibid. s 5(2)(b).

110 *R v O'Connor* [1987] VR 496.

111 Supreme Court of Victoria, 2017. See Section 6.6 for a discussion of the genesis of this Practice Note. The full Note is available at: https://www.supremecourt.vic.gov.au/law-and-practice/practice-notes/sc-cr-7-expert-reports-on-mental-functioning-of-offenders.

112 Supreme Court of Victoria, 2017, s 1.4.

113 Supreme Court of Victoria, 2017, s 4.1.

114 Ibid. s 4.2.

115 Ibid. s 4.4.

116 Ibid. s.7.3.

117 See, for example *Wright v R* [2015] VSCA 88; *DPP v Haberfield* [2019] VCC 2082.

118 Supreme Court of Victoria, 2017, s 7.4.

119 Ibid. s 6.4.

120 Ibid. s 6.1.

121 For example in *Avan v R* [2019] VSCA 257 the offender posted parcels containing asbestos to various embassies and consulates, due to the deluded belief that this would enhance their firefighting abilities. The court held that his moral culpability was reduced because the offending 'was influenced by deranged altruistic and humanitarian motives'. Similarly, in *Marks v R* (2019) VSCA 253 the offender made a bomb threat on an aircraft due to the delusional belief that the aircraft would be in serious peril if it was not forced to return to the airport. The court held that he had limited culpability, as he lacked 'an ulterior motive deserving of condemnation'.

122 See, for example *R v Miller* [2015] VSC 180.

123 Supreme Court of Victoria, 2017, s 7.5.

124 Ibid. s 7.6.

125 Ibid. s 7.7.

126 Ibid. s 7.8.

127 Jones, 1994, p. 14.

128 Freckelton, Reddy and Selby, 1999, p 3.

129 Supreme Court of Victoria, 2017, s 4.1.

130 Ibid. ss 5.1–5.2.

131 Ibid. s 5.4.

132 Jones, 1994, p. 92.

133 Supreme Court of Victoria, 2017, s 6.3.

134 Ibid. s 6.1.

135 Ibid. s 6.5.

136 Ibid. s 6.6.

137 Taylor et al., 2012.

138 Supreme Court of Victoria, 2017, s 6.7.

139 Supreme Court of Victoria, 2016; County Court of Victoria, 2017a, s 24.

140 *Supreme Court (General Civil Procedure Rules) 2015* (Vic) r 44.03; County Court of Victoria, 2017a, rr 20.1-20.2.

141 See: https://www.ranzcp.org/files/resources/college_statements/practice_guidelines/ppg11-medical-examinations-in-medico-legal.aspx.

142 *Evidence Act 2008* (Vic) s 79.

143 Ibid. s 4(2).

144 Supreme Court of Victoria, 2017, s 4.6 note 3.

145 Freckelton, Reddy and Selby, 1999.

146 Ibid.

147 Trimble, 2004.

148 Davis, 2019.

149 Supreme Court of Victoria, 2017, Schedules A-B.

150 *Evidence Act 2008* (Vic) ss 4, 79.

151 *R v O'Connor* [1987] VR 496.

152 *Marks v R* [2019] VSCA 253; *Avan v R* [2019] VSCA 257.

153 But see Jones, 1994, pp 128–164 for an exception to this.

154 *Cabassi v Villa* (1940) 64 CLR 130; *Young v Hones* [2014] NSWCA 337.

155 While unclear, it seems likely that this is a financial decision that arises due to a lack of sufficient funding.
156 *Mune v R* [2011] VSCA 231, [31].
157 Supreme Court of Victoria, 2017, s 4.5.
158 Ibid. s 11.2.
159 Ibid. s 11.3.
160 Ibid. s 11.5.
161 Ibid. s 11.4.
162 Ibid. s 11.5.
163 Ibid. s 12.
164 Ibid.
165 This has been acknowledged by the Victorian government following an extensive 'Royal Commission into Victoria's Mental Health System': https://finalreport.rcvmhs.vic.gov.au. The Victorian Government has committed to a substantial expansion of Thomas Embling Hospital.
166 Freckelton, Reddy and Selby, 1999, p. 4.
167 Ibid. p. 13.
168 See, for example *R v Miller* [2015] VSC 180.
169 Both authors of this chapter were members of the FEWG.
170 Perhaps because of its relatively small size, Victoria is marked by a high level of collegiality within and across the professions of psychiatry, psychology and the law. The establishment and growth of ANZAPPL have been at least as important as the discipline-specific colleges in fostering these healthy relationships.

References

Adult Parole Board of Victoria (2018). *Parole Manual.* Melbourne: Adult Parole Board of Victoria.

Bartholomew, A. (1986). *Psychiatry, the Criminal Law and Corrections: An Exercise in Sciolism.* Bundalong: Wileman Publications.

Davis, M.R. (2019). *The great divide: Is evidence-based forensic practice even possible?* Paper presented at the joint conference of the Australian and New Zealand Association of Psychiatry, Psychology, and Law (ANZAPPL) and the Royal Australian and New Zealand College of Psychiatrists Faculty of Forensic Psychiatry, Singapore, November 2019.

Department of Health and Human Services (2016). *Victoria Police Protocol for Mental Health: A Guide for Clinicians and Police.* Melbourne: Department of Health and Human Services.

Director of Public Prosecutions for Victoria (2019). *Policy of the Director of Public Prosecutions for Victoria.* Melbourne: Director of Public Prosecutions for Victoria.

Freckelton, I., Reddy, P., and Selby, H. (1999). *Australian Judicial Perspectives on Expert Evidence: An Empirical Study.* Carlton: Australian Institute of Judicial Administration Incorporated.

Jones, C. (1994). *Expert Witnesses: Science, Medicine and the Practice of Law.* Oxford: Clarendon Press.

Judicial College of Victoria (2020). *Victorian Sentencing Manual.* [online]. Available at: https://resources.judicialcollege.vic.edu.au/article/669236 [Accessed 20February2020].

Mullen, P., Briggs, S., Dalton, T., and Burt, M. (2000). Forensic mental health services in Australia. *International Journal of Law and Psychiatry*, 23, pp. 433–452.

Richardson, E., and McSherry, B. (2010). Diversion down under – programs for offenders with mental illnesses in Australia. *International Journal of Law and Psychiatry*, 33, pp. 249–257.

Royal Australian and New Zealand College of Psychiatrists (2015). *Professional Practice Guideline 11: Developing Reports and Conducting Independent Medical Examinations in Medico-legal Settings.* Royal Australian and New Zealand College of Psychiatrists.

Senate Select Committee on Mental Health (2006). *A National Approach to Mental Health – From Crisis to Community: First Report.* Canberra: Commonwealth of Australia.

Taylor, P.J., Graf, M., Schanda, H., and Vollm, B. (2012). The treating psychiatrist as expert in the courts: Is it necessary or possible to separate the roles of physician and expert? *Criminal Behaviour and Mental Health*, 22, pp. 271–292.

Trimble, M. (2004). *Somatoform Disorders: A Medicolegal Guide*. Cambridge: Cambridge University Press.

Walvisch, J. (2010). Sentencing offenders with impaired mental functioning: Developing Australia's "most sophisticated and subtle" analysis. *Psychiatry, Psychology and Law*, 17(2), pp. 187–201.

Walvisch, J. (2017). Defining "mental disorder" in legal contexts. *International Journal of Law and Psychiatry*, 52, pp. 7–18.

Walvisch, J. (2018). "Mental disorder" and sentencing: Resolving the definitional problem. *Journal of Law and Medicine*, 26, pp. 159–169.

Walvisch, J. (forthcoming). Sentencing offenders with self-induced mental disorders: Towards a theory of meta-culpability*Psychiatry, Psychology and Law*.

Walvisch, J., and Carroll, A. (2017). Sentencing offenders with personality disorders: A critical analysis of *DPP v O'Neill*. *Melbourne University Law Review*, 41, pp. 417–444.

Walvisch, J., Carroll, A., and Marsh, T. (2021). Sentencing and mental disorder: The evolution of the Verdins principles, strategic interdisciplinary advocacy and evidence-based reform. *Psychiatry, Psychology and Law*, pp. 1–21.

Chapter 7

A German perspective

Johannes Kaspar and Susanne Stübner

7.1 Introduction

7.1.1 The legal system

The German legal system contains the common division of the three main branches of civil, public, and criminal law. The criminal procedure in Germany is not adversary but inquisitorial, that is, the courts are actively involved in investigating the facts of the case (and are legally obliged to do so, § 244 section 2 of the German Criminal Code of Procedure (*Strafprozessordnung, StPO*). The trial only has one phase with a decision both on the facts of the case and on the legal consequences at its end. Decisions are made by courts, which consist of professional judges together with (in more severe cases) lay judges; independent juries do not exist in the German criminal procedure.

The most important criminal offences, general rules on criminal liability and the system of criminal sanctions are regulated in the German Penal Code (*Strafgesetzbuch, StGB*). Criminal sanctions in Germany can be divided into one of two major categories: penalties (*Kriminalstrafen*, §§ 38 et seqq. StGB) on the one hand and measures of rehabilitation and incapacitation (*Maßregeln der Besserung und Sicherung*, §§ 61 et seqq. StGB) on the other hand. Whereas the former are supposed to serve the aim of retribution in the first place, the latter are supposed to serve mere preventive and curative purposes. Because of this dual structure, the German sanctioning system is called a twin-track system (*zweispuriges System*).

Penalties are dominated by the guilt principle (*Schuldprinzip*) that is based on human dignity (Art. 1 section 1 of the German Constitution [*Grundgesetz, GG*]). It demands that no punishment can be imposed without 'culpability', that is, on persons who are not considered responsible for their actions due to their young age under 14 years (§ 19 StGB) or due to certain mental disorders (§ 20 StGB). It also demands that the amount of punishment must not exceed the amount of guilt fulfilled by the offence. Measures of rehabilitation and incapacitation are not bound by these requirements, they can be (and are) imposed on persons without criminal responsibility or with substantially reduced culpability due to mental illness, and they are not measured with regard to the amount of guilt fulfilled by the offence but are based on preventive and curative needs, that is, the risk of future crimes by the sanctioned person. They are limited by the constitutional principle of proportionality that is (in a rather declaratory manner) expressly regulated in § 62 StGB. This in principle quite clear picture is blurred by the fact that some preventive measures (like preventive detention, §§ 66 et seqq. StGB or the hospitalisation in an addiction treatment facility, § 64 StGB) can be imposed on fully responsible offenders in addition to a penalty. In cases of substantially reduced responsibility (*verminderte Schuldfähigkeit*, § 21 StGB), hospitalisation in a psychiatric hospital (§ 63 StGB) can be imposed next to a (mitigated) penalty. As will be shown, forensic assessment is relevant (and in some cases even

DOI: 10.4324/9781351266482-7

A German perspective 147

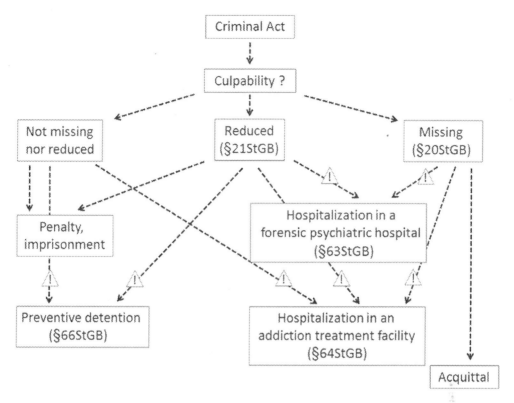

Figure 7.1 Possible outcome after criminal offences dependent on existing, reduced, or missing culpability. Triangles with exclamation marks symbolise existing dangerousness, which is also a prerequisite for the order of the respective measure.

required by law, see infra) in both 'tracks': questions of culpability but also questions of assessing the 'dangerousness' or the risk of recidivism of offenders respectively have to be answered both with regard to penalties and to measures of rehabilitation and incapacitation (for an overview over different possible outcomes of criminal proceedings dependent from culpability and assumed dangerousness of the offender, see Figure 7.1).

The prerequisites of criminal liability and criminal sanctions in both tracks are regulated by Federal law like the earlier-mentioned Penal Code (StGB). The execution of sentences, however, falls under the competency of the 16 German states. This is why there is a multitude of different regulations on the execution of prison sentences (*Landesstrafvollzugsgesetze*) or of measures of rehabilitation and incapacitation (*Maßregelvollzugsgesetze; Sicherungsverwahrungsvollzugsgesetze*) on the state level. For the purposes of this contribution, we will focus on the example of Bavarian regulations as both authors are located in Bavaria; with respect to the topic of forensic assessment, there are no remarkable differences between regulations on the state level.

7.1.2 The related tradition of forensic assessment

In a very brief summary, the concepts for dealing with mentally disordered offenders in Germany – like many socio-cultural developments – have their roots in Greek philosophical (Aristoteles) and Roman legal traditions.[1] In most regions which corresponded to later Germany, it was already forbidden in the Middle Ages to impose a death penalty on the mentally disordered. Based on the legal philosophical considerations of Samuel Pufendorf in the seventeenth century, the concept of freedom of will as the basis of human responsibility emerged. In the eighteenth century, it was increasingly recommended that doctors be consulted to assess and distinguish between various diseases. In the nineteenth century, another influential school of thought emerged, that of 'degeneration doctrine'. The extent of a disorder was equated with the degree of degeneration; and finally, a 'devolution theory' (*Entartungslehre*) emerged, which equated mental disorder and crime in terms of its genesis; the most prominent current in this regard at the time came from Italian psychiatry, especially personified by Cesare Lombroso.

Although these theories were not scientifically tenable, they became a fatal amalgamation in Germany in the first half of the twentieth century against the background of National Socialism with its ideologies. In this context, many politically undesirable persons were classified as psychiatrically ill, and many mentally disordered persons were in turn eliminated, such as Jewish, homosexual, and other persons unwelcome to the system. Many psychiatrists were instrumentalised and/or guilty during National Socialism. The examination of this historical burden still continues.[2] The horrors of this time are deeply rooted in the collective consciousness and unconscious. Even today, many people in Germany still have a deep mistrust and great, archaic-seeming fears of psychiatric institutions, which certainly go back at least in part to this difficult legacy. In the 1970s, the general wave of liberalism led to an emphasis on social psychiatry. And sometimes real problems that can arise as a result of mental illness have been ignored. Modern psychiatry in Germany had to fight very intensively for a new and realistic self-image and a good perception of others. This is still very difficult, especially for forensic psychiatry in Germany. Overall, there is a great sensitivity to state influence.

The current situation in general psychiatry – as probably in other countries – is characterised by the topic of further developments of disease concepts which shows in the discussion on the reform of the upcoming International Classification of Diseases (ICD) in its 11th version. The ICD, published by the World Health Organisation, represents the standard system of diagnostic criteria in German-speaking countries, whereas the Diagnostic and Statistical Manual of mental disorders by the American Psychiatric Association (DSM) plays a secondary role. Another current issue is the influence of scientific knowledge, especially in English-speaking countries. The general determinism–indeterminism debate, which would affect forensic psychiatry but is a rather philosophical question is going on. Forensic assessments are strictly based on the legal texts and are subject to a tight pragmatism, meaning that the question of determinism–indeterminism is not addressed. The legal texts regulating missing or reduced culpability were created in the 1970s. The characteristics described and required do not correspond to psychiatric diagnoses (see infra), but do in a certain sense reflect the state of psychiatric knowledge at that time. Until 2021, the legal text also contained very old-fashioned and rather stigmatising terms which could be translated as 'idiocy' (*Schwachsinn*) and 'abnormality' (*Abartigkeit*). Only recently, they have been replaced by the more contemporary and neutral terms of intelligence reduction (*Intelligenzminderung*) and disorder (*Störung*) (for a description of the reform process see Schiemann, 2019).

7.2 Short overview of the role of assessment in sentencing offenders

7.2.1 Sentences and execution

Taking a closer look at different sentences and their execution, we can distinguish between the two tracks mentioned above. The two main types of penalties are fines (*Geldstrafe*) and imprisonment (*Freiheitsstrafe*). The only additional ancillary penalty (*Nebenstrafe*) under German law is the driving ban in § 44 StGB.

Measures of rehabilitation and incapacitation can themselves be divided into two groups. The first group consists of non-custodial measures that are not linked with any kind of imprisonment or hospitalisation: the supervision order (§§ 68 et seqq. StGB), the driving disqualification order (§ 69 StGB) and the order of professional disqualification (§ 70 StGB). The other group consists of the three custodial measures which have already been mentioned above. In a way, they all combine the purposes of incapacitation and rehabilitation (or therapy respectively): placement in a psychiatric hospital for mentally disordered offenders (§ 63 StGB), placement in an addiction treatment facility for offenders with addiction problems (§ 64 StGB) and preventive detention for fully culpable persons – or in rarer cases and special constellations also persons with substantially reduced culpability – who committed grave offences (§§ 66 et seqq. StGB) and seem to have a general 'inclination' (*Hang*) to commit such crimes in the future. Each of the six earlier-mentioned measures requires that the offender is considered to be an ongoing danger for society (which obviously makes prognostic assessment necessary).

Juvenile Criminal Law is applicable for offenders between 14 and 18 years (and in some cases also for offenders up to 21 years who are considered to be immature, § 105 Juvenile Court Act [*Jugendgerichtsgesetz, JGG*]). It focuses very much on the purpose of preventing future offences by educating juvenile offenders (§ 2 section 1 JGG). The scope of possible sanctions is much broader compared to general criminal law, and there is much more discretion and flexibility on the side of the courts. There are three main categories of sanctions: Supervisory measures (*Erziehungsmaßregeln*) according to §§ 9 et seqq. JGG; disciplinary measures (*Zuchtmittel*; according to §§ 13 et seqq. JGG) and youth penalties according to §§ 17 et seq. JGG.

Generally, penalties are executed within regular prisons (with some specialisations depending on the type of offences and offenders). There are special prisons for female and juvenile offenders, for example. Youth detention (§§ 16, 16a JGG) as short-term imprisonment is executed in special detention facilities independent from regular youth prisons. For adult offenders, there are further specialisations like the distinction between facilities for short-term or long-term prison sentences. Even though prison inmates are fully culpable offenders, 'treatment' of offenders (in a broad sense) is considered to be one major aim of executing prison sentences. Art. 2 Bavarian Prison Act (*Bayerisches Strafvollzugsgesetz, BaySt VollzG*), for example states that the prisoner shall be enabled to lead a future life 'in social responsibility without committing criminal offences (objective of treatment)'. Art. 3 BayStVollzG regulates that 'treatment' in this sense is not limited to therapeutic measures. It comprises 'all measures that are apt to lead to a future life without delinquency'; inter alia, treatment in this sense also contains school- and job-related education, work and paedagogical measures. In addition, all prisons have medical departments and medical services, so that every inmate is given a thorough medical examination in the course of his sentence and can be given medical treatment if necessary. Psychological services are also available. Specific medical services, including psychiatric consultations, are available on request. Only very few, usually very large prisons have their own prison hospitals, rarely including psychiatric departments, in which inpatient and 'outpatient' psychiatric treatment can be provided. In principle, almost all common treatment measures that are provided in general psychiatric hospitals are available here;[3] however, certain treatment elements such as ergo- and milieu-therapeutic measures or stress tests etc. are hardly used under prison conditions and can only play a minor role.

Special facilities integrated into the regular prison system are socio-therapeutic institutions (see Art. 11, 116 BayStVollzG). They are a mandatory therapeutic measure for offenders who committed certain severe sexual offences (Art. 11 section 1 BayStVollzG); furthermore, they aim at offenders who seem to be at risk of committing grave violent or sexual offences in the future (which obviously requires a prognostic decision), Art. 11 section 2 BayStVollzG. Individual and group therapy measures are used here; the stay usually lasts two years and is timed at the end of the sentence so that a release can be prepared and arranged from here.

Custodial measures of rehabilitation and incapacitation are executed in specialised institutions independent from the prison system. The measure of § 63 StGB is executed within specialised psychiatric hospitals. Its aim is to heal the offender or at least improve his or her condition to a degree that he does not pose a danger to the public anymore, Art. 2 section 1 s. 2 no. 1 Bavarian Act on the Enforcement of Therapeutic Measures (*Bayerisches Maßregelvollzugsgesetz, BayMRVG*). The treatment order in § 64 StGB is executed within closed addiction treatment facilities. Its objective is to heal offenders from their addictive 'inclination' (*Hang*) or to prevent them from falling back into the inclination for a considerably long time and to dissolve the underlying destructive attitudes (Art. 2, section 1, s. 2 no. 2 BayMRVG). During hospitalisation in a forensic-psychiatric hospital or in an addiction treatment institution, all therapeutic measures of general psychiatry are available in principle,[4] that is measures of psychopharmacotherapy, psychotherapy, specialised addiction treatment, socio-therapy and other complementary therapies. In addition, some special crime therapy interventions are available. A key goal of treatment is crime prevention. The main difference in clinical practice compared to general (non-forensic) psychiatric institutions is that safety aspects must always be taken into account, which is also expressed in the fact that certain structural precautions must be taken and security personnel are also available.

Until 2011, preventive detention (§§ 61 et seqq. StGB) was in many cases executed within regular prisons, and detainees were treated very similar to regular prison inmates. Fuelled by judgements of the European Court of Human Rights (ECHR), the German Constitutional Court (*Bundesverfassungsgericht, BVerfG*) declared this practice to be unconstitutional in 2011. The Court argued that preventive detention had become too similar to a penalty and was not sufficiently orientated at intensely treating and releasing detainees as soon as possible, which was considered to violate their liberty rights. The court demanded that comprehensive therapeutic efforts had to be undertaken not only regarding actual, but also potential detainees during their stay in prison. As a consequence, the former regulations on preventive detention had to be reformed (which was completed in 2013). Now, § 66c StGB regulates that preventive detention is executed in facilities offering comprehensive and individual treatment programs for each offender. New separate facilities had to be installed or even built, with more staff and therapeutic efforts. Preventive detention is enforced in only 13 specialised institutions across Germany. In Bavaria, for example there is just one facility in Straubing (next to a high-security prison).

In the course of this development, a new category of preventive measure was introduced, the so-called therapeutic hospitalisation (*Therapieunterbringung*), which was regulated in a special act (*Therapieunterbringungsgesetz, ThuG*). It was meant for offenders who had to be released from preventive detention for legal reasons, even though they were still considered to be dangerous. It is a rather strange, hybrid type of measure that is ordered by civil courts and executed in separate institutions apart from the prison system. Prerequisites are that the offender is suffering from an 'unsound mind' (*psychische Störung*) and that because of this condition he is at risk of committing severe crimes such as murder, aggravated assault, or rape, § 1, section 1 no. 1 ThUG. The legislator deliberately made use of the terminology of Art. 5 lit. e of the European Charter of Human Rights in this context to avoid legal concerns by the ECHR. In practice, therapeutic hospitalisation did not become relevant at all as the Constitutional Court only allowed it under circumstances where also further execution of preventive detention remained possible.[5]

7.2.2 Decisions within sentencing and execution

Within sentencing, there is a considerable number of different kinds of decisions that require forensic assessment of some sort (of which we will present the most important ones in the following).[6] Following the procedural order, we can distinguish the imposition of a sanction, its execution, the question of temporary leave, and termination. A prolongation of criminal law sanctions is not possible under German law, neither with respect to penalties nor to preventive measures. The latter are terminated dependent on certain upper time limits and the prognostic question of future delinquency (see supra). Prison sentences with fixed terms are terminated at the latest if the sentence has been completely served – a further prolongation would be a violation of various principles, including the principle of guilt and the protection of legal force.

7.2.2.1 Imposition

The imposition of penalties requires full or at least partial culpability of the offender. A forensic assessment of this question is not always necessary, but only in those cases, where intoxication or mental disorder (§ 20 StGB) seem to have played a role. In practice, however, such an assessment is regularly carried out in cases of very severe crimes such as murder or homicide and usually for sexual offences. Figure 7.1 gives a schematic representation of the potential outcomes of criminal proceedings as a function of culpability.

If preventive detention is imposed, usually a sentence must first be served. If hospitalisation in an addiction treatment facility is imposed, there may be an accompanying sentence, which has then usually to be served before treatment begins.

Under Juvenile Criminal Law, the official Youth Court Act Guidelines (*Richtlinien zum JGG, RL-JGG*) generally suggest forensic assessment (inter alia) in cases where the offence might be related to a mental disorder or where the offender shows remarkable psychological, mental, or physical peculiarities (see § 43 Nr. 8 RL-JGG). These guidelines are based on an agreement by the Judicial Authorities of the German Federal States. They are not legally binding but mere recommendations; nonetheless in general they are obeyed in practice.

In addition to the assessment of culpability according to § 20 StGB, § 3 JGG requires a positive statement by the court that the offender is responsible for the criminal act which depends on his or her level of moral and intellectual maturity.[7] In practice, this question is not always assessed by forensic experts but rather intuitively by the courts. This might also be a consequence of the quite hesitant wording of § 3 RL-JGG: only if there are 'serious doubts' concerning the young offender's responsibility, forensic assessment should be 'considered', with strict regard to the principle of proportionality.

Youth penalties according to § 17 section 2 alt. 1 JGG can only be imposed if the juvenile offender has shown 'harmful inclinations' (*schädliche Neigungen*) to repeatedly commit serious crimes in the future, which is a prognostic question. Another topic is the application of Juvenile Criminal Law to young adults between 18 and 21 years (*Heranwachsende*). According to § 105 JGG, this is the case if the offence could be considered typical 'youth misconduct' (*Jugendverfehlung*) or if at the time of the act, the offender was still equivalent to a juvenile in terms of his moral and intellectual development.[8]

The imposition of all custodial measures of rehabilitation and incapacitation (on which we will focus here) is based on a prognosis of future offences (see also infra 2.3). § 63 StGB requires that the offender represents a danger to the general public because it is expected that he or she will commit grave unlawful acts in the future. Similarly, but with a slightly lower threshold, § 64 StGB requires the danger that the offender will commit serious unlawful acts as a consequence of his or her substance addiction. § 66 StGB demands an 'inclination' (*Hang*) to commit severe offences in the future. All these prognostic decisions require forensic assessment. In addition, § 63 StGB requires that the offender's culpability was missing or at least substantially reduced due to a mental disorder (§§ 20, 21 StGB).

7.2.2.2 Execution

Prison sentences up to two years do not necessarily have to be executed, but can be suspended on probation (§§ 56 et seqq. StGB; for juvenile offenders cf. §§ 21 et seqq. JGG) under the prerequisite of a favorable criminal prognosis. The court has to examine if there are reasons to believe that the sentence itself will serve as a sufficient warning to the convicted person and that he or she will commit no further offences even without having to serve the sentence.

A similar regulation exists concerning §§ 63, 64 StGB: according to § 67b StGB, these measures can be suspended on probation from the very start if special circumstances justify the expectation that their preventive purpose can also be achieved in this manner – which does not happen very often in practice as in many cases the negative prognosis which is necessary for the imposition (see supra) excludes the possibility of suspending the measure from the beginning.[9] Recent reforms have brought a change in this regard, however: if early preliminary measures – for example during a temporary accommodation in connection with § 126a StPO – have been taken, they may suffice to grant probation according to § 67b StGB.[10]

7.2.2.3 Leave

All Prison Acts of German Federal States contain regulations on a temporary leave from prison. The first possibility is privileges – in Bavaria for example according to Art. 13 BayStVollzG – which comprise short-term absences from prison with or without accompanying personnel. The second one is the so-called 'vacation' (*Urlaub*) according to Art. 14 BayStVollzG. Both alternatives are meant to be part of the treatment process and not to interrupt the formal enforcement of the prison sentence. They are only granted if there is no danger that prisoners will abuse their leave to commit criminal acts (13 section 2 and Art. 14 section 1 s. 2 BayStVollzG). This has to be examined especially thoroughly in cases in which the inmates had committed severe violent or sexual offences (Art. 15 BayStVollzG). Comparable regulations on privileges and vacation exist for the measures of hospitalisation in a psychiatric hospital and in an addiction treatment facility (Art. 16 BayMRVG): a leave is granted if the detainees are not at risk of abusing it for further offences;[11] due to the principle of proportionality, however, some risks have to be taken in this regard,[12] especially in cases of long-term hospitalisations (which is also true for the question of termination, see infra).

Vacation from preventive detention is not possible; the Bavarian Act on the Execution of Preventive detention (*Bayerisches Sicherungsverwahrungsvollzugsgesetz, BaySvVollzG*) however comprises regulations on privileges (§ 54 BaySvVollzG) and long-term-leaves up to six months in order to prepare the convict's release (§ 58 BaySvVollzG). They are granted if there are no concrete hints that the detainee will abuse his or her leave to commit criminal acts (§ 54 BaySvVollzG) – which is supposed to be examined 'especially thoroughly' by a forensic expert (§ 57 section 1 BaySvVollzG).

7.2.2.4 Termination

Prison sentences can be terminated after at least one-half (in most cases: two-thirds) of their duration; the rest of the sentence is then suspended on probation (*Reststrafenaussetzung*). This is possible if the convict gives his consent and if suspension seems justifiable taking into consideration the safety interests of the general public (§ 57 StGB) – which in the end boils down to the prognostic question of future delinquency. Accordingly, lifelong imprisonment is suspended under these circumstances if at least 15 years have been served and the gravity of guilt of the offence (*Schwere der Schuld*) does not oppose a suspension (§ 57a StGB).

Custodial measures of rehabilitation and incapacitation are terminated if certain time limits have been reached and/or if further execution can be suspended on probation due to a favourable prognosis. According to § 67d section 2 StGB the court grants suspension if it is to be expected that the detainee will not commit serious criminal acts outside of custody. Another possibility of terminating the measure of §63 StGB in particular is regulated in §67d section 6 StGB: Once the measure has lasted six years, its continuation is (as a rule) no longer proportionate and has therefore to be terminated unless there is a danger that the detainee will, as a result of his or her condition, commit serious offences causing severe emotional trauma or physical injury to the victims or exposing the victims to such risks. Furthermore, preventive detention and the measure of § 63 StGB are terminated after ten years if there is no danger that the offender will commit serious offences causing severe emotional trauma or physical injury (§ 67d section 3, § 67d section 6s. 3). Generally, the German Constitutional Court has stressed that proportionality becomes more and more important the longer a certain measure has lasted.[13]

7.2.3 Concepts to be assessed

The main criteria or concepts have already been briefly mentioned above. They can roughly be divided into two groups: first, the assessment of the personal status of the offender in terms of culpability, immaturity or responsibility and second, a prognostic assessment of the danger of future crimes.

7.2.3.1 Retrospective status-based criteria

The first group contains the following retrospective status-based criteria (as laid down in the respective legal provisions):

- Culpability (§ 20 StGB): It is missing if the offender suffers from one of four expressly listed mental disorders (*Eingangsmerkmale*): pathological mental disorder, profound disturbance of consciousness, intelligence reduction or any other serious mental disorder. Furthermore, this condition must render the offender incapable of appreciating the unlawfulness of his or her actions (*Einsichtsfähigkeit*) or of acting in accordance with this appreciation at the time of the commission of the offence (*Steuerungsfähigkeit*).
- Substantially reduced culpability (§ 21 StGB): It requires that the capacity to act in accordance with the appreciation of the unlawfulness of the act is substantially reduced at the time of the commission of the offence due to one of the reasons indicated in § 20 StGB.
- Unsound mind (§ 1 ThuG): it requires a mental disorder of some sort including personality disorders. The threshold of the seriousness of one of the mental disorders listed in § 20 StGB does not have to be reached.
- Responsibility (§ 3 JGG): It is given if, at the time of the offence, the juvenile offender has reached a level of moral and intellectual maturity sufficient to enable him to understand the wrongfulness of the act and to conduct himself in accordance with this understanding.
- Immaturity (§ 105 section 1 alt. 2 JGG): It requires that an overall assessment of the offender's personality, taking account of his living environment, demonstrates that at the time of the offence he was still equivalent to a juvenile in terms of his moral and intellectual development. The exact criteria are not defined by law, but in practice,

certain lists of criteria have been developed, for example the so-called Marburg guidelines (*Marburger Richtlinien*).[14]

7.2.3.2 Prospective criteria

The prospective criteria of the second group mentioned in the respective legal provisions are the following:

- Assessment of risk of (any) future delinquency: future crime (without any legal specification) has to be taken into account in different legal decisions like a suspension of a sentence on probation (§ 56 StGB) or use of privileges/short-term leaves from prison (Art. 13, 14 BayStVollzG), application of preventive detention (Art. 54 section 2 BaySvVZG) or hospitalisation in forensic hospitals (Art. 16 BayMRVG).
- Safety interests of the general public (§§ 57, 57a StGB): any future crime severe enough to outweigh the interest of the offender to be released (which is based on his liberty rights).
- Risk Assessment of grave future delinquency (§ 67 d section 2 StGB)
- 'Harmful tendencies' (§ 17 JGG). In several rulings, the German High Court (*Bundesgerichtshof, BGH*) defined them as deficiencies of the juvenile offender (caused genetically, by lack of education or exterior influences) that constitute the danger that he or she will commit further serious offences (above the level of petty crime) without longer intensive education.[15]
- The danger for the general public because of the expectancy of particularly severe offences (§ 63 StGB), that is criminal acts which will result in the victims suffering or being exposed to the considerable danger of severe emotional trauma or physical injury or which will cause serious economic damage.
- Expectancy of serious offences due to an 'inclination' (*Hang*) to consume alcohol or other intoxicating substances (§ 64 StGB). The exact type and nature of the expected offences are not defined by law and remain unclear – only petty crime is clearly excluded. The imposition is only possible if there is a concrete chance of healing the offender or at least of protecting him or her from falling into relapse for a considerable time and therefore of preventing serious addiction-based offences.
- The danger for the general public due to an 'inclination' (*Hang*) to commit severe offences (§ 66 StGB; see also § 67d section 3 for preventive detention and § 67d section 6 for hospitalisation in a psychiatric hospital), that is criminal acts which will result in severe emotional trauma or physical injury to the victim.
- Very high danger of the gravest sort of violent or sexual offences due to the offender's unsound mind (§ 1 ThuG; § 316 f section 2 Introductory Law to the Criminal Code [Einführungsgesetz zum StGB, EG-StGB]).

7.2.3.3 Specific demands concerning assessment

In this section, specific demands and prerequisites for the assessment of some of the earlier-mentioned criteria, which are the most important ones in practice, are described.

For the assessment of psychiatric prerequisites for the application of §§ 20 or 21 StGB, it must be examined whether the diagnoses – at the time of the presumed offence – were qualitatively and quantitatively so pronounced that they can be assigned to one or more characteristics (*Eingangsmerkmale*) of the legal paragraph. Although this classification is the responsibility of legal expertise, the psychiatric expert is required to make a proposal based on the forensic literature. It has also to be checked whether, at the time of the offence, mental functions were impaired by the diagnosed disorder to such an extent that the person concerned was incapable of appreciating the unlawfulness of his or her actions (*Einsichtsunfähigkeit*) or of acting in accordance with this appreciation (*Steuerungsunfähigkeit*). This assessment is also ultimately the responsibility of legal expertise, but once again the expert is requested to explain the psychopathological abnormalities and their possible effects. In this respect, the term 'two-stage' is often used with respect to the examination of 1) diagnoses (medical) and characteristics (legal) and 2) psychopathological abnormalities (medical) and functional impairments (legal).[16] However, the procedure is much more complicated in reality. A medical diagnosis does not automatically correspond to a legal characteristic, but must first be checked for its qualitative and quantitative features. Only if the actual psychopathology and/or the psychosocial effects of the disorder (structural-social concept of disease[17]) are correspondingly severe can the presence of a legal characteristic be assumed. An acute psychosis, for example in the context of schizophrenia, offers a so-called 'psychopathological reference system'[18] in this respect: here, both the assignment to the characteristic and the psychological functional impairments are clearly recognisable. It is more difficult, however, in the case of personality disorders or paraphilia, for example: here it must be examined very carefully, how serious the actual burdens of disease are.[19] Many parameters need to be taken into account, such as the relationship with the victim, the alleged offence in the context of the suspected offender's biography, personality or previous delinquency, behaviour in other, comparable situations and in contexts unrelated to the offence, and pre- and post-crime behaviour. Possible acts of concealment or long, complicated criminal actions make it ordinarily unlikely that control mechanisms were severely impaired. All these factors must be examined and considered by both the forensic-psychiatric expert and the court. Although both disciplines, legal and medical, have to consider these factors in a differentiated way, there is surprisingly little literature on the subject in both sciences. However, possible conspicuous features in this respect may have been what originally prompted the court to commission an expert opinion in the first place. In this respect, the circle is complete.

Moving on to the assessment of risk and protective factors, a general prerequisite is experienced in the exploration of offenders, competence in one's own empirical science field and criminological knowledge. Standards for prognostic assessment have been the subject of intensive scientific efforts in many countries in recent years. Not long ago, an interdisciplinary group of several leading German legal scholars, forensic psychiatrists, psychologists and criminologists drafted a consensus paper that summarises in two parts the most important key points of recommendations for the commissioning, preparation and interpretation of criminal prognostic reports (see infra).[20] A detailed presentation of all aspects would go beyond the scope of this paper. In brief, using the file information, exploration and investigation results, elementary areas must be analysed, such as development, personality and social behaviour, possible disorders, possible pre-delinquency, the current crime scene and its framework and developmental conditions, the course of events since the crime and perspectives. Discrepancies – for example, between statements and file content or between the subject's statements to different investigators or at different times – should be considered.

The information can also be collected and evaluated with experience-based, standardised risk assessment tools. Such a procedure is used in most cases. The instruments record particularly important and frequent risk factors whose general prognostic relevance can be considered proven by empirical studies. In recent years, many such tools have been developed for different indications. By now, several 'generations' of instruments are already available, including actuarial instruments and those of the so-called structured professional judgement. There is no end in sight regarding the development of new instruments. However, selection, application and interpretation of the results require a profound knowledge of the methodological possibilities and limitations of the instrument in question. For a criminal prognostic statement, a precise study of the individual case is carried out (idiographic approach), which is combined with empirical knowledge of risk factors and recidivism rates for different offences, types of delinquency, offender types, mental disorders, and age groups (nomothetic approach). Empirical knowledge is not exhausted in standardised instruments for risk assessment or personality diagnosis but exists in all empirical research results. The individual case must be located within this range of experience described by empirical data.

A delinquency hypothesis will be developed based on an analysis of the information about the crime itself (course and background, also concerning other significant acts), the context (acute, situational factors that were relevant in the hours and days before and after the crime, and environmental factors, which shaped the life situation in the days to months before the crime, the embedding of the delinquency event in the general biography as well as inter-actional aspects), personality-specific parameters (personal development and image, attitudes, self-concept, behaviour patterns as well as the willingness to act) and disease- or disorder-specific factors. On the basis of the delinquency hypothesis, it is then possible to investigate which of these circumstances still exist and could pose a danger. Based on these considerations, an individual risk management plan can also be developed.

In addition to the exact circumstances of the index delinquency, which are considered in the formation of the delinquency hypothesis, general empirical figures are also taken into account, such as offence-specific recidivism rates.[21] Particular attention is paid to anamnestic data, for example, whether there were particularly early behavioural problems or previous violent delinquency and what the stability of employment and social relationships was like. A further task is to examine the course of events since the crime. This allows further statements about the personality, development processes and his or her potential for change. Special attention is paid to criminogenic behavioural willingness, protective factors, and an assessment of the course of any therapy. It is considered, which prognostically relevant risk or protective factors are unchanged, attenuated or increased compared to the time of the offence, and how this can be specifically identified. Finally, it is examined whether the risk factors could be sufficiently compensated for by appropriate measures of aftercare, and if so, what kind of conditions must be imposed. The clarification of future life perspectives and the social reception area are decisive tasks of risk assessment (e.g. work, living, partnership, sexuality, sports, leisure, contacts with relatives, former friends, and acquaintances).

An example of a measure in which prognostic assessment is very important is forensic-psychiatric hospitalisation according to § 63 StGB. In addition to missing or substantially reduced culpability, a further prerequisite for imposition is that the offender is dangerous to the general public due to his condition, as serious offences are to be expected. In this respect, proportionality must be taken into account. These normative assessments are not the task of the psychiatric expert but are the responsibility of legal expertise. The task of the expert is to provide the court with assistance in the decision-making process. This means that he or she must try to convey (or at least to keep available as required) as much information as possible about the suspected offender and his personality but also about possible diagnoses, their effects, interactions, complications, forms of progression, and treatment options, both in general and in this specific, individual case. He must also prepare and communicate prognostic assessments.[22] Finally, every decision about leave and easing restrictions requires prognostic considerations, which of course also have to be made again in a particularly comprehensive manner in preparation for the decision about release or suspension on parole.

§ 64 StGB can be applied regardless if substantially reduced or completely missing culpability according to §§ 20 or 21 StGB is assumed.[23] A necessary condition is an inclination (*Hang*) to consume alcoholic beverages or other intoxicating substances in excess. The term 'inclination' is not a medical verbalism and is not congruent with diagnostic items. According to case law, this is understood to mean that a pattern of consumption has been established which has caused harmful effects in some way (not limited to health-related damage, as defined by the ICD-10 for diagnosing 'harmful use'). A further condition is that the offence must have been committed in connection with the inclination. Traditionally, this has been referred to as acquisitive crime, but case law has consistently held that much more indirect or only partly conditional causes are sufficient. It also requires that there is a further risk of criminal offences due to the inclination. Therefore, an assessment of the prognosis is also demanded here (see supra). The requirements for the connection between danger and inclination are again seen very broadly in practice. It is only in sentence 2 of the corresponding law that another prerequisite is named, which falls strictly and solely under medical expertise: there must be a prospect of success for the therapeutic measures, which can be offered in weaning treatment. However, this prerequisite is also weakened and again left to normative evaluation because the legal text explicitly states that not only the prospect of recovery is regarded as a success but also that the person concerned can be saved for a 'considerable' long time from falling back into the inclination and thus from delinquency.

7.2.4 Forensic assessment and procedure

7.2.4.1 Initiation of forensic assessment

Generally, the legislator assumes that courts themselves do have the necessary knowledge to examine all facts required for their legal decisions.[24] If this is not the case, however, they are obliged to formally obtain an expert opinion which follows from the principle of the official investigation, § 244 section 2 StPO. As for the question whether necessary knowledge of facts is lacking, courts can exercise some discretion. In practice, certain circumstances may prompt the prosecution or the court to commission a psychiatric assessment. These include the severity or nature of the offence, the circumstances of the committed crime or the person of the suspected offender.[25] An expert opinion is for example usually obtained for capital or sexual offences, for particularly conspicuous circumstances or scenarios, but also if there are indications of a psychiatric disorder or intoxication, for example based on observations by witnesses or police officers or on the suspect's previous history. Most status-based and prognostic questions mentioned above do require profound psychological or psychiatric expertise which the courts regularly do not have.[26] This is why in practice, expert opinions and forensic assessment are very frequent in these areas.

For some grave and important decisions, the legislator has even expressly regulated that courts are obliged to obtain an expert opinion, for example

- Imposition of custodial measures of rehabilitation and incapacitation (§ 246a section 1 StPO; § 415 section 5 StPO; for therapeutic hospitalisation see § 9 ThuG)
- Suspension of lifelong or long-term prison sentences for severe offences on probation (§ 454 section 2 StPO)
- Suspension of custodial measures of rehabilitation and incapacitation on probation (§ 463 section 3 StPO)
- Temporary detention of offenders in order to prepare a forensic assessment (§ 81a section 1 StPO)

Generally speaking, it is the competency and responsibility of the court to mandate and choose the expert (§ 73 section 1 StPO) and supervise his or her work (§ 78 section 1 StPO). During the preliminary proceedings, however, the public prosecutor can also assign experts (§ 161a StPO), which is done quite regularly,[27] for example in cases with doubtful culpability. In many of these cases, courts accept the choice of the public prosecutor,[28] which is understandable in terms of procedural efficiency; nonetheless, this practice somehow contradicts the strong position of the court laid down in § 73 section 1 StPO.[29] The defendant (or his attorney) may suggest certain experts to the court, but there is no right to be examined by a particular person.[30] It is possible, however, for the defendant to assign other experts on his own account and present their opinion to the court.

If the court holds that a particular expert opinion is insufficient, it can order another evaluation by the same or another expert (§ 83 section 1 StPO). If a certain expert has been successfully declined by the defendant or the public prosecutor, the court can also assign another expert (§ 83 section 2 StPO). Furthermore, due to the circumstances of the individual case, the principle of official investigation (§ 244 section 2 StPO) might lead to the obligation to obtain another expert opinion.[31] In exceptional cases such as the very grave decision of imposing subsequent preventive detention (*nachträgliche Sicherungsverwahrung*, § 66b StGB) or therapeutic hospitalisation, the court is obliged by law to obtain two expert opinions in the first place (§ 275a section 4 s. 2 StPO; § 9 ThuG). Given the general problem of lack of qualified evaluators (see infra) and the fact that disagreement between the two experts is rare, the benefit of these regulations is doubted.[32]

7.2.4.2 Procedure of forensic assessment and division of competencies

When an expert receives an appraisal assignment, he must first check whether it falls within his area of expertise and whether he can carry out the assignment in a reasonable time.[33] Then, as a rule, an examination appointment is arranged. The files of the preliminary proceedings – and of previous cases of law enforcement, if applicable – are carefully evaluated with respect to the psychiatrically relevant aspects. At the beginning of an expert examination, the respondent must be informed that he is not obliged to provide information and that he may not suffer any legal disadvantage if he remains silent. Furthermore, he must be informed that his statements to the expert as well as the results of his examination are not subject to doctor–patient confidentiality and that those experts who are heard by the court as witnesses do not have the right to remain silent.

As far as possible, a detailed exploration is carried out, including an anamnesis of the biographical and sexual development, the somatic, psychiatric, and consumption-related past history, the current social and financial situation as well as the past history of delinquency and information on the facts of the case. A thorough psychiatric examination shall be carried out, including a psychopathological status assessment and ordinarily a physical including a neurological examination. The written report shall contain the relevant extract from the file, the reports of the person and the results of the examination. It may be necessary to obtain further information, such as previous medical reports or results of additional examinations, possibly in consultation with the court. Any existing diagnoses must be presented and coded according to a valid diagnostic system (currently: ICD-10, possibly also DSM-5). A written expert opinion is always preliminary; participation in the main hearing is part of the expert opinion preparation and any further information must be included in the result. Finally, only the expert opinion which is reported personally and orally in the main hearing is valid.[34]

It is important to stress that the final decision on questions like culpability or the danger of future delinquency falls under the competency and responsibility of the courts alone.[35] It is up to them, not the forensic experts, to decide on these (in the end: legal) matters which combine empirical and normative elements, only taking into account (but not blindly following) the expert opinion.[36] This division of competencies between courts and forensic experts should be regarded from the start, even when formulating the specific questions to be addressed by the expert.[37] Even if the court urges the expert to answer legal questions he or she should refuse to cross this border.[38]

7.3 Safeguards for the quality of forensic assessment

7.3.1 Requirements in law and policy

Very general and fundamental legal requirements can be found within constitutional law that relate to all state measures intruding into liberty rights. This is obviously the case with all measures of criminal law discussed before that are based on forensic assessment. The principle of proportionality is the most important one of these requirements. It is not expressly regulated in the German Constitution but acknowledged as being a valid principle of constitutional law that is derived from the rule of law. It demands that intrusions by the state into liberty rights have to be apt, necessary, and appropriate to fulfil legitimate goals (e.g. the prevention of future crimes). Prison sentences or measures of rehabilitation and incapacitation are (obviously) an infringement on the right to personal freedom (Art. 2 section 2 GG). The German Constitutional Court (*Bundesverfassungsgericht*) has rightly stressed that a high quality of assessment is necessary to guarantee proportionality of state sanctions. If, for example, an offender is hospitalised due to a prognosis of serious future crime which is actually wrong (in other words: if we are dealing with a so-called 'false-positive' case, which is, according to several empirical studies, not a rare incident)[39], the measure of hospitalisation is in reality neither apt nor necessary (let alone appropriate) to contribute to the aim of prevention. In these constellations, it is very important that prognosis is not only based on intuition or subjective assessment by the judge but on professional experience by experts. The Constitutional Court spoke of an obligation for the courts to clarify the circumstances of a case 'as good as possible'.[40]

This is why the legislator (as a 'safeguard' in this respect) has regulated that expert opinions are mandatory in some of the earlier-mentioned cases, especially concerning the imposition or suspension of measures of rehabilitation and incapacitation (§§ 246a, 463 section 3 StPO) or the suspension of lifelong or long-term prison sentences (§ 454 section 2 StPO). For the assessment of culpability, a comparable provision is missing. But as mentioned above, courts tend to initiate expert opinions very frequently in this area as they are (as a rule) lacking psychological or psychiatric expertise; in doing so, they adhere to the earlier-mentioned principle of official investigation (§ 244 section 2 StPO). In some cases, forensic assessment is at least recommended by legal provisions or executive guidelines such as the earlier-mentioned RL-JGG within Juvenile Criminal Law (see e.g. § 43 Nr. 8 RL-JGG).

Given the high importance of the decisions in question (also from the perspective of constitutional law), there are surprisingly little legal provisions regarding the quality of assessments. Much is left to the discretion and personal attitudes of the judges on the one hand (based on the principle of free consideration of evidence, § 261 StPO) and the experts on the other hand. The judge (and before him the public prosecutor) can pick quite freely the expert they want to commission with the assessment (§ 73 StPO), even though this is a quite neuralgic decision for the future course and outcome of the procedure.[41]

The opinion of the defendant is irrelevant in this regard; as mentioned above he has no right to be examined by a particular person. The fact that he refuses to cooperate with the expert from the beginning has no direct impact on the court's decision.[42] However, the defense may urge the court to commission a second assessment by another evaluator (or take into account an assessment privately commissioned by the defence) if they can argue that the second evaluator will come to better results because of superior expertise or research methods[43] – this can (at least as an exception) also include cases where the defendant refuses to cooperate with the first evaluator, opening up the possibility of a better and more thorough assessment by another evaluator favoured by the defence.[44]

Art. 70 section 2 of the official guidelines for public prosecutors (*Richtlinien für das Straf- und Bußgeldverfahren, RiStBV*) regulates (as a recommendation) that prosecutors should grant defendants and their attorneys the right to express their opinion before choosing a particular evaluator. In practice, however, this is sometimes neglected.[45]

There are no explicit regulations concerning certain methods or instruments for the assessment or concerning the necessary content of the written or oral expert opinion used by the courts. The law only states that courts should somehow lead and supervise the assessment (§ 78 StPO), without naming relevant criteria. The German High Court (BGH) has stressed in various verdicts that it is the responsibility of the evaluator himself to decide upon the extent and the methods of exploration.[46] When it comes to crucial decisions (e.g. privileges for detainees within preventive detention or sexual and violent offenders), we can find some appeals by the legislator that the assessment has to be undertaken 'especially thoroughly' by the forensic expert (Art. 57 section 1 BaySvVollzG, see also Art. 15 BayStVollzG) – which is of course rather vague and questionable in terms of practical effects or judicial control.

What does exist (as a 'policy requirement' in a broad sense) are the earlier-mentioned so-called minimum requirements (*Mindestanforderungen*) for the assessment of culpability and the prognosis of future delinquency. Some of them had already been demanded by BGH,[47] for example the need for transparent and traceable assessment. More detailed requirements were compiled and published by a (private) group of psychiatrists, psychologists, legal practitioners and criminologists in 2005 and 2006 respectively.[48] Recently, a new and updated version of prognosis minimum requirements has been published, which have now been referred to as 'recommendations' (*Empfehlungen*).[49] The legal part of these recommendations deals with the various legal constellations and framework conditions in which a criminal prognostic assessment must be made and the course of proceedings from a legal perspective. An attempt is also made to provide guidance for the evaluation of an expert opinion.[50] The empirical part gives recommendations for information gathering, processing, critical evaluation and presentation of the results, in each case taking into account the respective legal aspects. Various methodological problems are presented and possibilities of approaches to pragmatic solutions to the current state of scientific knowledge are shown.[51]

It is fair to say that they are the most important safeguard for the quality of assessment that exists in Germany. The problem is that they are a mere professional recommendation that is not legally binding. And it is needless to say that compliance with formal standards and certain minimum requirements is (unavoidably) no guarantee for a high-quality assessment with regard to its content.[52] However, some High Courts (including the BGH) have started to use these requirements as a benchmark for the quality of forensic assessment and the way courts are dealing with it.[53] Another potential advantage for forensic experts is that compliance with these widely acknowledged requirements will most likely exempt them from criminal liability for negligent behaviour if a released offender commits a severe crime[54] as well as from possible civil law claims (§ 839a German Civil Code [*Bürgerliches Gesetzbuch, BGB*]).[55]

It is also worth mentioning in this context that a group of various psychiatric associations, led by the German Society for Neuroscientific Assessment (*Deutsche Gesellschaft für Neurowissenschaftliche Begutachtung, DGNB*), developed general guidelines for psychiatric and psychosomatic assessment, which were published by the Association of the Scientific Medical Societies in Germany (*Arbeitsgemeinschaft der Wissenschaftlichen Medizinischen Fachgesellschaften e.V.*).[56] The manuscript focuses on questions of social law but contains a number of generally valid statements and indications that can also be useful in the assessment of specific criminal law issues. The DGNB also offers a structured curriculum (and also acts in a commercial sense in this respect) and issues a certificate, which is widely recognised in social law contexts but is still hardly known in the area of criminal law.

7.3.2 Disciplinary and ethical requirements

As an ethical requirement, it is acknowledged (e.g. within the earlier-mentioned 're-commendations') that experts should inform the offender about the aim and possible consequences of the assessment and that it is not protected by doctor–patient confidentiality[57] (see supra) – which is more of a safeguard concerning rights of the offender, not directly the quality of the assessment. In order to avoid potential conflicts of interest, the therapists treating the patient should not, as a matter of principle, act as assessors in the same case.

7.3.3 Requirements for the evaluator

The law itself contains few explicit regulations concerning the person of the evaluator and his qualifications.

One example is § 74 StPO (in connection with § 24 StPO) which deals with possible biases of the evaluator due to circumstances like a personal relationship with the offender etc. The law aims at securing a neutral and objective assessment. A refusal of the evaluator based on § 74 StPO can be filed by the public prosecutor and the defendant. For (to some extent) similar reasons, the evaluator himself can refuse the assessment if he has a right to refuse to give evidence (§ 76 StPO). This is an exception to the general duty of forensic experts to accept judicial requests for assessment (§ 75 StPO).

An important field where some regulations on specific personal features of the evaluator do in fact exist is the question if hospitalisation in a psychiatric hospital should be continued (§ 67e StGB). According to § 463 section 4 s. 3 StPO, the evaluator must not have been involved in the treatment of the patient and must not have worked within the respective institution. Furthermore, he should not have been the last evaluator in this case. The law was introduced in 2016 as a result of the so-called 'Mollath' case, where (possible) judicial mistakes led to 7 years of hospitalisation for an offender whose mental disorder as well as his dangerousness remained doubtful.[58] In order to strengthen proportionality, the legislator implemented some constraints and safeguards, including the requirement that evaluators should change over the course of time and should be 'external' ones, that is not involved in the treatment of the person in question. The danger of personal involvement of the evaluator leading to biases should thus be avoided. Furthermore, it was regulated in § 463 section 4 s. 5 StPO that assessment should only be undertaken by medical or psychological experts with sufficient forensic-psychiatric expertise and experience, therefore excluding criminologists as potential evaluators.[59]

In general, forensic questions are mostly directed to forensic psychiatrists. Forensic psychiatrists have the broadest basic knowledge and are considered to be competent in medical, psychological and criminological questions. However, more and more questions are directed at psychologists, sex medicine experts, criminologists or even social pedagogues in rare special sub-questions. This development is based on the one hand on the lack of qualified doctors; on the other hand, psychologists have also developed appropriate forensic training curricula, and criminologists themselves have special empirical knowledge, for example. In this respect, it can make sense to combine different expert knowledge, for example in an alternating assignment of different experts. According to § 9 section 2 ThuG, assessments in the area of therapeutic hospitalisation 'shall' be undertaken by psychiatrists or (at least) have to be undertaken by medical doctors with experience in the field of psychiatry.

Another potential 'personal' safeguard is the fact that the evaluator has to do the assessment in person; he is not allowed to delegate this task to other persons without the consent of the initiator.[60] At the same time, the commission has to be addressed to certain persons and not entire institutions.[61]

Generally, there are no formal legal requirements regarding a special and documented expertise in forensic assessment. In order to remedy this deficiency and also to combat the corresponding abuses, professional associations have decided to take countermeasures. In this way, since 2000, the leading German professional association of psychiatrists (*Deutsche Gesellschaft für Psychiatrie, Psychotherapie, Psychosomatik und Nervenheilkunde, DGPPN*) has been offering a certificate for 'Forensic Psychiatry'. It is meant to establish certain professional standards for experts working in this field. A list of all certified experts is available on the website of DGPPN,[62] which was bound to be used as a source of information for public prosecutors and judges (but also defence lawyers,[63]) looking for evaluators. However, only about 200 assessors throughout Germany actually do have such a certificate. This number alone suggests that the list is of secondary importance in practice. Only much later than DGPPN did the official bodies of the medical associations of the German Federal states also develop a corresponding certificate, which is called 'focus' ('*Schwerpunkt*') and represents a further qualification for specialist training. The Bavarian State Medical Association ('*Bayerische Landesärztekammer*'), for example did not offer such a qualification measure until 2004.[64]

Speaking of professional qualifications, forensic psychiatrists and their professional associations have to struggle with worries concerning the next generation.[65] The training is long, difficult and elaborate. Among medical students, psychiatry is considered as being less attractive, as the earning potential is low and the stress is high. This situation is even more acute in the field of forensic psychiatry. Despite many efforts, for example on the part of the DGPPN, which organises training events such as the so-called 'Summer School' to get young psychiatrists interested in forensics, the response remains low. The path seems too laborious and full of responsibility.

Medical studies alone take at least six years, the training as a medical specialist another six years, the forensic specialisation requires another several years. It also takes a very long time to gain experience in the field: especially at the beginning, the preparation of an expert opinion is a very long and costly process, often months pass until the main hearing in court, and it is not possible to experience many such procedures in a short time.

The subject of forensic psychiatry is also of limited attractiveness from a scientific point of view: since the subject is strictly bound to the legislation of the respective country, publications are rarely of international interest and must be published in national journals. Epidemiological studies are difficult to conduct, one has to deal with special groups of persons (such as prisoners), which may only be researched under strict rules and regulations.[66] The essential and interesting questions such as criminal recidivism are methodologically difficult to research in view of rare events, small case numbers and necessarily long periods of time to be followed. This is why these specialist issues do not have high impact factors.

Forensic science is also unattractive for universities, which are increasingly in competition with each other in terms of impact factors and third-party funding, as the so-called 'excellence' universities are awarded and funded. Rapid success cannot be achieved. Chairs and professorships in forensic psychiatry will not be filled again.

On the other hand, forensic assessment requires many special skills and knowledge; among other things, because it is based on profound medical and psychiatric expertise, because it requires a high degree of linguistic accuracy and, last but not least, requires a paradigm shift between the different scientific disciplines, from the medical to the jurisprudential way of thinking. In 2015, the DGPPN therefore even felt compelled to publish a memorandum on strengthening and expanding forensic psychiatry at universities.[67] However, the calls went unheard and the situation has even worsened since then.

Despite the stated measures for quality assurance that have been undertaken in recent years, studies on the quality of expert opinions, for example with regard to the fulfilment of the formal and content-related minimum requirements described by the earlier-mentioned expert group[68] unfortunately show very heterogeneous and sometimes alarming results.[69] As a consequence, not least against the background of the changes in legislation in recent years, the gap between a growing need for qualified evaluators and their actual availability is widening.[70]

Probably not least due to the general lack of doctors and especially forensically qualified physicians, expert opinions in Germany will increasingly be provided by other, non-medical disciplines, such as psychologists or criminologists (for discussion see section 7.6), who were also much more strongly represented in the drafting of the 'recommendations' in 2019[71] than they were in 2006 when the 'minimum requirements' were created,[72] when only one legal psychologist was represented among the extended authorship.

7.3.4 Enforcement of requirements

As could be shown, there are but a few explicitly regulated 'hard' criteria concerning the quality of forensic assessment and – correspondingly – there is no elaborate system of strict control or enforcement of certain requirements. It is the responsibility of the court to convince itself that the evaluator has sufficient experience and expertise and that the assessment meets certain quality standards (which are not expressly regulated by law, as mentioned above). If the judge concludes that the assessment is not sufficient (or even deficient), which has to be explained,[73] he or she can either commission the same evaluator to make amendments and improvements or order another evaluator (see § 83 StPO).

If an expert opinion is commissioned by the Public Prosecutor (§ 161a StPO), the latter has to check as early as possible whether there are doubts concerning the competency of the evaluator and if in this case another evaluator should be commissioned (see 72 Nr. 4 RiStBV).

When the court comes to the conclusion that an assessment is practically worthless due to its deficiencies, the evaluator might lose at least parts of his claims for remuneration.[74]

7.4 Safeguards 'against' the limited quality of forensic assessment

7.4.1 Questioning the assessment by the defense

There are different ways for the defense to deal with (in their view) deficient assessment. First of all, in the course of the trial or even the preliminary proceedings, the defense (as well as the public prosecutor) can argue to the court that the assessment is deficient, for example because the evaluator is not competent in this field or maybe even because the earlier-mentioned 'minimum requirements' have not been met. The court has then to decide (according to § 244 section 4 StPO, which leaves room for judicial discretion) if it follows this opinion and commissions another assessment or not. The position of the defense is rather weak in this regard.[75] There are no formal rules concerning this type of complaint by the defense; according to the leading legal opinion (also among High Courts), a formal complaint

(*Beschwerde*, §§ 304 StPO et seqq.) against the choice of a certain expert is not possible as it is a mere preparatory decision prior to the judgement in the sense of § 305 StPO.[76]

If this way is not successful, another possibility for the defense is to commission a competing assessment or an assessment that critically evaluates the used methods (*methodenkritisches Gutachten*) on its own (and at its own expense). These so-called 'party assessments' (*Parteigutachten*) are not very popular among forensic experts, however: neutrality and objectivity are an issue,[77] and in the end, courts will tend to follow the other 'official' assessment anyway.

Apart from that the defense can of course appeal the legal decision as a whole, that is with the argument that it was based on a deficient assessment.[78] Financial matters are relevant as the defendant has to pay for the costs of litigation in case he is not successful with his appeal. Financial legal aid in a strict sense (*Prozesskostenhilfe*) does not exist in German criminal law (contrary to civil law), but in severe and complicated cases (like the ones where forensic assessment is regularly commissioned), the defendant has the right to an assigned counsel (*Pflichtverteidiger*) who is paid for by the state.

Private, non-judicial ways of complaining about possibly wrongful assessment do not exist, other than in the field of potential medical malpractice, where medical associations of the 16 German states have installed independent arbitration bodies (*Schiedsstellen/Gutachterkommissionen*) where patients can claim that they suffered harm by treatment errors.

7.4.2 Questioning the assessment by the court

It is the legal duty of the court to critically examine the qualification of the evaluator and the quality of the assessment. For that reason, the evaluator is obliged to disclose and explain his scientific approach, his methods and hypotheses to the court.[79] The depth and intensity of judicial examination, however, differs from court to court. The earlier-mentioned 'minimum requirements' are a helpful tool for the courts in this regard, even though their use is not mandatory and not all judges are actually aware of them. If the court has doubts and questions concerning the assessment, it will ask the evaluator to come up with amendments or a clarifying additional statement. The court may dismiss the expert opinion if the expertise of the evaluator is doubtful, if the opinion is based on false factual assumptions, if it is contradictory or if there is another expert with superior methods.[80]

A further possibility for the court is to order a special assessment that critically evaluates the methods used within a doubtful assessment. In principle, this seems like a good idea; in practice, however, this happens only rarely. One reason could be that the evaluator finds him- or herself in a particularly delicate position. His task is not only to take into consideration prior assessments (which is a standard element of every assessment) but to criticise the work of colleagues he might be personally involved.

The German High Court and the German Constitutional Court have stressed in various verdicts that it is a legal mistake (which leads to the annulment of the verdict) if the court just blindly follows the position of the forensic experts without showing that it critically examined the content of the assessment and thus came to its own conclusions.[81] As only the verdict and its content and not the assessment as such are the object of judicial revision, the verdict must contain a summary of the most important elements of the assessment.

To the best of our knowledge, there are no comprehensive statistical figures showing how often courts deviate from the results of forensic assessment. In our experience, deviation happens but is very much dependent on the question at stake. Some studies show that at least concerning the assessment of culpability, courts tend to follow the results of the assessment.[82] Practice shows that with other factors like the symptomatic connection (e.g. between addiction and offence; § 64 StGB), deviation from the expert's opinion happens more frequently, especially in cases where experts deny the connection whereas the courts deem the minimum requirements to be fulfilled.

7.4.3 Other questioning of the assessment

Special bodies that might interfere and challenge an assessment in single cases do not exist in Germany.

7.5 Safeguarding the quality of decision-making when confronted with disagreement between experts

7.5.1 Dealing with disagreement

We are not aware of any studies showing which decisions are the most controversial ones in Germany. But of course, both the question of culpability and the prognostic question of future delinquency are very crucial for the outcome of the trial. Therefore, in many of these cases, the defense at least tries to influence the assessment or (if they are not satisfied) will challenge it by means mentioned already in section 7.4.1.

As has been shown, generally there are no strict formal procedural rules dealing with matters of forensic assessment. This also relates to the question of dealing with a disagreement between different assessments. Also in this regard, it is very much up to the court's discretion how to deal with this situation. It may just follow one assessment and dismiss the other one, which has to be spelled out in the explanatory statement of the verdict.

Another possibility (which actually happens in practice) is the commissioning of a superordinate assessment (*Obergutachten*), regularly by experienced and renowned experts. These assessments are of course not legally binding for the court, which has to make up its mind on its own also in this regard.[83] And it is up to its discretion whether it considers such an assessment to be necessary or not. In the earlier-mentioned infamous "Mollath" case, the court expressly refused the commission of a superordinate assessment even though there was disagreement between forensic experts on the questions of culpability and dangerousness of Mr. Mollath.[84]

A further possibility is the order of an assessment that critically evaluates the methods used within disagreeing assessments, which happens rarely in practice, maybe also because of the reasons mentioned in section 7.4.2.

7.5.2 Best practices

In case of disagreement, a regular and approved measure are the earlier-mentioned superordinate assessment. But of course, even this method has its flaws: additional costs, a possible delay of proceedings and the question, if the superordinate assessment itself is of high quality, which again has to be answered by the judge in the end. Given the strong position of the courts in most of the earlier-mentioned decisions, it is obviously helpful (if not necessary) for the judges to possess psychiatric, psychological, and criminological knowledge. On this foundation, the judge him or herself is (ideally) competent enough to discriminate deficient assessments from ones with high quality and therefore to decide which assessment he accepts as a basis for his decision. What is needed (and would contribute to a 'best practice') in our eyes is a strong emphasis on measures of interdisciplinary education and advanced training for all professions involved, facilitating communication, and exchange between experts on both sides (see section 7.6).

7.6 Critical reflections

The starting point for a critical reflection is an awareness of the huge importance forensic assessment does have in the course of criminal proceedings. The decisions at stake here (like prison sentences or hospitalisation) bring about grave intrusions into the liberty rights of the affected person. Therefore, not least for reasons of constitutional law (including the principle of proportionality), a high-quality forensic assessment is of the utmost importance.

Against this background, it is surprising (and deplorable at the same time) that under German law, only quite a few explicit regulations exist concerning the area of forensic assessment in its concrete practical shape. There is only a broad legal framework leaving most crucial questions (When is an evaluation necessary? Who evaluates with which methods? How can deficient assessments be identified?) up to the discretion of the courts. Even taking into account that the formulation of general criteria on an abstract level is a hard task, this almost complete transfer of responsibility from the legislator to the judiciary is problematic and leaves unnecessary leeway for doubtful decisions and in addition for inequality and arbitrariness. A critical point in this regard is that the influence of forensic experts is not always the same: in practice, there exists every possibility, including the extreme positions, that the experts' assessments and the result of their forensic evaluation are adopted completely uncritically, unquestioned, and unchecked, or even that they are not considered at all. Both extremes can have very problematic consequences.

In recent years, there have been improvements in this regard. The German High Court has ruled several times that judges have to clarify within the reasoning of their verdicts why they came to their conclusions, neither blindly following nor completely neglecting the outcome of forensic assessment. In addition to that, German High Courts including the Constitutional Court have increasingly (and rightly) stressed the importance of forensic assessment and the need for certain minimum standards based on constitutional and criminal procedure law (see supra). Whereas the content of these verdicts remained quite general, more detailed 'minimum requirements' for the assessment of culpability and future delinquency have been compiled and published by an interdisciplinary group of leading experts joined together on their own initiative in 2005 and 2006 (see supra).[85] Whereas their content is widely acknowledged and has brought useful orientation for forensic experts and courts at the same time, their character as 'mere private', legally non-binding recommendations has been emphasised by critics. Recently, as mentioned earlier, a new version for prognostic assessment (partly in response to this criticism now entitled 'recommendations') has been published.[86] A step forward could be to somehow integrate these standards into the legal framework, for example by introducing a regulation where they are mentioned as a necessary point of reference.[87]

Another very important point in practice is the evaluator and his personal qualification. Even though it is self-evident and stressed by the High Courts that the forensic expert has to be sufficiently qualified, there are very few regulations where this is described more concretely (see e.g. § 463 section 4 s. 3; § 9 section 2 ThuG). Again, there is the problem of formulating abstract standards, but the legislator could (as a first step) at least explicitly regulate that the expert should have sufficient knowledge and experience in the respective area of assessment.[88] Another idea would be to regulate that experts with state-approved certificates by professional associations should, not exclusively, but primarily be commissioned – a comparable regulation exists for publicly appointed evaluators in § 73 section 2 StPO. Such a regulation would on the one hand stress the importance of qualification, but leave enough flexibility, on the other hand, taking into account that there is a huge lack of qualified evaluators.

In order to avoid one-sidedness and to guarantee a broad factual basis for the court's decision, a stronger involvement of experts from different disciplines (such as psychiatrists and psychologists[89] or criminologists[90] or professionals with special expertise in sexual medicine) or, in complicated cases, of experts from one discipline but with different approaches[91] should be considered. In our opinion, this would especially make sense in areas where a frequent assessment has to be undertaken (see e.g. § 67e StGB). The law should encourage or at least not impede 'diversification' of assessment in this sense (even if the earlier-mentioned qualification and capacity problem is a strong argument against binding rules in this regard).

A practical problem is the quite strong influence of the public prosecutor on the choice of experts (which are regularly accepted by the courts) together with a rather weak position of the defense in this regard. Going beyond the mere recommendation of 70 RiStBV, the defense should at least always get the chance to be heard before the expert is chosen (which can be a crucial decision concerning the outcome of the assessment). A draft proposal of the German Ministry of Justice in 2004 contained such a regulation but was dismissed in the end.[92] In addition to this minimum requirement, further efforts of reaching a consensus between public prosecutor, court, and defense should be discussed,[93] even though this is a complex matter: the acceptance of the evaluator by the defendant can obviously contribute to the quality of the assessment, not least because full cooperation of the defendant is more likely in these cases. On the other hand, it seems not to be possible to give the person concerned 'the power' to choose an expert, because this could also influence the procedure in a one-sided way. In this respect, the courts are – also understandably – adamant. In practice, the question is handled differently from court to court and region to region: some judges are open to proposals by the defense and an open discussion in this regard, while others insist on their strong and decisive position granted by § 73 StPO. According to reports by practitioners, a Bavarian court has developed the method of proposing three experts to the defence and let them choose one. Despite the fact that this practice grants them at least some power of co-decision, it has been criticised by defence lawyers that the circle of experts the court chooses from in the first place was rather small, so in the end, the court's influence remained quite strong.[94]

What remains as a general problem (despite all efforts by professional associations in recent years) is the earlier-mentioned lack of qualified experts that are largely based on structural problems (see supra). As long as this is the case, more and binding regulations aiming at a high-quality assessment by the legislator will not work in practice. What is strongly needed are more measures of education and advanced training,[95] starting at the universities. Forensic psychology, but even more so forensic psychiatry should be strongly promoted and made more attractive to students. After graduation, further advanced training should be offered. Since – as explained above – this is currently not recognised by the medical faculties or is counteracted by other constraints, a positive impulse by others, especially the law faculties, and the promotion of corresponding measures by politicians would be welcome.

A major problem both in gaining forensic experience and in assessing the quality of expert opinions is that the expert usually has no information about what has become of his opinion. As a rule, the expert leaves the hearing after his expert opinion has been rendered by the court. He learns nothing about the reception by the offender, the defence lawyer, the public prosecutor's office or the court itself. Nor does he usually obtain a copy of the judgement. He does not know what was adopted, critically discussed or rejected from his remarks.[96] If a verdict is appealed with reference to certain areas of assessment, it is not always clear (from the perspective of the evaluator) if the assessment itself or the way the judge made use of it is supposed to be wrongful. The central point of many forensic expert opinions is a statement on crime prediction. However, the expert rarely learns anything about the actual criminal recidivism of the concerned person. One reason for this is, of course, that such statements can only be made after many years. However, there is also no system that would give the expert feedback to confirm or refute his prognostic assessment. Only by chance does the expert learn about the further course and development of individual cases. Generally, most investigations and measures for quality assurance only refer to process or structural quality and not to the quality of results.[97]

Admittedly, the necessary quality check itself also poses a problem as formal criteria can be checked easily and quickly, whereas an assessment of content aspects already requires a thorough examination of the individual case in all its complexity. Nonetheless, the introduction of measures guaranteeing as much systematic feedback for evaluators as possible would be helpful. As hinted above, qualification measures should include an interdisciplinary approach.[98] This seems eminently important:[99] the process of successful interaction and communication between the professional groups is facilitated if the way of thinking, the procedure and the understanding of the role of the other position are at least to some extent known and consciously reflected upon. In medical studies, for example, legal basics are only briefly taught; it may take many years before the doctor is – consciously – confronted with legal issues in his practical work, and the little he learns is then long forgotten. So it can happen that a doctor may well be pressured or tempted, for example by a lawyer of his patient, to issue biased or even nonsensical certificates (such as for 'legal capacity' ['*Geschäftsfähigkeit*'] or others). For doctors, a role conflict is inherent in their work as consultants to a certain extent: they originally acquired their skills to heal. An assessment may well have a cathartic effect, but the primary purpose is different; at best, a diagnostic purpose is still a genuine medical activity. Medical science and law have very different terminologies and thought structures. But their socialisation is also completely different: among lawyers, a culture of dispute is cultivated and disputes are practiced and carried out. In contrast, people working in medical professions, especially psychiatrists, are more concerned with harmonisation and de-escalation.

The relationship between lawyers and doctors is not easy per se, and there is consideration of who is more afraid of whom. Both professions as such have a patriarchal understanding of roles, which can and must be questioned, and criticised, but which must also be brought to bear again and again in certain professional situations: both the judge and the doctor are required to take on a hierarchical position. For a physician, for example, it can already be very peculiar to find himself in the courtroom in a spatially subordinate position and then perceive that his explanations are not accepted at first, but are primarily completely put to the test. If, however, it is taken into consideration that the court bears the ultimate responsibility and must check everything for plausibility and comprehensibility and that, from the point of view of the defendant concerned, this represents his fundamental rights and that the procedure is an essential principle of the rule of law and should, as far as possible, protect against any arbitrariness, the internal logic and consistency becomes clear. This allows a different understanding and easier and better acceptance even if the court does not follow the expert's assessment.

For these reasons, forensic experts should have the necessary knowledge to understand the legal requirements (and boundaries) of their task. Vice versa, judges should have at least basic knowledge of forensic psychiatry, psychology, and criminology to enable them to critically examine forensic assessments (which is their legal duty anyway). Such advanced training could even be made mandatory for judges by changing the German Judges Act.[100] In our experience, both sides can (and actually do) benefit from interdisciplinary training; existing problems of communication[101] can thus be reduced. In our eyes, interdisciplinary intervision would be a very promising and maybe ideal way to overcome the problems described above: representatives of the different professions involved could meet outside of concrete criminal proceedings, could talk about their experiences and explain their views to the other side. In our opinion, it would be desirable to set up joint chairs for forensic psychiatry and law, which would deal intensively with the establishment of further education.

A German perspective 169

Of course, all measures proposed are no guarantee for a better quality of assessment in any single case. Formal requirements can be met, and still the assessment might be highly deficient. Mandatory training might be visited without an actual willingness of changing one's attitudes and professional habits. To put it in other words: like in other areas very much depends on the individual human beings and their subjective ethos, which can not directly be influenced by the legislator. What he can do is at least give a more detailed legal framework in order to restrict excessive judicial discretion – or, to put it more positively, to give more orientation and guidance to judges and forensic experts at the same time. As we tried to show, the German law and the forensic situation have some weaknesses in this regard and should be improved.

Notes

1 See also reference works for forensic psychiatry and/or history of medicine, such as Kröber et al., 2009; Müller and Nedopil, 2017; Groß, 2019.
2 See, for example Schneider, 2012.
3 For an overview, see for example Breuer, Endres, and Groß [2022]; Groß [in press].
4 Müller et al., 2017.
5 Schreiber and Rosenau, 2015a.
6 Other relevant decisions are a transfer to another measure (§ 67a StGB) or the execution of a measure before a prison sentence (§ 67 section 2 StGB).
7 Cf. Klosinski, 2008; Günter, 2015.
8 Cf. Günter, 2008.
9 Cf. Kaspar, 2007.
10 Müller-Isberner et al., 2015.
11 For example Stübner, Groß and Nedopil, 2006.
12 Steinböck, 2018.
13 Cf. several decisions of the German Constitutional Court, for example BVerfGE 70, 297; BVerfG, decision of August 26, 2013, 2 BvR 371/12 – NJW 2013, 3228, Mollath case.
14 See Günter, 2015.
15 See, for example BGH, decision of November 17, 1987, 1 StR 382/87.
16 See for example Schöch, 2007; Schreiber and Rosenau, 2015a.
17 Rasch, 1986.
18 Saß, 1985.
19 Boetticher et al., 2005.
20 Boetticher et al, 2019; Kröber et al., 2019.
21 For an overview see Groß, 2004; for German data see Harrendorf, 2007 and Jehle et al., 2016
22 Kröber et al., 2019.
23 For details see Seifert, 2015. In July 2022, the Federal Justice Department published a draft for a reform of § 64 StGB; the explicit aim is a stronger focus on offenders that seem to be not only in need of, but also "apt" for a successful therapy. The draft tries to clarify the connection between disorder and crime; furthermore, the possibility of release on probation after (only) half the time of the sentence has been served is about to be abolished in order to avoid an improper incentive for offenders and their lawyers to strive for a detention under § 64 StGB.
24 Rössner, 2015.
25 Müller and Nedopil, 2017.
26 Schreiber and Rosenau, 2015b.
27 Rössner, 2015.
28 Schreiber and Rosenau, 2015b.
29 Tondorf and Tondorf, 2011.
30 Boetticher et al. 2019 with references to several court rulings.
31 See, for example BGHSt 18, 375.
32 Habermeyer, 2015.
33 For the procedure of preparing the expert opinion see also Boetticher et al., 2005 and Kröber et al., 2019.

34 Schreiber and Rosenau, 2015b. Exceptions from this rule (e.g. cases where the expert will not be able to appear in court for a longer time) are regulated in § 251 StPO.
35 See, for example Rössner, 2015.
36 BGHSt 7, 239 et seqq; see also Schreiber and Rosenau, 2015a.
37 Saß, 2007.
38 Müller and Nedopil, 2017.
39 See, for example Müller, Haase and Stolpmann, 2013.
40 BVerfG, decision of August 26, 2013, 2 BvR 371/12 - NJW 2013, 3228, Mollath case; see also BVerfGE 70, 297, 308; Ahmed, 2017.
41 Konrad, Huchzermeier and Rasch, 2019; see also Rössner, 2015.
42 BGHSt 44, 26 et seqq.
43 Müller and Nedopil, 2017.
44 Ahmed, 2017.
45 Ahmed, 2017.
46 BGHSt 44, 26, 33; BGH NStZ 1999, 630.
47 BGHSt 49, 45.
48 Boetticher et al., 2005 and 2006.
49 Boetticher et al. 2019 and Kröber et al., 2019.
50 Boetticher et al., 2019.
51 Kröber et al., 2019.
52 Foerster and Dreßing, 2015; see also Konrad, 2010.
53 See, for example BGH, the decision of November 11, 2017, 2 StR 375/17.
54 Orlob, 2013 and Nedopil, 2018. For a recent case example of criminal liability, see Kaspar 2020.
55 See Gaidzik 2015.
56 AWMF, 2019.
57 Boetticher et al., 2005; Venzlaff et al., 2015; Müller and Nedopil, 2017; Konrad, Huchzermeier and Rasch, 2019; Kröber et al., 2019.
58 Kaspar, 2013; Kaspar and Schmidt, 2016.
59 Criticised by Brettel and Höffler, 2016.
60 Saß, 2007; BGH StV 2011, 709.
61 Schreiber and Rosenau, 2015b.
62 See https://www.dgppn.de/mitglieder/zertifzierungen/forensische-psychiatrie.html
63 See Tondorf andTondorf, 2011.
64 Orlob, 2013.
65 Müller and Nedopil, 2017.
66 WMA, 2018.
67 Briken et al., 2015.
68 Boetticher et al., 2005 and 2006.
69 Kury and Wertz, 2017; Prüter-Schwarte, Lutz and Kuhnert, 2019; Fiedler et al., 2019.
70 For example Stübner, 2015; Kaspar, 2013.
71 Boetticher et al., 2019; Kröber et al., 2019.
72 Boetticher et al., 2006.
73 Rössner, 2015.
74 BGH NStZ-RR 2006, 156 et seqq; Konrad, Huchzermeier and Rasch, 2019.
75 Tondorf and Tondorf, 2011.
76 Criticised by Ahmed, 2017.
77 Müller and Nedopil, 2017; Konrad, Huchzermeier and Rasch, 2019.
78 BGH StV 2003, 430; for details see Tondorf and Tondorf, 2011.
79 BGHSt 45, 178.
80 BGH NStZ 1999, 630 et seqq; Müller and Nedopil 2017.
81 BVerfGE 109, 133 – 2 BvR 2029/01; BGH, decision of January 27, 2016, 2 StR 314/15; for the assessment of witness credibility see BGHSt 45, 146 et seqq. See also Schreiber and Rosenau 2015a; Müller and Nedopil, 2017.
82 See, for example Verrel, 1995; for further references see Baltzer, 2013; from the perspective of the defence Ahmed, 2017.
83 Konrad et al., 2019.
84 See BVerfG, the decision of August 26, 2013, 2 BvR 371/12 margin no. 14.
85 Boetticher et al., 2005 and 2006.

86 Boetticher et al., 2019; Kröber et al., 2019.
87 Boetticher, 2018.
88 Boetticher, 2018.
89 See Rasch et al., 2019; BGHSt 50, 121, 129.
90 See Brettel and Höffler, 2016.
91 Schreiber and Rosenau, 2015a.
92 Rössner, 2015.
93 Schreiber and Rosenau, 2015b; Tondorf and Tondorf, 2011.
94 Ahmed, 2017.
95 Baltzer, 2013; Konrad, Huchzermeier and Rasch, 2019.
96 Wolf, 2017.
97 See also Habermeyer, 2017.
98 Tondorf and Tondorf, 2011.
99 As presented, for example in a lecture on the further training of lawyers Stübner, 2017.
100 Wolf, 2017.
101 See, for example Baltzer, 2013; Tondorf and Tondorf, 2011.

References

Ahmed, A. (2017). Sachverständige im Straf(verfahrens)recht. In: H. Pollähne, C. Lange-Joest C (Eds.), *Achtung: Begutachtung!*. Münster: LIT-Verlag, pp. 179–193.

Arbeitsgemeinschaft der Wissenschaftlichen Medizinischen Fachgesellschaften (AWMF) e.V. (2019). *Begutachtung psychischer und psychosomatischer Störungen.* Registernummer 051 – 029. Available at: https://www.awmf.org/leitlinien/detail/ll/051-029.html [Accessed on May 14, 2020].

Baltzer, U. (2013). Wie frei ist die Beweiswürdigung des Gerichts bei der Bewertung psychiatrisch-psychologischer Sachverständigengutachten. In: A. Dessecker, and W. Sohn (Eds.), *Rechtspsychologie, Kriminologie und Praxis.* Wiesbaden: Kriminologische Zentralstelle, pp. 15–30.

Boetticher, A., Nedopil, N., Bosinski, H., and Saß, H. (2005). Mindestanforderungen für Schuldfähigkeitsgutachten. *Neue Zeitschrift für Strafrecht*, 25(10), pp. 57–62.

Boetticher, A., Kröber, H.-L., Müller-Isberner, R., Müller-Metz, R., and Wolf, T. (2006). Mindestanforderungen für Prognosegutachten. *Neue Zeitschrift für Strafrecht*, 26(10), pp. 537–544.

Boetticher, A. (2018). Die Bedeutung von Mindeststandards für Schuldfähigkeits- und Prognosegutachten für die Strafjustiz. In: M. Dudeck, and F. Steger (Eds.), *Ethik in der Forensischen Psychiatrie und Psychotherapie.* Berlin: Medizinisch Wissenschaftliche Verlagsgesellschaft, pp. 35–43.

Boetticher, A., Koller, R., Böhm, B., Brettel, H., Dölling, D., Höffler, K., Müller-Metz, R., Pfister, W., Schneider, U., Schöch, H., and Wolf, T. (2019). Empfehlungen für Prognosegutachten. *Neue Zeitschrift für Strafrecht*, 39(10), pp. 553–573.

Brettel, H., and Höffler, K. (2016). Der aktuelle "Entwurf eines Gesetzes zur Novellierung des Rechts der Unterbringung" und seine Auswirkungen auf die Begutachtungspraxis. *Zeitschrift für Medizinstrafrecht*, 2, pp. 67–71.

Briken, P., Dudeck, M., Kröber, H.-L., Leygraf, N., Müller, J.L., Nedopil, N., Osterheider, M., Retz, W., and Rösler, M. (2015). *Memorandum: Stärkung und Ausbau der Forensischen Psychiatrie an den Universitäten!*. Available at: https://www.dgppn.de/_Resources/Persistent/57661cf836dbf6a3966c1dcc8e9e1f3245fea7fe/Memorandum_Universitaere_Forensischen_Psychiatrie.pdf [Accessed on May 11, 2020].

Endres, J. and Groß, G.(2022). Psychisch auffällige Gefangene. In: J. Endres, and S. Suhling (Eds.), *Behandlung im Strafvollzug. Ein Handbuch für Praxis und Wissenschaft.* Wiesbaden: Springer Verlag.

Fiedler, F., Steinböck, H., Yundina, E., Gros, J., and Stübner, S. (2019). Qualitätsmerkmale bei der Schuldfähigkeitsbegutachtung. Unpublished lecture held at 34th Münchner Herbsttagung der Arbeitsgemeinschaft für Methodik und Dokumentation in der Forensischen Psychiatrie (AGFP); *Abstract in: Forensische Psychiatrie und Psychotherapie, Werkstattschriften*, 26(3), pp. 330–332.

Foerster, K., and Dreßing, H. (2015). Aufgaben und Stellung des psychiatrischen Sachverständigen. In: U. Venzlaff, K. Foerster, H. Dreßing and E. Habermeyer (Eds.), *Psychiatrische Begutachtung* (6th ed.). München: Urban & Fischer, pp. 3–13.

Gaidzik, P. (2015). Haftungs- und strafrechtliche Verantwortung des Gutachters. In: U. Venzlaff, K. Foerster, H. Dreßing, and E. Habermeyer (Eds.), *Psychiatrische Begutachtung* (6th ed.). München: Urban & Fischer, pp.78–86.

Groß, G. (2004). Deliktbezogene Rezidivraten im internationalen Vergleich. http://deposit.ddb.de/cgi-bin/dokserv?idn=970628404

Groß, G. (2019). Psychiatrie in der Justizvollzugsanstalt. Lecture held at kbo-Isar-Amper-Klinikum, Haar bei München.

Groß, G. (2022). Psychopharmaka im Justizvollzug. In: J. Endres, and S. Suhling (eds.), *Behandlung im Strafvollzug. Ein Handbuch für Praxis und Wissenschaft.* Wiesbaden: Springer Verlag.

Günter, M. (2008). Der § 105 JGG: Entwicklungspsychologische Erkenntnisse und gutachterliche Praxis. *Forensische Psychiatrie, Psychologie, Kriminologie,* 2(3), pp. 169–179.

Günter, M. (2015). Strafrechtliche Begutachtung von Jugendlichen und Heranwachsenen. In: U. Venzlaff, K. Foerster, H. Dreßing, and E. Habermeyer (Eds.), *Psychiatrische Begutachtung* (6th ed.). München: Urban & Fischer, pp. 579–605.

Habermeyer, E. (2015). Die Begutachtung der Gefährlichkeitsprognose. In: U. Venzlaff, K. Foerster, H. Dreßing, and E. Habermeyer (Eds.), *Psychiatrische Begutachtung* (6th ed.). München: Urban & Fischer, pp. 413–426.

Habermeyer, E. (2017). Mindestanforderungen an psychiatrische und psychologische Gutachten. In: H. Pollähne, and C. Lange-Joest (Eds.), *Achtung: Begutachtung!*. Münster: LIT-Verlag, pp. 101–114.

Harrendorf, S. (2007). *Rückfälligkeit und kriminelle Karrieren von Gewalttätern.* Göttingen: Universitätsverlag Göttingen, Institut für Kriminalwissenschaften.

Jehle, J.-M., Albrecht, H.-J., Hohmann-Fricke, S., and Tetal, C. (2016). Legalbewährung nach strafrechtlichen Sanktionen. *Eine bundesweite Rückfalluntersuchung 2010 bis 2013 und 2004 bis 2013.* Berlin: Bundesministerium für Justiz und Verbraucherschutz.

Kaspar, J. (2007). Aussetzung und Erledigung der Unterbringung in einem psychiatrischen Krankenhaus nach §§ 67 b und d StGB. *Forensische Psychiatrie, Psychologie, Kriminologie,* 1(3), pp. 217–225.

Kaspar, J. (2013). Der Fall Mollath und die Folgen – zur Reform der Unterbringung in einem psychiatrischen Krankenhaus gem. § 63 StGB. In: M. Dudeck, J. Kaspar and M. Lindemann (Eds.), *Verantwortung und Zurechnung im Spiegel von Strafrecht und Psychiatrie,* pp. 103–134. Baden-Baden: Nomos.

Kaspar, J. (2020). Anmerkung zum Urteil des BGH vom 26.11.2019 2 StR 557/18, *Juristen Zeitung,* 75(19), pp. 955–964.

Kaspar, J., and Schmidt, P. (2016). Engere Grenzen nur in engen Grenzen – zur Novellierung des Rechts der Unterbringung gem. § 63 StGB. *Zeitschrift für Internationale Strafrechtsdogmatik,* 11(11), pp. 756–762.

Klosinski, G. (2008). Zu den Voraussetzungen des § 3 JGG aus jugendpsychiatrischer Sicht. *Forensische Psychiatrie, Psychologie, Kriminologie,* 2(3), pp. 162–168.

Konrad, N. (2010). Schlechtachten trotz Einhaltung der "Mindeststandards für Prognosegutachten". *Recht & Psychiatrie,* 30, pp. 30–32.

Konrad, N., Huchzermeier, C., and Rasch, W. (2019). *Forensische Psychiatrie und Psychotherapie* (5th ed.). Stuttgart: Kohlhammer.

Kröber H.-L., Dölling D., Leygraf N., and Saß H. (Eds.). (2009). *Handbuch der Forensischen Psychiatrie, Band 4 Kriminologie und Forensische Psychiatrie.* Darmstadt: Steinkopff Verlag.

Kröber, H.-L., Brettel, H., Rettenberger, M., and Stübner, S. (2019). Empfehlungen für Prognosegutachten: Erfahrungswissenschaftliche Empfehlungen für kriminalprognostische Gutachten. *Neue Zeitschrift für Strafrecht,* 39(10), pp. 574–579.

Kury, H., and Wertz, M. (2017). Zur Qualität forensisch-psychiatrischer und -psychologischer kriminalprognostischer Gutachten - Ergebnisse einer empirischen Untersuchung. In: H. Pollähne, and C. Lange-Joest (Eds.), *Achtung: Begutachtung!*. Berlin: LIT-Verlag, pp. 115–152.

Müller, J.L., Haase, K.A., and Stolpmann, G. (2013). Recidivism and characteristics of highly dangerous offenders being released from retrospectively imposed preventive detention: An empirical study. *Behavioral Sciences & The Law,* 31(3), pp. 359–380.

Müller, J.L., and Nedopil, N. (2017). *Forensische Psychiatrie* (5th ed.). Stuttgart: Thieme Verlag.

Müller, J.L. (2019). Ansätze zur Reform der Unterbringung in einer Entziehungsanstalt. *Forensische Psychiatrie, Psychologie und Kriminologie,* 13(3), pp. 262–271.

Müller, J.L., Saimeh, N., Briken, P., Eucker, S., Hoffmann, K., Koller, M., Wolf, T., Dudeck, M., Hartl, C., Jakovljevic, A.K., Klein, V., Knecht, G., Müller-Isberner, R., Muysers, J., Schiltz, K., Seifert, D., Simon, A., Steinböck, H., Stuckmann, W., Weissbeck, W., Wiesemann, C., and Zeidler, R. (2017). Standards for treatment in forensic committment according to § 63 and § 64 of the German criminal code: Interdisciplinary task force of the DGPPN. *Der Nervenarzt*, 88(1), pp. 1–29.

Müller-Isberner, R., Eucker, S., Rohner, A., and Eusterschulte, B. (2015). Unterbringung im Maßregelvollzug gem. § 63 StGB. In: U. Venzlaff, K. Foerster, H. Dreßing, and E. Habermeyer (Eds.), *Psychiatrische Begutachtung* (6th ed.). München: Urban & Fischer, pp. 363–387.

Nedopil, N. (2018). Qualitätssicherung und Mindestanforderungen (auch) als ethisches Desiderat. In: M. Dudeck, and F. Steger (Eds.), *Ethik in der Forensischen Psychiatrie und Psychotherapie*, pp. 27–34. Berlin: Medizinisch Wissenschaftliche Verlagsgesellschaft.

Orlob, S. (2013). Begutachtung im Maßregelvollzug. In: M. Dudeck, J. Kaspar, and M. Lindemann (Eds.), *Verantwortung und Zurechnung im Spiegel von Strafrecht und Psychiatrie*, pp. 39–72. Baden-Baden: Nomos.

Prüter-Schwarte, C., Lutz, M., and Kuhnert, H.-J. (2019). Die Qualität von Schuldfähigkeitsgutachten im Maßregelvollzug untergebrachter Patienten. *Der medizinische Sachverständige*, 115(5), pp. 203–209.

Rasch, W. (1986). *Forensische Psychiatrie*. Stuttgart: Kohlhammer.

Rössner, D. (2015). Strafprozessrecht. In: H.-L. Kröber, D. Dölling, N. Leygraf, and H. Saß (Eds.), *Handbuch der Forensischen Psychiatrie, Band 1: Strafrechtliche Grundlagen der Forensischen Psychiatrie*. Darmstadt: Steinkopff Verlag, pp. 379–423.

Saß, H. (1985). Ein psychopathologisches Referenzsystem zur Beurteilung der Schuldfähigkeit. *Forensia*, 6, pp. 33–43.

Saß, H. (2007). Grundlagen des Zusammenwirkens von Juristen und psychiatrischen/psychologischen Sachverständigen. In: H.-L. Kröber, D. Dölling, N. Leygraf, and H. Saß (Eds.), *Handbuch der Forensischen Psychiatrie, Band 1: Strafrechtliche Grundlagen der Forensischen Psychiatrie*. Darmstadt: Steinkopff Verlag, pp. 424–433.

Schiemann, A. (2019). Weg mit dem Schwachsinn – zur längst überfälligen Ersetzung der Begriffe "Schwachsinn" und "Abartigkeit" in § 20 StGB und der verpassten Chance einer umfassenden Reform der Schuldfähigkeitsfeststellung. *Kriminalpolitische Zeitschrift*, 4(6), pp. 338–346.

Schneider, F. ed. (2012). *Psychiatrie im Nationalsozialismus – Gedenken und Verantwortung. Psychiatry in National Socialism. Remembrance and Responsibility*. Berlin: Springer.

Schöch, H. (2007). Die Schuldfähigkeit. In: H.-L. Kröber, D. Dölling, N. Leygraf, and H. Saß (Eds.), *Handbuch der Forensischen Psychiatrie, Band 1: Strafrechtliche Grundlagen der Forensischen Psychiatrie*. Darmstadt: Steinkopff Verlag. pp. 92–158.

Schreiber, H.-L., and Rosenau, H. (2015a). Rechtliche Grundlagen der psychiatrischen Begutachtung. In: U. Venzlaff, K. Foerster, H. Dreßing, and E. Habermeyer (Eds.), *Psychiatrische Begutachtung* (6th ed.). München: Urban & Fischer, pp. 89–152.

Schreiber, H.-L., and Rosenau, H. (2015b). Auswahl und Hinzuziehung eines Sachverständigen. In: U. Venzlaff, K. Foerster, H. Dreßing, and E. Habermeyer (Eds.), *Psychiatrische Begutachtung* (6th ed.). München: Urban & Fischer, pp. 153–163.

Seifert, D. (2015). Unterbringung im Maßregelvollzug gem. § 64 StGB. In: U. Venzlaff, K. Foerster, H. Dreßing, and E. Habermeyer (Eds.), *Psychiatrische Begutachtung* (6th ed.). München: Urban & Fischer, pp. 389–403.

Steinböck, H. (2018). Vollzugslockerungen und Verhältnismäßigkeit. In: F. Schmidt-Quernheim, and T. Hax-Schoppenhorst (Eds.), *Praxisbuch Forensische Psychiatrie. Behandlung und ambulante Nachsorge im Maßregelvollzug* (3rd ed.). Bern: Hogrefe Verlag.

Stübner, S. (2015). Die Reformbemühungen im Bereich des § 63 StGB aus psychiatrischer Sicht. *Neue Kriminalpolitik*, 27(1), pp. 13–24.

Stübner, S. (2017). *Schuldunfähigkeitsbegutachtung* bei S. Stübner S and T. Kamm. Bayerisches Staatsministerium der Justiz. München: Fortbildungstagung für Richter und Staatsanwälte.

Stübner, S., Groß, G., and Nedopil, N. (2006). Inpatient treatment of mentally ill offenders: Results of a survey on clinical decision making about easing restrictions. *Criminal Behaviour & Mental Health*, 16(2), pp. 111–123.

Tondorf, G., and Tondorf, B. (2011). *Psychologische und Psychiatrische Sachverständige im Strafverfahren* (3rd ed.). Heidelberg: C.F.Müller.

Venzlaff, U., Foerster, K., Dreßing, H., and Habermeyer, E. (2015). *Psychiatrische Begutachtung* (6th ed.). München: Urban & Fischer.

Verrel, T. (1995). *Schuldfähigkeitsbegutachtung und Strafzumessung bei Tötungsdelikten.* München: Wilhelm Fink.

WMA (2018). *Declaration of Helsinki - Ethical Principles for Medical Research Involving Human Subjects.* Available at: https://www.wma.net/policies-post/wma-declaration-of-helsinki-ethical-principles-for-medical-research-involving-human-subjects/ [Accessed on May 12, 2020].

Wolf, T. (2017). Sachverständigengutachten im Straf- und Strafverfahrensrecht. In: H. Pollähne, and C. Lange-Joest (Eds.), *Achtung: Begutachtung!.* Münster: LIT-Verlag, pp. 153–177.

Chapter 8

A Swedish perspective

Tova Bennet, Malin Hildebrand Karlén, and Lena Wahlberg

8.1 Introduction

8.1.1 The legal system

The Swedish legal system belongs to the family of civil law and its primary source of law is statutory law. Preparatory works (in particular governmental bills) and precedents are important secondary sources, helping to interpret the meaning of the legal statutes. The judiciary system includes courts of different kinds. Criminal cases are decided by the general courts (district courts, courts of appeal, and the Supreme court), whereas cases concerning coercive mental health care are decided by the administrative courts (administrative courts, administrative courts of appeal, and the Supreme administrative court). In addition to the general and administrative courts, there is a number of specialised courts, including environmental courts and labour courts.

Not only legally qualified judges but also lay judges form part of the courts and participate in decisions on matters of both law and fact. Juries, however, are used only in cases concerning breach of the press law.[1] Expert judges occur in the special courts, but not in the general and administrative courts. The Swedish process is predominantly adversarial. As a main rule, the parties are responsible for presenting the evidence and the court for assessing its value. In some areas of law, however, the process displays certain inquisitorial elements. This is, for example, the case in criminal proceedings, where not only the parties but also the court can appoint experts to shed light on questions of fact. A scientific expert is supposed to state her opinion without taking a stance on matters of law.[2]

The standard of proof depends on the case and the matter at hand. In criminal cases, the defendant's guilt must be proven 'beyond reasonable doubt'.[3] With few exceptions, all evidence is admissible[4] and the court's evaluation of evidence is free, the main rule being that the court shall determine what has been proven in the case 'after evaluating everything that has occurred in accordance with the dictates of its conscience'.[5] The fact that the free evaluation of evidence is the governing principle means, among other things, that the court is not bound by an expert's opinion but shall make its own decision after having made an independent assessment of the opinion's evidentiary value.

Unlike many other jurisdictions, Swedish law does not recognise the insanity defense. Defendants who lacked the capacity to understand the nature of their actions are not considered legally insane or unaccountable. Instead, a defendant's mental state is considered at the sentencing stage, where inpatient psychiatric treatment (i.e. forensic psychiatric care) is available as a criminal sanction. The choice of sanction is made on the basis of forensic psychiatric expert assessment used as evidence by the court. Forensic psychiatric investigations (FPI) in Sweden are ordered by the court and thus merely intended to inform the

DOI: 10.4324/9781351266482-8

choice of sanction. However, apart from questions related to a court's choice of sanction, Sweden's principles of free admissibility and free evaluation of evidence allow for the consideration of FPI as evidence at other stages of a criminal trial. This means that courts can use reports by forensic psychiatric experts with respect to any legal issue which engages a defendant's mental state, for example when determining whether a defendant satisfies the *mens rea* of the crime charged.

8.1.2 The related tradition of forensic psychiatric investigation

8.1.2.1 The historic development of the law on defendants with a mental disorder

Under Swedish criminal law, individuals are considered legally responsible and liable for their intentional unlawful actions, regardless of their mental state at the time of the crime. The current Penal Code 'Brottsbalken' (BrB) took effect in 1965 and since then there has been no possibility of an acquittal on the basis of legal insanity in the Swedish criminal justice system. All defendants are treated as if sane and are subjected to the same evaluation of intent (*mens rea*). Prior to the introduction of the BrB, the previous Penal Code of 1864 (Strafflagen) included a distinction between an 'accountable' (sw. *tillräknelig*) and 'unaccountable' (sw. *otillräknelig*) defendant.[6] This concept of 'unaccountability', an equivalent to legal insanity in other jurisdictions, was abolished in 1965 when the BrB came into force.[7]

The reform drew from legal and political debates that were influenced by the 'positive school' of criminology and can be linked to Scandinavian legal realist ideas[8], as well as the major social and economic policy reform in Sweden from the 1930s onward, initiated by the social-democratic government.[9]

One of the main proponents of this reform was Olof Kinberg (1873–1960), the first professor of forensic psychiatry in Sweden. Kinberg referred to accountability as a metaphysical concept that should have little to do with the empirical institution that he thought the criminal justice system to be. Instead, scientific progress within the field of forensic psychiatry should be employed to explain and eventually 'cure' society of criminal behaviour.[10] According to Kinberg, psychological states of exception should only be considered when society chooses between its protective measures, in order for the latter to be as efficient as possible.[11] Not all of Kinbergs ideas were adopted. The BrB has been described as a compromise between 'treatmentist' ideas (i.e. to treat the individual to prevent risk for a future crime) of individual prevention and a 'classical' approach to criminal responsibility and proportionality between crime and sanction.[12] In the preparatory works of the 1962 Penal Code, it was stated that the most compelling argument against holding severely mentally disordered criminal offenders accountable was the belief that they should not be imprisoned. With the introduction of forensic psychiatric care as a penal sanction 1965, the practical need for distinguishing between the accountable and the unaccountable was no longer pressing.[13] Ivar Strahl (1899-1987), a professor of criminal law in Uppsala at the time, characterised the preparatory works as based on mainly humanitarian and practical, rather than philosophical, considerations.[14] The introduction of the BrB entailed that 'accountability' (i.e. legal sanity) as a requirement for criminal responsibility was removed. The mental states that comprised the definition of unaccountability (i.e. insanity) in the previous penal code were instead introduced in the regulation of sanctions, where such a mental state would trigger an imprisonment prohibition. With the introduction of the BrB, the sanction of forensic psychiatric care was also introduced as an alternative sanction for defendants diagnosed with a mental disorder.

8.1.2.2 Recent legal development with an impact on forensic psychiatric investigations

With the introduction of the BrB, the group of defendants that were exempted from punishment according to the former accountability standard was more comprehensive than today, for example, including states of drug-induced psychosis and a more liberal inclusion of personality disorders. Since 1965, the medico-legal concepts that delimit the group of offenders that are exempted from punishment have undergone three major changes.

First, in a legislative reform in 1992, the concept 'severe mental disorder' (SMD, sw. *allvarlig psykisk störning*) was introduced to replace the previous definition of mental states that invoked the imprisonment prohibition. The purpose of the reform was to narrow the group of defendants that were exempted from imprisonment, as well as harmonise all requirements for involuntary psychiatric treatment, within and outside of the criminal justice system.[15] The second change followed a dilemma that appeared in legal practice. In 1995, the Supreme Court tried a case that highlighted what has been described as a 'gap' in the Swedish model.[16] This case concerned a soldier who shot and killed seven people and injured three under the influence of an alcohol-induced psychotic state. The soldier was considered to have a severe mental disorder at the time of the offence but was found to have recovered by the time of the court hearing. According to the current regulation, the court was then prohibited from sentencing him to prison. At the same time, forensic psychiatric care was not an available sanction, since the soldier did not fulfil the requirement of a need for compulsory psychiatric care. As a result, the court was not able to sentence the soldier to any form of a custodial sentence. The Supreme Court solved the dilemma by ruling that the imprisonment prohibition did not apply to the soldier because his mental state at the time of the crime had been 'self-induced', and he was sentenced to life imprisonment.[17] Due to the fact that there was no explicit legal exception regarding voluntary intoxication, this solution required a re-interpretation of the concept of SMD to not include alcohol- and drug-induced psychosis. This interpretation was later made explicit in another Supreme Court case decided in 2001[18], where it was also clarified that temporary states of psychosis that were not self-induced were included in the definition of SMD.

The development of the concept of SMD can be understood in relation to what has been described as a 'neo-classical' turn in Swedish criminal law, where classical ideas are yet again taking precedence over individual prevention.[19] Part of this development is recurring criticism of the Swedish model, and several governmental enquiries have proposed a re-introduction of the insanity defense.[20] A few high-profile cases bringing attention to the above described 'gap' in the law, as well as a general move towards more focus on proportionality between crime and sanction, led to the third important reform in 2008.[21] With this reform, the imprisonment prohibition was delimited to offenders who due to an SMD 'lacked the capacity to understand the nature of the act or to act in accordance with such an understanding'.[22] The preparatory works state that the aim of the reform was to increase flexibility in sanctioning, and thereby increase the possibility of proportionality assessment in certain cases, while at the same time taking the defendant's need for treatment into account.[23]

The result of the reform is a presumption against, but not a prohibition of, sentencing defendants who committed a crime under the influence of SMD to imprisonment. It was however considered principally impossible to extend the possibility of imprisonment as a sanction also to 'the most severely mentally disordered offenders'.[24] A more narrow 'absolute' imprisonment prohibition was therefore introduced for these offenders that 'lacked the capacity to understand the nature of the act or to act in accordance with such an understanding'. This formulation is similar to common definitions of legal insanity and was indeed originally presented in a committee report in 2002 suggesting the very same formulation as a new definition of legal insanity.[25] The exemption is also explicitly intended to be interpreted in the same way as the proposed insanity standard but is still only relevant in relation to the choice of sanction.[26]

The new and limited imprisonment prohibition includes an explicit exception for self-induced states of SMD. The reform has thereby clarified that the concept of SMD now includes both temporary and self-induced mental states.[27] The reform also created a new task for forensic psychiatric experts who work with these investigations. The limited imprisonment prohibition requires that a distinction can be made between SMD and the 'the most severely mentally disordered offenders'. The former being essentially a delimited version of an insanity standard of the old penal code merged with prerequisites for involuntary psychiatric treatment in the administrative context, and the latter a new and further delimited equivalent of an insanity standard focusing on the capacity to understand the nature of one's actions and also the ability to control one's actions in accordance with such an understanding.

In summary, the medico-legal concepts that identify the defendants who are subject to exemptions have changed and developed in relation to both general policy changes and practical implications in legal cases. The current definitions of SMD and capacities respectively, are connected to ideas about criminal responsibility but are structurally formed mainly in relation to concerns regarding individual prevention. The latest reform of 2008 can be described to further blur the public interests and legal principles that form the foundation for both the legal and the forensic psychiatric assessment; the need for treatment, principles of criminal responsibility and sanction, and public protection. The tradition of forensic psychiatric investigations has been influenced by these legal changes. For information on the current state of forensic psychiatric assessment, see section 8.2.4.

8.2 Short overview of forensic psychiatric investigations in sentencing offenders

8.2.1 Sentences and execution

In the Swedish criminal justice system, forensic psychiatric expert evidence is mainly of relevance to the question of disposition, or choice of sanction. Contrary to most other jurisdictions, the legal assessment of criminal responsibility is restricted to establishing *mens rea* (criminal intent or negligence) in relation to an unlawful act (*actus reus*). Various grounds for justification and excuse are available, but there is no possibility of excuse on the grounds of legal insanity. If the defendant suffers from an SMD, this will instead be considered at the sanctioning stage, where a lack of capacity to understand and control one's actions accordingly limit the possibility of sentencing an offender to imprisonment. Then, coercive forensic psychiatric inpatient care is available as an alternative criminal sanction.

Notwithstanding the absence of a legal insanity doctrine, an FPI can play a crucial role in the sentencing decision. A defendant who suffers from an SMD may be sentenced to imprisonment only if there are extraordinary reasons to do so, which includes consideration of the defendant's need for psychiatric care.[28] According to the preparatory works, the notion of SMD refers to conditions of distorted perceptions of reality including, for example, dementia and severe depression.[29] If, due to the SMD, the defendant lacked the capacity to understand the nature of the act or to act in accordance with such an understanding, the person may be sentenced to imprisonment only if they themselves caused the inability (by, e.g. self-induced intoxication).[30] If imprisonment is not an available sanction, the defendant may instead be sentenced to forensic psychiatric care, provided that the person is in need of such coercive institutional care.[31] If the defendant committed the crime under the influence of the disorder, and if there is a risk that the person will relapse into criminality of a serious kind, the court may also prescribe a special discharge review.[32] These decisions are made by a general court, as part of the criminal trial. If, however, the general court prescribes a special discharge review, the risk of recidivism must be assessed by an administrative court before the person can be discharged from forensic psychiatric care. With the exception of the Supreme court and the Supreme administrative court, both legally qualified and lay judges participate in the proceedings in general and administrative courts. However, no expert judges take part in these decisions. Expert knowledge must instead be imported from, and communicated to the court by, external experts.

When no special discharge review is prescribed, the defendant may be sentenced to forensic psychiatric care after having been examined by a specifically assigned physician.[33] The court may, however, order an FPI to assist in the assessment of whether the defendant meets the conditions for forensic psychiatric care. An FPI is a comprehensive assessment, involving the joint participation of experts from several professional disciplines (see section 2.4) and is compulsory if the defendant is to be sentenced to forensic psychiatric care with a special discharge review.[34]

Questions about whether the defendant suffers from an SMD and whether the person had an ability to understand the meaning of the act/control her action accordingly are distinct from the question about the defendant's criminal intent, or *mens rea*. The existence of an SMD does not exclude either intention or negligence. Perhaps surprisingly, criminal intent is not even ruled out by the defendant's inability to comprehend the meaning of the act (at least not in theory – for example the defendant's delusional belief that the person they attacked was a hostile spy does not exclude a criminal intent to harm that person).[35] Even so, questions about *mens rea* are closely related to questions about whether the defendant suffers from an SMD and whether they had an ability to understand the meaning of the act. Specifically, the intent is said to require that the offender was conscious, or aware, of what he/she doing, which – like SMD and ability to understand – is a question about mental state.[36]

When the court orders the FPI, it can ask the experts whether the defendant a) committed the act under the influence of SMD, b) whether they lacked the capacity to understand the meaning of their actions, and c) were capable to act in accordance with such an understanding.[37] Although these questions do not directly address the defendant's *mens rea*, the answers to them can be of relevance in determining whether the defendant had the *mens rea* required for the crime charged and the courts are, due to the principles of evaluation of evidence, free to use the forensic information in any part of the legal assessment.[38] In our discussion on quality challenges and safeguards in Swedish law, we will focus on the question whether the defendant suffers from an SMD, and touch upon the other questions in passing.

The expert's task within FPIs in the Swedish justice system is hence both similar and different compared to that of most other jurisdictions. The similarities concern the task to evaluate the defendant's mental state and capacities at the time of the crime, as well as assessing the need for treatment and risk for recidivism at the time of the FPI. The differences are related to the legal and practical implications of the outcome of the assessment, and a somewhat ambiguous legal construction where a conclusion equivalent to that of legal insanity in other jurisdictions is of relevance only to the choice of sanction and, at least in theory, not a factor in determining criminal responsibility.

For persons over the age of 15 (i.e. reached the age of criminal responsibility), the law is the same as for adults when it comes to forensic psychiatric care. In Sweden, it is a very rare occurrence to conduct an FPI with a person aged 15–18, but it does happen and then almost always for crimes that include deadly violence. There are no special forensic psychiatric care units for young persons, so when young persons are sentenced to forensic psychiatric care by the court, they receive forensic psychiatric care among adults. Young persons (below 21 years of age) who have undergone FPI, but whose psychological function has not been deemed in line with SMD, can be sentenced to secure youth care.

8.2.2 Decisions within sentencing and execution

Forensic psychiatric investigations are conducted by experts at the National Board of Forensic Medicine and used by the general courts to aid in their decision regarding sentencing a person to prison or to forensic psychiatric care. When a person has been given a lifetime prison sentence, they can apply to the court to have the remaining time decided but to do this, a forensic psychiatric risk assessment is conducted by experts at the National Board of Forensic Medicine to inform the court's decision regarding the risk of recidivism. When a person has been sentenced to forensic psychiatric care (with a special discharge review), the administrative court decides whether to grant the person's application for permissions outside the hospital or to terminate the forensic psychiatric care. For these decisions, the psychiatrist responsible for the person's forensic psychiatric care gives their opinion on the request, principally regarding the risk of recidivism. If the person was sentenced to forensic psychiatric care without a special discharge review, it is the psychiatrist responsible for the person's treatment alone who decides these issues (i.e. the administrative court is not involved in this decision).

8.2.3 Concepts to be assessed

8.2.3.1 Severe mental disorder: A discussion

As seen above, several legal decisions depend on the possibility to determine whether the defendant had and/or has an SMD. The evaluation of SMD is based on a balanced evaluation of several different factors that together result in the decision of whether a person's psychological state may be said to be in line with how the concept of SMD is construed in Swedish law. According to The National Board of Health and Welfare (Socialstyrelsen), a government agency under the Ministry of Health and Social Affairs SMD is primarily a state of psychotic nature, meaning psychological states with a disrupted reality monitoring and symptoms such as delusions, hallucinations and confusion.[39] Also, severe depression with suicidal thoughts disrupted the ability to orient him/herself due to cerebral injury. Personality syndromes, dementia, crisis reactions, developmental disorders (e.g. autism spectrum disorder) may also be considered SMD depending on how severe the person's reality monitoring is disrupted by this mental state. Kleptomania and pyromania with a strong compulsive aspect, sexual perversions (e.g. genuine paedophilia and sexual sadism), as well as psychic disorders with extremely odd thought content and/or very low psychosocial functioning, may in some cases (but relatively rarely) be considered as SMD.

The presence of SMD is decided both on the basis of the type of disorder and its degree. Some disorders are always considered severe as a type (e.g. schizophrenia) but need not be severe in its present degree, while for example autism spectrum disorder need not be severe regarding the type of disorder but can be severe due to its degree. In addition to the definition of SMD formulated by the National Board of Health and Welfare, the National Board of Forensic Medicine relies on regulations and guidelines[40] and preparatory documents[41] regarding psychiatric compulsory care to consider in their evaluation of whether a state is to be considered in line with the judicial concept SMD. Nevertheless, SMD is ultimately a legal concept, and the final assessment is made by the courts, in relation to how the concept is defined in preparatory works and in precedent cases.[42]

The concordance between this definition of SMD and different mental states in terms of diagnoses are easier in some cases than in others. Hence, as is implicitly outlined in praxis, it is probably easier to define SMD by what psychological state it should correspond to than to try to define it through lists of diagnostic terms for different mental states which in their inherent definitions correspond to different degrees of mental disorder severity. The states which often are considered SMD, and which could be considered SMD, are most difficult to create clear guidelines and definitions for (i.e. since exceptions may apply in the individual case). The Government Bill 1990/91:58 states that 'it is not possible to through a list or in another way in legal text state more precisely which psychological states that could indicate forensic care. (…). In an interpretation [of the SMD-concept, the clinician] is referred to certain precedents and to the evolving praxis'. Hence, identification of these conditions requires a considerable clinical experience and expertise within the field as well as constantly keeping oneself updated with evolving diagnostic research and with societal and governmental changes in attitudes in the care vs. imprisonment question.

As indicated by the argument above, the diagnostic definition of SMD is based on linguistic issues in the current diagnostic praxis since SMD requires that the diagnosis used to determine SMD in a specific case needs to capture how the loss of reality (of uncertain temporal extension) outside the afflicted person's own willful control is applicable within the unique circumstances of the case. This has been proven to be more straightforward for certain psychiatric diagnoses which by their symptomatic and/or phenomenological definition entail such states, but harder for other diagnoses. Consensus between FPI experts regarding SMD seems to be considerably larger when the diagnoses that by definition incorporate psychotic states were applicable, but more variable when it concerned diagnoses which do not automatically entail this, such as borderline personality disorder.[43] Therefore, regarding the diagnoses where consensus is lower, the FPI expert needs to consider the aspects of the situation at the time of the crime and its interaction with the person's characteristics as well as the nature of his/her mental disorder more closely.

However, since the type of disorder (here: diagnosis) is not specified but the degree of loss of reality has to be substantial, the degree of mental disorder takes precedent over type. That some types of disorders (e.g. psychoses) are more frequently represented than others merely reflect that their structure more often incorporates a more severely thought disturbed state than other types (e.g. phobia). To illustrate this point further, loss of reality monitoring is not a criterion for diagnosing depression, still severe depression may evolve into a state where reality monitoring is lost and may constitute an SMD.

Only for a very small proportion of persons with clinically relevant psychiatric symptomatology, their type and degree of 'thought disturbance' are so profound that it can be considered SMD. This is in line with current research on psychopathology in general (e.g. the HiTOP model) which emphasises the view of psychic disturbance on a continuum from 'no thought disturbance' to 'profound thought disturbance', and as the degree of disturbance increases, the more diagnostic labels are likely to be considered to match a person's different psychiatric symptoms.[44] Based on statements within the more operationally oriented guiding documents created by the National Board of Forensic Medicine, it is indicated that both type, degree and functional impact of the psychic disturbance are important to consider within the evaluation, but as previously mentioned (and indicated by the preparatory works), degree of lack of insight is more important than in what diagnostic 'form'/type this lack of insight comes. In light of the present research which states that this dimensional perspective on psychopathology is a more accurate characterisation of the nature of the psychiatric

182 Tova Bennet et al.

disorder (and the importance of a case-by-case evaluation based on research evidence/best practice), the definition of psychiatric disorder and how it should be operationalised that is used within the National Board of Forensic Medicine in Sweden can be considered to be an evidence-based practice on a both theoretical and praxis level.

8.2.3.2 The distance/proximity between forensic psychiatric investigations and legal concept

To provide legally relevant information in a specific case, the forensic psychiatric experts responsible for the assessment must know which of the questions that the court wants to be answered. Swedish law requires the court to state reasons for investigation,[45] and lists questions that an FPI generally must address.[46] These questions include, for example, whether the defendant suffers from an SMD, lacked the capacity to understand the nature of the act, or to act in accordance with such an understanding, and whether the person is considered at risk of relapsing into serious criminal behaviour. For a person to be sentenced to forensic psychiatric care, a criterion is also that the person should be considered to be in need of psychiatric treatment that cannot be given in any other manner than through forensic psychiatric care. Clearly, an experienced FPI expert will be accustomed to these questions. However, the meaning of these questions is not straightforward but depends on the meaning of the legal terms that they make use of. As noted in the discussion of the SMD concept above, these terms often allow different interpretations. There is no unequivocal definition of the important notions of a 'severe mental disorder' or 'ability to understand'. The government bill from 1990 provides examples of some conditions, such as dementia and serious depression, that *can* constitute serious mental disorders and mentions the importance of a distorted reality monitoring as a common denominator.[47] The government bill from 2007, however, rather links the notion to the patient's need for care (which fits well with the abolition of the imprisonment prohibition proposed in the latter bill).[48] As pointed out by Malmgren et al., in clinical psychiatry, the term 'severe' is instead associated with factors such as bad prognosis, grave difficulties in daily living, great discomfort, etc.[49] Hence, there is no guarantee that the forensic psychiatric experts will interpret this term in its proper legal sense. On the contrary, there are indications that the interpretation of the notion in psychiatry and forensic social work is affected by theoretical and practical considerations of relevance in these disciplines.[50] Deferring the interpretation of the legal notion to the FPI experts is problematic, however, since it potentially gives the investigators the role of deciding when, and on what grounds, a person should be sent to prison, which clearly is a question for lawmakers and courts. As long as the law and the court do not define the precise legal meaning of the notion, this is nevertheless an inevitable consequence, since those who apply the notion must use some interpretation of it. An analogous problem concerns the level of certainty required for reaching the conclusion that a person suffers from an SMD. It is only natural that this depends on the FPI expert's opinion on whether it can be considered worse to conclude that someone who does not suffer from an SMD does suffer from an SMD (i.e. false-positive/Type I error), or vice versa (false-negative/Type II error). The problem, however, is that the question of how to deal with the uncertainty relating to this question is a legal matter, which ought to be handled by legal standards dealing with uncertainty.

There is therefore a significant risk that the FPI, instead of helping the court to answer the legal question 'Is it shown [according to legal standards] that the defendant suffers from an SMD [in a legal sense]', provides an answer to the question 'Is it shown [according to the forensic investigators' standard] that the defendant suffers from an SMD [in the forensic psychiatric expert's sense]'.[51] This kind of error, *to provide the right answer but to the wrong question*, is sometimes referred to as a Type III error, and is particularly likely in the communication across disciplines, where the same terms can have different meanings. The risk for Type III errors is general and does not arise only in relation to the notion of SMD. Consider, to take another example, the notion of 'consciousness', which, as we have seen, is relevant for assessing whether the defendant acted with legally relevant intent. Case law provides clear examples of how FPI experts have interpreted the notion of consciousness differently from the legal judges. Some judges, who have noticed the discrepancy in interpretation have rejected the experts' interpretation and disregarded their conclusions in this respect, whereas others seemingly have let a discrepancy between the traditional legal interpretation and the suggested psychiatric interpretation in the case in question to pass unnoticed.[52]

Another example concerns the evaluation of the defendant's capacity to understand and control the meaning of their act, an evaluation that is perhaps the least straightforward one from the medical perspective. This assessment is often presented in terms of factors that speak for the defendant having the relevant capacity, and factors that speak against the defendant having capacity. In some, but not all, reports, a conclusion is also presented.[53] Although a presentation in terms of reasons for and against, accompanied by a conclusion might be perceived as an ideal basis for the legal evaluations, several problems can still arise in the communication between the two disciplines. It can be difficult for the court to ascertain how the reasons presented differ in (medical) importance and how the conclusion follows from the reasons presented. Discrepancies in how the notion of 'capacity to understand' is interpreted might become more visible when the reasons for the conclusion are elaborated, but it might still be difficult for the court to challenge the medical assessment if a specific conclusion is presented. Furthermore, regarding this specific example, the legal question is not to what extent the defendant had capacity, but whether the defendant lacked capacity or not. However, the medical conclusion presented is often that the defendant had a limited, or reduced, capacity, a conclusion that might be difficult to translate into the legal context.[54]

The obvious solution to the risk for Type III errors is a transparent communication, where the court provides a clear definition of the questions that it asks, and the investigators state the reasons for the answers they give. In the sections that follow, we will return to this important point.

8.2.4 Forensic assessment and procedure

In Sweden, the praxis of performing some kind of FPI has a history dating back to the early twentieth century, but it was in 1946, that forensic psychiatry was established as a medical specialty and FPIs were then performed at specifically assigned investigative units. Today, all FPIs are court-ordered, and have been performed by the National Board of Forensic Medicine, a branch of the Ministry of Justice, since 1992.[55] The Board is organised in three departments and one headquarter. The three departments are forensic medicine, forensic psychiatry and forensic genetics/chemistry. The department of forensic psychiatry conducts all forensic psychiatric evaluations by order of the court, normally at either of the department's two evaluation centres. There are two forms of evaluations the court can order, a short assessment termed §7-evaluation (the type most frequently used by the court) and a comprehensive assessment termed FPI. For the persons who undergo an FPI, almost all have first been through the short assessment. The short assessment, §7-evaluation, is conducted in almost all cases where the court requires aid from forensic psychiatric expertise. This initial assessment is made only by a forensic psychiatrist (or a psychiatrist trained by the National Board of Forensic Medicine) and consists of a medical evaluation, most often based on a medical examination, a clinical interview, and often clinical records, criminal record and other relevant documents if available. Approximately 1200 §7-evaluations, and 450–500 comprehensive evaluations are conducted each year, and 200–300 offenders per year are recommended for forensic psychiatric care.[56] The comprehensive FPI is conducted if the result of the §7-evaluation is inconclusive, if it is not considered sufficient to make a reliable assessment, or if the court for some other reason has not requested a §7-evaluation. As previously mentioned, a comprehensive FPI is always required for a sanction of forensic psychiatric care with a special discharge review. The court can ask for a FPI in cases where it has been decided by the court that there is convincing evidence that the act was committed by the defendant, or in some instances, based on the defendant's confession of having committed the act. Moreover, the FPI can only be ordered in cases where a custodial sanction can be expected. The FPI is typically made over a period of four weeks by a multidisciplinary team that includes a specialist in forensic psychiatry, a forensic psychologist, a forensic social worker, and a representative of the staff from the psychiatric ward where the person stays during the general four-week period of FPI. Most defendants (approximately 75%) are in custody and evaluated according to this praxis (i.e. as inpatients), and the remaining group are evaluated as outpatients who visit the evaluation centre (typically during two full days, but this can vary due to the complexity of the case). The FPI results in a report consisting of a separate written assessment from each of the professionals within the assessment team, as well as a summarising report written by the forensic psychiatrist within the assessment team who is the person with overall responsibility for the FPI. All this material is handed over to the court, covering a medical, psychological, and social assessment of, and answer to, the questions posed by the court. The conclusions from the report are presented during the successive proceeding where the sentence is to be decided. If the court considers it necessary, the court can order any of the experts that have been involved in the person's FPI team (but most often the forensic psychiatrist responsible for the FPI) to attend the proceeding and further explain their conclusions.

The central aim of the FPI in Sweden is to provide a basis for the court's decision on whether a defendant should be sentenced to imprisonment or forensic psychiatric care.[57] Forensic psychiatric care as a sanction is available only if the defendant has an SMD and is in need of involuntary inpatient psychiatric care.[58] The sanction is indefinite, and can be combined with a requirement for a special discharge review if it is established that there is a 'risk of relapse into severe criminality'. If the defendant has committed a crime under the influence of an SMD, there is a presumption against imprisonment as a sanction. This presumption is rebuttable if there are 'extraordinary' reasons, which mainly refer to situations where a serious crime has been committed under the influence of a temporary SMD that is no longer present at the time of the evaluation. There is however an 'absolute' imprisonment prohibition in cases where defendants, due to an SMD, 'lacked the capacity to understand the nature of the act or to act in accordance with such an understanding'. In such a case, the defendant can be convicted of an intentional crime, but imprisonment is never an available sanction.

The questions that are the subject of the forensic psychiatric evaluation are the following:[59]

1 Does the defendant have a severe mental disorder?
2 Are the medical prerequisites for involuntary psychiatric inpatient care (regarding the defendant's 'mental condition and personal circumstances') satisfied?
3 Is there a risk of relapse into severe criminality?
4 Was the act committed under the influence of a severe mental disorder?
5 Did the defendant, due to a severe mental disorder, 'lack the capacity to understand the nature of the act or to act in accordance with such an understanding'?
6 Did the defendant, through self-induced intoxication or in any other similar way, cause the severe mental disorder or the lack of capacity?

Questions 1–2 determine the possibility to sentence the defendant to forensic psychiatric care, question 3 determines whether a special discharge review can be prescribed (for which positive answers to questions 1–4 also are necessary pre-conditions), and questions 4–5 determine whether the imprisonment prohibition applies.

To diagnose a psychiatric disorder (a medical concept) and evaluate SMD (a judicial concept) are both often complex procedures which requires much training, including comprehensive supervision by experienced clinicians, in both areas. As Anckarsäter et al. (2009) state based on Robert Cloninger's (1999) research, 'none of the commonly used mental disorder categories has yet been identified as a taxon that is clearly delineated from the normal variation or from other disorders'. Except for rare neurological disorders, a specific aetiology for mental disorder, and diagnostic methods to establish the presence of mental disorder other than clinical interviews, assessment of behaviour and/or self-reported lifetime symptoms is generally not present, or productive, in a substantial amount of cases. Hence, to be able to evaluate the presence of SMD, the principal methods used in assessment of mental state and functioning at the time of the crime and the FPI through considering, for example, archival information, cognitive tests, medical tests and self-reports in many different areas of life.

8.3 Safeguards for the quality of forensic psychiatric assessment

8.3.1 Requirements in law and policy

In addition to evaluating whether the person's mental state has been in accordance with the concept of SMD, risk assessments of relapse in serious criminality are one of the court-ordered questions that Swedish FPIs most often include. Swedish law requires that the assessment of whether there is a risk that the defendant will relapse into criminality of a serious kind must be made using a structured method based on science and proven experience.[60] 'Science and proven experience' is a poorly defined but frequently used standard in Swedish regulations concerning the medical professions. The standard, which has been part of the Swedish regulation of healthcare since the 1890s, is sometimes interpreted as a blunt reference to actual medical practice (i.e. to what doctors and other medical professionals normally do.) However, and as some of us have argued elsewhere,[61] we think that the standard is better interpreted as a requirement that medical decision-making (e.g. diagnoses and treatment decisions) be based on sufficient evidence (including not only scientific evidence but also evidence stemming from clinical practice).[62] According to this interpretation, what qualifies as 'sufficient' evidence depends on what is at stake in the particular decision, and can eventually become a question for a court to decide. The Swedish notion of 'science and proven experience' is hence kindred but not identical to the concepts of 'scientific evidence' and 'clinical expertise' in evidence-based medicine (the EBM model and related models).[63]

The overview of the risk assessment literature presented in chapter 2 of this book, makes it clear that there are substantial gaps in the scientific evidence pertaining to questions of mental state and recidivism that are relevant to sentencing. In Sweden, a systematic review published 2005 by the Swedish Agency for Health Technology Assessment and Assessment of Social Services Sweden, concluded that the best psychiatric risk assessments can predict the risk for recidivism with a probability of 25% for false positives and 30% for false negatives.[64] As is well known, group heterogeneity poses a serious threat to the possibility of making adequate assessments of individuals.[65] According to the report, there is no evidence that current risk assessment methods give reliable results for women.[66]

It is a general legal requirement that medical reports be clear and simple, and that the meaning of terms that are not generally known is explained. The law requires that an FPI accounts for circumstances that complicate the assessment,[67] and, more generally, that health care workers issuing a certificate or a report must not make statements on matters on which they do not have sufficient knowledge. For these requirements to be met, however, it must be observed by the investigators that the terms used in their own disciplines need not have the same meaning in law and that the standards of proof to be used in a legal setting differ from those used in medicine and other non-legal disciplines. There is an obvious risk that these differences, as it were, get lost in translation, which could result in a false agreement on what are the matters actually at stake.

8.3.2 Disciplinary and ethical requirements

8.3.2.1 Safeguards against the difference between psychological and legal concepts

The problems relating to how conceptual uncertainty and heteronymous terms can hamper the forensic psychiatric expert's understanding of the court's questions are mirrored in the courts' understanding of the FPI report. Thus, if the same terms are used in the FPI report as in the questions posed by the court, but means something else in the assessment than in the law, there is a real risk that the court will not fully grasp the meaning of the assessment and that the judgement will be based on the forensic experts' interpretation and value judgements. As already mentioned, there are examples in the case-law of how courts have indeed observed such differences in how the SMD concept is interpreted, but also many cases in which the potential differences in interpretation seem to have passed unnoticed.

Clearly, the same term can have different meanings in, say, psychiatry and social work too, but problems relating to different conceptual apparatuses that arise within the FPI are at least partly mitigated by a legal requirement that two of the three professions that are part of the FPI team (the clinical psychologists and forensic social workers) clarify the reasons for and against their particular conclusion regarding the court's questions. These requirements are stated in the regulation on FPI issued by the National Board of Forensic Medicine.[68] This regulation contains no corresponding requirement to state the reasons for and against the conclusions presented in the FPI report.[69] However, in a regulation on healthcare certificates, which is issued by the National Board of Health and Welfare, and only partly binding on FPIs it is stated that such certificates shall make clear not only what circumstances and information the assessment is based on, but also on what ways the information supports the assessment and conclusions.[70]

8.3.2.2 Awareness of common biases and consequential safeguards

First, the internal quality of the FPI depends not only on the certainty of the available scientific and/or clinical evidence, but also on whether the conditions under which the defendant has been observed are representative, and on whether the investigators have made an adequate assessment given the observation and evidence at hand. Second, the proximity between the information provided by the FPI and the questions that the court wants to be answered depends on whether it is clear to the investigators what the court wants to know and whether an FPI can answer the court's questions. Third, and finally, the court's capacity to make proper use of the information, depends on whether the court grasps the meaning of the information in the FPI report, and whether there are legal tools to handle the potential gaps between the information provided by the FPI report and the court's questions.

Below, we will point to potential challenges in relation to each of these questions, and discuss whether and how these challenges can be satisfactorily dealt with by the current legislation and practice. The discussion makes no claim to completeness but will highlight problems that we believe are particularly important or of interest to legal and psychiatric practitioners as well as students within these areas.

A crucial aspect of an FPI is the process of decision-making. Hence, the ability to engage in critical thinking, and a context that facilitates this, are essential to all expert making forensic psychiatric assessments. As a clinical FPI expert, awareness of stereotypes, heuristics and cognitive as well as affective biases is helpful to mitigate their effects, but research on decision-making has shown that erroneous decisions can nevertheless be made even by the most educated and experienced assessor.[71] Since several of these processes occur without the experts being aware of them and are involved in how information is perceived and interpreted, the expert cannot always know how biases affect their decision-making.[72]

Psychological and psychiatric assessment is concerned with the clinician, to understand the person being evaluated, taking a variety of information from multiple sources and considering this information in the context of a person's history, referral information, and observed behaviour. This is conducted to answer the court's referral questions and to communicate findings to the court as well as to the person being evaluated. Such an assessment methodology, both regarding content and process, can be considered to be evidence-based since it is recommended by researchers within the field of decision-making within legal contexts as well as clinical expertise in a legal setting to counteract classic cognitive errors (e.g. heuristics, Type I decision-making).[73]

Safeguards can both relate to the individual assessor as well as to formal, ethical and methodological aspects. Several safeguards to counteract many kinds of bias and other cognitive errors are currently employed within Swedish FPIs, and the most important are described below.

Examples of safeguards against expectancy-based bias stemming from learning and experience, as well as stemming from the structure of the human mental apparatus, are that in Sweden, the FPI is conducted in collaboration between different professions.[74] That experts in psychiatry, psychology and sociology apply their knowledge and theories from their respective areas of knowledge and make their own evaluation of the person's mental state in parallel, is in line with a pluralistic approach to psychiatric disorder. To take clear personal responsibility for one's own conclusions can also be considered a safe-guard based on previous research. Furthermore, the fact that the assessors during the person's time of evaluation repeatedly discuss the progress of their respective assessments together with ward personnel (i.e. where the person stays during the assessment), increases the chance for each assessor to consider his/her own knowledge of the person from a different theoretical/professional perspective. This praxis counteracts a singular focus on information from one's own theories and professional experience. The professional team discussions are also an opportunity for the assessors to engage in the position of devil's advocate against the conclusions made by the other team members, as well as having their own opinions scrutinised by the other team members within such a discussion. This gives all experts an opportunity to counteract blind use of heuristics, quick decision-making and discover weak aspects in one's own chain of reasoning by considering alternative explanations. Another important general safeguard in place, that prevents both group-think within the team as well as expectancy-based bias from individual learning and experience, is the second-opinion process used within the National Board of Forensic Medicine. This process can be employed more formally within FPIs, using 'shadow-teams' (i.e. two professional teams that make parallel assessments of the person undergoing FPI). However, in the majority of cases, a more informal version of this praxis is used where the expert engages a colleague from the same profession, but outside the current

FPI team, who is asked to review the assessment, evaluating the basis for the conclusions made in the assessment, as well as check whether the results are clearly and unambiguously presented in the expert's report.

Situational factors adhering to whether the defendant has been observed under circumstances that are representative is another aspect crucial to consider within the assessment process. It goes without saying that the defendant will be observed under circumstances that differ considerably both from those under which the crime was committed and those under which the sentencing decision is made. Moreover, an observation can be too brief or shallow to allow for certain inferences about the defendant's mental state. It is therefore crucial that the person is observed under conditions that are as representative as possible. Swedish law requires that an FPI is made as soon as possible.[75] As previously mentioned, an FPI is comprehensive and may take up to four weeks if the defendant is in custody (otherwise up to six weeks) and even longer if there are extraordinary reasons.[76] In practice, however, the point in time and the limited duration of an observation can both raise doubts about its relevance.[77] Consequently, the requirement that forensic experts account for circumstances that have complicated their assessment is key to safeguarding the quality of their conclusions.[78] To accommodate the difference in circumstances during the person's stay at the unit, the team gathers information from as many sources as possible to compare the obtained data and gain a comprehensive picture of the person's mental state and functioning historically, in close connection before and after the present crime, and during the stay in custody as well as in the department ward. Similarities and discrepancies in the person's behaviour are analyzed in light of how the person himself/herself understands them, changes in life circumstances and mental health, the degree of non-social and social stimulus that the person is exposed to in the different circumstances and how he/she react to these.

8.3.2.3 Different sources of data

During the twentieth century, the evaluation methods that are favoured within forensic psychiatric assessments in Sweden have changed. Although some methods used at the beginning of the twentieth century have been completely discarded (e.g. bodily measurements), many methods have rather been accumulated into today's comprehensive 'toolbox' than completely discarded (e.g. tests of cognitive functioning, but naturally the kind of tests used to ascertain such a function have developed over time according to research). Nevertheless, due to changing societal and political attitudes as well as changes in research's emphasis on theoretical frameworks and the development of new methods, the focus of data collection and how data is used within these evaluations has shifted. For example, on a more overarching level, the focus on identifying simulation during the FPIs in Sweden during the first half of the twentieth century has shifted into a focus on identifying those persons feigning health (i.e. hiding psychotic symptoms) at the end of the twentieth century.[79] The focus on the nature of the committed crime and its relevance for the evaluated person's mind and personality (i.e. that it exists a strong connection between the type of crime and a specific illness or disorder) has also successively been reduced during the last decades of the twentieth century. This has decreased the emphasis in today's FPI reports regarding the type of crime, modus operandi, planning, the possible consequence of a fixation (i.e. that these issues no longer is deemed as an equally important expression of the offender's inner life relevant to the question of SMD).[80] As a consequence, in today's FPI reports in Sweden, the crime is described less and the offender described more.

An example of the importance of using different sources of data to ensure the most comprehensive picture of the person available is the issue of personality assessment. For personality assessment, there is no ready gold standard that allows the evaluating psychologist to establish this with certainty.[81] Research has shown that psychologists cannot use, for example, self-, teacher-, spouse, or peer-ratings as a singular methodology, because the information from these different perspectives agrees only modestly. Thus, every single source of information may diverge substantially from every other possible source, and it is impossible to say that, as a rule, one is more 'true' than another. This emphasises the importance of gathering data from multiple sources before drawing conclusions since each source contributes with its own unique piece of information.[82] This kind of research results emphasise the value of combining psychiatric and psychological testing methods in FPIs. Research also emphasises that using tests is only one part of achieving an evidence-based assessment. Clinical expertise is another part, vital to optimise accuracy in conducting and interpreting the results from the information gathering phase, which decrease the risk for misdiagnosis and the risk of missing conditions that should be diagnosed.[83] Hence, interpretation of tests based on actuarial methods, depends to a considerable degree on the skill and judgement of the clinician, which further emphasises the need for expertise among the clinicians who are making FPIs.

Risk assessments can also be made within Swedish FPIs if the court has asked the question if there is a risk of relapse into serious criminality. The risk assessment instruments most commonly used include actuarial information (i.e. a historic inventory of the presence of known factors increasing the risk of relapse) and dynamic information (i.e. what known risk factors increase the risk of relapse that is present for the person at the time of the assessment). Examples of general risk assessment instruments used are HCR20-V3 and LSI, while more specific risk assessment instruments are also often used (i.e. in addition to these more general instruments) based on the person's personality profile, criminal history or psychiatric history (e.g. SARA, Static-99, Psychopathy Check List-Revised). Risk assessment procedures also in many cases include an assessment of protective factors, principally by using the instrument SAPROF. To consider both risk factors and protective factors when conducting risk assessment, may also nuance the decision-making process regarding what will increase the person's risk of relapsing and prevent this from happening (i.e. diminish the risk of a sole cognitive focus being applied on either risk or on ameliorating factors by the assessor). Hence, to consider the assessed person's history and current situation both from the perspective of risk and of protective factors should based on the previously presented research on decision-making, help the assessor gain a more balanced understanding of the person and can be regarded as a certain safe-guard. Nevertheless, since the level of risk changes, especially conclusions based on instruments which at least include dynamic risk factors whose influence could be lessened by different kinds of interventions, it is important that the risk of re-offending should be evaluated regularly and that the FPI conveys this kind of information to the court.

8.3.2.4 Teamwork

The established process within FPI praxis in Sweden is that while the §7-evaluation (i.e. initial assessment) is made only by a forensic psychiatrist, the FPI (i.e. comprehensive assessment) is almost always conducted by a team involving at least three professional groups (i.e. psychiatrist, psychologist, and social worker). However, only for persons who are detained will there be the information source clinical observations from the ward, and also the additional report to the court made by the staff at the unit during the person's approximate one-month stay there. For the remainder of the group (i.e. not detained) that undergo FPI, no such observational data from the time of the FPI exists. As a consequence, the FPI report given to the court will look different, since for the persons who were detained, a written report of their mental state and functioning at the unit will also be included. The team structure is the common methodology during FPIs and it is well established within the National Board of Forensic Medicine, Department of Forensic Psychiatry. The structure of the teamwork, and its procedure, generally follow the same pattern. The first team meeting is held as soon as possible after the client arrives at the unit to undergo their FPI. At this team meeting, a summary of the case is typically discussed, including what has happened (according to the information given by the court, e.g. material from the police investigation) and what needs to be investigated (i.e. based on the court's questions). The second team meeting, generally held approx. two weeks into the client's stay at the unit, a discussion regarding the results from the assessments made by each professional so far is held to keep each other informed regarding what has emerged from the different investigations. During the third, and final, team meeting, each of the professionals presents their final decision regarding the court's posed questions. After this, the forensic psychiatrist has the final say in what the conclusions of the FPI, regarding the court's questions, should be. However, if any of the other team members disagree, they can state this within their own FPI report (i.e. all professional FPI reports are submitted to the court together with that of the forensic psychiatrist). After this, the person undergoing FPI is informed of the outcome and informed that if he or she disagrees and wants to get a second opinion the person can via their lawyer initiate a review by the Swedish National Board of Health and Welfare.

8.3.3 Requirements for the evaluator

In Sweden, FPIs are made by health care workers and several legal requirements relate to the competence and objectivity of the individual assessors. To begin with, health care workers must not issue a certificate unless they have the competence needed to do so.[84] More specifically, a §7-evaluation must be made either by a physician who is a specialist in forensic psychiatry or by a physician who is a specialist in psychiatry, has experience in forensic psychiatric investigations and has been appointed by the National Board of Forensic Medicine to make such evaluations.[85] An FPI must as a rule, be carried out by a team consisting of forensic psychiatrists, forensic social workers, psychologists and ward personnel. If, for some reason, the investigation is carried out in a different manner, the reasons for this must be stated within the FPI report.[86] The report itself must be given by a forensic psychiatric specialist at a forensic investigation unit, or by some other forensic psychiatrist appointed by the Board.[87] It is a general requirement that health care workers must be objective in the collection of data when making a report or issuing a certificate. Moreover, the Swedish Administrative Act lists general reasons for disqualification, thereby prohibiting assessors from dealing with cases where their impartiality can be called into question.[88]

Regarding safeguarding expert competence and knowledge of evidence-based practice within one's field, basic formal professional requirements to work at the National Board of Forensic Medicine, Department of Psychiatry as an expert are the following. Certified psychologists, certified medical doctors, and certified social workers,[89] and all three professional groups continuously receive training in different instruments, methodology etc. through both internal and externally led courses with the purpose of developing specialised competence in the field of forensic psychiatric assessment. A majority of the psychiatrists and psychologists, for whom there also exists a state-certified specialist competence, also partake in courses within this education[90] to further develop their expertise within the field. An internal system is also in place to ensure that each new assessor works with FPIs under supervision by a senior assessor during his/her first 30 cases, which are required to vary in character (e.g. include several different forms of SMD and different kinds of crimes) to make sure that the new assessor has encountered several different varieties of evaluation-processes regarding SMD before starting to conduct FPIs without supervision. Regarding organisational safeguards relating to the written assessment, based on the legal description of what kind of states within the law should be considered to be the SMD, a formalised document is always used to create the written FPI report. This formalised document clearly outlines what should be included in the respective profession's written FPI report, and how these conclusions should be presented, as well as in the overarching assessment made by the responsible forensic psychiatrist. This kind of structure can be considered a safeguard against the court missing the basis on which the FPI conclusions are drawn due to its standardisation.

8.3.4 Enforcement of requirements

When it comes to enforcement of the mentioned requirements, no mechanisms are to be mentioned in addition to those explained above and used in court, as explained in section 8.4.

8.4 Safeguards 'against' the limited quality of forensic assessment

8.4.1 Questioning the assessment by the defense

In Sweden, FPIs are commissioned by the court and conducted by a state authority, the National Board of Forensic Medicine. In other words, they are not commissioned by parties to the criminal proceedings or conducted by experts selected by the parties. It is possible, but very uncommon, that the parties present their own expert evidence alongside the state's official investigation.[91] It can be difficult for the parties involved to question the FPI. Moreover, since a considerable portion of all forensic psychiatrists in Sweden today work (or have worked) within the National Board of Forensic Medicine, it is also difficult to find alternative experts. To get a second opinion, parties can request that the court orders a review of the FPI by the National Board of Health and Welfare, but there is no guarantee that the court will grant such a request (i.e. if the court considers a second opinion unnecessary). If the parties present their own expert evidence (e.g. an assessment made by an external clinical psychologist), the principles of free admission and free evaluation of evidence apply.

In cases where the FPI report has only influenced the court's decision regarding sentencing, and where forensic psychiatric care and imprisonment are deemed by the parties to be equally severe sanctions, the parties rarely question the FPI. However, such questioning may be more common in the future. This is attributable in part to the defence's heightened awareness of the fact that the length of incarceration in forensic psychiatric care for most crimes significantly exceeds the alternative prison time served. It can therefore often be in the interest of the defendant to be convicted to imprisonment instead of psychiatric care. Another reason why parties might become more likely to question FPIs is the fact that courts increasingly rely on FPI reports when determining a defendant's guilt. An FPI report can include information that speaks against, or in favour of, an acquittal and the parties might subject such FPI reports to particular scrutiny.[92]

8.4.2 Questioning the assessment by the court

As noted above, the FPI is not necessarily the final word, and there are safeguards designed to prevent assessments of poor quality from influencing the sentencing decision. The court can ask the National Board of Health and Welfare to give an opinion on the FPI or, if needed, make a complementary investigation.[93] Moreover, according to the principle of the free evaluation of evidence, it is up to the court to make an independent assessment of the investigation(s) and make a final decision on its evidentiary value.[94] In practice, however, empirical studies have shown that courts most often make decisions in line with the conclusions that forensic psychiatric experts have drawn on whether a person suffers from an SMD and is in need of forensic psychiatric care.[95] The situation is different, of course, when the National Board of Health and Welfare has another opinion, which does not concur with the conclusions made by the FPI. In this case, the Swedish Supreme Court has stated that the Board's opinion should normally be regarded as more reliable than the FPI, but that the court nevertheless must make a comparison and consider the differences in opinion.[96] The court must also consider other relevant material, and should decide, on the balance of probabilities, whether the defendant suffers from an SMD.[97] The court's sentence can be appealed, but once the verdict has gained legal force, the decision made based on the FPI regarding the patient's need for care will not be re-examined.

The court's capacity to fully understand the meaning of the FPI report is potentially threatened by the fact that the judges normally do not have any psychiatric or psychological education. Except for what is the case in some special courts in Sweden, such as the environmental courts, judges with expertise from other disciplines are, as already mentioned, not employed in the general courts. However, as mentioned above, if in doubt regarding the conclusions or information presented in an FPI report of a specific case, the court can call the responsible forensic psychiatric expert to the proceeding to have him/her clarify the lines of reasoning or conclusions drawn from these within their report to the court. Furthermore, a more general and recent safeguard regarding this problem (and also a safeguard for diminishing the risk of Type III-errors, to give the right answer to the wrong questions) is an initiative that has been made during recent years to promote a better understanding between forensic psychiatric experts and legal professionals. To do this, these professionals meet in seminars and discuss their experiences of perceived problems and/or uncertainties regarding the questions asked by the court and the answers given by the forensic psychiatric experts (e.g. what aspects are relevant to the court and the forensic psychiatric experts should answer, and how the court should interpret important psychiatric terminology etc.).

If the court does indeed observe that there is a discrepancy between the information provided in the FPI and the questions asked by the court, or that the investigation for some other reason does not fully answer these questions, it must decide how to bridge the gap and handle the ensuing uncertainty. As already indicated, the court can in this situation ask the National Board of Health and Welfare to give an opinion on the FPI or even to make a complementary investigation, but the uncertainty that nevertheless remains will, as in other legal contexts, be dealt with the use of presumptions and standards of proof. For example, the Swedish Supreme Court has stated that if the defendant suffered from an SMD when the crime was committed, it can normally be presumed that the crime was committed under the influence of the disorder (even if this is not evident from the FPI).[98] The Supreme Court has also said that because the question about whether the defendant suffers from a mental disorder does not concern guilt, it is inappropriate to use the standard 'beyond reasonable doubt' to deal with uncertainty in this regard. Instead, the question of whether the defendant suffers from a severe mental disorder shall be determined on the balance of probabiliy.[99]

8.4.3 Other questioning of the assessment

In Sweden, no external body (i.e. not part of the case in question) can provide submissions etc. to challenge the case or in another manner interfere in this process.

A Swedish perspective 193

8.5 Safeguarding the quality of decision-making when confronted with disagreement between experts

8.5.1 Dealing with disagreement

The forensic psychiatrist has the final say in what the overarching conclusions of the FPI should be. However, as stated above, if any of the other FPI team members disagree, they clearly mention this within their own written report. After this, the person undergoing FPI is informed of the outcome and informed that if he or she disagrees and wants to get a second opinion the person can via their lawyer initiate a review by the Swedish National Board of Health and Welfare. The forensic psychiatrist in charge of the FPI can also expressly recommend that the court asks for such a second opinion, which is done when for some reason the FPI results have been deemed more inconclusive than usual (e.g. a typologically especially unusual case, or lack of information to base the FPI on such as if the person refuses to meet the team members and there is no previous documentation regarding the person to consider).

To get a second opinion, the party that wants this can ask the court for an appeal at the National Board of Health and Welfare, but there is no guarantee that the court will grant this (i.e. if the court considers this unnecessary). If the parties present their own expert evidence (e.g. an assessment made by an external clinical psychologist), the general principle is that all evidence is admissible and that the courts' evaluation of evidence is free. If the FPI and the second opinion given by the National Board of Health and Welfare come to different conclusions regarding SMD, the court usually relies on the second opinion. Often, there are objective reasons for this choice, such as that more time has elapsed to observe the client or that other new information has emerged in the meantime, generating a more solid information basis for the second opinion.

8.5.2 Best practices

In addition to the practices mentioned above, there are no other best practices to mention specifically here.

8.6 Critical reflections

8.6.1 Current threats to the quality of the forensic assessment

Regarding the internal quality of FPIs, the overall structure of the work in practice meets several of the recommended safeguards presented in research on decision-making in general. The pluralistic approach employed, regarding content, data sources, type of professions involved as well as the inter-professional collaboration on the assignments, is also in line with current recommendations on how a evidence-based assessment procedure within the psychological and psychiatric field should be conducted. Nevertheless, this is a complex and vulnerable structure, relying on the expertise of the professionals, their willingness to be open and critical towards their own conclusions (as well as respectfully so towards that of other professionals to facilitate a fruitful discussion), and finally that the professionals have enough time to discuss and engage in focused analysis while working with the assessment. Since stress is detrimental in all these areas, this is crucial to avoid. Otherwise several of the important safeguards that the structure relies on will not function and this may endanger the rule of law. In line with this, adhering to the systemic factors, one hazard adheres to the position of the FPI within the structure of the judicial process. Being a part of the justice system carries with it that the organisation cannot control the influx of court-ordered FPIs. This means that sometimes the experts need to conduct several FPIs in parallel, while at other times there are considerably fewer to handle at the same time. To ensure that safeguards are in place to guarantee the quality of the evaluation is comparable between such different workloads, the team structure, the content of the team meeting, the structure of the teamwork and the content of the evaluation is fixed and stated in organisational guidelines. However, the pressure of doing these evaluations quickly can arise from different sources, which should always be considered as an increased risk that bias, use of heuristics as well as premature conclusions occur more frequently and undermine the evidence-based approach of clinical assessment in FPIs.

8.6.2 Concluding remarks

The legal definition of SMD does not reduce the legal concept to specific psychiatric diagnoses or medical definitions. The ensuing vagueness is intended to make the legal concept capable of accommodating future developments of psychiatric knowledge and to ensure that the concept is applicable in each unique case. However, the discussion above suggests that different conceptual apparatuses, and the possibility of the same terms having different meanings in different disciplines, create a real risk of misunderstanding between the forensic psychiatric experts and the courts. A particular challenge in this respect is posed by the potential vagueness or 'open texture'[100] of legal terms and concepts. Legal vagueness is not unique to this domain but is perhaps particularly problematic when the terms are used in the communication with other disciplines, to medico-legal concepts since it forces the experts from the other discipline to make their own interpretation of the term, whereas the meaning of these terms in a legal setting strictly speaking is a question of law that ought to be decided by the court and not by the forensic expert. Vagueness in the law, therefore, seems to blur the division of labour between courts and forensic experts. Moreover, and as we have seen, it is sometimes not even clear what is the legal function of a term. A clear example is the notion of SMD and the tension regarding the function of this notion being to determine whether a person needs care, or whether he/she should be held criminally accountable. To the extent that this is an open question, it seems as if it is likewise an open question of not only what the term 'SMD' more precisely should entail, but also whether lawyers or FPI experts are best apt to determine this. In our view, it is therefore crucial that it be clarified – from a legal point of view – what the important legal notions in this area of law more precisely mean, or at least what they *could* potentially mean, so that the investigator can provide information of relevance to the legal assessment. However, due to the comment in the preparatory works regarding the consideration of current legal praxis when determining SMD, it is also important to note that such an agreement on the meaning of SMD between legal practitioners and FPI experts is an ongoing process, that bilateral discussions are continuously held regarding this issue so that praxis evolves in parallel with research on psychiatric disorders.

Related to this recommendation described above, another fundamental key to dealing with these problems and minimising the risk for Type III errors – the error to provide the right answer but to the wrong question – is a clear and transparent communication between the court and the forensic experts.[101] To uphold the rule of law and to guarantee that legal norms are applied in a predictable and purposeful manner, both courts and FPI experts need to clearly define both their fundamental terms and the basis for their conclusions. In our opinion, there is also reason to consider the possibility of using expert judges in proceedings of these kinds. The use of expert judges can be expected not only to facilitate dealing with potential conceptual differences between the legal questions and the information provided by external experts but also to help the legally qualified judges to better understand the meaning of that information.[102] At least, the issues discussed in this chapter show the great importance of a continuous discussion between forensic psychiatric assessment experts and legal practitioners (here principally judges, prosecutors and lawyers), for example within annual joint seminars, to keep each other appraised of new developments within their respective field relevant to FPI praxis to ensure a common understanding of key issues.

Notes

1 Regulation on freedom of the press (TF, 1949:105), 7:4–5.
2 See, for example Wahlberg and Dahlman, 2021.
3 NJA, 1980, p. 725.
4 There are some exceptions. For example, written witness testimonies are normally not admitted and the court may reject evidence that is deemed clearly irrelevant, see The Swedish Code of Judicial Procedure, 1942:740, chapter 35, sections 14 and 7.
5 The Swedish Code of Judicial Procedure (1942:740), chapter 35, section 1.
6 Chapter 5, section 5 of the Penal Code stated that a person who committed an act 'under the influence of insanity, mental deficiency or other mental abnormality of such a profound nature, that it must be considered on a par with insanity' was considered unaccountable for the act. (sw: 'Ej må någon fällas till ansvar för gärning, som han begår under inflytande av sinnessjukdom, sinnesslöhet eller annan själslig abnormitet av så djupgående natur, att den måste anses jämställd med sinnessjukdom'.) The Penal Code, 1946, chapter 5, section 5.
7 The term 'tillräknelighet' is here translated to 'accountability'. Other possible translations are 'imputability' (Lernestedt, 2009), or 'capacity of liability' (SOU, 2002:3). Legally, the concept of accountability is in most aspects equivalent to concepts of 'legal insanity' in other jurisdictions, but there is no linguistic equivalent in Swedish law to the phrase 'legal insanity'.
8 Bjarup, 2005.
9 See, for example Lernestedt, 2009; Svennerlind, 2009; Qvarsell, 1993.
10 See Kinberg, 1935.
11 Kinberg, 2017, p. 203.
12 Wennberg, 2002; Lernestedt, 2009.
13 For an account of the discussion preceding the enactment of the Penal Code, see Lernestedt, 2009.
14 Strahl, 1976, p. 77.
15 Prop. 1990/91:58.
16 NJA, 1995, p. 48.
17 NJA, 1995, p. 48.
18 NJA, 2001, p. 899.
19 See Lernestedt, 2009.
20 The latest one is SOU 2012:17, see for descriptions and discussions of different aspects of the proposal; Radovic, Meynen and Bennet, 2015; Bennet and Radovic, 2016; Gooding and Bennet, 2018.
21 See Lernestedt, 2009.
22 Prop. 2007/08:97.
23 Prop. 07/08:97, p. 14.
24 Prop. 07/08:97, pp. 25 f.
25 SOU, 2002:3.
26 Prop. 2007/08:97, p. 26.
27 Despite this, it is important to note that in the considerable majority of cases, self-induced intoxication at the time of the crime does not lead to an FPI recommendation of forensic psychiatric care, but if the person for example still maintained sufficiently severe symptoms of paranoia due to drug-induced psychosis at the time of FPI, the person could be recommended care.
28 BrB, 30:6.
29 Prop. 1990/91:58, pp. 86 f. and 453 f.
30 BrB, 30:6, section 2.
31 BrB, 31:3.
32 BrB, 31:3 section 2: Act 1991:1129, on forensic psychiatric care.
33 Section 4 Act 1991:1137, on the forensic psychiatric investigation.
34 Section 3 Act 1991:1137, on the forensic psychiatric investigation.
35 See, for example Morse and Hoffman, 2006.

36 Bennet and Radovic, 2016; Gooding and Bennet, 2018.

37 Penal Code chapter 31, section 3; Act 1991:1137, on the forensic psychiatric investigation, section 1.

38 Recent studies show that forensic psychiatric reports are used in this way and can have a decisive impact on the outcome of the legal assessment of *mens rea*. See Bennet, 2020.

39 SOSFS, 2008:18.

40 HSLF-FS, 2015:31.

41 Prop. 1990/91:58.

42 See primarily Prop. 1990/91:58 pp. 86 f, 453 f; and NJA, 2004, p.702.

43 Sturup, Sygel and Kristiansson, 2013.

44 Kotov et al, 2017. This is also in line with a classic view of psychopathology, described by Karl Jaspers (1883–1969) at the beginning of the twentieth century among others, of a dimension of psychosis where there is no thought disturbance at one end and profound thought disturbance at the other.

45 Act 1991:1137, section 1:2.

46 HSLF-FS 2015:31, chapter 2, section 6.

47 Govt. Bill 1990/91:58, pp. 87ff.

48 Govt. Bill 2007/08:97, p. 18.

49 Malmgren et al., 2010.

50 Examples of this are the interpretation of SMD within the guiding document used within the National board of forensic medicine for the social worker's investigation where the recommendation of SMD from this profession encompasses the person's psychosocial functioning.

51 Mitroff and Featheringham, 1974; Wahlberg, 2010, p. 16.

52 See, for example RH, 2008:90.

53 Bennet and Radovic, 2016.

54 Bennet and Radovic, 2016.

55 See Bennet, 2020.

56 National Board of Forensic Medicine, 2018; 2020. Specifically, in 2020, 1152 §7-evaluations and 529 FPIs were conducted and 303 clients were considered to have an SMD at the time of their offence.

57 See for an overview Svennerlind et al., 2010; Grøndahl, 2005.

58 Regarding the concept of severe mental disorder in Swedish law, see Kullgren et al., 1996; Malmgren et al., 2010.

59 HSLF-FS 2015:31, chapter 2, section 6 (albeit in different order).

60 HSLF-FS 2015:31, chapter 3, sections 9 and 13.

61 See, for example Wahlberg and Sahlin, 2017.

62 For more information about the meaning and function of the Swedish standard 'science and proven experience', see for example Wahlberg and Persson, 2017; Dewitt et al., 2021.

63 For a comparison of the Swedish notion and EBM, see Persson et al., 2019.

64 SBU, 2005, p. 62.

65 See, for example Kravitz et al., 2004.

66 SBU, 2005.

67 HSLF-FS 2015:31, chapter 4, section 7.

68 HSLF-FS 2015:31, chapter 3, sections 8 and 12.

69 Cf. HSLF-FS 2015:31, chapter 4, section 2.

70 HSLF-FS, 2018:54, chapter 6, sections 4 and 8.

71 For example Dror, 2020; Bornstein, 2017.

72 Dror, 2020; Bornstein, 2017.

73 For example Bornstein, 2017; Dror, 2020.

74 This structure, to have a team of different professionals participating in the FPI, is stated in guidelines for the National Board of Forensic Medicine.

75 Act, 1991:1137, on the forensic psychiatric investigation, section 6 §1 and the National Board of Forensic Medicine's Regulation on the forensic psychiatric investigation, 2015:31, chapter 2, section 6.

76 Act, 1991:1137, on the forensic psychiatric investigation, sections 6, 2, and 3.

77 See, for example, the statements by the forensic experts in RH, 2008:90, p. 8.

78 The National Board of Forensic Medicine's Regulation on the forensic psychiatric investigation, 2015:31, chapter 3, section 6.

79 Börjesson, 2000.

80 Lidberg, 2000.

81 Bornstein, 2017.

82 Interestingly, validity for many psychological tests is indistinguishable from those observed for many medical tests, again highlighting the importance of using multiple kinds of data sources. For example, validity coefficients in the 0.3–0.5-range has encompassed MMPI-2, MMCI, Rorschach, PCL-R, as well as EEG, CT, MRI, and SPECT, and the ability to detect dementia is at least as good with neuropsychological tests as it is with MRI. See Bornstein, 2017.

83 Bornstein, 2017.

84 HSLF-FS, 2018:54, chapter 3, section 1.

85 HSLF-FS, 2018:54, chapter 3, section 5.

86 HSLF-FS, 2015:31, chapter 2, section 3.

87 HSLF-FS, 2015:31, chapter 2, section 2.

88 The Administrative Procedure Act, 2017:900, section 16.

89 Certification for all these professions is made after the person has concluded university training in respective professional programs and has applied to, and been approved by, the Swedish National Board of Health and Welfare.

90 For medical doctors, a specialisation in forensic psychiatry involves first a specialisation qualification in psychiatry (five years of clinical training, courses and a scientific report), and thereafter a specialisation qualification in forensic psychiatry (2.5 years of clinical training in forensic psychiatry and courses). For clinical psychologists, it involves five years of clinical practice, courses and a scientific report, all within the field of specialisation.

91 One example of a defendant's reliance on independent expert evidence is a Supreme Court case (NJA, 2009, p. 234) concerning the aggravated assault. The defendant claimed to have acted in self-defence and presented a statement by a psychologist who was an expert on crisis and stress management. The psychologist stated that the situation within which the aggravated assault occurred was so stressful for the defendant that he could not reasonably have controlled his actions. While the lower courts convicted the defendant, the Supreme Court decided on acquittal taking the psychological expert evidence introduced by the defendant into account.

92 The Supreme Court recently acquitted a defendant charged with aggravated assault on the basis of an FPI; NJA, 2020, p. 169). The court concluded that the defendant, due to a severe mental disorder, was not aware of what he was doing to the extent that is required to form *mens rea* (criminal intent).

93 Section 18 Regulation, 2015:284, with instruction for the National Board of Health and Welfare; Section 12 Act 1991:1137, on the forensic psychiatric investigation.

94 Penal Code 30:6 §2.

95 See, for example Vahlne Westerhäll and Princis, 2013; Wahlberg et al., 2015.

96 NJA 2004 s. 72, p. 13.

97 Act on Forensic Care sections 16 and 16a. If a special discharge review is not required, the chief physician shall discharge the patient when conditions for forensic care no longer apply (Act on Forensic Care, section 13). However, the care will end automatically after four months, unless the chief physician applies to the administrative court for prolongation (Act on Forensic Care, sections 12 and 12a). It is not possible to apply for a reconsideration of a sentence regarding forensic psychiatric care (Prop. 2007/08:97, pp. 32–33), but it is possible for the patient to apply for the court's consideration of whether the pre-conditions for special discharge review still are applicable.

98 NJA, 2004, p. 702, p. 721.

99 NJA, 2004, p. 702, p. 720.

100 Hart, 1994, p. 135.

101 See also Malmgren et al., 2010.

102 Paloniitty & Kangasmaa, 2018.

References

Anckarsäter, H., Radovic, S., Svennerlind, C., Höglund, P., and Radovic, P. (2009). Mental disorder is a cause of crime: the cornerstone of forensic psychiatry. *International Journal of Law and Psychiatry*, 32, pp. 342–347. doi: 10.1016j.ijlp.2009.09.002

Bennet, T., and Radovic, S. (2016). On the abolition and re-introduction of legal insanity in Sweden. In S. Moratti, and D. Patterson (Eds.), *Legal Insanity and the Brain: Science, Law and European Courts*. Portland, Oregon: Hart Publishing Ltd, pp. 169–206. 10.5040/9781509902347.ch-007

Bennet T. (2020). *Straffansvar vid atypiska sinnestillstånd*. Nyköping: Norstedts Juridik AB.

Bjarup, J. (2005). The philosophy of Scandinavian legal realism, *Ratio Juris*, 1(18), pp. 1–15.

Bornstein, R.F. (2017). Evidence-based psychological assessment. *Journal of Personality Assessment*, 99, pp. 435–445. doi: 10.1080/00223891.2016.1236343

Börjesson, M. (2000). Det rättspsykiatriska centralarkivet i historisk belysning [The forensic psychiatric central archive in a historical light]. In L. Lidberg (Ed.), *Svensk rättspsykiatri, [Swedish forensic psychiatry]*, Stockholm: Studentlitteratur, pp. 421–442.

Dewitt, B., Persson, J., Wahlberg, L., and Wallin, A. (2021). The epistemic roles of clinical expertise: an empirical study of how swedish healthcare professionals understand proven experience. *PLoS ONE*, 16(6): e0252160. 10.1371/journal.pone.0252160

Dror, I. (2020). Cognitive and human factors in expert decision making: six fallacies and the eight sources of bias. *Analytical Chemistry*, 92, pp.7998–8004. 10.1021/acs.analchem.0c00704

Gooding, P., and Bennet, T. (2018). The abolition of the insanity defense in sweden and the united nations convention on the rights of persons with disabilities: human rights brinksmanship or evidence it won't work? *New Criminal Law Review*, 21, pp. 141–169.

Grøndahl, P. (2005). Scandinavian forensic psychiatric practices–an overview and evaluation, *Nordic Journal of Psychiatry*, 59, pp. 92–102.

Hart, H.L.A. (1994). *The Concept of Law*. Oxford: Clarendon.

HSLF-FS (2015):31. *The National Board of Forensic Medicine's regulation on forensic psychiatric investigation [Rättsmedicinalverkets föreskrifter om rättspsykiatrisk undersökning]*. Stockholm: Socialstyrelsen. ISSN 2002-1054, Artikelnummer: 2015-12-31.

HSLF-FS (2018):54. *The National Board of Health and Welfare's regulations on to issue certificates within health services [Socialstyrelsens föreskrifter om att utfärda intyg i hälso- och sjukvården]*. Stockholm: Socialstyrelsen. ISSN 2002-1054, Artikelnummer: 2018-12-35.

Höglund, P., Levander, S., Anckarsäter, H., & Radovic, S. (2009). Accountability and psychiatric disorders: how do psychiatric professionals think? *International Journal of Law and Psychiatry*, 32, pp. 355–361. doi: 10.1016/j.jijlp.2009.09.004

Kinberg, O. (1935). *Basic Problems of Criminology*. Copenhagen: Levin & Munksgaard.

Kinberg, O. (1917). *Regarding the So-Called Accountability [Om den så kallade tillräkneligheten]*, Stockholm: Nordiska Bokhandeln.

Kotov, R., Krueger, R.F., Watson, D., Achenbach, T.M., Althoff, R.R., Bagby, M.R., … Zimmerman, M. (2017). The Hierarchical Taxonomy of Psychopathology (HiTOP): A dimensional alternative to traditional nosologies. *Journal of Abnormal Psychology*, 126, pp. 454–477. doi:10.1037/abn0000258

Kravitz, R.L., Duan, N., and Braslow, J. (2004). Evidence-based medicine, heterogeneity of treatment effects and the trouble with averages. *The Milbank Quarterly*, 82, pp. 661–687.

Kullgren, G., Grann, M., and Holmberg, G. (1996). The Swedish forensic concept of severe mental disorder as related to personality disorders: an analysis of forensic psychiatric investigations of 1498 male offenders, *International Journal of Law and Psychiatry*, 19, pp. 191–200.

Lernestedt, C. (2009). Insanity and the 'gap' in the law: Swedish criminal law rides again. *Scandinavian Studies in Law*, 54, pp. 79–108.

Lidberg, L. (2000). Förord. In L. Lidberg (Ed.), *Svensk rättspsykiatri, [Swedish Forensic Psychiatry]*. Stockholm: Studentlitteratur, pp. 15–18.

Malmgren, H., Radovic, S., Thorén, H., and Haglund, B. (2010). A philosophical view on concepts in psychiatry. *International Journal of Law and Psychiatry*, 33, pp. 66–72.

Mitroff, I.I., and Featheringham, T.R. (1974). On systemic problem solving and the error of the third kind. *Behavioral Science*, 19, pp. 383–393. 10.1002/bs.3830190605

Morse, S.J., and Hoffman, M.B. (2006). The uneasy entente between legal insanity and mens rea: Beyond Clark v. Arizona. *Journal of Crime & Criminology*, 97, pp. 1071–1150.

National Board of Forensic Medicine (2018). *Annual Report*. Stockholm: Rättsmedicinalverket.

National Board of Forensic Medicine (2020). *Annual Report*. Stockholm: Rättsmedicinalverket.

National Board of Forensic Medicine (2015:31). *Regulation on forensic psychiatric investigation*. Stockholm: Rättsmedicinalverket.

Paloniitty, T., and Kangasmaa, S. (2018). Securing scientific understanding: expert judges in Finnish administrative judicial review. *European Energy and Environmental Law Review*, 4, pp. 125–139.

Persson, J., Vareman, N., Wallin, A., Wahlberg, L., and Sahlin, N.-E. (2019). Science and proven experience: a Swedish variety of evidence based medicine and a way to better risk analysis? *Journal of Risk Research*, 22, pp. 833–843.

Prop. 1990/91:58. *The government's proposition regarding psychiatric involuntary care.*

Prop. 2007/08:97. *Sanctions for offenders with psychiatric disorder.*

Qvarsell, R. (1993). *Without Reason and Volition: Regarding the View of Criminality and Mental Illness [Utan vett och vilja: Om synen på brottslighet och sinnessjukdom]*, Stockholm: Carlssons Bokförlag.

Radovic, S., Meynen, G., and Bennet, T. (2015). Introducing a standard of legal insanity: The case of Sweden compared to The Netherlands. *International Journal of Law and Psychiatry*, 40, pp. 43–49.

SOU [Swedish Government Official Reports] (2002:3). *Mental disorder, crime and responsibility [Psykisk störning, brott och ansvar]*.

Stockholm: SBU (2005). *Risk assessments within psychiatry: Can violence in society be predicted? [Riskbedömningar inom psykiatrin: Kan våld i samhället förutsägas?]*.

SOSFS (2008:18). *Socialstyrelsens föreskrifter och allmänna råd om psykiatrisk tvångsvård och rättspsykiatrisk vård.*

SOU (2012:17). *Psykiatrin och lagen – tvångsvård, straffansvar och samhällsskydd.*

Strahl, I. (1976). *Allmän straffrätt i vad angår brotten.* Norstedt: Stockholm.

Sturup, J., Sygel, K., and Kristiansson, M. (2013). *Rättspsykiatriska bedömningar i praktiken – vinjettstudie och uppföljning av över 2000 fall. RMV-rapport 2013:1.* Rättsmedicinalverket Stockholm.

Svennerlind, S. (2009). Philosophical motives for the Swedish criminal code of 1965. *Philosophical Communications, Web Series*, 42. Gothenburg: University of Gothenburg.

Svennerlind, C., Nilsson, T., Kerekes, N., Andiné, P., Lagerkvist, M., Forsman, A., Anckarsäter, H., and Malmgren, H. (2010). Mentally disordered criminal offenders in the Swedish criminal system. *International Journal of Law and Psychiatry*, 33, pp. 220–226. doi: 10.1016/j.ijlp.2010.06.003

Vahlne Westerhäll, L., and Princis, L. (2013). Medicin och juridik vid psykiatrisk tvångsvård. *Förvaltningsrättslig tidskrift*, 4, pp. 387–422.

Wahlberg, L. (2010). *Legal Questions and Scientific Answers: Ontological Differences and Epistemic Gaps in the Assessment of Causal Relations.* Lund University.

Wahlberg, L., Dahlman, C., Sarwar, F., Sikström, S., and Åkerman, S. (2015). Rättslig prövning av skälen för sluten psykiatrisk tvångsvård: Bör domstolarna lita på den medicinska expertisen? *Förvaltningsrättslig tidskrift*, 4, pp. 629–646.

Wahlberg, L., and Dahlman, C. (2021). The role of the expert witness. In C. Dahlman, A. Stein and G. Tuzet (Eds.), *Philosophical Foundations of Evidence Law*, Oxford: Oxford University Press.

Wahlberg, L., and Sahlin, N.-E. (2017). Om icke vedertagna behandlingsmetoder och kravet på vetenskap och beprövad erfarenhet, *Förvaltningsrättslig tidskrift*, 1, pp. 45–66.

Wahlberg, L., and Persson, J. (2017). Importing notions in health law: science and proven experience. *European Journal of Health Law*, 24, pp. 565–590. 10.1163/15718093-12453308

Wennberg, S. (2002). Psychiatric disorder, crime and responsibility – For and against the commitees suggestions [Psykisk störning, brott och ansvar - För och emot psykansvarskommitténs betänkande]. *Svensk Juristtidning*, 34, pp. 576–587.

Chapter 9

A Dutch perspective

*Michiel Van der Wolf, Hjalmar Van Marle, and
Sabine Roza*

9.1 Introduction

9.1.1 The legal system

To understand the subtleties of the Dutch penal law system related to forensic assessment, a few interrelated procedural characteristics are of great importance in shaping its context. These are addressed in this paragraph. Of course, more substantive characteristics related to sentencing, such as criminal responsibility and the nature of sentences may be of equal impact on the contents of the assessment, but these will be addressed more thoroughly in the remainder of this chapter.

As in most continental European jurisdictions, the criminal process may be best characterised as an inquisitorial system, in which the judge is the driving force in fact-finding, in contrast with adversarial justice systems, generally stemming from the Anglo–American common law tradition, in which parties play that role. As a consequence, in inquisitorial systems the judge is not merely the referee but the independent and 'incorruptible' inquirer, while in adversarial systems there is a greater emphasis on playing fair through equality of arms and an active defense by the accused.[1] The Dutch jurisdiction has been described in the past as the most inquisitorial jurisdiction in Western Europe.[2] However, especially under the influence of the European Convention on the Protection of Human Rights and Fundamental Freedoms (since 1950) and the jurisprudence of the European Court of Human Rights (ECHR) in Strasbourg (France), more and more adversarial elements are being added to the system.[3] Even though the Court does not judge legal systems, individual cases may give rise to changes within a system.[4] For example, both in practice and legislative reforms the issue of fitness to stand trial is increasingly under the attention. This evidently also has relevance to forensic assessment; at least it is of great influence in adversarial justice, while absent in some inquisitorial systems. It is already remarkable that the Dutch system even has such a doctrine in place since 1926, but originally this had a more pragmatic background related to the responsibility doctrine and the (im)possibility for commitment to a psychiatric hospital if the offender became disordered after committing the crime. However, since a few decades, fairness is recognised as its main legitimation.[5] For the subject of this chapter the most important consequence of the inquisitorial system is that forensic evaluators (as expert witnesses) are officially doing the assessment on behalf of the court instead of the parties.

A basic trust in authorities and pragmatic efficiency are two fundamentals of the Dutch welfare state. They explain why the principle of immediacy – which requires that all evidence is presented in court in its most original form – plays a limited role in practice. Witness testimony, including expert-witness testimony, is generally dealt with through paper reports – for eye witnesses, for example, reports of their statements to the police –, and are not voiced by the

DOI: 10.4324/9781351266482-9

(expert-)witness in the courtroom.[6] Trust and pragmatism are also part of the explanation for the fact that the criminal trial consists of one phase, in which both fact-finding and sentencing take place. In order for forensic assessment to be ready before the trial, very early in the criminal process case selection has to take place, and defendants are being evaluated without the establishment of fact (and consequent culpability). As an important part of the assessment is criminal responsibility based on the mental status at the time of the offense, this feature of the system could be problematic for defendants who dispute the charges.[7]

That the percentage of the population's trust in judges is still highest of all authorities, and also higher than in many other jurisdictions, explains why – outside of academia – no need seems to be felt for further democratic legitimation of judicial decision-making, for example through juries or other lay-judges. The high level of trust seems to be associated with the perceived level of procedural justice.[8] As a consequence of all the characteristics above, admissibility of expert evidence is not a major issue. The professional judges are expected to be able to assess the quality of the evidence and weigh its conclusions accordingly. The division of legislative, judicial, and executive powers, however, hands decisions concerning the execution of sentences to the Ministry of Justice and Security and the Public prosecutors office. Some other decision-making bodies within the execution of sentences are more judicial, but consist also of other professionals (i.e. psychiatrists and psychologists), like the Council for the Administration of Criminal Justice and Protection of Juveniles, the body that for example deals with appeals against decisions of the Ministry concerning the execution of sentences in individual cases.

Again pragmatism and trust play their part as grounds for a large discretionary competence of the prosecutor to not prosecute criminal offences. For example, the widely known policy of tolerance, which is used to 'legitimize' the use of marijuana or a diligently planned and performed euthanasia, is based on this competence.[9] But it is also grounds for the possibility to not prosecute a mentally disordered offender to favour civil commitment, as a kind of diversion.[10] Empirical research shows that this is generally only done in case of less severe offences.[11] Using this competence conditionally may also be used as an out-of-court settlement, with in- or outpatient treatment among the possible conditions. Other out-of-court settlements with the Prosecution exist, both consensual and non-consensual, but they differ from plea-bargaining as no guilty plea is required.[12]

9.1.2 The related tradition of forensic assessment

The historic developments concerning forensic assessment mentioned in Chapter 2 are also identifiable in the Netherlands. Whereas insanity used to be regarded as something also a lay person could see, in the late Middle Ages cases are known in which law practitioners would use medical books to assess insanity themselves, like that of Volker Westwoud from 1674.[13] When psychiatry became a more specialised discipline, including more rigorous scientific evaluation, its influence on criminal law grew. The development of treatment and assessment for forensic patients went hand in hand, and in a sense has been interrelated for almost 150 years. In 1884 new legislation on coercive treatment of mentally disordered people was introduced (the 'insanity law', the first edition was from 1841) while in 1886 the new Criminal code was enacted as the follow-up of the Code Pénal (1811) from the Napoleontic times.[14] The connection between those new laws was the person of Johannes Nicolaas Ramaer (1817–1887), a medical doctor and from 1842 medical superintendent of different asylums for the insane.[15] He was the adviser of the Ministry of Justice in the development of both laws and as a doctor he introduced a better health care and legal protection in the asylums and prisons. It became common for courts to ask doctors, working in those institutions, for advice on legal matters. This was also triggered by the fact that as the psychiatric discipline evolved, more subtle disorders were recognised, which were not as easily recognisable for judges. Especially the category of 'monomania' became popular, a form of partial insanity conceived as single pathological preoccupation in an otherwise sound mind, as these patients acted rational, but for one psychological function. It was no coincidence that the oldest case traceable in which a psychiatrist testified in court, was that of a pyromaniac girl in 1839. She was acquitted for setting fire to a haystack.

From the case of Volker Westwoud onwards, who was convicted for manslaughter, insanity did not necessarily mean acquittal, but could also lead to a form of preventive detention. When the modern criminal law school emerged at the end of the nineteenth century – which emphasised causes of crime based on advancements in biological, psychological, and sociological knowledge – preventive sentencing became more popular and justified. A pivotal moment in the history of forensic assessment in the Netherlands was the introduction in 1928 of the entrustment order called the TBR (from 1988 onwards: TBS), by which offenders could be sentenced to a commitment in a high-security psychiatric hospital when they were a 'danger for the public order and/or security', due to a mental disorder which diminished the responsibility for the offense. The disorder and diminished responsibility were necessary to reach a compromise with the classical school in criminal law, which was based on proportionate retribution to the extent of guilt. It only allowed for such a safety measure next to incapacitation in penitentiary institutions, because diminished responsible offenders kept getting lower sentences even though they were more likely to reoffend.[16] As this safety measure was basically indeterminate, but had to be prolonged every two years by the court, more assessment was required, in this case from the psychiatrist of the TBR-asylum, later called 'clinic' and since the turning of the twenty-first century 'center'.

When after World War II the attitude towards psychiatric patients became more therapeutically optimistic – group therapy and relevant psychotropic drugs were discovered in the meantime – and humane, the TBR became more frequently used. Its criteria turned into the dominant questions for pre-trial assessment, and an observation clinic to support this assessment was instituted in 1949 as well as a selection clinic in 1952. Selection was necessary because similar to criminal law, forensic psychiatry 'schools' also emerged with their own frame of reference on treatment and assessment, among which a psychodynamic school, a phenomenological school, and a behavioural school could be distinguished.[17] Clinics were differentiated accordingly, and private clinics invested in by the Ministries of both Justice and Health. When towards the end of the twentieth century the treatment model shifted from cure to control, TBS-clinics became more eclectic. The necessity of efficiency was also related to a large increase in the number of patients, leading also to an increase of psychologists within forensic treatment. This backdrop explains why the TBS-clinics became early adapters of risk assessment instruments for back-end decisions: prolongation or termination of the order. Since 2008, the Forensic Care Act (FCA) supports the movement to a broader mental health field for forensic treatment, paid for solely by the Ministry of Justice and Security (which is a telling addition in 2010!), ranging from outpatient treatment as a condition for non-prosecution to inpatient treatment in a high-security TBS-facility, and everything in between.

Likewise, the pre-trial assessment has undergone several quality-enhancing changes over the years. After World War II, the forensic assessment was detached from the treatment clinics, through the establishing of local institutions named Forensic Psychiatric Services for every judicial district and the abovementioned observational clinic. These institutions and the observational clinic were merged in 2008, so that assessment is now governed by a centralised organisation: the Netherlands Institute for Forensic Psychiatry and Psychology (NIFP). The centralised NIFP was established by the Dutch Government to provide more unity in the quality of the assessments for the courts. How this is done, will be elaborated in the next paragraphs. Of course, standardisation is important in unifying. This development was already visible at the end of the twentieth century, when for example a first standard set of questions for the assessment was introduced as well as a Likert scale for the assessment of criminal responsibility, instead of everyone formulating their own questions or using their own words to describe the strength of the causal relationship between disorder and offence.[18] Maybe also because risk assessment research has had more focus on back-end sentencing decisions, structured assessment was introduced fairly late to pre-trial assessment. Up until today discussions on scientific reasoning, nomothetic versus idiographic, for example, can become quite emotional among evaluators, especially when it comes to risk assessment.

Another important governmental body for safeguarding the quality of forensic assessment is the Netherlands Register of Court Experts (NRGD), which was introduced by the Experts in Criminal Cases Act in 2010. Even though the act had a background in miscarriages of Justice related to fact-finding, it also applies to behavioural scientific experts making evaluations for sentencing.[19] *A fortiori*, Forensic Psychiatry and Psychology is by far the largest discipline represented in the register, within 2019 508 out of 604 court experts in total, i.e. 84% of the total number of registered court experts.[20] It underlines the quantity of forensic assessment, and thereby the relevance of its quality.

9.2 Short overview of the role of assessment in sentencing offenders

9.2.1 Sentences and execution

9.2.1.1 The Dutch sentencing system

The Dutch sentencing system may be characterised as a twin-track of retrospective, retributive penalties, on the one hand, and prospective, preventive measures, on the other hand. The penalties and measures however differ mainly in theory. In recent decades, the objectives of custodial penalties and safety measures have grown closer together.[21] This is partly because of the compromises between classical and modern theory, of which the TBS-order itself is an example, but also because one of the main arguments for the distinction – intentional versus unintentional suffering – is rather unsatisfactory from both a pragmatic and a moral point of view.[22] More important is the fact that in the 1950s when the TBS-order was executed with a lot of liberties for the patients, it was not regarded as sufficient for public protection, and instead lengthy prison sentences were imposed on dangerous offenders. The Supreme Court allowed this practice, so that the severity of punishment is no longer only tailored to the extent of guilt, but may also be tailored to the extent of dangerousness.[23] This discretionary competence for judges is understandable, as it is almost total in sentencing. There are only maximum sentences in place per offence and there are no mandatory sentences. The recently enacted prohibition of community service for severe violent or sexual offences (or in case of recidivism) seems to keep judges from sentencing too mild but is also often avoided by giving a prison sentence for the duration of the pretrial detention already served.[24] Recidivism in general may be an aggravating factor for raising the maximum sentence, as well as confluence of multiple offences tried together, for which only one penalty may be imposed. Again it is pragmatics over principle that excludes the option of a back-to-back-sentence conviction. From the side of the judges themselves, judicial 'points of reference' for sentencing have been formulated for the most common offences, as the word 'guidelines' was considered to be too much in friction with their discretionary competence.[25] The prosecution does have guidelines in place for both their prosecutorial decisions and their sentence demands.[26] The discretionary competence includes the choice of penological goals of the penalty in a single case, as long as these (especially restriction of liberty) are well motivated, and – even after conviction – no sentence may be applied for example if due to personal circumstances penological goals can no longer be reached.[27]

The twin-track system was originally very much related to the concept of criminal responsibility, but this dogmatic stronghold has similarly weakened under the influence of pragmatics. Non-responsible offenders may still not be given a penalty, but they may be given a safety measure. Ever since the first Dutch Criminal Code (CC) from 1886, a safety measure of placement in a psychiatric hospital (not the same as the imposition of a TBS-order) existed, especially for the non-responsible. It has been replaced in 2020 by the possibility for the criminal court to warrant coerced civil care in any stage of criminal proceedings for whomever meets the criteria laid down in the civil (in name, but administrative in function) mental health laws. Non-responsible offenders may be sentenced to a TBS-order if they meet the criteria of having committed a severe offence and being considered (very) dangerous. Diminished responsible offenders may be sentenced to a combination of a penalty, generally a prison sentence, for the part they are responsible, and a TBS-order, for the part that they are (bio-psychologically) determined to be dangerous. Since a supervision order was enacted in 2018, the combination of a prison sentence and a supervision order is also possible for offenders considered fully responsible. Furthermore, it depends on the contents of the sentences at hand whether they can or may be combined.[28]

Another relevant feature of the Dutch sentencing system is that for juveniles between the ages of 12 (the age of criminal accountability) and 18, specific sentences are in place. The rationale is primarily determined by the pedagogical/educational aim of sentencing and has to be least restrictive to allow the minor to make a new start in life after serving the sentence. However, for two groups exceptions may be made. Adult sentences may be applied to 16–17 year olds, if they meet aggravating criteria. Vice versa, juvenile sentences may be applied to 18–23 year olds ('adolescents'). This latter exception is called 'adolescent criminal law', was introduced in 2014, and was based on the dual rational of accountability (neuroscientific evidence that the brain is maturing until around the age of 24) and prevention. The central notion was to provide an effective and offender-oriented manner of sentencing which does justice to the committed offense and which takes into account the personal circumstances of the offender, including his/her developmental phase. Although Dutch law recognised the relationship between incomplete (biopsychosocial) development of adolescents and young adults, and recognised the superior effectiveness of the offender-oriented and pedagogical juvenile justice system in terms of better reintegration into society and prevention of re-offending, juvenile criminal sentencing is still only rarely applied to young adults.[29]

In sum, the Dutch sentencing system has evolved away from its former dogmatic rigidity to a highly flexible system in many aspects. The upcoming wish (or demand) in recent decades to further reduce reoffending, to fill all the gaps that may allow for risk to peep through – the pursuit of absolute certainty – has led to an increase in sentencing options, especially through new safety measures, many of which target specific groups of offenders. Since measures are much less bound to dogmatic restrictions than penalties, and are founded in the wish to counter 'undesirable situations',[30] they are prone to be used and created in risk society politics. To be able to follow such developments, for some recently added sentences the years of enactment are provided as additional information in the next paragraph.

9.2.1.2 Relevant sentences

Examples of penalties are the prison sentence, the community service, and the fine. A prison sentence may be a life sentence for a very selective set of offences (including murder), while the maximum period of a temporary prison sentence is 30 years. Sentences may (in part) be imposed conditionally, so that the execution is being suspended as long as conditions are met for a certain timeframe (probation period). In suspended sentences, special conditions may be imposed, such as inpatient or outpatient treatment, not necessarily *de iure* but indeed *de facto* only as long as the offender agrees to the conditions. Even though no forensic assessment is required for imposing a (partially conditional) penalty, such a special condition of a suspended prison sentence, is actually the most frequently recommended legal framework for forensic psychiatric treatment.[31] Partially conditional penalties cannot be used for the most severe offences, as a complete suspension is possible for prison sentences up to two years and a partly suspension is possible for prison sentences between two and four years.[32] In practice, in 90% of the cases of suspended penalties in which special conditions are being imposed, some kind of assessment, possibly also by probation, is in place.[33] If the condition entails inpatient treatment, the judge has to decide upon imposition on its maximum length. This decision cannot be delegated to the probation services.

Similar to penalties, measures can be both monetary and liberty restricting. The monetary measures include compensation of damage, confiscation of illegally obtained benefits or extraction of dangerous objects. Other measures target dangerous people and are called safety measures in literature.

The before mentioned TBS-order can be imposed in case of severe offences, dangerousness, and no or diminished criminal responsibility, and can be prolonged infinitely every two years by the court of imposition.[34] In case of diminished responsibility, TBS may be imposed in combination with a penalty. The order can also be imposed conditionally (instead of coerced commitment). In case of conditional TBS, the possible additional sentence is restricted to five years imprisonment and the total duration of the TBS-order is capped to nine years. A conditional TBS-order can however be changed into an unconditional TBS-order if conditions are breached or if '*the safety of others, or the general safety of persons or goods demands it*'. The unconditional TBS-order has a variant of limited duration of four years when it is imposed for offences which are not directed at or cause risk for the inviolability of the human body – a term which covers violent and hands-on sexual offences. For the imposition of all the variants of the TBS-order, a recent and multidisciplinary (of which at least a psychiatrist) forensic assessment has to be in place. Specific rules regarding defendants who refuse to cooperate in the evaluation exist to avoid as much as possible that the formal criterion of assessment would be considered unmet.

A safety measure targeting repetitive (petty crime) offenders was enacted in 2003. This 'ISD measure' permits the placement in a custodial treatment facility (e.g. for drug addicts) for two years '*if the safety of persons or goods demands it*'. The imposition of this safety measure formally requires a forensic assessment, but – other than for the TBS-order – this does not have to be provided by a psychiatrist and/or clinical psychologist as establishment of a mental disorder is not required. In practice, probation officers advise about utility, necessity and feasibility of the ISD measure. In case of diagnostic questions, a specific ISD-trajectory consultation or diagnostic investigation can be provided by any independent psychologist or psychiatrist, not required to be registered as a court expert. This is similar to the possibility for a suspended ISD measure can be imposed, as well as for the option for the court to provide itself with an intermediate check of the continuation of the order.[35]

Since 2012, liberty of offenders can be restricted with location and/or contact bans for a maximum of five years, for '*protection of society or to prevent criminal offences*'. No forensic or behavioural assessment is needed for such imposition. Since 2018, an indeterminate supervision order exists called the 'Measure of Influencing Behavior or Restricting Liberty' (GVM), which can be imposed in case of violent or sexual offences in combination with a prison sentence or a TBS-order. After TBS the order is most logical in combination with one of the two modalities of the TBS with a maximised duration, i.e. the conditional TBS (max. nine years) and the unconditional capped TBS for non-violent offences (max. four years). The criterion of dangerousness as meant in the GVM-measure resembles that of the TBS-order, although no (relation to a) mental disorder is required. The order needs to be imposed during sentencing, but another judicial decision is needed for the execution of the order at the end of the combined sentence. In this second judicial decision, the initial duration is set, up to five years, after which prolongations for periods up to five years are possible. For execution and prolongation a different dangerousness criterion is in place (see paragraph 9.2.3). For imposition, execution, and prolongation, forensic assessment by the probation service is required.[36]

Up to 2020, non-criminally responsible offenders could be placed in a psychiatric hospital, not necessarily a secured facility, for the maximum duration of one year. In a legislative change, this safety measure has been replaced by its successor (art. 2.3 of the Forensic Care Act, FCA). The new regulation provides the criminal court the opportunity to warrant coerced psychiatric, psychogeriatric, or intellectual disability care, when the criteria of the civil mental health laws (also new since 2020) are met, in any stage of the criminal process – prosecution, trial/sentencing, and execution of sentences. As it is no longer limited to the trial phase, or restricted to non-criminally-responsible offenders, the option of confluence with other sentences – in practice mainly suspended prison sentences – or legal frameworks is created, as well as the combination with an acquittal. Since the new civil mental health laws, it has become possible to only warrant, for example, coerced medication, instead of only coerced admission in a mental health institution. The maximum duration of the warrant is six months but can be prolonged if the criteria are still met. The criterion of dangerousness differs from before, and now includes 'serious disadvantage' for others and self. Other differences include formal criteria of the medical expert advice. Before 2020, a multidisciplinary forensic evaluation by at least one psychiatrist used to suffice, but for imposition of coerced civil care a medical declaration and treatment plan from the receiving facility are necessary. Whereas placement in a psychiatric hospital before 2020 could be imposed under criminal law also in the case of limited treatability of the underlying mental condition, the new legislation created new barriers. Coerced treatment is not only required to be proportionate but should also be effective, including expected improvement of the psychiatric condition. Therefore, if a receiving mental health facility – usually not equipped for reduction of the risk of reoffending, but merely for the treatment of the psychiatric condition – concludes that coerced treatment will probably be ineffective, it usually refuses to offer a treatment (plan) and/or refer the patient to another (secured) centre.

For juveniles (and, as mentioned, some adolescents/young adults), the Criminal Code provides separate sanctions. The most common sentences for adults have their equivalent for juveniles, albeit with a (much) lower maximum. Prison sentences for juveniles below the age of 16, can be at maximum one year, for 16–17-year-olds at maximum two years. The equivalent of the TBS-order, known by the public as 'youth-TBS', is called 'placement in an institution for juveniles' (PIJ). This PIJ measure is carried out in special wards in the same facilities as the juvenile prison sentence but can have a longer duration. The safety measure is imposed for a minimum of two years and can be prolonged up to a maximum of seven years. A maximum duration is in line with the aims of the juvenile criminal justice system, which is to provide education and give the convict a real second chance by avoiding lengthy detention. Life sentences are therefore not possible for minors convicted under juvenile criminal law. Other sanction modalities of rehabilitation and restriction of liberty in the community exist in the juvenile sentence arsenal, including a 'Measure of influencing behaviour'. Placement in psychiatric hospitals via 2.3 WFZ is not possible, although civil mental health laws also include minors from the age of 12 years onwards. On the other hand, opportunities under civil youth law, such as supervision orders and coerced placement in youth care institutions, are often combined with sanction modalities. The aims of education and rehabilitation ensure that in juvenile justice there is always some sort of forensic assessment in place. The NRGD acknowledges separated registration for court experts reporting about juveniles. Probation services and the Council for Child Protection are always involved.[37]

9.2.1.3 The execution of these sentences [38]

The described sentences are executed in four 'systems' or 'pathways' with specific legislative frameworks for the internal legal position: 1. the penitentiary system, governed by the Penitentiary Principles Act (PPA), 2. the TBS system, governed by the TBS-care Principles Act (TPA), 3. the (forensic) mental health system, governed by civil (mental) health laws, different for voluntary care, coerced care for persons with mental disorders, and coerced care for persons with psychogeriatric conditions or intellectual disabilities, 4. the community. Even detainees may be treated within all three intramural systems, for example through transfer. In the execution phase of offenders in these three systems, the Ministry of Justice and Security is the most common decision-maker. Treatment is also being paid for by this ministry during execution. The Forensic Care Act (FCA) is merely an 'organizational' act, labelling which care is being paid for by the Ministry of Justice and Security. The act now covers almost thirty legal frameworks within the criminal law sphere, which can be divided roughly in care related to the TBS-status, care as a condition in a conditional legal framework, and care for both provisional and prison detainees. Especially the last two categories cover multiple phases within the criminal process: the prosecution (including provisional detention), the trial (sentences imposed which involve care), and the execution of sentences (including safety measures). As a consequence several actors may decide on forensic care, like the prosecutor, the court, and the Minister, as competencies are divided over the course of the criminal process. Community reintegration, under supervision of the probation services, is generally within a conditional legal framework, like conditional release, in which the ex-detainee needs to adhere to certain conditions in order to not be placed (back) into detention.

In all systems, special facilities exist for treatment. Within the penitentiary system, the most notable institutions for forensic care are the so-called Penitentiary Psychiatric Centers (PPC's), of which there are at present four locations within penitentiary institutions throughout the country. The TBS-system consists of seven Forensic Psychiatric Centers (FPC's), of which two are governmental institutions and five private institutions. Within the forensic mental health system, the facilities with the highest security – albeit one level less secure than FPC's – are Forensic Psychiatric Clinics (FPK's), five in total. There are also a number of Forensic Psychiatric Departments in psychiatric hospitals (FPA's). Within the realm of addiction care, there are separate clinics and departments in place with similar levels of security. Furthermore, any mental health facility that meets the criteria may have a contract with the Ministry of Justice and Security for delivering forensic care. For treatment and care within the community, forensic outpatient clinics exist, as well as many homes for assisted living designated for forensic care.

So again, flexibility is a core characteristic of the execution of sentences, especially when it comes to administering forensic care, which is recognised in policy as the way to reduce reoffending. Even if such care or treatment is not automatically part of the sentence, it may still be provided through transfers between systems. Treatment aims and possibilities however differ between systems. Treatment in penitentiary institutions should cover general mental health care based on the WHO standard of equivalence of care compared to the community, basically including crisis intervention, stabilisation, and motivational treatment to provide a starting point for more in-depth psychotherapy after the prison sentence. In FPC's the treatment is of high intensity, including a long-term trajectory of slow but steady re-integration, and aimed at reducing risk. The aim of risk reduction is similar throughout the forensic mental health system although with less security and possibly less intensity, while treatment in the general mental health system treatment is primarily aimed at (recovering from) the mental disorder.

9.2.2 Decisions within sentencing and execution

9.2.2.1 Front-end sentencing decisions as part of the trial

The first type of front-end sentencing decisions that comes to mind is of course the imposition of sentences by the court. The relevant sentences are described in paragraph 9.2.1.2, including if any type of forensic assessment is required for such imposition. Preliminary to this decision, however, a decision has to be made about the culpability of the offender, as for example, the absence of culpability on the basis of a mental disorder (non-criminal-responsibility) renders penalties out of reach. Dogmatically related is the decision, for defendants of a certain young age (as described in paragraph 9.2.1.1), on the application of adult or juvenile sentences. As mentioned before as well, the criminal court may, either alternatively or additionally to a (minor) sentence, choose to warrant civil commitment. In sentencing, first of all a decision has to be made about the type of sentence, or the combination of sentences.

With regard to penalties, a decision has to be made about the height of the sentence within the maximum established by law. As mentioned earlier, diminished responsibility (based on a mental disorder) may be used as a mitigating factor, while dangerousness (either or not based on a mental disorder) or recidivism may be used as aggravating factors. Behavioural advise on these concepts is generally received by the forensic assessment(s) for the trial.

When a suspended/conditional sentence (including safety measures) is chosen, a decision has to be made about the type of conditions. The probation services generally advice on these issues and courts rely heavily upon these reports (as part of the quintessential practical enforceability). If one of the conditions is forensic care, a department within the NIFP is in charge of indicating the required level of security and treatment intensity. Of course if relevant, the evaluators doing the forensic assessment for the trial may advice on these matters, as they will also advice on the necessity and feasibility of the type of treatment and the legal framework. Many suspended/conditional sentences or liberty restricting safety measures may be declared immediately executable, meaning that appealing the verdict does not suspend the execution. These decisions often require sanction-specific, and different, criteria for dangerousness. Electronic monitoring may be ordered to control location bans as a restrictive condition in many sanction modalities.[39] A final decision for suspended penalties is the choice of the probation period. In general, it can have a maximum of three years, but in case of high risk for reoffending with a violent or hands-on sexual offence, or in case of high risk for an offence against the wellbeing of animals, it can be up to 10 years.[40]

9.2.2.2 Mid-way sentencing decisions within execution

After the judicial sentence, the executive branch or administration – prosecution, Ministry, directors of institutions, probation services – becomes the authority. First, it has to decide on placement within custodial sentences. Placement in forensic care institutions requires some psycho-legal information on risk and treatment needs which is gathered internally (by the NIFP). At present, there is no general risk screening for detainees, although a recent pilot with a newly created instrument was successful.[41] Decisions on transfer from prison to external institutions are made by the director of the penitentiary institution, on advise of a multidisciplinary prison team meeting, in which a psychiatrist (provided by the NIFP), psychologist, medical doctor, nurses, and social workers. So-called selection officers from the Ministry are able to transfer detainees within the penitentiary system, for example from a regular ward to a PPC, and transfer to either the TBS-system or the (forensic) mental health system.[42] A transfer from the TBS-system to the (forensic) mental health system is possible as well.

Within the TBS-system, transfers to other TBS-facilities are quite common, via the general route for placement in forensic care. Differentiated wards exist for offenders who need extreme risk management (including the risk for escape), or long-term forensic psychiatric care (LFPZ), formerly known as 'longstay' wards. These former 'longstay' wards are infamous, because the TBS-treatment is no longer aimed at rehabilitation through reduction of risk. Even though at the moment in practice there is more flow through the facility than its public stigma of 'life sentence in disguise' suggests, there are additional legal safeguards in place concerning placement and continuation of placement, which has to be reviewed every two years. There is a special multidisciplinary advisory committee for placement on long-term wards, which checks the application by the TBS-facility, while placement and continued placement also require independent multidisciplinary forensic assessment. In the end, however, the Minister decides. This decision may be appealed to the 'Council for the administration of criminal justice and protection of juveniles' (RSJ), which deals with appeals to many decisions by the Minister in the execution of sentences, as well as appeals to decisions of complaints committees in individual institutions, or certain decisions on coerced medication. Other important decisions in the execution of the TBS-order are those on leave. Over the decades an extensive system of leave has developed which is used as a treatment instrument in an individual case and ideally gradually becomes less restrictive. Phases include accompanied leave, unaccompanied leave, and 'transmural' leave, with which someone can live outside the institution but still follows treatment inside. Every new phase in the leave system has to be warranted by the Minister. Again, an independent multidisciplinary advisory committee judges the application for leave by the TBS-institution. On that advice, the Minister decides. Only the decision to revoke a warrant for leave is eligible for appeal, a general negative decision on an application is not. In a way, all these decisions are a product of a sequence of forensic assessments, as already the application of the institution, as well as the advice of the committee, may be regarded as such.

Some decisions during the execution are in the competence of the judiciary. These are first of all decisions related to deprivation of liberty, such as prolongation of the TBS-order, the intermediate check on the ISD-order, and decisions on changing conditional sentences into unconditional sentences (for example prison, TBS, PIJ, or ISD). Many of these decisions can be appealed by a specialised judicial body called the Penitentiary Chamber, in which three judicial members are accompanied by two behavioural scientific members. For the prolongation of the unconditional TBS-order at least an advice from the clinic is required, and every four years an independent multidisciplinary assessment. For prolongation of the conditional order an advice from the probation services and a psychiatrist are required.[43] Even though the law does not require establishing a mental disorder for prolongation, in legal practice this is used as a criterion nonetheless as a basis for risk and treatment. For the PIJ-order, comparable requirements are in place. Some decisions for which a judicial decision is necessary are related to restriction of liberty, such as the execution and prolongation of the GVM, as well as many back-end decisions.

9.2.2.3 Back-end sentencing decisions regarding execution[44]

At the end of sentences involving deprivation of liberty, frameworks involving restriction of liberty exist for a gradual community reintegration. Such frameworks of supervision often consist of conditions, under which someone is allowed (back) into the community, and which are being supervised by the probation services. Of course all conditional frameworks require consent to the conditions, even though the conditions could even mean inpatient treatment in a forensic mental health facility. The most obvious framework related to prison is conditional release.[45] Since July 2021 the eligibility for parole is no longer after serving two-thirds of the (long) prison sentence, but only two years before fully serving the sentence. The possibility for parole was pushed back to better communicate the retributive aspect of the sentence to victims and society. It is expected that judges will counter this development by imposing lower sentences.[46] As this was also the moment for transfer to a TBS-institution in case of a combination sentence with prison, this will mean longer detention before the treatment can start. In 2018, another hole in the dike was closed by enabling prolongation of the probation period for conditional release, again and again for two years, in case of high risk for violent or hands-on sexual offences or burdensome behaviour towards victims or witnesses.[47] This indeterminacy within the track of penalties is dogmatically a novelty. Life sentence in the Netherlands is in principle indeed 'for life', even though this is determinate in a way. There is no tariff system in the law, but to adhere to the European Court of Human Rights' requirement of perspective, a legal safeguard was enacted in 2017, in which a committee will advice the Minister about rehabilitative options for a lifer after 25 years of imprisonment. In this advice, risk is also a factor. Any potential rehabilitative efforts would then have to be fit in a general, but rarely used, legal framework of a (conditional) pardon, which is officially a decision by the Crown.[48]

Conditional release is also a possibility with regards to the TBS-order.[49] The GVM supervision order may be used as a back-end decision after a prison sentence or TBS, but only if it is already imposed at the trial. It is the only framework of restriction of liberty that does not require consent. All conditional release possibilities may be revoked by a court, as not adhering to conditions of the GVM may also lead to deprivation of liberty as a sort of punishment.

Even if all the criminal justice frameworks are to expire, art. 2.3 FCA civil commitment may be used to keep someone off the streets, of course only when the individual meets the criteria from civil mental health law, which may be problematic if the framework is only used to avoid reoffending (see paragraph 9.2.1.2). It is more frequently used in case of termination of the TBS-order, than after a prison sentence, but can also be used for individuals detained in a PPC at the end of their sentence, who need further coercive treatment after their imprisonment in the general mental health system.

Within youth sentences, also conditional release options exist. For the sentence of 'youth detention' a judge can even order it at any time during the execution of the sentence. As indeterminacy is not in line with the principles of youth justice, such frameworks are all limited in time. Only one back-end decision in this case is the exception. If, after seven years of PIJ *'the safety of others, or the general safety of persons or goods demands'*, the PIJ measure may be changed by a court into a TBS-order for adults. For this decision, in terms of assessment, only an advice by the youth institution is required.[50]

9.2.3 Concepts to be assessed

9.2.3.1 Relevant psycho-legal concepts

As the possibility of a TBS-order was traditionally the dominant reason for forensic assessment, it is no coincidence that the formulated standard set of questions for forensic assessment in service of the trial are very much in line with the criteria for imposition of the order. The questions are on:

1 The current presence of a disorder
2 The presence of that mental state during the offence
3 The influence of the disorder on behaviour and choice-making during the offence
4 The corresponding (level of) criminal responsibility for the offence
5 The risk for re-offending
6 The required treatment in behavioural terms and in terms of the legal framework

The questions evidently show that translations are required from psychodiagnostics to psycho-legal diagnostics. Even though the TBS-order is no longer the dominant outcome of the evaluation, and for most other frameworks there is no legal requirement of having a disorder, it still remains the point of reference for the forensic diagnostic evaluation by psychiatrists and psychologists. A pilot with a set of questions without diagnosing a disorder has recently been conducted. Assessments by the probation services in service of the trial focus much less on psychodiagnostics. In case of adolescent/young adult defendants, a question is added on the eligibility for juvenile justice. The standard set of questions for juvenile defendants is comparable, with more emphasis on developmental and educational or pedagogical aspects.

During the execution of sentences, especially risk and need for treatment remain important concepts, for example for decisions on leave or transfer respectively. For placement on an LFPZ ward, treatment prognostics come into play. For back-end sentencing decisions, again risk is the most important concept.

9.2.3.2 Mental disorder

Until 2020, the criterion for mental disorder in both criminal and civil law was 'a defective development or pathological disorder of the mental capacities'. Except for some minor editorial changes this criterion did not change since the first Dutch Criminal Code in 1886. Apparently, it sufficed for a long time, due to the fact that it was broad – acknowledging both a developmental and pathological cause for mental dysfunctioning –, not phrased in language of medical and/or behavioural disciplines and therefore could adapt to all changes and fashions within those disciplines. In case law it has been ruled that the criterion is not restricted to DSM-classifications, and could include a wider range of mental dysfunctioning.[51] Forensic assessors phrased their conclusions in both clinical diagnostical terms and in a classification.

This adaptability was particularly important because in Dutch law the criterion is a legal criterion, which has to be established by the court, possibly based on the answer to the relevant question in the forensic assessment, but it is not bound by this 'advice' and may substitute its own view on the matter. This does not often happen, but is more common in cases in which defendants refuse to cooperate with the evaluation and evaluators are unable, or hesitant, to diagnose a mental disorder. As refusal to cooperate is often prompted by the wish to avoid a TBS-order, for which a disorder has to be established, the old criterion has only been kept in place for the imposition of that order (and the equivalent in juvenile justice, PIJ). In doing that the legislator wanted to avoid that no such safety measure could be imposed, even though the protection of society would demand it. This legislation was triggered by an infamous case of re-offending of a dangerous offender (Michael P.) who was able to avoid a TBS-order by refusing to cooperate with the forensic evaluation. Even more legislative changes were enacted, such as the possibility to request old medical records. A special multidisciplinary committee was installed to assess the relevance of these records for forensic evaluation, but it has not yet had any cases in practice.[52] The ECHR has acknowledged the possibility of establishing the legal criterion by the court in cases of refusing defendants as grounds for imposition of the TBS-order.[53] The evaluator is asked to explain what the attitude of the defendant was towards the evaluation, and if he refused to cooperate, to what extend, and in what way this impacted the answering of the questions.

However, as in new civil mental health laws the criterion for mental disorder was changed into more 'modern' language, also in all other provisions of criminal law, the new criterion is now 'mental disorder, psychogeriatric condition or intellectual disability'. This enumeration is explained by the fact that in 2020 separate civil mental health laws were created for coercion within the psychiatric side of the mental health system and within the institutions for psychogeriatric and mental disability care, and is therefore solely pragmatic and without too much contents. In practice, however, the distinction is quite hard as a lot of disorders that do not literally fall under these categories have to be added in lower provisions, while co-morbidity between disorders (which is highly frequent within individuals) makes the distinction even more difficult. Although the intention was to not alter the principle in criminal law that it is the court that has to establish the criterion, the new terminology, more in line with the DSM-classification system, seems to shift the competence for establishment more to the behavioural disciplines.

9.2.3.3 Criminal responsibility[54]

The literal translation of the Dutch term for criminal responsibility *'toerekeningsvatbaarheid'* is something like 'susceptibility for attribution'. Attribution has a broader meaning within criminal law in light of the question whether offence behaviour can be attributed to the accused. It underlines the legal competence in deciding on the matter. Nevertheless, there has been elaborate discussion about the competence of forensic assessors to give advice to the court on this concept, as susceptibility seems to suggest a rather fixed capacity of the personality. Of course, non-responsibility is strictly related to the particular offence and not a permanent trait. In practice, the division of competences is not that rigid that the evaluator may give no advice about criminal responsibility. The only provision related to the concept is on non-responsibility: *'A person who commits an offense for which he cannot be held responsible due to a mental disorder, psychogeriatric condition or mental disability shall not be punishable.'*[55] It lacks any specific test as to which specific abilities should be impaired, as there was no consensus to be reached on the subject. Therefore the Dutch concept is an example of requiring a general (not specified) relation between the disorder and the offence. As such an open criterion allows for almost all sorts of causal relations between the disorder and the offence, which have been formed in legal doctrine, case law, and assessment practice, including internationally known criteria on cognition and volition.

This general causal criterion leaves room for (gradations of) diminished responsibility. The Dutch legislator however chose, in order to ensure consensus between classical and modern theorists, not to mention diminished responsibility in the criminal code, but in practice it plays an important role. The gradual or dimensional approach to responsibility may indeed have more 'face validity', but automatically adopts problems in the reliability of assessment. Indeed the Dutch experience has shown that even something like 'percentage responsibility' can be developed in practice, but there are far too many gradations than can scientifically be distinguished.[56] At present the debate has focused for almost a decade on five versus three gradations, ever since the guideline from the Dutch Association of Psychiatry in 2013 seemed to suggest that five gradations (including severely and somewhat diminished) cannot reliably be distinguished.[57] Non-responsibility is generally reserved for cases of psychotic motivations, in which the offence may solely be explained by the disorder without any circumstantial factors. Many personality disordered or sexually deviant offenders are considered to have (somewhat) diminished responsibility.

In the execution of sentences criminal responsibility does not play a role. Of course other capacity issues may arise, for example, related to coerced medication, but these are not specific for sentencing law.

9.2.3.4 Dangerousness

In the Dutch Criminal Code, dangerousness is not defined by a fixed definition. A lot of criteria have already been mentioned in paragraphs 9.2.1 and 9.2.2, as there are risk-criteria in place for all kinds of decisions in sentencing. They differ in contents and strength, both in aim and in required likelihood. But these cannot consistently be related to the severity of the consequences of certain decisions. The highest bar, both in aim and in contents, for example, seems to be for extending the probation period of a conditional sentence to 10 years: '*if it must be seriously taken into account*' (likelihood) that reoffending will take place of an '*offence which is directed at or cause risk for the inviolability of the human body*' (aim). It would be more understandable if this were the criterion for the TBS-order, in fact, why wouldn't such a person receive a TBS-order? However, the bar for receiving a TBS-order is, in terms of dangerousness, lower, defined as '*if the safety of others, or the general safety of persons or goods demands the imposition of the measure*'. Even stranger is the fact that another criterion for that same decision on the probation period is '*if it must be seriously taken into account that the convicted person will again commit an offence that harms the health or welfare of one or more animals*'. Here a political – or electoral – agenda, of a few political parties that have made animal welfare their issue, peeps through into the criminal law. Similarly, in the recent civil mental health laws the agenda of patient interest groups is visible in avoidance of the stigmatising word – and its broad definition – dangerousness, in favour of 'a significant risk for serious disadvantage'. In civil law disadvantaging oneself is an additional criterion to those of others and society in criminal law. Of course, the diverse and inconsistent use of risk criteria is a result of the expanding sentencing arsenal with the impossible aspiration of controlling any risky situation.[58] Creating a logical and consistent system would require a complete revision of the sentencing provisions in the CC.

In the CC no provisions are in place for how the establishment of these criteria should be carried out, apart from requiring it to be multidisciplinary. Only for imposition of the TBS-order, the provisions state that other reports regarding the personality of the defendant, the seriousness of the offence, and the frequency and seriousness of former offences are taken into account by the court.[59] This is the remainder of a discussion in Parliament on whether or not to require relating the assessment of risk to these factors. As also a mental disorder is required, there is a debate in case law whether there should be a relation between the disorder and the dangerousness. This debate is also topical amongst evaluators, as traditionally the dangerousness is derived from the established relation between disorder and offence, while risk assessment research suggests that disorders in general are not a strong predictor for recidivism.[60] For civil commitment the risk has to be related to the disorder, meaning that a general risk for (re-) offending does not suffice. In the standard questions for criminal pre-trial evaluation a compromise may be seen, in which the risk should also be described in terms of known risk and protective factors, other than arising from the disorder. Risk assessment in the Netherlands has traditionally been developed in relation to decisions in the execution of the TBS-order and back-end decisions. Those are situations in which there is a lot more clinical information present to draw from, than in case of pre-trial evaluation. There is still a lack of validated instruments for risk assessment that match the specific criteria during the trial phase.

9.2.3.5 Other relevant concepts

In relation to the last question of the pre-trial evaluation, concerning need for treatment, concepts such as treatability and responsivity are implicitly taken into account. Regarding civil commitment, also if warranted by a criminal court, effectiveness of the coerced care is an additional legal criterion. In the execution of a prison sentence (or provisional detention), need for treatment is relevant for decisions on internal or external transfer to a treatment facility. Traditionally, the criterion for external transfer was 'unfitness for detention' on a regular ward. In practice, this is still important, as the need for care or treatment is less noticed if a detainee easily manages his/her stay in the prison unit.

Finally, for 18–23 year-old-defendants, an additional question is added to the standard set of questions for pre-trial assessment on the eligibility for the application of juvenile sentences. Vice versa, for 16–17-year-olds, forensic assessors are asked to advise about the application of adult sentences. In practice, behavioural experts almost never find any reason to explicitly advise a juvenile to be convicted as an adult, and the severity of the offence is the most prominent reason for criminal courts to apply adult criminal law in the case of a 16- or 17-year old offender. The other way around, the advise to convict a young adult as a juvenile, is more frequently given by forensic behavioural experts. As the central notion behind 'adolescent criminal law' was to provide an effective and offender-oriented manner of sentencing, which does justice to the committed offence and which takes into account – as the law mentions – the personal circumstances of the offender, including his/her developmental phase, this may be considered a psycho-legal concept. Even though the legislator recognised the relationship between incomplete (biopsychosocial) development of adolescents and young adults, and recognised the superior effectiveness of the offender-oriented and pedagogical juvenile justice system in terms of better reintegration into society and prevention of re-offending, juvenile sentencing is still only rarely applied to young adults.[61] This is partly due to the lack of clear guidelines, both for behavioural experts as for legal practitioners in the criminal law system. Public prosecutors have developed a list of indicators that can be used as a basis for the decision to request the application of juvenile criminal law for young adults, including still living at home, still going to school, needing support because of mild intellectual disabilities and openness to educational support. Contraindications are the severity of the (alleged) offence and the criminal record of the young adult. Still, many public prosecutors (and judges) rely on intuition and experience. Social workers from the probation organisations often advise in an early stage, and recommend on applying juvenile criminal law, including (preventive) detention of the young offender in a juvenile institution instead of adult jail. Most behavioural experts use a standard weighing list as developed by the NIFP, thereby weighing concepts such as cognitive and adaptive skills of the adolescent and the (expected) responsivity of the adolescent to pedagogical interventions. Contraindications include the criminal record of the offender, a 'criminal lifestyle', psychopathic traits, and pedagogical impossibilities. Nevertheless, the concepts and dimensions to conclude with

A Dutch perspective   215

regards to developmental delays in the young offender are still being discussed. Furthermore, the need to review contraindications as well as the starting point in the application of the law (adult criminal law for 18 years and older unless, instead of juvenile criminal law unless) is still debated, as no young adult under the age of 25 is fully or completely developed, neither biologically (brain maturation) nor psychologically.

9.2.4 Forensic assessment and procedure

With regards to forensic assessment in service of the trial, it is often the public prosecutor who decides whether forensic assessment is needed, and if so, by which behavioural discipline(s). As soon as a defendant is taken into custody, police officers, probation workers, and, for juveniles, the Council for Child Protection, can signal any mental problems, and advise the public prosecutor to ask for a comprehensive forensic behavioural evaluation. After three days, all (alleged) offenders are arraigned to an examining magistrate. At this point in time, psychiatrists or psychologists working for the NIFP are often consulted to do a short reviewing evaluation and provide a behavioural advise for further forensic assessment. The nature and severity of expected psychiatric disorders, nature and severity of the (alleged) offence, as well as the expectancy regarding a possible verdict of TBS or PIJ, guide the necessity and multidisciplinarity of the assessment.

The kind of the assessment will eventually be chosen by the public prosecutor, or, in case any questions on mental state or personality of the offender remain during the ongoing criminal process, by the examining magistrate or trial court, possibly on request of the defense counsel. If a sentence that requires multidisciplinary evaluation is not to be expected, a monodisciplinary evaluation suffices. In such a case, the nature of both the mental state and the offence points towards which discipline should be chosen. For example, one may expect a different examination of an individual with primarily psychotic or bipolar disorder than with a person with a personality disorder, or with interpersonal violence at home compared to violence within street gangs. Finally, the intensity of the examination decides between an examination in a cell in the remand prison or at an office of the NIFP (the so-called ambulatory examination) or a clinical observation in the Pieter Baan Centre (PBC) or the juvenile counterpart, to be ordered by a judge. An observation will last for six weeks in general, which time can be doubled whenever needed, for example, in the case of those persons who refuse to cooperate. Possibly, in case of group offences, as the interactions between the members of the group seem to be decisive for the aggressive outcome, a group observation may be organised. Observation within the PBC also includes a comprehensive survey of the social network of the defendant, by a trained social worker.[62] Rather new is the possibility of such a 'triple' variant, in combination with a multidisciplinary ambulatory examination, to prevent a clinical observation (because of pragmatic reasons such as a waiting list and the costs). As such the views of three behavioural experts (psychiatrist, psychologist, and social worker) will come together for a consensus meeting, comparable to a final observation meeting within the PBC. All biopsychosocial aspects of the defendant and the situational aspects of the offense will play a role in the decision about place, time, and involved experts. Methodologically it is important that both judges and behavioural experts know what the influence of the setting of the examination is on the outcome of its results. Clinical observations as well as ambulatory examinations may include further specialist diagnostics and reports from a neurologist, neuropsychologist, or other specialties, for example, in case of (suspected) psychogeriatric disorders or acquired brain injuries.

All evaluations lead to one or more written reports, which are discussed in court, but usually not with the authors themselves. Naturally, either one of the parties or the court itself can ask the expert to further testify verbally in court, if there are any questions. In general, about 90% of the conclusions of the PBC evaluations are followed by the courts.[63] This percentage is lower for ambulatory evaluations, which is partly explained by the fact that these are cases with less severe offences or problems, creating more sentencing alternatives.[64] In about 20% of adult cases brought before a criminal court, forensic assessment by NIFP evaluators was performed. For juvenile cases, this is about 11%, which can also be explained by the fact that the Council for Child Protection writes reports as well.[65]

Within the execution of the TBS-order the prosecution is also competent in requiring forensic assessment as it has to be submitted to the court along with their request for prolongation. This is similar for both an evaluation from the TBS-facility or probation service, and a four-year report from independent NIFP evaluators.[66] For decisions on leave or transfer (to an LFPZ ward), the initiative is taken by the TBS-facility as they make an application to the Ministry. The screening being done for transfers within the correctional system is already explained in paragraph 9.2.2.2.

9.3 Safeguards for the quality of forensic assessment

9.3.1 Requirements in law and policy

The requirements that exist in law and policy can be divided in (a) general requirements for expert evidence for all forensic expertise in the CCP, (b) requirements for what type of forensic assessment should be done for a few impactful decisions within sentencing (mainly in the CC, already mentioned in paragraph 9.2), and (c) requirements in policy about what instruments to assess risk with for a few decisions within the execution of sentences.

Regarding the general requirements for experts, at the end of paragraph 9.1.2, it was already mentioned that since 2010 more extensive regulations for expert evidence can be found in the CCP.[67] The most fundamental change was the introduction of a register for experts (NRGD). As its rationale is mainly to safeguard the quality of the expert, its procedure will be discussed in paragraph 9.3.3. Some other requirement on the quality of the expertise can be found in the CCP. An examination needs to be in an area on which the expert possesses specific or particular knowledge. A written report is required – except when a judge specifically asks for an oral report –, which is truthful, complete, and to the best of the expert's knowledge. The report should be reasoned and '*if possible, the expert will indicate which method he has used, to what extent this method and its result can be considered reliable and what skills he has in applying the method*'.[68] Most behavioural scientific forensic evaluators, however, do not specifically comment on the reliability of their general diagnostic method, other than describing reliability and validity of one or more standardised assessment instruments or mentioning reliability issues in auto- or heteroanamnesis.

As mentioned in paragraph 9.2, for a few decisions a multidisciplinary forensic assessment is required. Even though the order existed since 1928, this requirement for the imposition of the TBS-order came into force in 1988. In that same legislative change many legal safeguards against disproportionate deprivation of liberty were introduced, for example, the appeal possibility to the decision on prolongation, and the independent multidisciplinary evaluation after six (now four) years (more on those in paragraph 9.4.2). The multidisciplinarity requirement for imposition was also very much rooted in the wish for more legal protection (initiated in the 1970s), but was specifically motivated to ensure 'maximum scientificity and due diligence'.[69] The option of requiring assessment in an observation clinic for all defendants was even discussed, but that was deemed unpractical. The demand that one of the examining disciplines is a psychiatrist may be viewed in light of the status of the medical profession (at that time). Later, this requirement was similarly applied to conditional TBS, PIJ, and the transfer of a prisoner to a TBS-facility. In the text of the provision, it is stated that the report should be done by the experts 'together or each separately'. No specific motivation was given for these wordings, leading to a discussion whether multidisciplinarity was meant as having expertise and counter-expertise together. In practice it is almost often 'together', as there is generally a deliberation between the two experts, sometimes also together with experts from the NIFP and probation officers. Experts generally strive for consensus, but dissensus is possible and should be discussed in detail in the written reports. Arguably both a team assessment and a counter-expertise may count as safeguards for the quality of an assessment. A final safeguard for quality is that the assessment may not be older than one year before the trial, unless all parties agree.[70] In practice, assessments are generally finished shortly before the trial, so this provision is mostly relevant for a possible appeal.

In policy regulations, some requirements exist for the use of standardised risk assessment instruments. Since 2008, in the aftermath of the parliamentary inquiry report after incidents with TBS-patients on leave, it is required for TBS-leave applications to use instruments of standardised clinical judgement.[71] Later, this became also required in the prolongation advice format or LFPZ-application format for example. In the aftermath of an infamous case, Michael P., similar requirements would be demanded for the placement of a detainee in a (forensic) mental health facility. Since 2019, offenders of severe violent or sexual offences need a formal risk assessment and offence analysis before their potential transfer to a mental health facility during the prison sentence. The risk assessment instrument has to be tailored to the offence at hand, and the assessment cannot be older than six months.[72]

9.3.2 Disciplinary and ethical requirements

Under this heading, first the efforts of the NIFP to ensure the quality of forensic evaluations are addressed. Thereafter, relevant guidelines from scientific associations and the code of conduct from the NRGD are discussed. These are all mostly applicable to the evaluation in service of the trial. However, many aspects will also be applicable to assessment within the execution of sentences, although differences will be mentioned if relevant.

The NIFP may be involved in case selection. Even though it is the duty of the prosecution to decide which cases require forensic assessment, efforts are underway to discuss cases together with behavioural or legal experts from the NIFP. After an attempt to use a standardised instrument for case selection,[73] which was never completely adopted in practice, these deliberations seem to be an efficient way to already involve expertise into the decision. If a case is selected, the NIFP matches the case with a suitable evaluator. Since (especially psychiatric) evaluators are scarce at present, there are practical limits to the matching process. Juvenile and adult evaluations require specialised knowledge as well as registrations, while young adults (18–23-year-olds) may be examined by both specialties. With regard to specific cases, such as sex offenders, evaluators who are trained in using tailored risk assessment instruments are preferred.

Another important instrument for safeguarding the quality of an individual report is a so-called 'feedback' procedure. All forensic reports are, before they are sent out to the legal parties, reviewed by a colleague behavioural expert and a legal expert working at the NIFP. These reviewers provide the forensic assessor with constructive criticism on the traceability and readability of the report, and the feasibility and applicability of the advices. It remains however the responsibility of the assessor whether s/he processes and adapts the comments, thus guaranteeing independence as an important ethical requirement – and in line with his/her own liability under disciplinary law. In the PBC the whole evaluation, including the conclusions, is being discussed with a peer and a legal expert in team meetings.

A more general safeguard which is already mentioned is the standard set of questions. The NIFP makes sure that with every change in legislation, this frame of questions is updated via expert meetings, including members of the public prosecution offices and courts. Moreover, there are regular deliberations with judges to test whether the set of questions is adequate for legal practice. In that sense, the NIFP is like a spider in a web, deliberating also with the disciplinary associations, NRGD (see next paragraph), the Prosecution and Ministry, for example about hours and financial compensation. The standard number of hours was recently updated to 23 hours for the psychiatrist and 27 hours for the psychologist (who is using more standardised instruments, questionnaires, tests). As an important part of the quality, as in usefulness for legal practice, is to have the report finished in time (before the trial), the NIFP keeps track of processing time as well. Finally, the NIFP provides education and supervision to become a registered expert, refresh courses, further training, assistance to and tools for evaluators, as for example a 'format' for the report (for all types of evaluations), which is being recommended but not obliged. After description of the diagnostic data collection and interpretation, including the conversation about the analysis of the offence, the format ends with forensic considerations and answers to the questions.

Although forensic psychiatry has been well connected to general psychiatry, it took until 2012 for the Dutch Psychiatric Society (NVvP) to set out disciplinary guidelines for forensic examination and reporting (a second version is now under construction, in which the NIFP is also involved).[74] For psychological evaluation, the Dutch Institute for Psychology (NIP) at present does not have a guideline, but the governmental NIFP has formulated some disciplinary recommendations, written down in a guideline in 2018.[75] Both the psychiatric and psychological guidelines build on existing guidelines for methodology in general psycho-diagnostics, and add recommendations on (the translation to) the forensic context. Both cover adult and juvenile justice. An important aspect related to quality that is covered in both guidelines is the differential diagnostic considerations. It is stressed that the disorder may not be based on the indictment. Furthermore, methodology on how to assess criminal responsibility and risk is covered extensively, as well as some ethical issues.

Some relevant aspects of health law are not applicable to reporting to the court. For example, confidentiality does not exist in the relation between forensic expert and examinee, which differs essentially from the usual patient-doctor relationship in society. Whereas a pre-trial evaluator is not allowed to have such a relationship, in the current nor in the past, the advisor from the TBS-facility on prolongation of the order generally does have a treatment relationship. The examinee, as a part of his legal position, should be pointed at this difference and also at the fact that he cannot stop the report from being transferred to the court. Although the examinee does not have the right to block the report, s/he has the right to read it at first hand, by which the examinee can point to some factual inaccuracies (such as date of birth or number of siblings) or may respond verbally or in writing to the contents of the report. The examinee's response to the content of the report is added to the report. Evaluators are required to provide clear information about the examination, their role in the trial process, the rights of the examinee, and the issued report, after which the examinee is able to provide informed consent for the examination.

As mentioned before, in the case consent has been refused, the expert witness still has to write a report to the court, not only informing about the refusal but also about the reasons (if available) for that, and all the attitudes and behaviours s/he has witnessed from the examinee. The examining psychiatrist and psychologist remain as professionals subordinate to the disciplinary law and behavioural codes of their profession, even though they act on behalf of the court. Expert witnesses should be independent, impartial, and competent professionals. Other obligations for the expert, as mentioned in the Code of conduct of the NRGD,[76] include: remain within the limits of your assignment and your expertise, report every significant (attempt to) influence the execution of your assignment, ensure the required quality of the evaluation, keep the gathered information available for counter-expertise, ensure a comprehensible, properly reasoned, verifiable and timely report (be prepared to submit your report to fellow professionals for assessment), supplement a provided report as far as necessary on the basis of further information, maintain and develop your professional competence.

9.3.3 Requirements for the evaluator

Requirements that are in place to safeguard the quality of the evaluator in general are training and registration. However, these are more or less connected, as accomplishing the forensic training by e.g. the NIFP leads to an initial registration in the NRGD. The total duration of theoretical training courses is nine months for one day a week, during or after which at least five different forensic reports are written under supervision of a trained and registered supervising colleague. Registration takes place after a written and oral exam in which three reviewers, including a representative from the NRGD, assess the applicant on at least three of the applicant's forensic reports. Prior or partly during the training to become a forensic expert, applicants should have completed training and registration as a psychiatrist or as a health care psychologist (which takes a total of at least 10.5 or 6 years respectively).

Assessors who act as an expert in a criminal case should be registered in the NRGD. Only in exceptional cases, non-registered experts can be appointed to report by an examining magistrate, usually in the case of special expertise for example on the type of disorder. Every five years a registered expert is required to re-register, during which the applicant should report on further training and followed conferences and the number of hours of intervision with other behavioural experts. There is also an association for forensic evaluators, which aids in reaching these goals, just like the NIFP. During re-evaluation, representatives of the NRGD again evaluate at least two (anonymous) forensic reports written by the applicant. In the Resolution Register Expert in Criminal Cases,[77] the criteria for a positive decision on the application are mentioned. They include: sufficient knowledge and experience in both the own discipline and the legal context, able to write an understandable report, again timely, and once more independent, impartial, diligent, skilled, and honest. These requirements are preceded by a criterion for the discipline itself. It should be: a well-defined area of expertise of which it is plausible that meaningful, objective, and reliable information can be provided on that basis and that, in the opinion of the Board, has been developed in a such a way that the findings can be tested and justified on the basis of shared standards. Interestingly, most disciplines acknowledged by the NRGD have substantive additional standards in place, including legal psychology, while the extra standards of the clinical behavioural disciplines are mostly procedural.[78] It underscores the exceptional position of these disciplines, both in terms of difficulty to be judged like (other) empirical disciplines, and in terms of its traditional value for the practice of criminal law.

9.3.4 Enforcement of requirements

The requirements for the quality of the evaluator under 3.3 are of course enforced by the (re-) registration procedure of the NRGD itself. Experts may loose their registration, or receive a conditional registration, if the standards are not yet completely met. However, being a registered expert, does not automatically mean that all your reports are of sufficient quality (if only because re-registration is done on cases that someone can select him/herself). For every individual evaluation, even when registered, an expert is appointed by a magistrate. If a court is not satisfied that the quality of the evaluation is sufficient, it will for example leave the report out of consideration, as it did in a case of someone who claimed to be an expert in non-verbal communication and micro-expressions, but draw conclusions outside that area of expertise.[79] When more reports are present in a case, the court may use arguments on quality of the report, to dismiss its conclusions in favour of those of a report which is deemed of higher quality.

Disciplinary 'malpractice' cases, based on health law, regarding forensic assessment are scarce. Only disciplines that fall under the Professions in Individual Health Care (BIG) can be liable. Therefore, assessments by probation services for example cannot be challenged through this way. Some case law exists on cases in which the evaluation was completely done on file information and the examinee was never seen. However, in cases of defendants refusing to cooperate, the attempt to talk to someone can qualify as 'seen' already, after which conclusions may be drawn for example on information from files, observation or conversations with network members.[80] Also some case law exists on the right to correct information. If a complaint is filed against an evaluator, the norm applied is generally whether this was an act or omission contrary to the care that the healthcare practitioner should exercise in that capacity.[81] To judge how an evaluator should act will probably be based on the guidelines as mentioned earlier in paragraph 9.3. A concern is that disciplinary committees often do not have enough 'feeling' for the forensic population, among which are also a few frequent complainers.[82] Even though complaints are generally not considered well-founded, the procedural hassle for the evaluator is enormous, while a founded complaint may lead to serious consequences from a fine or (a warning to) being removed from the BIG-register.

9.4 Safeguards 'against' the limited quality of forensic assessment

9.4.1 Questioning the assessment by the defense

In the Dutch inquisitorial trial procedure, expert witnesses are called by the court itself. However, the parties may apply to the court for calling the expert witness. If the expert has also written a report, this is generally granted. First the court questions the expert, but after that the prosecution and defense counsel are allowed to ask questions as well. Regarding forensic assessment the counsel can also take other initiatives. Counsel can apply for forensic evaluation to the prosecution, the examining magistrate, or later the trial court.[83] Moreover, the defense can take the initiative to suggest a particular (registered) expert already for the initial assessment, for example, if the defendant trusts this expert.[84] This may also aid not refusing to cooperate with the assessment. These provisions apply for both an initial assessment, as well as a counter-expertise. Of course, if there already is an initial report, the court will judge an application for a second report differently. The criterion used in case law is whether the court considers itself sufficiently informed.[85] It proves to be quite hard for the defense to motivate why counter-expertise is necessary, especially if the report comes from the highly esteemed PBC. The questioning in the trial may also be used for this argument.

Two other options that exist in the CCP to test the quality of an expert evaluation are not often used for behavioural scientific assessment. First of all, a controlling expert may be appointed by the defense, also to be present during interactions with the defendant.[86] This accompaniment is less imaginable in case of a diagnostic interview than in case of DNA-analysis for example. The alternative of audio(visually) recording such interviews, is also uncommon. Another option is to have the report evaluated by another expert.[87] It has been argued that these options should be explored more, for example in having an observing expert present during a meeting between the evaluating experts, or in the PBC, in which the conclusions are discussed, to monitor the process.[88]

Another possibility the defense may use, commissioning an assessment itself, is not provided for by law. In practice, a few difficulties have to be overcome regarding this adversarial initiative. First of all, via this route there is no option to have the defendant placed in the PBC. This has led to complaints from the perspective of equality of arms, which in this inquisitorial system is not completely applicable. Moreover, the costs of the evaluation have to be advanced by the defense (or defendant). If a report is eventually used in court, counsel can motivate afterwards that the costs have to be reimbursed by the State.[89] However, counsel generally wants to have the opportunity not to submit the report in the proceedings, for example, if the conclusions are not in line with the desired strategy, rendering reimbursement of the costs unsure. Especially this strategic use, and the uncertainty whether the report will be used in court, is one of the reasons that most experts are reluctant to evaluate individuals commissioned by the defense. For example, the idea that an assessment of high risk for violent reoffending will not reach the court, weighs on their conscience, apart from concerns about influencing attempts by the defense or to be viewed as a 'party-expert', or not having the quality safeguards from the NIFP in place.[90] Most of these concerns are or may be remedied. The NIFP has circled the policy that feedback will be provided also for reports commissioned by the defense, while a 'quick scan' of the initial report by an expert on request of the defense, whether other outcomes by a plausible outcome of a second evaluation, is being used by certain experts to mitigate the costs.

Of course, if there is an option for appealing the court decision, this would be a possibility to have another court look at the evaluation, or have a new evaluation in place. Most of these regulations apply, *mutatis mutandis*, to court decisions within the execution of sentences, such as prolongation of the TBS. The difference is that in such a proceeding the initial assessment is being done by the TBS-facility in charge of treating the offender. A placement on an LFPZ-ward may be for example appealed by the RSJ. But in general, from the perspective of the counsel there are very few options to effectively challenge the course of treatment.[91] The TBS-provisions allow for applying for transfers (also for second opinions) or for an observation in the PBC, for the necessity of which the Ministry has to be persuaded. In general, in contesting forensic assessment much depends on the initiative and specialist knowledge of the defense counsel. There is an association for TBS-lawyers to promote such knowledge, but not all TBS-patients have a lawyer that is part of that association, while it is legally the responsibility of the patient to have a good lawyer.

9.4.2 Questioning the assessment by the court

Indeed in this inquisitorial process, the court is leading in questioning the assessment, even if calling the expert to court was applied for by one of the parties. For the decision on calling the witness, a timely finish of the report is essential. As mentioned, it is not self-evident to call experts to court. Efficiency deliberations often lead to decisions based on written reports. Procedures for judicial bodies within the execution of sentences are also inquisitorial in nature. Since many questions already have been answered, questioning by the parties does not really have the nature of a cross-examination. As mentioned in paragraph 9.2 (especially 9.2.4) courts often follow the conclusions of the assessment, even though they have the competency to substitute their own conclusions. In paragraph 9.5 it will be discussed how courts could decide in case of differences of opinion. If the court does not consider itself sufficiently informed, it may commission expertise or counter-expertise itself.

The conclusions of the forensic evaluation are considered an advice. This means that it is only a part of the other facts and circumstances which the judges use in their sentencing decision. As the education of the expert witnesses tells them how to put their reports into words the judges can understand, as such the judges and public persecutors have their own options for training to understand forensic reporting at their education centre (SSR). There is also a knowledge circle for TBS and warranted care within the judiciary, in which relevant knowledge is shared and which also organises conferences. Membership of this circle is however not obligatory. Some larger courts have special teams in place for TBS-decisions, but courts with fewer judges have not. Although there have always been debates about strengthening the behavioural expertise within judicial bodies, even the court deciding on prolongation of TBS consists of three members from the judiciary. Only in the Penitentiary chamber, dealing with all sorts of appeals to court decisions within sentencing, two behavioural expert members are added to 'strengthen the expert element' in the decision. However, the fact that their influence in the secret deliberations for decision-making may not be (con)tested, has been criticised.[92]

9.4.3 Other questioning of the assessment

The Dutch legal system does not know a 'friend of the court' (*amicus curiae*), nor a possibility for intervention in a single case concerning the quality of forensic assessment by any others, including bodies mentioned earlier, like the NIFP.

Only regarding the execution of the TBS-order, the legislator has provided for obligatory counter-expertise, for example for prolongation and for (continued) placement on an LFPZ-ward. This is understandable, as the initial advice is being given (or application is being made) by the treating TBS-facility. In addition, the continuation of the order is considered a very severe infringement on the right to liberty, solely based on forensic assessment, and LFPZ-placement is considered a loss of perspective on liberty. The independent multidisciplinary advice for prolongation used to be after every six years, but on the grounds of the wish to reduce the mean duration of the intramural TBS-treatment, is now every four years. The decision on continuation of stay on an LFPZ-ward, including independent assessment, used to be every three years, and is now every two years (also to be in line with the timing of decisions on prolongation of the order itself).

The presence of behavioural experts in some decision-making bodies, like the RSJ (for appeals concerning decisions on the internal legal position, including transfers) and the Penitentiary Chamber (for decisions on the external legal position, the framework for deprivation of liberty), serves in a sense as a (peer) review on the expert assessment. The same applies to many advisory bodies (for example for TBS-leave, for pardoning a life sentence, et cetera).

9.5 Safeguarding the quality of decision-making when confronted with disagreement between experts

9.5.1 Dealing with disagreement

In a multidisciplinary evaluation, it may occur that the psychiatrist and co-reporting behavioural expert (mostly a psychologist) disagree on the conclusions. As mentioned in paragraph 9.3.1, they generally discuss the outcomes of their separate evaluations, and strive to consensus. However, if they cannot find agreement on (some of) the conclusions, the guidelines require them to both discuss and explain their differences in their respective reports. For the obligatory counter-expertise on the advice of the TBS-facility for prolongation or application for LFPZ-placement described in paragraph 9.4.3, the standard set of questions is already phrased in terms of agreement and explanation of any disagreement.

Even though disagreement may occur in any case, especially in exceptional cases of scientifically more uncertain matters, disagreement occurs more often. It is no surprise that a famous case in which about six evaluations were being done by several instances, was a case of double homicide by an asylum seeker after a change in his antidepressant medication. Complicating factors here were the intercultural and pharmacodynamic aspects. It led to very different conclusions on the presence of a mental disorder at the time of the offence and the level of criminal responsibility.[93] The case has also led to a complaint from pharmacological experts against one of the evaluators to the university he works for, however without any consequences.[94] As this obviously showed that the state of the discipline on the issue was one of uncertainty, the Court of Appeal was explicitly critical about the fact that even the PBC-report did not mention this.

> *After all, it is of great importance [...] to find out whether there are differences of opinion between the reporting experts themselves, and with other members of the interdisciplinary consultation, about the quality of the evaluation conducted and the conclusions drawn from that evaluation. Only such openness enables the court to assess the reliability and the traceability of the expert's report for the decisions to be taken. Whether a report stating differences of opinion between experts is useful for those decisions is at the discretion of the court, not of the experts.*[95]

That last remark is related to the idea among experts that judges are not helped with differences of opinion. With regard to the required openness of the experts about the state of scientific evidence, the appellate court also referred to the NRGD Code of Conduct in which it is stated that: 'If the findings within the relevant area of expertise can reasonably lead to differing interpretations or conclusions, the expert shall report this when providing information or when issuing that report.'[96] Again, it shows that the NRGD standards are tailored more to (natural) empirical sciences, because this standard may have to lead to a general disclaimer for behavioural forensic assessment. And in defense of the experts, little research is being done on difference of opinion.[97]

A first option for a decision-maker when confronted with conflicting conclusions is just to make a decision. An analysis of case law[98] suggests that most often one of the reports is being followed, with no particular favour for an initial or counter-expertise,[99] motivated by the fact that this report seems more reasoned and understandable. For example, when it is a report from the PBC, which is generally more elaborated as a team effort, this argument is used. In fewer instances the court substitutes its own, third, position on the matter. In cases of the obligatory counter-expertise of TBS-prolongation, in about half of the cases there is some disagreement. It is apparent that the independent experts reported more in favour of the individual. In about two-thirds of the cases, the court follows the independent expertise. This is partly explained by the difference in advising a prolongation of one or two years, which is quite a 'safe' decision. When it comes to disagreement on conditional release, the court follows the initial experts in about 50%. Even though courts seem prone to speed things up, arguments may then be that the TBS-facility knows the individual better because they see him everyday instead of in two meetings.

In literature, there is some support for courts' ability to break through the 'expert-paradox', which means that the court has to judge the quality of the expertise without having the expertise. The court may ask questions on the methods (and level) of acquiring knowledge and the state of the discipline.[100] However, when the decision-maker finds it too difficult to reason which advice to follow – the criterion of not considering to be sufficiently informed seems similarly applicable – it could ask for a third opinion, or more (as we saw in the discussed case).

9.5.2 Best practices

In literature, an expert meeting is suggested in case of differences of opinion, with a debate on the timing of this meeting, either prior to the trial or in front of the court – lawyers prefer the latter.[101] Such a meeting may show some similarities with the best practice that has come up within the execution of the TBS-order, in case treatment takes a very long time (it started out as a pilot for 15+ years) for example because of an impasse in the treatment. The Ministry introduced a so-called 'care conference', which is a case conference, with all the parties involved: Ministry, clinic, patient, lawyer, third experts, probation service, possible follow up facilities, et cetera. Quite often, disagreement about the diagnosis or the course of treatment is such an impasse. It shows to be a highly valued instrument and quite effective in reaching its goals: out of the box brainstorming, shared problem ownership, and taking trajectories responsibly forward.[102] Lawyers may request such a conference, just as they may also request an official meeting with the clinic, which often already helps in aligning the patient and the clinic.

9.6 Critical reflections

In the body of this chapter some critical reflections have already been made, which are briefly summarised here. From the positive side, it should be mentioned in advance that the Dutch tradition of forensic assessment is deeply rooted in the practice of criminal law, is frequently used, and has quite an impact on decision-making. Forensic care is and has been extensively used, in a highly flexible sentencing system, creating a lot of decision-making in which expertise is requested. Many parties are involved in trying to safeguard the quality of this expertise.

Critical comments have been made concerning the ever-growing sentencing arsenal, with the impossible aspiration of reducing all re-offending risk. The consequential sprawl of different dangerousness criteria is, both in terms of substantive and procedural requirements, inconsistent with the severity of the consequences. It also does not easily match the existing instruments for (standardised) risk assessment, while in many cases psycho-legal concepts do not have to be established with the aid of behavioural expertise at all. Many discussions on relevant concepts, especially regarding criminal responsibility, are typical for the Dutch context. Similarly, the inquisitorial justice system and the strive for consensus, may overestimate the reliability of the expertise (underestimate difference of opinions) and render the assessment less scrutinised. The strongest safeguard for the quality of assessment, the register and its procedure, do not necessarily ensure the quality of assessment in a single case. The instruments in the CCP for that, as well as the standards of the NRGD, are tailored more to the (natural) empirical sciences and are not always applicable for clinical behavioural expertise. Even though this has had a positive effect in opening up the tradition of too little transparency about the state of the discipline, there is more to gain and tailor. Obvious recommendations are: more research on the quality of forensic assessment and reporting, further interdisciplinary training of all the parties involved in sentencing, and a continued debate involving all these parties on how to further safeguard the quality of forensic assessment within the particular disciplines at stake, in all its elements, both in service of the trial and within the execution of sentences.

Notes

1 Van Koppen and Penrod, 2003.
2 Nijboer, 2000.
3 See Mevis and Van der Wolf, 2021.
4 Schwikkard, 2008.
5 Van der Wolf et al., 2010.

A Dutch perspective 225

6 Groenhuijsen and Selçuk, 2014.
7 Outside the issue of assessment, this feature is also under debate when it comes to victim impact statements, which also only influence the sentencing decision, but may have psychological consequences for both victim and offender if the defendant is afterwards found not guilty of committing the crime and as a result no decision on sentencing is made. Keulen et al., 2013, with a Summary in English.
8 Grootelaar and Van den Bos, 2018.
9 Mevis, 2015.
10 Van Marle et al., 2012.
11 Gremmen, 2018, with a Summary in English.
12 Jacobs and Van Kampen, 2014.
13 Parts of this paragraph are based on Van der Wolf, 2013 (in Dutch).
14 Strange as it may sound, this legislation introduced by the occupier remained in force after regaining sovereignty.
15 J.N. Ramaer was, with colleagues, also co-founder of the Dutch Society of Medicine (KNMG; in 1849) and the Dutch Psychiatric Association (NVvP; in 1871).
16 See for more background on the origins of the TBS-order: Van der Wolf and Herzog-Evans, 2014.
17 See Koenraadt, 1987, who refers to the Groningen school and Utrecht school.
18 See Van der Wolf and Van Marle, 2018.
19 See Hoving, 2017, with a Summary in English.
20 Nauta, Abraham and Pieters, 2020, in Dutch.
21 Van der Wolf and Herzog-Evans, 2014.
22 De Keijser, 2011.
23 SC 10-09-1957, *NJ* 1958, 5. See Van der Wolf and Herzog-Evans, 2014.
24 De Ridder et al., 2018, with a Summary in English.
25 See, also for this terminology Tak, 2008, p. 137.
26 Van Wingerden and Drápal, 2018.
27 Art. 9a CC.
28 See Van der Wolf and Mevis, 2021.
29 See Schmidt, Rap and Liefaard, 2020.
30 Kooijmans, 2002, with a Summary in English.
31 Van Kordelaar, 2018, in Dutch.
32 Art. 14a CC.
33 Jacobs, Van Kalmthout, and Von Bergh 2006, with a Summary in English.
34 Art. 37a-38j CC.
35 Art. 38m-38p CC. See also Struijk, 2015.
36 Art. 38z CC. See also Struijk and Mevis, 2016.
37 See art. 77a–77gg CC.
38 Parts of this paragraph are based on Van der Wolf and Mevis, 2021.
39 See Hucklesby et al., 2016.
40 Art. 14b CC.
41 De Vries Robbé, Van den End and Kempes, 2021, in Dutch.
42 For a complete description of the possibilities, see Van der Wolf and Mevis, 2021.
43 Art. 6:6:12 CCP (Code of Criminal Procedure).
44 Parts of this paragraph are based on Van der Wolf and Mevis, 2021.
45 Art. 6:2:10 CCP.
46 Uit Beijerse et al., 2018, with a Summary in English.
47 Art. 6:1:18 CCP.
48 Van Hattum and Meijer, 2016.
49 Art. 38 g CC.
50 Art. 6:6:33 CCP.
51 CA Den Bosch 11-10-2011, *LJN* BT7167.
52 See art. 37a under 6–9 CC.
53 See Kooijmans and Meynen, 2017.
54 Parts of this paragraph are based on Van Marle and Van der Wolf, 2018.
55 Article 39 CC, own translation.
56 See Zeegers, 1981.
57 NVvP, 2013, in Dutch. A new guideline is in the making, so the discussion continues.
58 See Struijk and Van der Wolf, 2018, in Dutch.

59 Art. 37a under 5 CC.
60 See Bijlsma et al., 2019.
61 Schmidt, Rap, and Liefaard, 2020.
62 See Koenraadt, Mooij, and Van Mulbregt, 2007.
63 Boonekamp et al., 2008, in Dutch.
64 Canton, 2004, with a Summary in English.
65 Van Kordelaar, 2020, in Dutch. For cases in front of a three judges court, as for less severe cases one judge may suffice.
66 Art. 6:6:12 CCP.
67 See art. 51i-51m CCP.
68 Art. 51 l under 1 CCP.
69 See Van der Wolf, 2012, with a Summary in English.
70 Art. 37a under 3 CC.
71 Next to the HCR-20 an instrument was created specifically for the TBS-context, called HKT-30. Werkgroep Risicotaxatie Forensische Psychiatrie, 2002, in Dutch.
72 Artikel 5.2 van het Besluit forensische zorg.
73 Van Kordelaar, 2002, with a Summary in English.
74 NVvP, 2013, in Dutch.
75 NIFP, 2018, in Dutch.
76 NRGD, 2016.
77 Art. 12 Resolution Register Experts in Criminal Cases.
78 NRGD, 2018, in Dutch.
79 DC Zeeland-West-Brabant 27-01-2021, ECLI:NL:RBZWB:2021:280.
80 See Kempes and Van der Wolf, 2018, in Dutch.
81 Art. 47 under 1, a, Wet BIG.
82 Prinsen and Groothuizen, 2019, in Dutch.
83 Art. 150, art. 176, art. 315 under 3 CCP respectively.
84 Art. 227, under 2 CCP.
85 E.g. CA Arnhem 9-07-2011, ECLI:NL:GHARN:2011:BQ7584.
86 Art. 228 under 4 CCP.
87 Art. 230 under 2 CCP.
88 Hummelen, 2018, in Dutch.
89 Art. 591 CCP.
90 Drees et al., 2020, in Dutch.
91 See Van der Wolf et al., 2016, with a Summary in English.
92 See Van der Wolf, 2010, in Dutch.
93 See SC 12-12-2016, ECLI:NL:HR:2016:2838 and SC 14-3-2017, ECLI:NL:HR2017:417.
94 Van Wijngaarden, 2016, in Dutch.
95 CA Arnhem-Leeuwarden 11 December 2014, ECLI:NL:GHARL:2014:9618.
96 See III Ad II.5 NRGD Code of Conduct.
97 See Drees et al., 2020, in Dutch, for an analysis of case law, and Kempes and Van der Wolf, 2018, in Dutch, for a vignette study, supported by the NIFP.
98 See Drees et al., 2020, in Dutch.
99 Even though in the case law it could not be distinguished who initiated these counter reports.
100 See Giard and Merckelbach, 2018, in Dutch; and Hoving, 2017, with a Summary in English.
101 See Drees et al., 2020, in Dutch.
102 Oosterom et al., 2019, in Dutch.

References

Bijlsma, J., Kooijmans, T., De Jong, F., and Meynen, G. (2019). Legal insanity and risk: An international perspective on the justification of indeterminate preventive commitment. *International Journal of Law and Psychiatry*, 66, pp. 101462.

Boonekamp, J., Barendregt, H., Spaans, M., De Beurs, E., and Rinne, T. (2008). Hoe gebruikt de rechtbank de PBC-rapportage? Een onderzoek naar PBC-rapporten van 2000–2005. *Sancties*, 5, pp. 294–303.

Canton, W.J. (2004). *Gerapporteerd... en dan? Een onderzoek naar risicotaxatie, behandeling en recidieven bij personen over wie pro justitia is gerapporteerd*. (dissertation Amsterdam). Amsterdam: UvA.

De Keijser, J.W. (2011). Never mind the pain, it's a measure! justifying measures as part of the Dutch bifurcated system of sanctions. In: M. Tonry (Ed.), *Retributivism Has a Past: Has It a Future?*. Oxford: Oxford University Press, p.188.

De Ridder, J., Emans, B.J.M., Hoving, R.A., Krol, E., and Struiksma, N. (2018). *Evaluatie Wet beperking oplegging taakstraffen*. Den Haag: WODC.

De Vries Robbé, M., Van den End, M., and Kempes, M. (2021). *Onderzoeksrapport Pilot 'Risicoscreening in detentie*. Den Haag: DJI.

Drees, M., Huisman, C., De Jong, J., Olde Keizer, M., Rodenboog, S.D., Van Tongeren, P.E., De Wildt, P.E., and Van der Wolf, M.J.F. (2020). De gedragskundige contra-expertise in straf- en tbs-zaken: problemen en oplossingen. *Expertise en Recht* 2020-5, 5, pp. 178–187.

Giard, R.W.M., and Merckelbach, H. (2018). De ene deskundige is de andere niet. Hoe de rechter empirisch gefundeerd bewijs kan waarderen. *NJB*, 19, pp. 181–188.

Gremmen, E.M. (2018). *De kwetsbare psychisch gestoorde verdachte in het strafproces. Regelgeving, praktijk en Europese standaarden* (dissertation Rotterdam). Oisterwijk: Wolf Legal Publishers.

Groenhuijsen, M.S., and Selçuk, H. (2014). The principle of immediacy in Dutch criminal procedure in the perspective of European Human Rights Law. *Zeitschrift für die Gesamte Strafrechtswissenschaft*, 126(1), pp. 248–276.

Grootelaar, H., and Van den Bos, K. (2018). How litigants in Dutch courtrooms come to trust judges: The role of perceived procedural justice. *Law & Society Review*, 52(1), pp. 234–268.

Hoving, R.A. (2017). *Deskundigen in het strafproces* (dissertation Groningen). Oisterwijk: Wolf Legal Publisher.

Hucklesby, A., Beyens, K., Boone, M., Dünkel, F., McIvor, G., and Graham, H. (2016). *Creativity and Effectiveness in the Use of Electronic Monitoring: A Case Study of Five Jurisdictions*. EMEU-Report.

Hummelen, J.W. (2018). Gedragsdeskundig rapporteren op verzoek van de verdediging. *Expertise en Recht*, p. 9.

Jacobs, M.J.G., Van Kalmthout, A.M., and Von Bergh, M.Y.W. (2006). *Toepassing van bijzondere voorwaarden bij voorwaardelijke vrijheidsstraf en schorsing van de voorlopige hechtenis bij volwassenen*. Den Haag: WODC.

Jacobs, P., and Van Kampen, P. (2014). Dutch 'ZSM Settlements' in the face of procedural justice: The sooner the better?. *Utrecht Law Review*, 10(4), pp. 73–85.

Kempes, M., and Van der Wolf, M.J.F. (2018). Wat kan een gedragskundige nog adviseren bij een weigeraar? Een vignet studie. *Sancties*, 4, pp. 223–234.

Keulen, B.F., Van Dijk, A.A., Gritter, E., Kwakman, N.J.M., and Lindenberg, K.K. (2013). *Naar een tweefasenproces? Over voor- en nadelen van een strafproces in twee fasen, in relatie tot de positie van slachtoffer en verdachte*. Paris: Zutphen.

Koenraadt, F. (1987). Two centuries of psychiatry and criminal law. In D.N. Weisstub (Ed.), *Law and Mental Health: International Perspectives. Volume 3*. New York: Pergamon Press, pp. 1–6.

Koenraadt, F., Mooij, A., and Van Mulbregt, J. (Eds.) (2007). *Mental Condition in Criminal Law. Forensic Psychiatric and Psychological Assessment in a Residential Setting*. Amsterdam: Rozenberg publishers.

Kooijmans, T. (2002). *Op maat geregeld? Een onderzoek naar de grondslag en de normering van de strafrechtelijke maatregel* (dissertation Rotterdam). Deventer: Kluwer.

Kooijmans, T., and Meynen, G. (2017). Who establishes the presence of a mental disorder in defendants: Medicolegal considerations on a European court of human rights case. *Frontiers in Psychiatry*, 8, pp. 1–6.

Mevis, P.A.M. (2015). *Voluntary Euthanasia and Assisted Dying: The Position in The Netherlands*. Baron Ver Heyden de Lancey Lecture, University of Cambridge, 26 January 2015, online at https://www.delanceyfoundation.co.uk/#foundation-video-one

Nauta, O., Abraham, M., and Piepers, N. (2020). *Evaluatie College gerechtelijk deskundigen. Eindrapport*. Den Haag: WODC.

NIFP (2018). *Richtlijn ambulant forensisch psychologisch onderzoek en rapportage in het strafrecht (volwassenen en jeugdigen)*. Utrecht: NIFP.

Nijboer, J.F. (2000). The significance of comparative legal studies. In J.F. Nijboer and W.J.J.M. Sprangers (Eds.), *Harmonisation in Forensic Expertise: An Inquiry into the Desirability of and Opportunities for International Standards*. Den Haag: Thela Thesis, p. 1.

NRGD (2016). *Code of Conduct. Netherlands Register of Court Experts*. Utrecht: NRGD.

NRGD (2018). *Beoordelingskader forensische psychiatrie, forensische psychologie en forensische orthopedagogiek.* Utrecht: NRGD.

NVvP (2013). *Richtlijn psychiatrisch onderzoek en rapportage in strafzaken.* Utrecht: NVvP.

Oosterom, P., Bezemer, B., and Knoester, J.A.W. (2019). Zorgconferenties in de tbs – ervaringen opgedaan in het project '15-plus'. *Strafblad,* 2, pp. 32–36.

Prinsen, M., and Groothuizen, M. (2019). Leg het eindeloos klagen in de justitiële psychiatrie aan banden, *NRC Handelsblad,* 24 June 2019.

Schmidt, E.P., Rap, S.E., and Liefaard, T. (2020). Young adults in the Justice System: The interplay between scientific insights, legal reform and implementaion in practice in the Netherlands. *Youth Justice,* 21(2), pp. 172–191.

Schwikkard, P.J. (2008). *Possibilities of Convergence.* Deventer: Kluwer.

Struijk, S. (2015). Punishing repeat offenders in the Netherlands: Balancing between incapacitation and treatment. *Behavioral Sciences & the Law,* 33(1), pp. 148–166.

Struijk, S., and Mevis, P.A.M. (2016). Legal constraints on the indeterminate control of 'dangerous' sex offenders in the community: The Dutch perspective *Erasmus Law Review,* 9(2), pp. 95–108.

Struijk, S., and Van der Wolf, M.J.F. (2018). Gevaarscriteria in het strafrechtelijk sanctierecht: een risicovol ratjetoe. *Ars Aequi maandblad,* 67, pp. 938–947.

Tak, P. (2008). *The Dutch Criminal Justice System.* Nijmegen: Wolf Legal Publishers.

Uit Beijerse, J., Struijk, S., Bleichrodt, F.W., Bakker, S.R., Salverda, B.A., and Mevis, P.A.M. (2018). *De praktijk van de voorwaardelijke invrijheidstelling in relatie tot speciale preventie en re-integratie.* Den Haag: Boom juridisch.

Van der Wolf, M.J.F. (2010). 'Auprès de moi le juge'. Gedragskundigen als meebeslissers in de penitentiaire kamer. *Strafblad,* 8, pp. 126–136.

Van der Wolf, M.J.F. (2012). *TBS – veroordeeld tot vooroordeel. Een visie na analyse van historische fundamenten van recente knelpunten, het systeem en buitenlandse alternatieven* (dissertation Rotterdam). Oisterwijk: Wolf Legal Publishers.

Van der Wolf, M.J.F. (2013). Gedragskundige rapportage in historisch perspectief. In H.J.C. Van Marle, P.A.M. Mevis, and M.J.F. Van der Wolf (Eds.), *Gedragskundige rapportage in het strafrecht, Tweede herziene druk.* Deventer: Kluwer, pp. 131–164.

Van der Wolf, M.J.F., and Herzog-Evans, M. (2014). Mandatory measures: 'safety measures'. Supervision and detention of dangerous offenders in France and the Netherlands: a comparative and Human rights' perspective. In: M. Herzog-Evans (Ed.), *Offender Release and Supervision: The Role of Courts and the Use of Discretion.* Oisterwijk: Wolf Legal Publishers, pp. 93–234.

Van der Wolf, M.J.F., and Van Marle, H.J.C. (2018). Legal approaches to criminal responsibility of mentally disordered offenders in Europe. In K. Goethals (Ed.), *Forensic Psychiatry and Psychology in Europe. A Cross-Border Study Guide.* Basel: Springer International Publishing, pp. 31–44.

Van der Wolf, M.J.F., Van Marle, H.J.C., Mevis, P.A.M., and Roesch, R. (2010). Understanding and evaluating contrasting unfitness to stand trial practices. A comparison between Canada and The Netherlands. *International Journal of Forensic Mental Health,* 9(3), pp. 245–258.

Van der Wolf, M.J.F., and Mevis, P.A.M. (2021). Defendants and detainees with psychiatric disturbances in the criminal process and in the prison system in the Netherlands'. In P.H. Van Kempen, and M. Krabbe (Eds.), *Mental Health and Criminal Justice: International and Domestic Perspectives on Defendants and Detainees with Mental Illness.* Den Haag: Eleven, pp. 359–386.

Van der Wolf, M.J.F., Mevis, P.A.M., Struijk, S., Van Leeuwen, L., Kleijn, M., and Van Marle, H.J.C. (2016). *Op zoek naar nieuw evenwicht. Derde evaluatie van de Beginselenwet verpleging ter beschikking gestelden.* Den Haag: Boom Juridisch, WODC.

Van Hattum, W., and Meijer, S. (2016). An administrative procedure for life prisoners: Law and practice of royal pardon in the Netherlands. In D. Van Zyl Smit and C. Appleton (Eds.), *Life Imprisonment and Human Rights.* Oxford: Hart Publishing Ltd, pp. 141–165.

Van Koppen, P.J., and Penrod, S.D. (2003). Adversarial or inquisitorial. Comparing systems. In P.J. Van Koppen and S.D. Penrod (Eds.), *Adversarial versus Inquisitorial Justice. Psychological Perspectives on Criminal Justice Systems.* New York: Kluwer Academic, pp. 1–19.

Van Kordelaar, W.F. (2018). Veilig onder voorwaarden. *Sancties*, 6, pp. 265–280.

Van Kordelaar, W.F. (2020). Het psychologisch onderzoek pro Justitia. In F.A.M. Bakker, and H.J.C. Van Marle (Eds.), *De psychiatrie in het Nederlandse recht*. Deventer: Kluwer, pp. 93–119.

Van Kordelaar, W.F. (2002) *BooG Beslissingsondersteuning onderzoek Geestvermogens in het strafrecht voor volwassenen* (dissertation Tilburg). Deventer: Kluwer.

Van Marle, H.J.C., Prinsen, M.M., and Van der Wolf, M.J.F. (2012). Pathways in forensic care: The Dutch legislation of diversion. In K.T.I. Oei, and M.S. Groenhuijsen (Eds.), *Progression in Forensic Psychiatry: About Boundaries*. Deventer: Kluwer, pp. 105–120.

Van Wijngaarden, A. (2016). Klacht tegen RUG-deskundige in antidepressiva-rel. *Dagblad van het Noorden* April 20, 2016.

Van Wingerden, S., and Drápal, J. (2018). Dutch prosecutorial sentencing guidelines: an inspiration for other countries?. *Leiden Law Blog*, November 14, 2018.

Werkgroep Risicotaxatie Forensische Psychiatrie (2002). *Handleiding HKT-30 versie 2002*. Den Haag: Ministerie van Justitie.

Zeegers, M. (1981). Diminished responsibility. A logical, workable and essential concept. *International Journal of Law and Psychiatry*, 4, pp. 433–444.

Chapter 10

Comparative analysis

Michiel van der Wolf

10.1 Introduction

'Who only knows his own discipline, does not know this either',[1] a wise Dutchman once said. Even though it then referred to the subject of interdisciplinarity within social sciences, it is similarly applicable to the forensic disciplines at hand. As forensic assessment is in its core communication between behavioural experts on the one hand and legal experts on the other, it is often within this dialogue that one becomes aware of the peculiarities of one's own discipline, for example when questions are asked from across the table about what seems self-evident on this side. Indeed throughout the book, it can be seen that understanding how in a certain jurisdiction the quality of forensic assessment is being safeguarded, requires knowledge from both sides of that table. Interestingly, the introductory quote has also been applied to a comparison of cultures: 'Who only knows his own culture, does not know this either'.[2] Indeed, this relates to the purpose of the book – and one of the purposes of the series –, that in learning about how things are done in other jurisdictions, one understands better how and why things are done the way they are in the own jurisdiction. One could even become aware of what seems self-evident about one's own situation, but not necessarily is. This comparative analysis is written in service of that purpose. In many aspects it is the reader him- or herself, coming from a certain jurisdiction, who is the best judge of the own situation in light of the others. This chapter is not a summary of the book and therefore is not an alternative for reading the country chapters. It aims mainly to describe and try and explain similarities and differences, through collecting and arranging relevant bits of information from the country chapters. A normative evaluation is not intended, other than a comparison of the critical reflections mentioned by the authors of country chapters themselves. To that aim, it follows the same outline as that of the country chapters, followed by some conclusions. Of course for explanation through a law-in-context approach, as was mentioned in the introduction, ideally the societal and legal traditions would be fully explored, but in light of the subject at hand were limited to the legal system and the tradition of forensic assessment. As for understanding differences between countries the context is very important, it is given a relatively large amount of attention to start with.

10.1.1 The legal system

In describing the legal system within a reasonable amount of words, authors were given and took the liberty to focus on things they thought were important within the context of (safeguarding the quality of) forensic assessment for sentencing decisions. On an aggregate level, a few major distinctions can be made.

DOI: 10.4324/9781351266482-10

10.1.1.1 Federal versus unitary government

An obvious distinction between the countries in the type of government is that some are federations – Australia, Canada, the US, and Germany – while the others have a unitary government. As in federations multiple jurisdictions exist within a country, while some matters concerning sentencing – especially related to which authorities are the competent decision makers on certain matters – are not regulated on the federal level, trying to be complete in the presented information is an impossibility within the given framework. Authors from federations could for example choose to focus, next to the federate level, on an exemplary regional jurisdiction, like the Australian chapter on Victoria, and the German one on Bavaria.

The other option was to take more of a bird's eye view approach, zooming in on relevant aspects of several regional jurisdictions for example to show contrast between them, as it was done in the American and Canadian perspective. This approach may show better the complexity of the situation, as indeed, 'the international comparative law approach used by this book could just as fruitfully be applied to the numerous jurisdictions within the USA'. Both approaches show that the division of competencies between federal and regional authorities in sentencing matters is different between the countries for all three branches of government: legislative, executive, and judicial. In Germany for example, criminal liability and (the imposition of) sentences are regulated on the federate level, while the execution of sentences is regulated on the regional level. In Canada, the division is somewhat similar, with regions having authority over prisons, hospitals, and asylums, and the administration of courts of criminal jurisdiction. In Australia and the US, regions have a vast authority over criminal and sentencing matters. Nevertheless, in practice a more unitary approach may be taken, for example in Australia on the matter of how mental health problems are taken into account in the sentencing process, where the laws have recently converged after a landmark case in Victoria.

10.1.1.2 Adversarial versus inquisitorial justice, two-phase trial versus one-phase trial

A second dichotomy between the countries that is easily identified is the procedural difference between adversarial versus inquisitorial justice. The former is in place in the jurisdictions from the Anglo-American tradition, while the latter is dominant in the Continental-European jurisdictions. In the American and Dutch chapters, the characteristics of the respective systems are explained most elaborately, with the quintessential difference of either the parties or the judge/court being the driving force in the proceedings. In relation to forensic assessment, this has a few general implications.

First of all, in adversarial justice there is a lot more emphasis on playing fair through equality of arms. In adversarial procedures therefore also forensic expertise is presented on behalf of the parties, while in inquisitorial proceedings this is generally on behalf of the court. In inquisitorial systems, decision-makers are less often confronted with contrasting views by experts, which are sometimes even viewed as problematic, while in adversarial justice a so-called 'battle of experts' is more common. It can be derived from Chapter 2 that difference of opinion between behavioural experts may be exaggerated by adversarial justice, but that on the other hand due to the existing margin of error in forensic assessment sometimes multiple outcomes may be a more accurate depiction of the state of the art.

Secondly, equality of the parties also requires an active defense by the accused, making unfitness/incompetency to stand trial an important doctrine, which is of minor influence or even absent in inquisitorial justice systems. Even though the doctrine is not directly related to sentencing, it has been suggested that as 'forensic psychiatric energy' is divided over relevant aspects related to (criminal) law, the attention paid to unfitness may come at the expense of the attention to other psycho-legal concepts.[3] Indeed, in inquisitorial systems, issues of criminal responsibility and/or sentencing, risk and need for treatment attract almost all the attention, and possibly even more than in adversarial systems. Even though forensic expertise is of course not a zero-sum game, there are limits to its possibility for expansion, most obvious financially. The fact that criminal responsibility is procedurally differently engaged in both systems, and therefore also substantively dissimilar, may also account for a lesser attention to that doctrine in adversarial systems. This is especially true for the fact that part of the doctrine is embedded in the insanity plea or defense as part of the trial on merits/trial of fact and its possible consequences.[4]

Now that the trial of fact is mentioned, it is important to note that in all the adversarial jurisdictions a so-called two-phase trial is in place, with a sentencing trial only taking place after a guilty plea or conviction in the trial of fact. Of course, there are always exceptions to the rule like in juvenile cases in some US-states the trial is not bifurcated. In Germany and the Netherlands however, in one trial both facts and issues related to sentencing are covered. For forensic assessment related to sentencing, the consequence is that defendants are being evaluated without the establishment of fact or guilt. As in these jurisdictions an important part of the assessment is the level of criminal responsibility based on the mental status at the time of the offense, the one-phase trial is especially problematic for assessment of defendants who deny the charges. There have been many discussions in these countries about switching to a two-phase-trial, with arguments mainly circling around the effects of publicly discussing personal circumstances in service of sentencing without establishing guilt – protection of private life, presumption of innocence, unprejudiced decision-maker, et cetera –, the co-operation of the defendant (for example with the evaluation) and economic arguments. Even though it is suggested that it is economical to not discuss sentencing-related issues if guilt is in the end not established, calculations of the costs of changing an entire system have thus far been too weighty.[5] In other words, it is not a matter of principle that inquisitorial justice should have one trial. Moreover, even though Sweden in general has a one-phase trial, a sort of two-phase trial exists especially in cases in which a comprehensive forensic evaluation is required, which can only be carried out after a confession or establishment of 'convincing evidence'. In fact, the evaluation itself has two phases, with a short evaluation being allowed before such an establishment and a comprehensive evaluation after. The fact that adversarial systems generally have two-phase-trials also seems to be mainly a matter of tradition, which is probably predominantly based on the division of decision competencies between a jury (fact) and a judge (sentence), even though this distinction is no longer absolute in adversarial systems, while also inquisitorial systems may have juries or lay-judges.[6] In general, many elements of one system may be visible in the other, as for example in (some) adversarial systems judges may ask questions to (expert)-witnesses about facts or culpability, while in inquisitorial systems parties can ask questions as well.

The most important thing to note on the relation of adversarial justice and the two-phase trial in light of the subject of this book is that the sentencing trial may be less adversarial than the trial of fact. Given the above historical background, this may be explained by the fact that the decision maker is generally not a jury, even though for example in the US juries may have to decide on capital punishment or other 'enhanced' sentences. In Australia and England for example, it is mainly the defense that initiates a forensic evaluation for the sentencing trial, resulting in less of a 'battle' than is common in the trial of fact, for example on the issue of insanity. However, also in the sentencing trial, the expert evidence may of course still be challenged via adversarial procedures, such as cross-examination and opposing expert testimony.

Moreover, in Chapter 1 it is explained that in this book sentencing is considered in a broad sense, including not only front-end decisions on the imposition of sentences, which are made after a (sentencing) trial but also mid-way decisions and back-end decisions. As in adversarial systems, such decisions may be made by multidisciplinary Parole Boards – in the correctional system – or Review Boards – in the (forensic) mental health system, these hearings may be much more of inquisitorial nature, for example in Canada, where for example in Parole hearings lawyers are often not even present. This may be different in some US regions where civil commitment is decided on by juries.

10.1.1.3 Other relevant procedural differences related to forensic assessment

One of such aspects, the issue of admissibility, is of course related to the division in type of procedures in conjunction with the type of decision-maker. Rules for admitting (expert) evidence, for example in the US, are most stringent for trials – as juries may be considered less skilled in determining reliability of (expert) evidence themselves. However, typically they do not apply to adult sentencing or juvenile disposition hearings, while in contrast, they may apply to civil commitment hearings in some regions. In an inquisitorial system, such as the Dutch, even in the trial phase, the professional judges are expected to be able to assess the quality of the evidence and weigh its conclusions accordingly.

Another relevant procedural issue, the principle of immediacy – which requires that all evidence is presented in court in its most original form – is also mainly associated with adversarial justice. However, it may also be a sacred principle in inquisitorial systems, such as in Sweden. In the Netherlands, however, it plays a limited role in practice. Expert-witness testimony, for example, is generally dealt with through paper reports and not voiced by the expert witness in the courtroom, for efficiency reasons.

Some differences within inquisitorial systems also exist on another relevant issue, the division of competencies between the branches of government, especially the judicial and executive branches. For example, the discretionary competence of the public prosecutor, not to prosecute or to divert for example to the mental health system, is nil in Germany, while it is at the root of the typically Dutch policy of tolerance, and it is also common in adversarial justice. In the execution of sentences, generally the competence of the executive branch, especially in Germany special courts may have competence in matters of execution. On a related note, in most countries sentencing guidelines exist, which in some cases are initiated by the executive branch.

Of course, there are also differences between the countries in substantive criminal law, for example, systems of sentencing, which will be discussed in paragraph 10.2.1. That is also the place for discerning what the influence is of penal politics on sentencing (laws) in the respective countries, as an important macro context.

10.1.2 The related tradition of forensic assessment

Also on the issue of the tradition of forensic assessment, authors had the liberty to discuss what they thought was necessary in the context of the book. Even though they applied different focuses, some similar themes can be identified.

10.1.2.1 The (increasing) need for expert assessment

In most chapters, developments are mentioned that increased the need for forensic expertise in service of criminal law in the past. The Dutch and English chapters go furthest back in time, even further than where Chapter 2 ended around the turning of the twentieth century. Both point to developments in the psychiatric discipline, especially regarding diagnostics, in the nineteenth century, that rendered testimony on some forms of madness no longer feasible for lay-persons like judges or acquaintances. They also point to famous cases, the best example of course being the English M'Naghten case from 1843, which influence on the criteria for legal insanity stretches out to date over all the jurisdictions in the Anglo-American tradition and beyond. It underlines the well-documented impact of single cases on the practice of law and psychiatry, as well as on legislation.[7]

The chapters on the countries of the Continental-European tradition echo the impact of the Modern criminal law theory as described in Chapter 2, as a catalyst of the need for more assessment in the beginning of the twentieth century. As it built on advancements in biological, psychological, and sociological knowledge in identifying causes of crime it added an offender approach to the classical offence approach. In adopting a deterministic view it abandoned the classical ideas on free will and responsibility, for example resulting in sanctions tailored to dangerousness instead of the extent of guilt, so a prospective approach instead of a retrospective approach. Preventive, possibly indeterminate, sanctions called (safety-)measures were enacted in all three systems. In Germany and the Netherlands, compromises were struck with the classical school, for example through the concept of diminished responsibility and combinations of penalties and measures. In Sweden, it initially evolved similarly but eventually, in the shape of a new criminal code in 1965, adopted a very modern view, abandoning the concept of (non-)criminal responsibility altogether.[8]

Other than in Sweden, which maintained its policy of neutrality, World War II obviously had quite an impact on the German and Dutch context for forensic assessment. In the German chapter, it is described how the degeneration theory, which was also used within the mentioned theoretical discussions on criminal law for example in relation to the concept of diminished responsibility,[9] became a 'fatal amalgamation' against the background of National Socialism, and how the subsequent misuse of psychiatry during the war still impacts the image of, and trust in, psychiatry and especially forensic psychiatry, as it is intrinsically related to governmental power. In the Netherlands, especially the sense of (therapeutic) optimism and humanitarianism as a reaction to the horrors of occupation, led to an increasing use of preventive treatment measures and a vast expansion of forensic treatment facilities, increasing the need for assessment.

On a related note, in the Australian and English chapter it is also mentioned how developing forensic mental health treatment services, or secure units, impacted the need for assessment. Of course, in all these countries, such developments may be related to those in the target population, which is impacted by many societal factors.

And finally, almost in all countries, the impact of legislative changes on the need for or the contents of forensic assessment is stressed. In England, the 1959 Mental Health Act, which introduced a hospital order as a sentencing option, for example, meant that enabling treatment for offenders no longer had to be/and was less done through the unfitness or insanity doctrine.

10.1.2.2 The psychologist vis-à-vis the psychiatrist

In a few chapters, it is mentioned how the position of the psychologist evaluator changed in relation to that of the psychiatrist. In the US a landmark case in 1962 – in which it was held that psychologists could be qualified to testify about mental disorders in insanity cases – ushered in the now widespread legal acceptance of forensic psychologists as court experts. In the English chapter, however, it is described how it took until the late twentieth century to equally recognise the role of psychologist evaluators, as a result of the increased relevance of other personality factors, such as suggestibility. In the Netherlands, the text of a law from 1988 still stresses the need for a psychiatrist to be part of a multidisciplinary evaluation for imposing a safety measure without mentioning the psychologist, while in practice there is now a longstanding equal recognition, only somewhat differentiated related to the type of mental disorder. In Germany, an increase of involvement of psychologists in forensic expertise is from the last decades, also triggered by the lack of forensic psychiatrists.

Following the short summary of the American chapter: where the nineteenth century showed the rise of psychiatrists in service of justice, the twentieth century showed the rise of psychologists. And the authors add that in the twenty-first century, the rise can be observed in assessment by probation and parole officers or criminologists. As that holds true for many of the countries, the impact of this development on the applicability of disciplinary instruments for safeguarding the quality of assessment will be discussed in paragraph 10.3.2.2.

10.1.2.3 Quality enhancing developments

As this chapter follows the outline of the country chapters, and the remainder of the chapter is on the current state of affairs in safeguarding the quality of forensic assessment, some authors used this paragraph to describe how and why the quality has improved up until this point.

A first development, which is mentioned are the scientific advancements in risk assessment, also mentioned in chapter 2. The American chapter describes the development of the 'four generations' of instruments, the first being clinical judgement. The Canadian chapter rightfully notes its 'long and distinguished history in the development of psychological instruments for the risk assessment of violence and sexual violence'. With regards to that tradition, it refers to the strong relationship between forensic mental health services and universities. Secondly, many of the chapters refer to when and why bodies or associations became important in safeguarding the quality of forensic assessment, and which will start in the remainder of the chapter.

10.2 Short overview of the role of assessment in sentencing offenders

10.2.1 Sentences and execution

Authors were asked to list the sentences that are in place, which are relevant to forensic assessment. Instead of summing up what they have summed up, here some distinctions are identified which impact forensic assessment. Other systematic distinctions, such as minimum or maximum penalties, monetary versus custodial sentences, et cetera, are less-relevant to forensic assessment and not addressed here. The death penalty does have relevant connections to forensic assessment, but as it is only applicable to the situation in the US, it is not mentioned as a distinction here.

10.2.1.1 Determinate versus indeterminate sentences

In the German and Dutch chapter, their twin-track system of sentencing is explained, in which dogmatically 'penalties' are regarded as dominantly retrospective and retributive, while 'measures' are dominantly prospective and preventive in nature. The Dutch chapter acknowledges that what sounds dogmatically sound in theory – a (safety) measure is not considered punishment – may sound somewhat ridiculous in practice. Indeed, to the detainee at hand the restrictions will feel similarly punitive and criminal in nature. From the side of countries that are alien to this dogmatic distinction, the following comment has been heard in the past related to the concept of 'measures': 'if it looks like a duck, swims like a duck, and quacks like a duck, …'.[10] In the adversarial jurisdictions discussions on retribution versus prevention are predominantly drawn into that on the purposes of sentencing. Indeterminacy of sentences to ensure prevention is achieved through a flexible approach to the life sentence, with tariffs, extension of sentences, or a special status for dangerous offenders, like in Canada. In England and the US, especially for sex offenders, civil orders may come into play. Preventive sanctions may include detention (deprivation of liberty) but are also often community sentences or orders (restriction of liberty). Of course, indeterminacy may also be achieved through commitment to (forensic or civil) mental health care, which in some countries may be considered a sentence, like in Sweden, where it is actually the only possibility for indeterminacy (next to a life sentence). In several countries 'hybrid orders' exist in which a custodial and mental health 'track' are combined (e.g. England, Australia, Germany, the Netherlands), while in the inquisitorial systems this is related to the concept of diminished/reduced responsibility.

Of course, indeterminacy of a sanction – in whatever manner it is achieved – is often related to a criterion of dangerousness/risk and the need for prognosis, while for commitment to (forensic or civil) mental health, mental disorder, and possibly the level of responsibility (more retrospective) are required. These psycho-legal criteria evoke forensic assessment, even though this is not always required – especially concerning risk. Indeterminacy of course also entails the need for mid-way (prolongation) and back-end decision-making.

Most sentencing systems, especially in the adversarial realm, show the influence of penal politics in recent decades, with an increase of sentencing options for (types of) dangerous offenders. Possibly the dogmatic rigidity of the inquisitorial systems serves somewhat as a protection to this trend, even though this does not hold true for the Dutch more pragmatic and flexible approach to its system in recent decades. Out of all systems, the Swedish seems least preoccupied with risk.

10.2.1.2 Sentences for juveniles versus adults

All these countries have separate provisions for sentencing juveniles in place, with an ambition to divert or avoid (long) custodial sentencing as a relatively general characteristic. For some countries, it is explicitly mentioned that the educational, pedagogical, and rehabilitative goals of juvenile justice evoke relatively more forensic assessment, but not necessarily from the side of behavioural experts, as there are often services designated for juvenile justice involved. In relation to behavioural assessment, the question is whether these evaluators should be specialised in diagnosing juveniles.

Of course the legal minimum age for criminal liability differs. The age for the separation between juvenile and adult justice is generally the legal ages for adulthood/majority (typically eighteen), while most countries mention the possibility of exceptions. Some only mention the possibility of administering adult justice on certain juveniles (e.g. US, Canada), while the inquisitorial jurisdictions also mention the possibility of applying juvenile justice to young adults (up to 21 or 23 years of age). Decisions on these exceptions generally evoke specific forensic assessment on aspects of developmental psychology, (im)maturity, et cetera.

10.2.1.3 Correctional facilities versus mental health facilities

An important distinction in the type of facilities involved in the execution of sentences (including measures) is that between the correctional track and the (forensic) mental health track. Even though the book is on sentencing, some chapters do describe diversion schemes or mention the role of unfitness (to stand) trial, as possible entrances into the latter track before or during the phase of prosecution. Of course in the trial phase, all countries have provisions in place for the (criminal) court to commit an offender to the (forensic) mental health track, whether it is related to the trial of fact after a finding of legal insanity or NCRMD (see Canada) or related to the sentencing trial, after a finding of non- or diminished criminal responsibility or merely a (severe) mental disorder (like in England, Sweden or the Netherlands). Some countries, like the Netherlands, allow for a 'voluntary' placement in this track on the basis of a special condition in a conditional/suspended sentence. Finally, during the execution phase, most countries mention the option of transfer from the correctional facility to the (forensic) mental health track (and back), possibly related to psycho-legal criteria surrounding responsivity, treatability, the need for treatment, or even unfitness for detention.

The Netherlands traditionally has a third track in place in between the two tracks, specifically intended for execution of the TBS-order. On paper, many options for transfer between the three tracks exist, but in practice mainly transfer to the mental health track is used. It is mainly considered a third track because of a separate legal position, however in practice, it is mainly the high-security level that separates it from the (forensic) mental health track. Such differentiation in security level can be found in most countries, within the mental health track, some patients (for example in England or Canada) may even have a different 'high-security' status and legal position (with restrictions) within this track. Of course within the (forensic) mental health track in general more assessment is being done (more or less on a daily basis), related to decisions on treatment, leave, prolongation, et cetera. Depending on the subject and the jurisdiction these are for internal use, or for decisions by a Ministry, board, or court.

10.2.2 Decisions within sentencing and execution

In the respective paragraphs in the country chapters, all the front-end decisions, mid-way decisions, and back-end decisions for which forensic assessment may be used are listed. Many of these have already been discussed in paragraph 10.2.1, including the possible decision-makers. No additional relevant distinctions are to be made here.

10.2.3 Concepts to be assessed

In this paragraph especially (dis)similarities relating to the concepts that are generally assessed are mentioned, in terms of relation to certain decisions, or in terms of substance, or in terms of assessment methodology. In Chapter 2 issues related to the quality of assessment of these concepts are discussed.

10.2.3.1 Mental disorder

When a mental disorder, in whatever way it is phrased in the legal text, is a criterion in any sentencing decision, it is considered a psycho-legal concept. This is underlined by the fact that in most countries in the end it is the decision-maker who legally establishes the disorder, either or not advised by a forensic evaluator. Of course, the scope of the concept may differ on the basis of the terminology, but also on the basis of the (consequences of the) decision at hand. The Swedish developments are a good example in this context. After abolishing the responsibility doctrine in 1965 in favour of an imprisonment prohibition in case of presence of a mental disorder at the time of the trial. To narrow the scope of these consequences, in 1992 the concept was changed to 'severe mental disorder', with additional clarifications of what mental states qualify as such.

In Germany and the Netherlands the terminology of the concept has very recently changed to be more contemporary, less stigmatising – e.g. 'disorder' instead of 'abnormality' (Germany, 2021) – or more in line with terminology from the behavioural sciences (the Netherlands, 2020). As the latter has been criticised to limit the scope of the concept, while the former concept was explicitly meant to be legal terminology to underline the competence of legal decision-makers in establishing it, the old criterion 'a defective development or pathological disorder of the mental capacities' was only upheld for the decision of imposing a TBS-order. The main rationale was that in case of defendants who refused to cooperate with the evaluation, possibly leading to an absence of conclusions from the evaluator, the court could still establish the concept and keep society safe by imposing the measure.

The fact that for different decisions different concepts are in place, is also visible in common law jurisdictions, as in England different concepts are in place for the insanity defense, the diminished responsibility defense ('abnormality of mental functioning') or the imposition of a hospital order. In Australia, the so-called Verdins principles on what role mental health problems may play in sentencing, use a broad definition – 'mental disorder or abnormality or impairment of mental functioning' – covering all sorts of diagnoses, including situations in which no firm diagnosis may be established in legal practice. The Canadian concept of 'disease of the mind' is also broader – and materially different – from that prescribed in the DSM-5 for clinical assessment and treatment purposes, as (again) it is a legal concept and not a medical concept.

10.2.3.2 Criminal responsibility/legal insanity

More evidently a legal concept is the doctrine of criminal responsibility or legal insanity or culpability. Even so that in some jurisdictions, especially in the US, evaluators are not allowed to conclude on the ultimate legal issue, as this is considered trespassing on the terrain of competence of the legal decision-maker. In other jurisdictions similar discussions take place, and individual evaluators may refrain from such conclusions.

Criminal responsibility doctrines are different in form and matter, while the form also shapes the matter into substance. As discussed in the described adversarial systems (maybe with the exception of some US states), it is a defense during the trial phase. This form, due to the consequence of acquittal (and/or disposal) shapes a dichotomous concept of insanity. In England, since 1957, additionally a diminished responsibility defense exists on account of a mental abnormality, but only for persons charged with murder, pleading guilty to a lesser charge of manslaughter.

In the German and Dutch one-phase trial non-criminal responsibility serves as an excuse for the committed offence, after a finding of which no punishment can follow, while diminished or reduced responsibility is – or may be, in the Dutch less dogmatically sound denial of a complete punishment to the extent of guilt principle – a mitigating factor, creating a true graded culpability concept. The concept also traditionally plays a central role in sentencing, in the twin-track system of penalties and safety measures, even though in the Netherlands in recent years non-responsibility is no longer a criterion for commitment in a mental health facility by the criminal court. This is similar to the English hospital order, even though there recent case law and sentencing guidelines have located medical disposal options more firmly within a framework of determinations of culpability. Also in Canada and Australia culpability, as a more dimensional concept, plays a role in sentencing, for example as a mitigating factor.

In terms of substance, these culpability concepts come close to the Dutch concept of criminal responsibility, as it only requires a general causal relation between disorder and offence – somewhat like the product test. In most other jurisdictions, especially in its dichotomous use as a defense, a more specific relationship between offence and disorder is required, via additional (cognitive or volitional) impairments in mental functioning during the offence caused by the disorder, is common. Moreover, even though Sweden officially abolished the concept in favour of an imprisonment prohibition for persons suffering from severe mental disorder at the time of the trial, in what is described as a 'neo-classical turn' in 2008 they limited the scope of the prohibition to persons that 'lacked the capacity to understand the nature of the act or to act in accordance with such an understanding'. In adding these requirements, which preclude retrospective diagnostics again, the prohibition has almost become a criminal responsibility doctrine. These changes were made after high-profile cases showed unsatisfactory outcomes of not having such a doctrine in place. Discussions that other countries have related to criminal responsibility, Sweden has related to this prohibition, for example also in relation to self-induced mental states through drug use.

10.2.3.3 Dangerousness/risk

Traditionally, in the absence of culpability due to the mental state, dangerousness acted as a legitimation for deprivation of liberty, not as punishment but as protection of self and others. In the modern criminal law theory, dangerousness did not have to be related to diminished responsibility – as nobody was considered responsible – to legitimise preventive detention. In the 1930s Germany introduced a measure of preventive detention (Sicherungsverwahrung), for dangerous offenders that were not considered mentally disordered. However, still, for imposition of that measure something related to the personality is required: an 'inclination' (Hang) to commit serious offences. For many sentencing decisions in the involved countries, the internal cause of dangerousness is still of importance: ranging from a broadly defined mental disorder for imposing the Dutch TBS-order, to an 'unstable character' for the English life sentence, or a volitional impairment for some US sexually dangerous person (civil) commitments. The methodology for risk assessment in such situations may therefore be different from decisions, in which the cause for the risk is irrelevant. In most sentencing systems in recent decades (indeterminate) options for control have been expanded, by adding such criteria. In some criteria, more external clues for dangerousness are included in the legal definitions, such as (frequency) of reoffending criteria, which seem less dependent on expertise.

A common denominator among the countries is that, as new sentencing decisions including new risk criteria are added to the existing system, a wide range of definitions are in place, which are often inconsistently related to the target behaviour, to the severity of the decision, or probative requirements. For optimising the quality of assessment instrumentarium, see also Chapter 2, this lack of standardisation is a major obstacle. Another obstacle, as it is presented in the American chapter due to its relevance within that adversarial system, is that as new risk assessment instruments based on reoffending research, are more transparent about strengths and weaknesses, they may be more prone to admissibility challenges than for example clinical judgement.

In terms of substance, the described concepts in the respective countries range from 'vague statutory references' or very general risks to public safety, to very specific risks regarding the target behaviour, for example, the 'health or welfare of one or more animals'. Another distinction that can be found is that some definitions also include risk for psychological harm. Of course psychological harm caused by the index offence could be a factor in determining such risk, but may also be an independent, for example aggravating, factor in sentencing. Especially in the English chapter, it is discussed whether victim impact statements may be enough basis for such a finding or if also behavioural assessment is required. In the Netherlands, possibly because of this uncertainty there seems to be some reluctance towards including psychological harm in (risk) definitions, as most are restricted to physical violence.

Finally, in most countries it is mentioned that for civil commitment in addition to risk to others also the risk to self is incorporated.

10.2.4 Forensic assessment and procedure

In describing the proceedings to obtain forensic assessment, chapters focus almost exclusively on the trial phase. Evidently, in the execution phase, the decision at hand will more automatically trigger the necessary information to make that decision. In the trial phase, however, more (sentencing) options are open, so information is required also more broadly.

In the inquisitorial systems, it is quite common that for some impactful measures based on psycho-legal criteria forensic assessment is required. As in Sweden, there is often a short assessment, before a comprehensive assessment is being ordered. A comprehensive assessment is required for imposing coerced forensic mental health care. Similar requirements exist for certain safety measures in Germany and the Netherlands. For other decisions, for example on criminal responsibility, assessment may not be obliged but is necessary to answer the legal question at hand. In these inquisitorial countries assessments are typically court-ordered. So when the court wants to have the option of imposing a certain sanction for which assessment is required, it has to make sure the assessment has been done. Therefore, also fitting within an inquisitorial system, in Germany and the Netherlands, in preliminary proceedings also the prosecution may order the assessment in the common interest of having the assessment in place before the one-phase trial. Options for the defense are discussed in paragraph 10.4.1. In practice, some criteria related to the offender and the severity or characteristics of the offence may induce the initiation of an assessment.

As it has been described in paragraph 10.1.1.2 that in the adversarial jurisdictions the sentencing trial may be less adversarial than the trial of fact, in most jurisdictions the courts will order (behavioural) assessments – sometimes as a statutory requirement – for decisions they have to make (e.g. Canada), possibly on the basis of information that is presented to them by probation services or the National Health Service (e.g. England), or the department of Justice (Australia). Of course behavioural assessment may also be initiated by the parties, in case of the defense generally when legal aid allows it. The Australian sentencing trial seems to be most adversarial of the countries involved, as it is the responsibility of the parties – in practice mostly the defense – to bring any relevant matter, which it wants the judge to take account of, in the sentencing process under the attention. The burden of proof is higher for aggravating factors (beyond reasonable doubt) than for mitigating factors (balance of probabilities). In an inquisitorial system like the Dutch, the burden of proof for psycho-legal criteria related to sentencing is even lower: plausibility. In the US, for a sentencing trial information from an expert commissioned by one of the parties will often be shared with the other party, even overcoming assertions of attorney-client privilege. And for impactful decisions, such as capital cases or sexually dangerous person commitment proceedings, often by practice or by law, two evaluators (for risk assessment) are required, one retained by or appointed for each party. In some US states, certain decisions – like the conditional release of an insanity acquittee – actually require three forensic evaluators (including one appointed by the court).

10.3 Safeguards for the quality of forensic assessment

10.3.1 Requirements in law and policy

Safeguards for the quality of forensic assessment in law and policy can be divided in three types, as mentioned in the subparagraph titles below.

10.3.1.1 Requirements for the type of forensic assessment for certain decisions

Already mentioned in paragraph 10.2.4, these safeguards are directed at what type of assessment is necessary for a few impactful decisions within sentencing. As these requirements generally concern the type of assessment, instead of the quality of the assessment, they may not even have to be mentioned in this regard. However, it can be argued that the common requirement of multiple or multidisciplinary assessment is in service of (judging) the (inter-rater) reliability of the assessment. In Germany provisions can be found that for some crucial decisions (e.g. privileges for detainees within preventive detention or sexual and violent offenders), the assessment has to be undertaken 'especially thoroughly' by the forensic expert, which is deemed rather vague and questionable in terms of practical effects or judicial control, while for other decisions (e.g. on hospitalisation) a psychiatric evaluation is required and a report from a psychologist does not suffice. Of course, this is in service of the requirement of having the specific expertise for a certain assessment.

10.3.1.2 General requirements in (procedural) law related to forensic expertise

These requirements may be divided in provisions defining an expert and how the evaluation should be conducted and reported versus provisions on rules of evidence or how a court may assess the quality of an assessment and react to a substandard evaluation.

Beginning with the latter, paragraph 10.1.1.3 already explains how in adversarial jurisdictions admissibility, as part of the rules of evidence, is much more of an issue than in inquisitorial systems. On the other hand, when it comes to sentencing hearings, even in adversarial jurisdictions the rules of evidence of the trial of fact do not similarly apply, so that – like in Australia – judges may consider any evidence they consider to be of assistance to the sentencing task. Nevertheless, for Canada the law of evidence is mentioned as the primary safeguard for the quality and reliability of forensic assessments, even in the context of the subject of this book. It provides that opinion evidence – in the form of a forensic assessment or otherwise – is not admissible unless it satisfies certain conditions, as they are developed in case law. Such conditions generally apply to all sorts of forensic expertise brought before courts, not only behavioural expertise. However, in Australia (Victoria to be precise) some specific requirements related to behavioural forensic assessment for sentencing came forth out of the judiciary, albeit not through case law. Next to an expert witness code of conduct, since 2017 a Supreme Court of Victoria 'Practice Note' is in place, called *Sentencing Hearings: Expert Reports on Mental Functioning of Offenders*. It covers both explanations of substantively relevant issues and procedural requirements related to the expert and evaluation, and was created by a committee consisting of representatives from all relevant bodies and academics.

Remarkably for a common-law system, England has codified regulations in place for prescribing requirements for expertise, through a section in the Criminal Procedure Rules. Similar to inquisitorial systems without a two-phase trial, general requirements in such codes apply to all sorts of expertise and to both the phases of fact and sentencing. As most of these requirements are either of an ethical nature or a safeguard for the quality of the evaluator him- or herself, they are discussed in paragraphs 10.3.2 and 10.3.3. However, a common requirement present in such provisions that is directed to the quality of the assessment is that on the reliability of the methods used, which should be commented on in the report. For the Netherlands it has been argued that in behavioural expertise, these requirements are generally not adhered, as some of the idiographic methodology used is not easily explained. As Sweden has a two-phase assessment, certain requirements – especially for the comprehensive evaluation – are laid down in law. Some of these are related to reliability, such as the use of different sources of data – like also the Australian Practice Notes demand to not solely rely on self-reports – and teamwork, while others are more related to validity, such as that the evaluation has to be done as soon as possible and under conditions that are as representative as possible. For the report itself, requirements exist on transparency and traceability (e.g. Germany), clarity and simplicity, including the explanation of terms that are not generally known is explained (e.g. Sweden), give details of any literature or other information which the expert has relied on in making the report and of the substance of all facts given to the expert which are material to the opinions expressed in the report, or upon which those opinions are based (e.g. England).

10.3.1.3 Requirements on what risk assessment method or tool to use

As explained in Chapter 2, especially in risk assessment the methodology, or the use of tools, is eligible to be empirically researched in a way that leads to scores for predictive validity. Therefore, in some jurisdictions requirements exist in law or policy about what method/tools to assess risk with for a few decisions within sentencing. Swedish law requires the use of a structured method based on 'science and proven experience'. In the English chapter the example of Scotland is mentioned, where a specific Risk Management Authority was established, with a statutory duty to set standards for the assessment and management of risk related to the decision on an Order for Lifelong Restriction. It emphasises a formulation-based approach, based on a review of a comprehensive range of information and evidence. 'Assessors are expected to select empirically supported risk instruments and other relevant assessment tools that are appropriate to the individual case'. Only in some US jurisdictions and the Netherlands, it is mandated that certain risk assessment tools be used in certain sentencing contexts. In the US it includes criminogenic and violence risk assessment tools developed by the federal government for use in federal jurisdiction probation and prison decision-making, and Virginia's requirement that a particular sexual criminogenic risk assessment tool be used in sexually dangerous person screening. In the Netherlands it includes the use of structured professional risk assessment tools in applications of leave during the TBS-order and the use of structured risk assessment next to an offence analysis for transfer from prison to forensic mental health. Of course overall, even when the use of a certain tool is not mandatory, often risk assessment tools are used on the basis of disciplinary guidelines.

10.3.2 Disciplinary and ethical requirements

Disciplinary and ethical requirements show a great deal of overlap. In the context of the subject of this book, a distinction can be made between requirements of conduct related to evaluation in the forensic (criminal law) context and requirements of conduct related to the profession of the behavioural discipline at hand, in this case mainly the diagnostic process. The former can be mainly regarded as duties to the court (and/or parties or the proceedings in general), while the latter are mainly duties to the patient (or the interests of – the quality of health care in a broader sense). Examples of requirements may be found in which these duties align – like honesty – while there are also examples of requirements in which these duties conflict with one another – as for example confidentiality is overruled by the duty to report in the legal process. The former requirements may be regulated in criminal law (including case law) or policy, while the latter are generally found in health law. Both types of requirements may be found in Code of Conduct-type rules from regulatory bodies, as well as in guidelines from professional organisations. The purpose of this paragraph is not to give a complete overview of these duties, but to describe in what way these duties are being safeguarded in the different countries and how these duties may differ in relation to the context of these jurisdictions.

10.3.2.1 Duties related to the forensic context

Differences can be observed in the level on which these duties are regulated. Of course the level on which they are regulated determines the manner in which they can be enforced (see paragraph 10.3.4). In Canada and the US case law seems to be the most important source of these duties. In England, the mentioned Criminal Procedure Rules are 'highly prescriptive and detailed in defining the expert's duty to the court, and in specifying what a report must contain and what must be disclosed'. These rules, and the corresponding declaration, indeed seem much more detailed than is common in the codified provisions in the inquisitorial jurisdictions. In the Netherlands, this can in part be explained by the fact that the code establishes a Netherlands Register of Court Experts, with its own regulations and Code of Conduct. Another explanation may be found in the differences between the adversarial and inquisitorial system.

For example, the requirement of impartiality can be found in all countries, however, in an adversarial context it requires a much more detailed elaboration. For example in the Australian context, the mentioned Practice Note on forensic assessment for sentencing notes that 'the function of an expert witness is to assist the Court, not to advocate for the interests of a party', after which a detailed elaboration of related requirements follow, which is extensively covered in the chapter. Several of these requirements will not (soon) be found within an inquisitorial system like the requirement never to alter a report or an opinion at the request of the commissioning party, or report any such attempts, or when requested disclose the records of any examination to the other party. Related to the latter requirement is that of recording examinations in service of controllability of inferences made, which is frowned upon in an inquisitorial system based on trust (like the Netherlands).

An issue related to impartiality, but also to forensic requirements of giving unbiased opinion or avoiding conflicts of interest, as well as disciplinary requirements of confidentiality and non-maleficence, is whether or not the subject's treating practitioner may report to the court. Even though this issue is dealt with differently within jurisdictions, it is not related to the distinction between adversarial and inquisitorial justice. While in the US for example it is often considered a matter of principle, it is not an uncommon practice in England, even though guidelines will encourage the evaluator to report on it. In the Australian chapter, a compromise is mentioned that treating practitioners may only report on information relevant to treatment. However, in the Netherlands treating practitioners of patients within safety measures based on dangerousness, are explicitly asked to report on risk at prolongation hearing, with due consequences for the continuing therapeutic relationship, while in Germany the law explicitly mentions that it should be an evaluator not involved in the treatment.

As it is also the duty of the expert to respect the rights of the examinee, of course the right not to cooperate with an evaluation, derived from the principle not to cooperate with one's own conviction, which stretches out to sentencing, is worth mentioning here. Even though such a requirement is rights-based (like the right to be informed or to correction) and not related to safeguarding the quality of the assessment, of course it impacts the quality of the dialogue in court. Of course there is a distinction between a pathological or strategic refusal. In the Netherlands, it is even required to write a report on the refusal and on what may be concluded within the boundaries of the discipline, on which the court may still base impactful decisions like imposing a TBS-order. In Germany, a second evaluation may be issued after a first has been refused. This suggests that cooperation may depend on the expert at hand. In that sense, defense-initiated evaluations in adversarial justice are less likely to be refused.

10.3.2.2 Disciplinary duties

It is customary that many of such duties are set out in guidelines. A distinction can be made between guidelines from governmental regulatory bodies and professional organisations. In the Netherlands not only the mentioned Register is in place but also a National Institute of Forensic Psychiatry and Psychology (NIFP), with its own guidelines. And Sweden has a National Board of Forensic Medicine, which also issues regulations, for example on the comprehensive forensic evaluation. Both these bodies have created formats for reporting and have some sort of peer review system in place as a safeguard for the quality of a certain report, which is called 'feedback' in the Netherlands and a 'second-opinion process' in Sweden.

All countries have professional organisations in place, which have their own guidelines, and possibly codes of ethics or conduct in place. In Canada, professional regulatory oversight occurs at the provincial and territorial level. Of course guidelines are in principle not binding, but they may be incorporated in licensing statutes and regulations, giving such the force of law. Generally, associations will exist for psychiatrists or psychologists, while sometimes specific associations exist for forensic psychiatry and/or psychology, issuing own guidelines (like the American Academy of Psychiatry and the Law). While the general professional associations will have guidelines on treatment and diagnostics in place, they may also issue guidelines on providing forensic expertise (often in collaboration with relevant legal stakeholders). It is not uncommon that multiple laws and guidelines cover similar requirements within a single jurisdiction. The four ethical principles of the British Psychological Society provide a nice overview of the contents of most requirements: respect, competence, responsibility, and integrity. Staying within the limits of one's competence is a requirement often found in the forensic context. It raises the question for example whose competence it is to do a risk assessment. As such guidelines do not apply to other professions and are not even in place for criminologists or parole/probation officers performing risk assessments, this lack of quality safeguards and the lack of behavioural knowledge are especially scrutinised in the American and Dutch perspectives.

In Germany, the most important guidelines, called 'recommendations' or 'minimum requirements', in this context were actually created (starting in 2005, but updated) by a private group of psychiatrists, psychologists, legal practitioners and criminologists. They offer legal information and practical guidelines for the evaluator, including 'pragmatic solutions to the current state of scientific knowledge'. They are mentioned as the most important safeguard for the quality of assessment in Germany. Also, because some high courts have started to use these requirements as a benchmark for the quality of forensic assessment.

10.3.3 Requirements for the evaluator

The two most important safeguards for the quality of the evaluator are licensing or registration and training. The two are generally connected, as finishing a certain training results in a certain license, while continued practice and training are often prerequisites for continued registration. Differences can be observed in the level of specificity of the license or registration: clinical work, forensic clinical work, and court expert work. Moreover, differences can be observed in the necessity of having such licenses for court expert work.

Probably the most stringent specific registration is that of the Netherlands Register of Court Experts, as mentioned in the Code of Criminal Procedure. Only in extraordinary cases can someone be appointed as an expert who is not in the register. The register is only applicable to reporting for the criminal trial, not to decisions within the execution of sentences. Initial registration follows after accomplishing a specific forensic training of the NIFP and an exam in which also three reports are being judged by three reviewers. But the registration has to be renewed every five years, on the basis of new reports, while peer review and training requirements have to be met in the meantime. For the nine months of NIFP training only licensed psychiatrists and clinical psychologists are eligible.

In other countries only such licenses may suffice for acting as a court expert. In Sweden, forensic experience may be an additional criterion, while for being a team member for a comprehensive assessment one has to be employed by the National Board of Forensic Medicine. The Scottish Risk Management Authority mentioned earlier is also responsible for the accreditation of practitioners who are authorised to prepare a detailed 'risk assessment report'. Some US states, next to being a licensed health care worker in that jurisdiction, also require that mental health professionals acquire special certifications to engage in forensic work, while administrative agency may then keep a register of certified evaluators. But a judge ultimately decides whether a professional, proffered as an expert witness, is so qualified given the professional's education, training, experience, knowledge, or skill. In some countries, for example, certificates or titles may be earned for Forensic Psychiatry (e.g. Germany, Australia) and Forensic Psychologist (e.g. Australia), but it is not required to have such a formal 'forensic' qualification in order to be able to give evidence in court. Nevertheless, these specialisations can help to establish the quality of the witness. In Australia, while for the trial of fact, an expert witness must have specialised knowledge based on his or her training, study, or experience, the same restrictions do not exist at the sentencing stage, unless in a specific case the court chooses to direct that they apply. The Practice Note however requires specialised knowledge. In the Australian chapter the discussion is mentioned on whether experts should also work in clinical practice, as it used to be frowned upon if they didn't but no longer is. In most countries this is the case, as the amount of cases allows for it.

The level of post-graduate training differs per country as well. In England there is no single system of accredited training or qualification specifically for expert witness skills amongst psychologists and psychiatrists, so they are dependent on non-obligatory sources of training from commercial or membership-based organisations. Such organisations exist in most countries, for example facilitating more informal peer review programs or interprofessional dialogue (like in Australia). 'Access to high-quality training and continuing professional development is therefore available for expert witnesses who seek it, but not every expert witness will do so'. In Canada however, the high quality of postgraduate training that forensic mental health professionals receive, coupled with ongoing requirements of Canadian governing regulatory bodies for continuing professional development, is considered an important quality safeguard.

10.3.4 Enforcement of requirements

10.3.4.1 In the (sentencing) proceedings at hand

There are different ways through which the requirements discussed in the former paragraphs are enforced. In any decision within sentencing in the broad sense, the decision-maker at hand will decide on whether to admit, use, or how to weigh the expertise provided for the relevant decision on the basis of quality safeguards. But of course, as mentioned in the American perspective also the parties will help to 'safeguard forensic evaluation quality through challenges to forensic evaluators as being unqualified to function as expert witnesses, or challenges to the admissibility of their opinions as being the product of insufficient information or unreliable methods. They also challenge admitted expert testimony via cross-examination and the presentation of opposing expert testimony'. Of course, this is less of a safeguard when the expert does not give oral testimony in court, which is generally the case in the Netherlands. These options will be elaborated on in paragraph 10.4.1, including the laws of evidence on which they are based. In Germany, the court can have subsidiary reactions to the poor quality of evaluation like ordering improvements or withholding (part of the) remuneration for the evaluator if the evaluation is considered worthless. Of course, more general reactions may be appointing another expert, or a party appealing the decision made on the alleged poor quality report. In the Canadian and Australian chapters, a consequential dynamic of enforcing quality is described after expert evidence is not being admitted or used in court. The reputation of the forensic assessor might be adversely impacted, by the court writing a decision on the issue. As these are public, decisions of this nature are of interest to professional colleagues, and sometimes even attract media attention. 'In short, reputation matters, and judicial comments contribute to a process of natural selection wherein poorer quality expert evidence is likely to result in fewer future referrals for the expert involved. This quality assurance mechanism for expert evidence, although rarely commented upon, may in practice be the most important of all'.

10.3.4.2 Additional malpractice proceedings

In the Netherlands, an expert who performs too little evaluations, performs substandard or undergoes too little training or review, will not come through the (re-)registration process of the NRGD. Of course, this is not a safeguard for every individual evaluation and therefore only suffices when the substandard performance is structural. In addition, in most countries it is possible for professionals who engage in ethically or disciplinary substandard practice to be sanctioned by professional organisations. Expulsion from the organisation of course does not mean that one can no longer practice. That is different from decisions of licensing authorities or disciplinary courts, generally after a complaint from the examinee, but possibly also from judges or other participants in the court case, such as the expert from the opposing party (maybe after tactful confrontation). Additional training, suspension or revocation of licenses, or the right to practice are common sanctions. In the examples mentioned in the country chapters, the situation of diagnosing someone as disordered or dangerous without having examined the defendant in person is mentioned several times. Again, in addition, it may be possible for the evaluators to be sued in civil malpractice cases. This is rare in general, but even less common in the continental European jurisdictions. Of course liability depends on the conduct and on the rules related to immunity. In most countries, absolute immunity from civil liability is enjoyed for reports and testimony. However, US jurisdictions may still allow for potential liability for negligence in the actual conducting of a forensic evaluation. Also in England, this is a relatively new reality reversing a longstanding tradition of immunity for expert witnesses that protected them from retaliatory action by disappointed civil litigants or criminal defendants. The authors of the American chapter believe 'that the costs of defending against such lawsuits, regardless of whether a plaintiff's suit is likely to succeed, serve as a practical deterrent to mental health professionals from engaging in subpar practices'.

10.4 Safeguards 'against' the limited quality of forensic assessment

10.4.1 Questioning the assessment by the defense

10.4.1.1 Adversarial versus inquisitorial justice

The options for the defense to contest forensic behavioural assessment differ hugely between adversarial and inquisitorial justice systems (even though in both systems when all else fails the options from paragraph 10.3.4.2 remain). As the Canadian authors eloquently put it: 'courts rely on the mechanics of the adversarial process to bring to light any instances where proposed expert evidence falls short of that required for admissibility'. These mechanisms are twofold, as described in the American perspective. 'The first is cross-examination of the adverse expert by the attorney, potentially informed ahead of time by a retained expert consultant's review of the adverse testifying expert's work. The second is the presentation of countervailing expert evidence and testimony from a retained evaluating expert, or a non-evaluating expert on the generally applicable science'. In Australian legal practice however contesting is not the applicable word, as in sentencing hearings there is in the vast majority of cases a single expert, briefed by the defense. In the American system for the trial of fact, there may even be an admissibility hearing before the actual trial, in which the parties could argue the inadmissibility of the other party's expert's evaluation. As such a hearing may not be required for many sentencing and disposition matters, their spirit may be incorporated by judges in individual cases. There, another option for challenges to forensic evaluations can also be raised via argumentation on appeal or petitions for *habeas corpus* relief. In England however, appeals against sentence are rarely successful, as the judge is allowed a wide margin of discretion and the Court of Appeal will only interfere if the sentence was 'manifestly excessive or wrong in principle'. Procedurally barriers exist as well, as a person wishing to appeal needs leave to do so, while just the wish for behavioural evidence of higher quality is generally not enough of an argument. In Canada, a somewhat similar barrier (leave) for appeal exists through the limited ability to appeal from questions of fact. Even though in Canada, the admissibility of evidence is a question of law, and any party to the proceedings may advance an appeal on the basis of an alleged error of law, however, the decision to accept or reject the evidence itself, in whole or in part, is a question of fact. In words from the English perspective: 'This underlines the importance of ensuring as far as possible that clinical evidence at the trial is correct. It may not be possible to review it on appeal'.

As in inquisitorial justice there generally is a one-phase trial, combining the trials of fact and sentencing, it is understandable that there are no such obstacles for an appeal. In the Netherlands, especially the requirement that the evaluation is not older than a year, while appeal procedures may take longer, often results in a new evaluation. At the beginning of the proceedings in first instance, as the expert is generally appointed by the court, the defense may have some influence on the choice of expert through making a suggestion. Even though this is not a right of the defendant, and formal complaints are not possible, it may be granted. Of course after the evaluation, for example at the trial, the defense may try to argue that the expert evidence is of poor quality. While in Germany experts are more commonly present at the trial, for the Dutch attorney it is wise to call the witness to the hearing. Since in an inquisitorial system, the court asks the expert questions first, many questions will already have been answered, rendering the questioning by the parties without a true nature of cross-examination. A request for counter-expertise will only be granted if the courts 'finds itself insufficiently informed', which is generally not the case. Two other Dutch procedural provisions for testing the quality of an expert evaluation exist. First of all, a controlling expert may be appointed by the defense, also to be present during interactions with the defendant. As this accompaniment is less imaginable in case of a diagnostic interview than in case of DNA-analysis for example, this option is not often used for behavioural assessment. The alternative of audio(visually) recording such interviews, is also uncommon. Same is true for the option to have the report evaluated by another expert, even though this is more imaginable for behavioural assessment. In Sweden, such an option for a second opinion exists in requesting the court to order a review of the comprehensive evaluation by the National Board of Health and Welfare, but again the request will not be granted if the court considers a second opinion unnecessary. In all three inquisitorial

248   Michiel van der Wolf

jurisdictions the option exists for the defense to commission its own expert evidence alongside the State's official investigation, providing the case with a somewhat adversarial character (or even a battle of experts), however as this is alien to the inquisitorial system they may somewhat disrespectfully be called 'party-assessments' or 'party-experts', hinting at issues regarding impartiality. But there are other obstacles for the defense on this route, one being financial.

10.4.1.2 The possibility for legal aid

The costs of the 'party-assessment', at least in the Netherlands, have to be advanced by the defense (or defendant). If a report is eventually used in court, the defense can motivate afterwards that the costs have to be reimbursed by the State. However, the defense generally wants to have the opportunity not to submit the report in the proceedings, for example, if the conclusions are not in line with the desired strategy, rendering reimbursement of the costs unsure. These obstacles make these assessments unpopular among forensic experts, also as neutrality and objectivity are an issue, while in the end courts may be prone to follow the 'official' assessment anyway. Via this route defendants cannot be evaluated in an observation clinic, for example, leading to complaints from the perspective of equality of arms, which in inquisitorial systems is actually not completely applicable.

Nevertheless, even in adversarial systems, financial issues may hinder the commissioning of an expert by the defense at sentencing hearings. Ordinarily, the offender must bear the costs of (the attorney and) commissioning an expert to write a report or appear in court. However, where they lack means to fund an attorney or expert's involvement in their case, they may call on financial support. If the representing lawyer demonstrates legitimate grounds for the need for mental health expertise in order to assist the courts, these evaluations are generally funded, as is mentioned in the Australian perspective. It is noted in the Canadian perspective that 'mentally disordered individuals accused of a crime cannot necessarily be expected to have the personal resources or family support required to fund a robust legal defense'. As the amount of public funding available to counsel depends on the tariffs and guidelines in place in each Canadian region, and in some cases appear to be wholly inadequate in terms of both the rates of pay and the scope of compensable work, the situation in British Columbia was described by one lawyer as 'scandalous', representing a significant barrier to access to justice. In the US, case law at least provides for a due process right to a court-appointed mental health expert in responding to expert forensic evidence of future dangerousness as an aggravating factor for capital sentencing. With such court-appointed experts, defendants however may not enjoy the benefit of attorney-client privilege, such that the results of the evaluation cannot be kept from the prosecution even if unfavourable to the defendant.

10.4.2 Questioning the assessment by the court

In inquisitorial justice systems, the court itself will do most of the questioning of the experts. Procedures for judicial bodies within the execution of sentences are also inquisitorial in nature. As mentioned, it is not self-evident in the Netherlands to call experts to court, as efficiency deliberations often lead to decisions based on written reports. It is therefore necessary for the court to study the report way in advance so that experts may be called if there are any questions. If the expert is registered, it is less necessary to assess the quality of the evaluator, so that the quality of the report and conclusions remain as the subject of questioning. In Germany, however, it is the responsibility of the court in any case to convince itself that the evaluator has sufficient experience and expertise. In judging whether the assessment meets certain quality standards, there are no binding criteria, even though the mentioned 'minimum requirements' have been adopted by some courts as such. If the court has doubts and questions concerning the assessment, it can ask the evaluator for amendments or a clarifying statement. The court may dismiss the expert opinion (or give less or no weight to its evidentiary value), for example, if the expertise of the evaluator is questionable, if the opinion is based on false factual assumptions, if it is contradictory or if there is another expert with superior methods. In all inquisitorial systems, also the court can ask for a new evaluation, or a second opinion, critically evaluating the first evaluation. In Sweden, as mentioned, this will be done by the National Board of Health and Welfare. In practice, however, empirical studies show in these three jurisdictions that such instruments are hardly used and that the conclusions of the initial assessment are generally followed. In the Swedish perspective, it is noted that judges not only lack criteria by which to judge the evaluation but also lack knowledge on behavioural expertise. In some Dutch judiciary boards within the execution of sentencing, behavioural experts are present, however, similar to parole or review boards in some adversarial countries.

As in adversarial justice, as mentioned, the court relies on the characteristic mechanisms, they often incline against an activist approach. 'Instead, they rely on counsel in the discharge of their duties in the adversarial process to conduct the necessary questioning and bring to the court's attention any frailties in that evidence', as is mentioned in the Canadian perspective. That may even explain why in England, and in Australia for less serious matters, it is mentioned that in many cases written reports are considered without additional oral evidence. The court however ultimately has to decide on admissibility of evidence or the weight it has to be given in the decision. In all adversarial jurisdictions this is decided on aspects of the quality of the evaluator and the evaluation. In England, in practice it is unusual for an expert's credentials and methods to be extensively examined, and perhaps more common after listing their qualifications 'to hear uncomfortably courteous references to being "distinguished" or "highly experienced"'. On occasions, however, the expert's qualifications and methods will be sharply tested in cross-examination or by a judge.

For the substantive testing of the reliability of their reports, all adversarial jurisdictions have 'tests' or other tools for the decision-makers in place, which differ in specificity/applicability related to the sentencing context and detail. The Practice Note mentioned in the Australian perspective is specifically for sentencing, while in other jurisdictions tests for the trial stage are or may be applicable in that context. The latter tests may not be as stringently applied in the sentencing hearing, as the rules of evidence are often more leniently applied than in the trial of fact. In the American perspective it is mentioned that at the sentencing stage, expert evidence is generally admissible, so that it becomes a question of weight, which can vary based on the sufficiency of evaluator expertise, methodological reliability (or validity, as this is often assessed under the heading of reliability), relevance to specific legal questions, credibility or persuasiveness of the testimony. In proceedings before Canadian mental health Review Boards, the restrictions on the admission of expert evidence are more relaxed. This is attributed to the inquisitorial nature of the process, and in part a reflection of the expert nature of Review Boards, which include members with expertise and experience in psychiatry and mental health training. 'These members are well-equipped to critically engage with information presented in forensic assessments, and to question the assessor directly in the course of Review Board hearings'. Production of additional evidence, including further assessments, may be ordered if they find that the evidence falls short.

When it is up to legal judges to assess expert evidence they are supported by the mentioned tests or tools. In the Practice Note, the need for judges to critically assess the forensic mental health evidence is implicit: '[i]n order to evaluate what reliance to place on an expert report, the sentencing judge needs to know the purpose of the report, the relevant qualifications and expertise of the expert, the expert's opinions and the factual foundation of each opinion'. For evaluating the qualifications of the expert, the Practice Note includes two Schedules for assistance. They address matters such as the roles of the different professional organisations working in the area, and the meaning of the various titles, qualifications, and endorsements a judge may encounter. Not complying with the requirements of the Practice Note or the Expert Witness Codes of Conduct may lead to inadmissibility or limited weight. In England, extensive Criminal Practice Directions are in place as derived from the Criminal Procedure Rules, to aid the court in 'actively enquiring' into factors that may affect the reliability of the expert evidence. These factors go so far as to include identifying potential flaws in hypothesis, assumptions, data, methods (execution and appropriateness), inferences, and conclusions. In the Canadian '*White Burgess* test' for admissibility of expert evidence, after a first step testing relevance, the expert nature of the matter (outside the knowledge of the decision-maker), adherence to other laws of evidence, and qualifications of the expert, in a second step a cost-benefit analysis is required, balancing significance versus factors like introducing time, prejudice and confusion. The test is this stringent, among other things to avoid the expert to usurp the role of decision-maker. In the US chapter, it is mentioned that, next to legal admissibility tests, 'scholarly resources are available to assist legal professionals with more critically appraising and challenging forensic evaluations and related expert mental health testimony'. However, in practice available case law suggests for example that legal decision-makers are generally uncritical of both structured and unstructured risk assessment testimony. Little empirical evidence is available for more generalised inferences, however for certain decisions – such as imposing a hospital order in England or a sexually dangerous person commitment in a US state – a high level of concordance between evaluator opinions and court decisions exists. An English study from about 30 years ago concluded that psychiatric reports commissioned by defense solicitors had a higher likelihood of rejection than reports commissioned by courts, a finding which has a somewhat inquisitorial ring to it.

10.4.3 Other questioning of the assessment

Under this heading, other relevant provisions and practices could be mentioned. In the English perspective, specific provisions are mentioned that create a possibility for the prosecution if it considers that a sentence should be challenged because it is 'unduly lenient'. In the American perspective, the possibility is mentioned for professional societies and other groups to submit *amicus curiae* (non-party informational) briefs in appellate case that raise significant issues about forensic evaluation, especially dangerousness assessments. Well known examples have tended to call for respect for scientifically supported risk assessment practices, including an appreciation for the limits of the state of the science. However, courts may still admit clinical judgement as a risk assessment. In other countries, this practice has not been replicated in this context. In the Dutch perspective a provision for mandatory counter-expertise is mentioned regarding the execution of the TBS-order, for prolongation after every four years and for (continued) placement on a so-called 'longstay' ward. The obligatory independent advice is understandable, as the initial advice is being given (or application is being made) by the treating TBS-facility.

10.5 Safeguarding the quality of decision-making when confronted with disagreement between experts

10.5.1 Dealing with disagreement

Another way in which the limitations of forensic behavioural evaluation come to light is through disagreement between evaluators. Evidently, decision-makers in adversarial jurisdictions are more

Comparative analysis 251

accustomed to disagreement than those in inquisitorial jurisdictions, as being confronted with opposing opinions is actually part of the (safeguards of the) system. Nevertheless, in all jurisdictions some types of cases or decisions may especially evoke disagreement. These will be described first, after which possible ways of dealing with disagreement in the respective countries are discussed to try and ensure optimal decision-making, both from the side of the evaluators and from the side of the decision-makers.

10.5.1.1 Decisions or cases, which especially evoke disagreement

Two reasons may be identified that render certain cases or decisions more prone to disagreement. Obviously, the higher the involved stakes, the more scrutiny will be placed on unfavourable outcomes of evaluations from the perspective of the parties. In addition, decisions or cases, which touch on current scientific debates or difference of opinion among professionals, may incorporate that debate into the decision-making process.

Several examples of high stakes are mentioned, among which of course capital sentencing and sexually dangerous person commitment in the US. In England, disagreement can be particularly prominent in murder trials in which a defense of diminished responsibility is pleaded by the defendant but not accepted by the prosecution. In Canada, there are circumstances mentioned for which courts or Review boards may order a new assessment, including cases where fitness to stand trial is an issue. Cases, which evoke current scientific debate include risk assessment for front-end sentencing decisions, for reasons described in Chapter 2. Also adversarial allegiance/ partisan potential of evaluators that can manifest in the scoring of risk assessment tools, and multicultural generalizability issues in risk assessment, are hot debates in this respect. In the Dutch chapter, a case is mentioned in which about six evaluations were being done by several evaluators. The circumstances, a case of double homicide by an asylum seeker after a change in his antidepressant medication, touched on two scientific issues for which little evidence-based knowledge exists: multicultural aspects (again) and pharmacodynamic aspects.

10.5.1.2 Options for the evaluators

As for impactful decisions multiple, or multidisciplinary, or a team evaluation is required, also in inquisitorial systems disagreement will be experienced. Traditionally, the idea among experts was/is that decision-makers are not helped with differences of opinion. Therefore they have become accustomed to discussing the outcomes of their separate evaluations, in which they strive for consensus, before writing the final report. Even though this may also be considered as a safeguard, through a form of peer review, as a consequence, possible disagreement that existed initially is obscured from the decision-maker. In Germany, this has led to a debate about the added value of a second evaluator, also in light of the shortage of experts. Only when consensus deliberations do not lead to agreement on (some of) the conclusions, it is customary to both discuss and explain their differences in their respective reports. In Sweden, when a team performing a comprehensive evaluation does not come to a joint conclusion, the regulations state that the psychologist and social worker clarify their reasons for disagreement, as the psychiatrists as the final say over the overarching conclusions. If these are inconclusive, the psychiatrist can also recommend the court to get a second opinion from the National Board of Health and Welfare. Recommending a second opinion is of course something all experts could do when confronted with disagreement with a fellow evaluator.

In the US, in cases with multiple evaluators, depending on the jurisdiction and types of case, laws may either prohibit or permit consultation between the experts, but of course this is less common in adversarial proceedings. In the Canadian chapter, the following description is also applied to forensic psychiatry, an 'interpretative discipline in which degrees of certainty are not easily quantified or may not even be scientifically supportable'. It is therefore recommended not to use language in reports that overstates the expert's level of confidence, to develop language for the level of confidence experts have, make full and proper disclosure of any doubts they might have, or alternate diagnoses. A similar transparency is warranted for controversies and uncertainties in the science on which they rely. This requirement can be found in several regulations, phrased as 'if the findings within the relevant area of expertise can reasonably lead to differing interpretations or conclusions' (the Netherlands), 'summarise the range of opinion, and give reasons for the expert's own opinion' (England), and 'disclose the existence and nature of that disagreement or controversy' (Australia). The English Criminal Practice Directions actually direct the court to inquire whether such debates exist related to the question at hand.

10.5.1.3 Options for the decision-makers

Since, as mentioned, adversarial systems are more accustomed to disagreement between experts, they also have more (regulated or formal) options in place for decision-makers to deal with the situation. The simplest and most common one – actually also in inquisitorial systems –, is that they need not actually resolve disagreement between experts, but can just make a decision. They may reject or accept evidence in whole or in part, based on their own assessment of the strength and probative value of the evidence, resulting in preferring one assessment over another. What persuades them may be the more reasoned and understandable report, or the more conservative outcome, or 'the relative expertise of the assessor as well as their demeanor and conduct in the courtroom, particularly when under cross-examination' (Canadian chapter). The courtroom appearance of experts is also more likely in case of contested evidence. In the English chapter, it is mentioned that the context of adversarial criminal proceedings can add heavily to the burden of dealing with disagreement: 'Expert witnesses need the psychological ability constantly to perceive questioning and cross-examination as a search for truth and not experience it as attack or personal criticism. They also need constantly to respect the human tragedies that lie behind criminal trials, and not be invested in winning a contest'.

Another option that courts have is to commission their own, third, evaluation. In Canada, a court or Review Board may order such an assessment, in certain circumstances, where it has reasonable grounds to believe that such evidence is necessary – possibly due to disagreement. Beyond that, no formal options or alternate bodies are reported for the resolution of disagreement between experts. Outside the mentioned cases in which this is mandatory in certain US states, appointing a third expert is rarely used – similarly in England – mainly as it runs counter to the adversarial system. So by that rationale, only in the rare instance 'in which the traditional adversarial process has failed to permit an informed assessment', this option would be contemplated. Even though in most Victorian sentencing cases only one expert witness (the defense expert) is relied on, outside adversarial mechanisms as a first option and commission an independent report as a second, the Practice Note does contain three additional procedural provisions that can help resolve any disagreements which do occur. First, a direction can be made to the experts to discuss matters in advance, and 'prepare a statement for the Court of the matters on which they agree and disagree, giving their reasons'. Secondly, the courts may convene a special 'pre-hearing' prior to the sentencing hearing. In both cases, non-compliance from the side of the evaluator may lead to inadmissibility of the evidence. Thirdly, the courts can vary the order in which evidence is given in the sentencing hearing, so that the experts of both parties give their evidence consecutively.

In inquisitorial systems, as mentioned, it is also most common that the decision-maker just decides when confronted with disagreement. The advantage it has, in comparison with its adversarial counterpart, is that it can actively question all experts, after calling them to the hearing. In Dutch literature, there is some support for courts' ability to break through the 'expert-paradox', which means that the court has to judge the quality of the expertise without having the expertise, through questioning the methods (and level) of acquiring knowledge and the state of the discipline. Of course, as is underlined in the German perspective, in the explanatory statement of the verdict it will have to spell out the reasons for following one and dismissing the other evaluation. However, when the decision-maker finds it too difficult to reason which advice to follow it could ask for a third opinion, in the Netherlands on the grounds that it does not consider itself to be sufficiently informed. In Germany and Sweden there is an explicit possibility of commissioning a superordinate assessment. In Germany, regularly experienced and renowned experts are appointed. In Sweden, as mentioned, the National Board of Health and Welfare has this authority. In the Netherlands, it is not a formal option, but ordering the third evaluation to be done in the state's observational clinic may have the same effect. Even though the superordinate advice is not binding, it makes sense that the court follows that. In Sweden, objective reasons are often given for this choice, such as that more time has elapsed to observe the client or that other new information has emerged in the meantime, generating a more solid information basis for this superordinate second opinion. In Germany however, criticism has addressed the additional costs of this procedure in addition to a possible delay of proceedings and the uncertainty that the superordinate assessment is of higher quality. A subsidiary, more rare, option is therefore to appoint an expert to critically evaluate the methods used within disagreeing assessments (see the similar options in paragraph 10.4.2).

10.5.2 Best practices

Apart from the more formal options described above, one additional option that has come up in practice is described. In addition, the importance of interdisciplinary training for both evaluators and decision-makers is being stressed.

In Australia, an additional option in practice is that decision-makers can order the experts to give their evidence concurrently, colloquially known as 'hot tubbing'. This can only be done with the agreement of the parties, after deliberations on the procedure to adopt. It allows the experts to explicitly address one another's approach and findings, and respond to one another in real time. To date, the use of this power has been very limited in the criminal law context but has been used – also in the US – in the civil law context. In the Netherlands, a similar practice has been advocated in literature, with a debate on the timing of this meeting, either prior to the trial or in front of the court – defense lawyers prefer the latter. In the execution of the TBS-order, a comparable 'care conference' has been introduced in practice by the Ministry in case treatment takes a very long time for example because of an impasse in the treatment, possibly as a result of disagreement about the diagnosis or the course of treatment. All the parties involved with the case and external experts are invited to come to agreement about a future course. As these conferences are within the context of forensic treatment, it matches the suggestion in the English chapter, that in the context of clinical work the approach to dealing with uncertainty and differing views about assessment, diagnosis and treatment should be collaborative. The clinical context does not fit a well with adversarialism. Some suggestions in the American chapter, related to dealing with disagreement in the assessment context, also advocate distancing from the adversarial nature of proceedings, aware of the criticism this will trigger. Reducing the likelihood of disagreement from the outset may be achieved by greater utilisation of legal procedures (e.g. judicial orders) to ensure that experts are given access to the same information and follow the same basic procedures. Additionally, judges have occasionally required the recording of evaluations, as it can be a way for mental health and legal professionals to see for themselves how a particular expert's questions and evaluation procedures may have led to the expert's particular opinions. Also the use of 'blinded' experts, unaware of which party has retained them, or parties agreeing on mutual referral to a single evaluator are mentioned, to avoid 'the drift that may occur due to adversarial allegiance'.

In all chapters, the need for cross-training of the involved disciplines – 'training forensic evaluators about law, and legal professionals about forensic evaluation' – is underlined. In the US some states have instituted statewide training requirements, or evaluator certification programs, as a prerequisite to mental health professionals completing certain forensic evaluations, including some involving risk assessments. The English chapter stresses the importance of peer-group work for reviewing the quality and soundness of expert witness opinion, as well as for more focus on legal and ethical issues in specialty training schemes and research. In the German chapter the wish for a feedback loop from the judiciary on the decision of the case, or even from recidivism studies on prognostic assessment is expressed. On the side of legal practitioners, according to the English chapter, altering the style or approach of judges and advocates to be optimal for the purposes of revealing (and enabling witnesses to acknowledge) the strengths and weaknesses of their evidence, should be the focus of training. Finally, a 'judicial primers project' for the mental health field is suggested, to help the judiciary be better informed about areas of scientific knowledge relevant to this kind of expert evidence. In short, in the words of the German authors: 'What is needed (and would contribute to a "best practice") in our eyes is a strong emphasis on measures of interdisciplinary education and advanced training for all professions involved, facilitating communication and exchange between experts on both sides'.

10.6 Conclusions and critical reflections

Even though such a question was not posed to the authors, in most country chapters comments were made on what is considered the strongest safeguard for the quality of assessment in sentencing in that jurisdiction. Together with the critical reflections that were asked for, it paints a picture of how in that country quality is being viewed and safeguarded.

In adversarial jurisdictions, the corresponding mechanisms including opposing expert opinions and/or cross-examination are described as tools to test and contest the quality of forensic assessments. But jurisdictions differ in how adversarial proceedings within sentencing actually are, while the nature of the proceedings in front-end sentencing decisions may also be quite different from proceedings concerning mid-way or back-end decision-making. Therefore the law of evidence generally related to adversarial justice, more specific the stringent test of admissibility of expert evidence, is mentioned in Canada as the primary safeguard for the quality and reliability of forensic assessment in this context, while in the US expert evidence in the sentencing stage is generally admissible. In the Australian context, as at the sentencing hearing in practice there generally only is an expert on behalf of the defense, strengthening its adversarial nature by opposing evidence from the prosecution is advocated by the authors. While in the English and American perspectives, adversarial pitfalls related to the possibly personal nature of the battle of experts and so-called adversarial allegiance, actually result in all sorts of suggestions of inquisitorial nature to reduce disagreement and allow for optimal decision-making. Rules and regulations that are in place for the quality of expert evidence also vary in detail and in specificity for the sentencing context. The English and Australian regulations are quite detailed, with the difference being that the Victorian Practice

Note is more specific in its focus on both forensic behavioural assessment and the sentencing hearing. Given also its background in dissatisfaction with the quality of such assessment, and its interdisciplinary and ground-up approach, which has ensured buy-in of all relevant stakeholders, it is no surprise that the Practice Note is mentioned as the strongest safeguard in the context of this book. As it is a strong hold for the court in assessing admissibility, it may also cope better with the possible 'drifts' of adversarialism. Especially where admissibility is an important issue, like in Canada and Australia, reputation matters following the providing of inadmissible expert evidence, is seen as a quality assurance mechanism of underestimated importance. As the quality and the obligation of training, with a variable connection to licensing for forensic assessment work, may differ, they are given less or more weight within the country chapters as quality safeguards. Especially, in the English perspective, the voluntariness of training and the absence of a 'single, independent regulated register of expert witnesses on which the public can rely' are said to lead to great lack of uniformity as to the quality of evaluation and are therefore scrutinised.

In turning to the inquisitorial jurisdictions on the subject of a register, with its related procedures and mandatory nature, this is especially considered to be the strongest safeguard for the quality of forensic assessment in the Netherlands. Nevertheless, the Dutch authors stress that registration does not necessarily ensure the quality of assessment in a single case, while behavioural scientists may well escape some of the standards that seem to be more applicable to natural sciences. As inquisitorial systems view collaboration of evaluators – in Sweden and the Netherlands multidisciplinary – as an important safeguard of quality the strive for consensus may overestimate the reliability of the expertise, or underestimate difference of opinions, and render the assessment less scrutinised. In Germany, professional recommendations from a private interdisciplinary group, for example on the issue of risk assessment, are mentioned as the most important safeguard for the quality of assessment, also because some high courts have adopted some of their standards, making them more legally binding. The German authors point out however that compliance with formal standards and certain minimum requirements is no guarantee for a high quality of the assessment with regard to its content. They are also most critical of all towards their own system. Given the impact of decisions for which forensic assessment is used, they feel like the legislator should provide more explicit regulations as it depends too much on the discretion of decision-makers and leaves 'unnecessary leeway for doubtful decisions and in addition for inequality and arbitrariness'. They point out that on the one hand unquestioned and complete adoption of the evaluation often occurs, while the other extreme of not considering an evaluation at all is equally possible, which calls for restriction of excessive judicial discretion, or – positively put – for more guidance. In addition, they recommend more multidisciplinary assessment, also because of a vast scarcity of qualified forensic psychiatrists. This practical barrier, which is also highly topical in the Netherlands, may render any binding improvement of quality safeguards impracticable. There are historic reasons for the unattractiveness of the occupation, but they are intensified by current dynamics related to its poor scientific status, also due to methodological obstacles, and underpayment in light of the professions responsibilities and risks. In the Netherlands, the lack of reporting psychiatrists has already led to an increased use of psychologists and a pressure for time. In Sweden, the time pressure is equally felt, posing a risk for the quality of assessment, which benefits from discussions and focused analysis. A final risk for the quality of the interdisciplinary dialogue, which the Swedish authors mention, is the vague and 'open texture of legal norms and concepts'. Not only does it lead to misunderstanding, when related to risk it also hinders the development of evidence-based tools.

In optimising the quality of forensic assessment and the consequential legal decisions, all authors underline the importance of a continuous interdisciplinary discussion – both in and out of the courtroom – as both the legal context and the behavioural scientific state of the art keep developing. Not only to avoid misunderstanding but – as the begin quote suggests – in contrast it will help to know the own discipline (better). In most of the countries, the context of the interdisciplinary dialogue in sentencing is highly demanding, as risk-averseness and cost-effectiveness are competing and have tremendous effects on the sentencing arsenal and the possibilities of care for mentally disordered offenders, as well as on optimising decision-making. No doubt, the effects of the mentioned lack of legal aid in Canada, may be seen in other countries as well. And not only because of such practical barriers, as shortages of professionals and funds, with all the mentioned safeguards in place, all authors are aware that no country can claim with confidence that the measures in place can fully safeguard against error. Formal and minimal requirements can even be met in a poor quality evaluation. In the end, as is mentioned in several chapters, it all depends on 'individual human beings and their subjective ethos'. And even if that would all be up to standard, the state of the art of the discipline will still leave room for error.

Many differences between countries in safeguarding the quality of forensic assessment in sentencing, may indeed be attributed to the difference between adversarial and inquisitorial justice, and their different rationales in how to find 'fact'. Interestingly, in combatting the ex-crescences in this regard of both adversarial justice – the exaggeration of disagreement through battle and allegiance – and inquisitorial justice – the overestimation of agreement and reliability –, adversarial countries point towards inquisitorial safeguards and vice versa. Meeting in the middle, through hybridity in structures, may very well be optimal. Forensic assessment in adversarial justice may gain from collaboration, independence, and registration, while in inquisitorial justice openness and transparency about the state of the discipline and the possibility of alternate opinion, and guidance in scrutinising expert evidence by the decision-maker, may benefit the quality of assessment and decision. Both evaluators and decision-makers will have to do their part. However, some differences between countries sharing a similar justice system are accounted for through subtleties of the legal system or the tradition or development of forensic assessment, or events stirring concern about the quality of forensic assessment. Some of the mentioned safeguards could very well be adopted in other systems, but the reader will have to be the judge of that. 'Whoever knows another culture, will also know his own'.

Notes

1 It is mentioned as a quote of S.R. Steinmetz, who – active in the late nineteenth and early twentieth century – is considered to be one of the founders of the academic disciplines of sociology, social geography, and cultural anthropology in the Netherlands. See Van Heerikhuizen, 2008.
2 The use of the quote by Steinmetz in this context is from the inaugural lecture of a Dutch professor in transcultural forensic psychiatry Mario Braakman, 2021, p. 33.
3 Vice versa, this has been used to explain the disregard for the Dutch unfitness doctrine. See Van der Wolf et al., 2010.
4 A more elaborate and nuanced look at the concept will be described in paragraph 10.2.3.2.
5 Keulen et al., 2013, with a Summary in English, pp. 264–270.
6 Keulen et al., 2013, with a Summary in English, pp. 241–243.
7 See also Ford and Rotter, 2014.
8 More on this in paragraph 10.2.3.2.
9 See Van der Wolf and Herzog-Evans, 2014.
10 See Van der Wolf, 2016, where it is mentioned as a quote from an English author.

References

Braakman, M. (2021). *Culturele empathie: over Tantalus en andere beproevingen. Transculturele reglecties binnen de forensische psychiatrie* (inaugural lecture). Tilburg: Tilburg University.

Ford, E. and Rotter, M. (2014). *Landmark Cases in Forensic Psychiatry*. Oxford: Oxford University Press.

Keulen, B.F., Dijk, A.A. van, Gritter, E., Kwakman, N.J.M., and Lindenberg, K.K. (2013). *Naar een tweefasenproces? Over voor- en nadelen van een strafproces in twee fasen, in relatie tot de positie van slachtoffer en verdachte*. Paris: Zutphen.

Van der Wolf, M.J.F., and Herzog-Evans, M. (2014). Mandatory measures: 'Safety measures'. Supervision and detention of dangerous offenders in France and the Netherlands: A comparative and Human rights' perspective. In M. Herzog-Evans (Ed.), *Offender Release and Supervision: The Role of Courts and the Use of Discretion*. Oisterwijk: Wolf Legal Publishers, pp. 193–234.

Van der Wolf, M.J.F., Marle, H.J.C. van, Mevis, P.A.M., and Roesch, R. (2010). Understanding and evaluating contrasting unfitness to stand trial practices. A comparison between Canada and The Netherlands. *International Journal of Forensic Mental Health*, 9(3), pp. 245–258.

Van der Wolf, M.J.F. (2016). Legal control on social control of sex offenders in the community: A European comparative and human rights perspective. *Erasmus Law Review*, 2(9), pp. 39–54.

Van Heerikhuizen, B. (2008). "Wie alleen zijn eigen vak kent, kent ook dit niet. Over interdisciplinair denken." Retrieved 15 July 2021, from http://bartvanheerikhuizen.nl/2014/03/wie-alleen-zijn-eigen-vak-kent-kent-ook-dit-niet-over-interdisciplinair-2008/

Contributors

Tova Bennet, PhD, is a postdoctoral researcher at the Faculty of Law at the University of Bergen. She is also affiliated with the Center for Ethics, Law and Mental Health (CELAM) at the University of Gothenburg. Her research focuses on foundational questions of criminal law and their relationship with psychiatry, psychology, and philosophy. Her most recent publications have explored the prerequisites for criminal responsibility in cases of atypical mental states, such as psychosis.

Andrew Carroll, MA (Cantab), BM, BCh (Oxon), MMedSci, FRCPsych, FRANZCP, is an Associate Professor (Adjunct) at Swinburne University of Technology and a Consultant Forensic Psychiatrist at the Victorian Institute of Forensic Mental Health (Forensicare). He studied psychology as an undergraduate at the University of Cambridge before pursuing clinical medical training at the University of Oxford. He trained in psychiatry in Yorkshire before completing a research fellowship at Edinburgh University. He has worked as a forensic psychiatrist in both the public and private sectors in Australia for two decades. Currently, he works primarily in private medicolegal practice, doing forensic assessment work in both the criminal and civil fields.

Adrian Grounds, DM, FRCPsych, is an Honorary Research Fellow at the Institute of Criminology, University of Cambridge. He was previously University Senior Lecturer in Forensic Psychiatry at the Institute of Criminology, and Consultant Forensic Psychiatrist in the Cambridgeshire & Peterborough NHS Foundation Trust. He is a Sentence Review Commissioner and a Parole Commissioner in Northern Ireland, and a medical member of the First-tier Tribunal (Mental Health) in England.

Lauren Grove, MA, is a doctoral student in the PhD Program in Clinical Psychology at Montclair State University. Her research interests include juvenile transfer and juvenile competence.

Malin Hildebrand Karlén, PhD, is a researcher, research coordinator and certified clinical psychologist at the National Board of Forensic Medicine, Department of Forensic Psychiatry, in Gothenburg, Sweden. She is a licensed specialist within addiction psychology and within forensic psychology, Associate Professor of Psychology and senior lecturer within the field of addiction psychology at the Department of Psychology, University of Gothenburg, and assistant director of the cross-disciplinary research group Centre for Ethics, Law and Mental Health (CELAM), Institute of Neuroscience and Physiology, Department of Psychiatry and Neuroscience, University of Gothenburg, Sweden. Her main research interests are decision-making within forensic psychiatric assessment and care, as well as applied addiction psychology to the field of forensic psychiatry.

Johannes Kaspar, LLM, PhD, is a Professor of Criminal Law, Criminal Procedural Law, Criminology, and the Law of Criminal Sanctions at Augsburg University. He is one of the chief editors of the Journal *Neue Kriminalpolitik*. In 2018 he wrote an extensive expert opinion on the Reform of Sentencing Law in Germany for the 72nd *Juristentag*, the biannual Convention of German Legal Scholars and Practitioners. Apart from general questions of criminal law and penal theory, his main research interests include the relationship between constitutional law and criminal law, Restorative Justice, and the theory and practice of sentencing and criminal sanctions.

Sharon Kelley, JD, PhD, is an Assistant Professor of Research in the Department of Psychiatry & Neurobehavioral Sciences, and conducts forensic psychological evaluations at the Institute of Law, Psychiatry, & Public Policy, at the University of Virginia. Her research interests include juveniles and adults' capacity to waive *Miranda* rights and enter guilty pleas, false confessions, law enforcement interactions with individuals with mental illness, and using psychological research to improve the forensic sciences. Her clinical work includes conducting forensic evaluations with adults and juveniles examining a range of criminal and civil psycholegal issues.

Christopher M. King, JD, PhD, is an Associate Professor of Psychology and the Director of Clinical Training (PhD Program in Clinical Psychology) at Montclair State University. His research interests include forensic mental health assessment, correctional psychology, police and public safety psychology, and mental health law. He also works in part-time private practice providing clinical, forensic, and police and public safety psychological services.

Michelle S. Lawrence, LLM, PhD, is an Associate Professor and Director of the Access to Justice Centre for Excellence at the University of Victoria's Faculty of Law. She teaches and researches in the areas of criminal law, sentencing, and evidence. She holds graduate degrees in law and criminology, including an LLM from the University of Cambridge and a PhD (Criminology) from Simon Fraser University. She completed her doctoral work as a Trudeau Scholar. Her research has been published in leading Canadian journals, including the *Canadian Bar Review, Canadian Criminal Law Review, Criminal Law Quarterly*, and *Canadian Journal of Criminology and Criminal Justice*. Dr. Lawrence is a founding member of the UVic Access to Justice Centre for Excellence. She currently serves as an Alternate Chair of the British Columbia Review Board.

Hjalmar van Marle, MD, PhD, psychiatrist, professor emeritus of forensic psychiatry at the Erasmus Medical Centre and the Erasmus School of Law, Rotterdam, and former professor of forensic psychiatry at the Catholic University of Nijmegen, The Netherlands. Medical Superintendant of the Van Mesdag maximum security tbs-hospital and of the Pieter Baan Observation Centre of the Ministry of Justice. Psychoanalyst in forensic in- and out-patient clinics. From 1991 certified forensic expert witness for the Courts. Former member of the Council for Criminal Justice and Youth Protection. Member and chairman of the Dutch Association of Medical Specialist Reporting.

David W. Morgan, BSc (Hons), MB BCh, LLM, FRCPC, is a clinical assistant professor at the University of British Colombia, where he teachers and supervises postgraduate and subspecialty residents. His research interests include mental health law and ethics, rural and community forensic psychiatry, and youth sexual offending. He is a forensic psychiatrist with British Columbia Youth Forensic Psychiatric Services, where he is also the provincial clinical lead for youth sex offending treatment services and the regional clinical director for northern British Columbia. He lived in, and worked across, northern BC for eight years. Dr. Morgan also maintains a private practice in civil and criminal forensic psychiatry at the Broadway Forensic Group in Vancouver.

Nicola Padfield, QC (Hon), is a Professor of Criminal and Penal Justice at the Law Faculty, University of Cambridge, where she has worked for more than 30 years. She was Master of Fitzwilliam College, Cambridge from 2013 to 2019. Her main expertise is in sentencing law, including the law and practice of release from (and recall to) prison. She sat as a Recorder (part-time judge) in the Crown Court from 2002 to 2014, and is a Bencher of the Middle Temple.

Sabine Roza, MD, PhD, is a psychiatrist, tutor in forensic psychiatry at the Dutch Institute of Forensic Psychiatry and Psychology and medical director at the penitentiary institution in The Hague. She is also an associate professor of Forensic Psychiatry at Erasmus MC University Medical Center in Rotterdam. She is a registered expert witness for criminal courts (juveniles and adults) and supervises (trainee) psychiatrists in the training of forensic evaluators.

Brooke Stettler, MA, is a doctoral student in the PhD Program in Clinical Psychology at Montclair State University. Her research interests include forensic interviewing and forensic and correctional psychology.

Susanne Stübner, MD, PhD, is a Professor at the Department of Forensic Psychiatry of the Ludwig-Maximilians-University in Munich, and is also associated to Klinik für Forensische Psychiatrie in Ansbach. She frequently provides forensic psychiatric expertise before criminal courts. Her research interests include psychopathology, psychopharmacology, and risk management in forensic settings.

Michiel de Vries Robbé, PhD, is a psychologist and senior researcher at the Department of Child and Adolescent Psychiatry and Psychosocial Care, of the Amsterdam University medical center in The Netherlands. In addition, he is affiliated as a senior researcher with the Netherlands Institute of Forensic Psychiatry and Psychology and as an associate professor with the Department of Psychiatry and Behavioural Neurosciences of McMaster University, Hamilton, Canada. His research focuses primarily on risk assessment and its applicability and implementation in forensic practice. In particular he is involved in the development of risk screening and the assessment of protective factors for (violence) risk for adults, juveniles, and children. He is co-author of the Structured Assessment of Protective Factors for violence risk (SAPROF), the SAPROF-Youth Version (SAPROF-YV), the SAPROF-Child Version (SAPROF-CV), the Female Additional Manual (FAM), the Risk Screener-Violence (RS-V), and the Risk Screener-Youth (RS-Y).

Lena Wahlberg, LLD, is an Associate Professor of Jurisprudence at the Faculty of Law, Lund University. Her research focuses on ethical, conceptual, and methodological problems that arise in the interface of law and science, in particular in the legal regulation of health care. Her most recent publications deal with the meaning of the Swedish legal standard 'science and proven experience', with the importance assigned to scientific evidence in Swedish policy and decision-making during the pandemic, and with the role of the expert witness in legal proceedings.

Jamie Walvisch, BA (Hons), LLB (Hons), PhD (Monash), is a Senior Lecturer at the Melbourne Law School, University of Melbourne. Before becoming an academic, he worked at the Judicial College of Victoria, where he was responsible for developing and drafting the *Victorian Criminal Charge Book*, the main reference book used by judges and legal practitioners in Victorian criminal jury trials. Prior to that he worked at the Australian Institute of Criminology and the Victorian Law Reform Commission, where he co-authored reports on a wide-range of topics, including defenses to homicide, fraud, and electronic commerce-related crime and road rage. Jamie's current research focuses on the intersection between law and mental health, especially in the sentencing context. His PhD thesis, titled *Sentencing Offenders with Mental Illnesses: A Principled Approach*, examined the circumstances in which mental illnesses should be taken into account when sentencing offenders who are convicted of serious crimes.

Michiel van der Wolf, LLM, MSc, PhD, is a Professor of Forensic Psychiatry at the Institute of Criminal Law and Criminology at Leiden University and an associate professor in Criminal Law at the University of Groningen, in the Netherlands. He was trained as both a legal scholar and a clinical psychologist. In the latter capacity, he worked for two years as a trainee in a high-security forensic mental (TBS) hospital. On the legal practice side, he is a deputy judge at the criminal court of Amsterdam and the court of appeal in Leeuwarden. His research interests focus on the interface between law and psychiatry/psychology including forensic assessment and sentencing, from a legal, empirical, historical, and internationally comparative perspective.

Index

Academic training for forensic experts 122
accountability 73, 176–77, 204
accreditation 46–48, 52, 100, 134, 245
actuarial tools 19, 101
ADHD (attention deficit hyperactivity disorder) 126
admissibility of expert evidence 50, 65, 111, 201, 250, 254
advice, medical expert 206
Alcohol Treatment Orders 123, 129
American Academy of Psychiatry and the Law (AAPL) 15, 77
American Bar Association 85
American Judges Association 85
American Psychiatric Association 148
American Psychological Association 77, 81
APS (Australian Psychological Society) 123, 134, 136–37, 139
assault, aggravated 150
assessment
    behavioural 26, 205, 236, 239–40, 246–47, 255
    competency 16
    competing 164
    flawed 112
    individualised 20
    prognostic 149, 153, 155–57, 166, 168, 254
assessment context 23, 253
assessment instruments
    actuarial risk 114
    structured risk 21, 41
assessment methodology 187, 237
assessment of culpability 151, 159–60, 165–66
assessment tool 24
Australian and New Zealand Association for Psychiatry 122
Australian Courts 124
Australian criminal justice system 127
Australian Health Practitioner Regulation Agency 136
Australian judges 138
Australian law 121
Australian legal practice 247
Australian Psychological Society; *see* APS

autism spectrum disorder 24, 126, 180
AWMF (*Arbeitsgemeinschaft der Wissenschaftlichen Medizinischen Fachgesellschaften*) 161

balanced understanding 189
ban, constitutional 69
Bavarian Act 150, 152
Bavarian court 167
Bavarian Prison Act 149
Bavarian State Medical Association 162
Bayerische Landesärztekammer 162
Bayerisches Maßregelvollzugsgesetz 150
behaviour
    harmful 18–19, 23
    historical 185
    individual 23
    negligent 161
    social 155
behavioural (scientific) expertise 3, 222, 241, 249
behavioural experts 13, 214–15, 217, 219, 222, 230–31, 236, 249
behaviour observations 18
behaviour patterns 156
bell curve 12
best practice for courts 138
best practices 2, 56, 84–85, 115, 138, 165–66, 193, 253–54
beyond reasonable doubt 175, 192
biases
    affective 11, 187
    affiliation 11
biography, general 156
biological markers 13
bodies
    advisory 222
    disciplinary 100
    judicial 221–22, 248
    national 100
    official 162
    regulating 49
bounds of sentence 71
brain 6, 204
brain maturation 215

Index 263

branches
    executive 64–65, 208, 233
    judicial 64
    political 99
British North America Act 98–99, 116
British Psychological Society (BPS) 49, 244

Canada's territories 99
Canadian Academy of Psychiatry 100
Canadian Charter 99, 116
Canadian courts 107, 111, 113–14, 116
Canadian criminal justice process 115
Canadian criminal law 103
Canadian federal government 98
Canadian justice system 112
Canadian Medical Association (CMA) 116
Canadian universities 101
coerced care 207
cognitive disorders 14
community order 38–39, 41–42
community supervision 102, 110
competence 4, 6, 13, 15, 49, 82, 85, 155, 158, 190, 201, 212, 233, 238, 244
comprehensive range of information 49, 242
contesting assessments 79–80
counter-expertise 2–3, 217, 219–21, 223, 247
court decisions 81, 221–22, 250
court of appeal 36–38, 40, 54–56, 126, 129, 175, 223, 247
court orders 179, 191
court proceedings 108, 136
court testimony 49, 77
criminal acts 7, 151–54
Criminal Appeal Act 54
criminal cases 64–65, 68, 82, 175, 219
criminal intent 178–79
criminal jurisdiction 98–99, 231
Criminal Justice Act 37, 40, 42, 55
criminal justice process 35, 40, 104, 121
Criminal Procedure Rules 46, 48, 50, 99, 241, 243, 250
criminal responsibility doctrines 238–39
criminogenic risk 64, 66–67, 74–75, 78
criminogenic risk factor 75
criminologists 155, 160–63, 167, 235, 244
Crown Court 34–35, 39, 44–45, 54–55
custodial measures of rehabilitation 151, 157–58

dangerousness assessments 81, 250
dangerous person commitments 72–73, 75–76, 81, 84, 250–51
databases, big data risk assessment 24
decisions
    final 82, 159, 190, 192, 208
    prognostic 149, 151
decisions on prolongation 216, 222
defence counsel 108, 113
defendants, capital 69, 79

definition of violence risk assessment 17
delinquency 73, 149, 151–52, 154, 156–60, 165–66
development of treatment 201
diagnostic categories 13–14
diminished responsibility defense 43, 56, 238, 251
discretionary competence 203, 233
disordered offenders 4, 8, 15, 36, 39, 102, 147, 149, 177–78, 201
disorders, paraphilic 73, 109
dispositional options 73–74
Dutch Association of Psychiatry 213
Dutch attorney 247
Dutch concept of criminal responsibility 238
Dutch Criminal Code 213
Dutch Government 202
Dutch inquisitorial trial procedure 220
Dutch Institute for Psychology 218
Dutch judiciary boards 249
Dutch jurisdiction 200
Dutch law 204, 211
Dutch legal system 222
Dutch sentencing system 203–4
duties, expert's 46–47, 50, 243

ECHR (European Court of Human Rights) 150, 200, 210, 212
England 2, 8, 35–36, 39–41, 45, 232, 234, 236–38, 240–43, 245–47, 249–52
English Common Law 35
English criminal courts 36
English Criminal Practice Directions 252
English legal system 34
English-speaking countries 148
evaluation procedures 83, 85, 254
evidence
    fresh 54–55
    non-expert 68, 84
evidence-based sentencing 74, 86
expert evaluation 220, 247
expert opinion evidence 46, 50, 112, 116
expert psychiatrist 136
expert reports 50, 115, 129–30, 133–34, 137–38, 249
Expert Reports on Mental Functioning of Offenders 129, 241
experts
    clinical 43
    forensic psychiatric 176, 178, 182, 192, 194
    opposing 54, 75, 83–84
Experts in Criminal Cases Act 203
expert testimony 65, 67, 74, 78, 81, 83, 85–86, 245
Expert Witness Codes 133, 135, 241, 250
expert witness skills 50, 245

facilities
    federal 102
    penal 68
    secure 68

264 Index

factfinder, legal 76, 78
factors
  ameliorating 189
  clinical 104
  contextual 20
  historical 20–21
  precipitating 23
fairness 200
FCA (Forensic Care Act) 202, 206–7, 210
federal government jurisdiction 98
federalism 63
Federal trial judges 71
feedback 135, 139, 221, 244
  systematic 168
fees, expert's 52
Female Additional Manual (FAM) 24
field reliability 10, 14, 16, 82–83, 86
financial issues 248
fitness, impaired 53
fitness to practice 53
fixed sentence 70
focus
  cognitive 189
  insanity defense 72
forensic assessment
  behavioural 223, 241
  high-quality 122, 166
  impact 4, 235
  importance 166
  independent multidisciplinary 209, 216
  psycho-legal criteria 240
  substandard 112
forensic assessment and division of
    competences 158
forensic assessment by decision makers 9
forensic assessment of psycholegal concepts 1
forensic assessment practice 63
forensic assessment role 106
Forensic Behavioural Science 122
forensic care institutions 209
Forensic College 139
forensic dialogue 75
forensic disciplines 115, 230
forensic evaluation information
  holistic 69
  sensitive 79
forensic evaluations 63–64, 66–67, 71–73, 75, 77,
    80–81, 84–86, 212, 217, 220–21, 246–47,
    250, 254
forensic evaluators
  behavioural scientific 216
  multiple 82
  opposing 81
  proffered 78
Forensic Evidence Working Group 139
forensic examinations 218
forensic examinees 77
Forensic Mental Health Services 85

forensic methodology 110, 116
forensic neuropsychology 134
forensic pathologist 112
forensic practice 24, 78, 84
Forensic Psychiatric Centers 207
Forensic Psychiatric Departments in psychiatric
    hospitals 207
forensic psychiatric expertise 183
forensic psychiatrists
  accredited 134
  consultant 39
  qualified 255
  subspecialist 100
forensic psychiatry
  adolescent 53
  civil 100
forensic psychiatry subspecialty training 100
forensic psychology 10, 36, 66, 77, 84, 101,
    134, 167
forensic science 10, 35, 163
forensic treatment effectiveness 9
forensic work 78, 84, 135, 245
  civil 79
FPI (Forensic psychiatric investigations) 175–80,
    182–84, 186–94

gender 11, 19, 75
General Medical Council; see GMC
general requirements for experts 216
generations 19, 66, 156, 162
genuineness 131
German Civil Code 161
German Constitution 146, 159
German Constitutional Court 150, 153, 159, 164
German Criminal Code 146
German criminal law 164
German criminal procedure 146
German Federal States 151–52, 162
German High Court 154, 160, 164, 166
German legal system 146
German Ministry 167
German Penal Code 146
German sanctioning system 146
German Society for Neuroscientific
    Assessment 161
German states 147, 164
GMC (General Medical Council) 49, 53, 56
Greek ideas, ancient 7
ground of insanity 41
group heterogeneity 185
guardianship order 39, 41
guilt 8, 34, 65, 67, 151, 153, 192, 232
  establishing 232
guilt principle 146, 151, 238
guilty pleas 34, 201, 232

habeas corpus 79, 81, 247
harm

bodily 17
potential 111
serious 42
Hawaiian system 15
HCPC (Health and Care Professions Council) 49
health care workers 186, 190
Health Technology Assessment 185
heuristics 187, 194
Hippocrates 7
historical traditions 7
history
defendant's 43
medical 129
psychosocial 131
homicide 53, 69, 101, 151
Homicide Act 35
hospitalisation 146, 149–52, 154, 156, 159, 161,
166, 241
secure 68
hospital order 35–36, 39–40, 42, 44, 55, 234,
238, 250
House of Lords 37, 40
humanitarianism 234
human mind 107
human nature 11
Human Rights 150, 200
hypoglycemia 126

ICD (International Classification of Diseases) 148
impairments 125–26, 238–39
impartiality 9, 51–52, 132–34, 139, 190, 243
imprisonment prohibition 184, 237
indeterminacy 210, 236
indigent defendants 80
insanity defense 15, 72–73, 121, 175, 177, 238

judges
adversarial systems 232
advisory committee 209
deputy 1
federal district court 82
juvenile 74
professional 146, 201, 233
judicial agency 64
judicial commentary 135
judicial waiver 73
judiciary 42, 139, 166, 209, 222, 241, 254
jurors 40, 66, 76
juvenile cases 9, 65, 79, 216, 232
juvenile court 68, 73
Juvenile Court Act 149
juvenile court jurisdiction 73
juvenile criminal law 149, 151, 159, 206, 214–15
juvenile justice system 64, 69, 73–74

knowledge
criminological 155, 165
evidence-based 251

scientific 11, 99, 148, 160, 244, 254

legislatures 70–71
licensees 77–78
licenses 79, 244–46
life sentence 37, 42, 204, 206, 210, 222, 236
limited quality of forensic assessment 54, 79, 113,
136, 163, 191, 220, 246

malpractice cases 220
mandatory minimum sentences 70, 101
material time 106, 108–10, 116
maximum sentences 203
measures of rehabilitation and incapacitation
146–47, 149, 159
mental disorders in insanity cases 66, 234
Mental Health Act 34–36, 39, 41, 44, 46, 103, 234
mental health assessment 14, 121, 123, 127, 137–38
mental health conditions 128, 130–31
mental health evidence 122–23, 128–29, 134, 136,
139, 249
mental health expertise 131, 135–36, 248
mental health experts 122–23, 127–28, 130–31,
133–39
mental health treatment 38, 41
mental health treatment requirement (MHTR) 39,
41–42
mental state defenses 65, 72, 121
Mindestanforderungen 160
misuse of psychiatry 6, 234
mitigating evidence 69, 71, 80
multidisciplinary assessment 241, 255

National Board of Health and Welfare 180, 186,
190–93, 247, 249, 251, 253
National Health Service (NHS) 41, 45, 240
National Judicial College 85
National Socialism 148, 234
naturalistic study 14
negligence 53, 77, 178–79, 246
Netherlands Register of Court Experts 203,
243–44
neurological impairments 40
neuroscience 6, 36
NHS (National Health Service) 41, 45, 240
nomothetic research 12
non-capital criminal sentencing 74
non-criminal-responsibility 208
non-maleficence 50, 243
non-responsibility 16, 212–13
non-responsible offenders 204
norm, legal 194, 255
not guilty by reason of insanity 34, 68, 72
notification, advanced 76

occupation 234, 255
offences
alleged 108, 110, 155

severe 151, 154, 158, 201, 204–5, 216
offenders
long-term 98, 101, 105
serious 124
opinion evidence 111, 113, 138, 241
admissibility of 111
optimal decisions 82, 85
out-of-court settlements 201

participation, joint 179
parties, commissioning 130–32, 243
patients, restricted 42, 44
PBC (Pieter Baan Centre) 215, 218, 221, 223
Penitentiary Principles Act (PPA) 207
personality disorders, antisocial 13, 68
physical injury 153–54
post-traumatic stress disorder (PTSD) 126
PPA (Penitentiary Principles Act) 207
praxis 181, 183–84, 187, 194
pre-sentence reports 46, 105, 110, 129
prison sentences
lifetime 180
long-term 149, 158–59
suspended 205–6
professional societies 77–78, 81, 84, 250
proxies 13, 18
psychiatric conditions 132, 206
psychiatric evidence 35–36, 38–39
psychiatric reports 41–46, 53, 55, 250
psychodiagnostics 6–8, 10, 211
psycholegal concepts 1, 9, 13, 26
psychological assessment 37
PTSD (post-traumatic stress disorder) 126

qualifications
expert's 46, 52, 113, 133, 249
relevant 137, 249
quality
contextual 8–10, 15
perceived 136
procedural 8–9
safeguard forensic evaluation 78, 245
substantive 4, 8–9
quality assurance 135, 163, 168
questionnaires 218
questions
additional 214
central 107
court's 186, 190
criminological 162
open 194
standard 214
threshold 106–7

race 75
RANZCP (Royal Australian and New Zealand
College of Psychiatrists) 123, 134–37, 139

RCPSC (Royal College of Physicians and
Surgeons of Canada) 100, 116
reform 35, 41, 108, 125, 148, 176–78
Regional Reception and Assessment Centre
(RRAC) 102
release decisions 42, 68, 79
reliability of assessment 15, 213
reliability of expert opinion 50–51
remorse 131–32
report for sentencing 46
Resolution Register Experts in Criminal Cases 219
responsible offenders 146, 206
restriction orders 36, 39, 42, 44
risk assessment
clinical 42
formal 217
interpreting 17
risk assessment evidence, sexual criminogenic 68
risk assessment procedures 189
risk assessments for violence 105, 109
risk assessment tools 20, 25, 67, 77, 82, 101,
242, 251
standardised 155
structured professional 242
Risk for Sexual Violence Protocol (RSVP) 101
risk management 17, 20–21, 23, 67, 71–72, 74
Risk-Need-Responsivity (RNR) 75
risk of recidivism 75, 147, 179–80
risk of relapse 109, 184, 189
Rogers Criminal Responsibility Assessment
Scale 15
Royal College of Psychiatrists 49
RSVP (Risk for Sexual Violence Protocol) 101
rules of evidence 76, 78, 85, 111, 129, 241, 249

SAVRY (Structured Assessment of Violence Risk
in Youth) 20–21, 23, 25, 101, 105
security 36, 41, 71, 104, 201–2, 207–8
self-reports 133, 185, 242
sentence for high-risk offenders 121
sentence of imprisonment 39, 105
sentences
appropriate 35, 39, 129
community-based 71
extended 37, 41–42, 98
juvenile 204, 208, 214
proportionate 125
Sentencing Act 35, 37, 42, 123–24
Sentencing and Punishment of Offenders Act 37
sentencing commission 64, 70
sentencing court 39, 45, 101–5, 126–27
sentencing decisions
judicial 71
new 239
sentencing guidelines 36, 64, 70–71, 238
sentencing hearings 79, 99, 122, 128–29, 135, 137,
139, 241, 247–48

sentencing objectives 124
sentencing offenders 4, 37, 40, 67, 101, 123, 148, 178, 203, 235
sentencing process 40, 122, 125, 128, 136, 231, 240
sex offenders 16, 75, 217, 236
sexual violence 17–18, 101, 105, 109, 116, 235
structured risk assessment 11, 18, 242
superordinate assessment 165, 253
Swedish Administrative Act 190
Swedish Agency for Health Technology Assessment and Assessment of Social Services 185
Swedish criminal justice system 176, 178
Swedish criminal law 176–77
Swedish justice system 179
Swedish law 175, 179–80, 182, 185, 188, 242
Swedish National Board 190, 193
Swedish process 175
Swedish regulation of healthcare 185
Swedish Supreme Court 192

TBS-care Principles Act (TPA) 207
test for expert evidence 113
testifying 8–9, 78–79
testimony
    expert's 49, 81
    unstructured risk assessment 81, 250
training
    advanced 134, 166–67, 254
    postgraduate 112, 245
trial phase 206, 214, 233, 237–38, 240
two-phase trial 231–32, 241

unfit to stand trial 103
unsound mind 150, 153
utility, clinical 13

vagueness, legal 75, 194
validation studies 20, 24

validity
    face 15, 213
    limited 3, 13
variations
    legal 63
    normal 185
    regional 99
victim reports 38
Victoria Legal Aid 131, 136, 139
Victorian Court of Appeal 122, 125, 127, 139
Victorian Institute of Forensic Mental Health 122
video footage 110
violence
    domestic 104
    extremist 17
    honour-based 17
violence risk assessment 17, 72, 81–83, 85, 101, 235
violence risk assessment evidence 68
violent offenders 37, 102, 160, 241
volition, impaired 15
VPS (Victim's Personal Statement) 38
vulnerabilities, individual's 45

warrant 19, 41, 111, 204, 206, 208–9
weapons prohibitions 102
weight, evidentiary 68
well-behaved assessee 20
witnesses
    adverse 79
    medical 35
World Health Organisation 148

youth 45, 73–75, 104–5, 123
Youth Offending Teams (YOTs) 45
youth penalties 149, 151
youth prisons, regular 149

zweispuriges System 146

Printed in the United States
by Baker & Taylor Publisher Services